From Classicism to Modernism

From Classicism to Modernism

Western Musical Culture and the Metaphysics of Order

BRIAN K. ETTER

Ashgate

Aldershot • Burlington USA • Singapore • Sydney

Published by
Ashgate Publishing Limited
Gower House
Croft Road
Aldershot
Hants GU11 3HR
England

Ashgate Publishing Company
131 Main Street
Burlington VT 05401–5600 USA

Ashgate website: http://www.ashgate.com

British Library Cataloguing in Publication Data

Etter, Brian K.
    From Classicism to Modernism: Western Musical Culture
    and the Metaphysics of Order.
    1. Music—20th century—History and criticism.
    2. Avant-garde (Music).
    I. Title.
    780.9'04

Library of Congress Control Number: 2001091552

ISBN 0 7546 0285 0

This book is printed on acid-free paper

Typeset in Times New Roman by Express Typesetters, Farnham, Surrey and printed in Great Britain by TJ International Ltd, Padstow, Cornwall.

Contents

List of Tables

List of Music Examples

Preface

For nearly a century the avant-garde has defined the authority for new composition. This movement, extending from Schoenberg and his pupils to Boulez and Stockhausen, Penderecki and Crumb, and the academic composers influenced by them, dominates the modern conception of musical creativity. Serious music is held to demand new styles, new forms, and new ways of listening and hearing. This involves, specifically, the rejection among composers of the long tradition extending from the Baroque to the late masters of symphonic music, Shostakovich and Prokofiev. Yet the concert and operatic repertoire is largely devoted to the long tradition, represented in canonic works which appear increasingly problematic to critics today, but which audiences continue to love.

The need to accommodate and encourage musical creativity leads, then, to tensions in the concert hall: the works of the avant-garde are juxtaposed against works from the longer tradition, to the frequent discomfiture of audiences and performers alike. This juxtaposition creates a dichotomy of repertoires, but it also implicitly raises aesthetic questions about the nature of the two approaches to music. Yet such questions become muted by the fact that the avant-garde has so largely defined the creative side of contemporary musical culture.

The authority of the avant-garde also has implications for its representation in the historical and critical literature. For in general, critics and music historians have understood the avant-garde's historical importance as determinative for the direction of musical composition for the future.[1] That is, academic observers have usually understood the movement in the same way that it understands itself, so that the musical tensions of the twentieth century become defined by radical innovation and the opposition of tradition. The prevailing belief is that originality is always rejected in its day, but will someday come to be accepted. In this light even normal critical debate appears as illegitimate.

The arguments justifying the avant-garde are various and deserve to be taken seriously: this new music is seen by its proponents as the inevitable continuation of the tonal tradition, or as the necessary rejection of an exhausted tradition, or as a commentary on the evils of the twentieth century which could not be ignored. The arguments, however plausible in spite of apparent contradictions among them, never convince audiences to modify their tastes. But they also fail to suffice for a philosophical understanding of the avant-garde. For since its justification is bound up with its relation to the prior historical tradition, a philosophical understanding of the avant-garde will necessarily have to take its history into account. The questions remain:

Whence came the avant-garde into history? What is its relation to modernity? What is its inner, aesthetic logic?

The puzzles posed by the dichotomy of the tradition and the avant-garde have had their origin in the avant-garde's rejection of the tradition from which it claimed both descent and emancipation. But if the new music could be understood only by reference to the tonal tradition of the past, then parallel questions deserve to be asked of that tradition: What did tonality signify? How did it originate? What was its aesthetic logic? The critique of the tradition begun by the avant-garde appears plausible now precisely because the traditional aesthetic is not well understood. The long academic silence with respect to the aesthetic of the tonal tradition has largely continued; the twentieth century's exorcism of its aesthetic logic has left few means of recovering an understanding of the integrity it once possessed. This book, therefore, attempts to understand the dichotomy of concert music by recovering the origins and logic of both the tonal tradition and the modern avant-garde.

In sketching the above account of the core concerns of the book, I speak from within a particular musical culture – that of the United States – and from the dual perspective of both a scholar and a professional orchestral musician. Yet my experience attending concerts in European halls suggests that American musical life is not atypical among Western nations, and my perspective as a musician gives me first-hand knowledge of repertoire and programming decisions. Thus, to emphasize the essential point: although a purely academic knowledge of the history of music may point to an ever increasing fragmentation of styles and approaches in the twentieth century, the facts of musical life point rather to the continued centrality of the traditional orchestral and operatic repertoires. The tradition is still a vital presence, even if little is now written within its stylistic parameters. The recognition of this fact is a fundamental premise of this enquiry.

A few words need to be said in explanation of the terms and conceptual framework employed in this study. This book is a study in the history and philosophy of ideas about music. Because the determining questions are posed within what has been the prevailing understanding of the history of music, I take the dichotomy of the tonal tradition and the avant-garde as the typology best suited to conceptual clarity. Hence the principal title of the book: I employ the term 'classicism' to refer to what is casually, but not altogether incorrectly, referred to as 'classical music', and I use the term 'modernism' to refer specifically to the avant-garde movement of the twentieth century. This corresponds to the actual dichotomy of concert life that arose during the twentieth century and still remains in place.

Terms such as these are sometimes fraught with ambiguity, and the divergent ways philosophers, historians and art critics use the term 'modern' offers ample opportunity for misunderstanding. 'Modern' in particular may mean, depending on the discipline of inquiry, post-Renaissance, post-French Revolution, or post-Nietzschean; 'post-modern', then, arises as a desperate search for a term to distinguish the third alternative from the first. Fortunately, 'modernism' itself is used with more consistency in the history of the arts than 'modern'; it denotes both a chronology and an approach distinct from what went before. Chronologically, modernism in the arts had its origin at the beginning of the twentieth century; conceptually, its origin and essence remain masked behind the spirit of its revolution against the tradition. For the sake of clarity in this book, I shall seek consistency by taking 'modern' and 'modernism' to be related philosophically as well as chronologically: they shall denote the post-Nietzschean enterprise of the rejection of the inherited intellectual tradition. I shall restrict the use of the neologism 'post-modern' to the contemporary movement in the academy seeking to disestablish the received intellectual tradition from its privileged position. I note, however, that post-modernism in this sense is itself descended from the modernist impulse.

The concept of 'classical music', as embracing the Baroque, the Classical era and the Romantic effusions of the nineteenth century, may appear more problematic, but, again, there is a common concept providing a unity at the core: that is the idea of tonality in its traditional sense of tonal unity achieved by a functional harmony. The older term, 'the common practice period', recognized this dimension of harmonic unity amidst stylistic change. As we shall see, the dependence of this music on classical metaphysics provides an additional reason to conceive these periods of music history as governed by a common set of principles. 'Classicism' is thus a warrantable term.

For any reader troubled by a seemingly over-simple dichotomy of classical and modernist styles, I would point first to the way that apologists for the avant-garde have conceived the relation of modernism to history and the general culture. The self-understanding of the avant-garde is precisely in contrast to the received tradition, whatever the continuity that may also be claimed. But another perspective is possible: surely there was a mainstream of twentieth-century music, embracing the sometimes expressionistic and sometimes classically inspired works of Stravinsky, Bartók, Prokofiev and Shostakovich, as well as others such as Benjamin Britten, Ralph Vaughan Williams, Samuel Barber and Leonard Bernstein. This mainstream is music that is performed; it is accepted by audiences in ways that the avant-garde never has been. Were I writing a history of twentieth-century music, I would recast the conventional telling of it in this way. Yet it remains true that the driving force in twentieth-century musical history has been the avant-garde, and in particular its influence on Stravinsky, Bartók, and Shostakovich was great indeed.[2] The predominance of rhythm over melodic interest, the use of dissonance treated as sonority and non-functional harmonic language in this mainstream all testify to the departure from the classical tradition. Thus, the conceptual dichotomy of the recognizably tonal tradition and the revolutionary avant-garde has a justifiable foundation in historical reality; it establishes a basic typology for understanding the aesthetic issues. To achieve an understanding of the origins and aesthetic logic of each side of the dichotomy will illuminate the dynamic of history, if not all its details. The achievement of even this modest goal must have some merit in the present climate of musical confusion and aesthetic debate.

Yet the mainstream described above appears largely to have come to an end; what will take its place remains uncertain. The so-called minimalism of John Adams, Philip Glass and Henryk Gorecki fails as a substitute, appearing instead as a highly particularistic school of composition. But since there may be composers now who seek a place in the canon, and who find it difficult because the canon appears closed against virtually all new music, it is not out of place to reflect on the degree to which the tension between the modernist avant-garde and the tradition of classicism has created a climate little conducive to the reception of new music. If 'new' is understood as 'modernist', after a century of 'New Music' defined largely by the avant-garde programme, then it is little wonder that audiences automatically associate the two terms. If they are apprehensive of the avant-garde, they will be apprehensive of anything new; hence, the closure of the canon against new additions may well be one result of the domination of musical creativity by the ideology of the avant-garde. But it seems to me that this is not an altogether healthy situation; if an understanding of the assumptions of both the avant-garde and the prior tradition could clear the way for less suspicion on the part of both composers and audiences, perhaps a more vibrant musical life might result. Perhaps, too, the concept of a canon might appear less problematic than it does to many academicians today.

The foregoing remarks, cast more as the definition of an interpretive position than as formal argument, identify the core concerns of this book. Nevertheless, while they may suffice for the non-specialist reader, they necessarily raise certain questions in the context of current academic discussions of music, many of them arising in the post-modernist critique of the hegemony of Western culture and of the dominance of determinate traditions within that culture. The first question is why the concern of the book is limited to Western art music, that is, the concert and operatic repertoires. Especially inasmuch as there are so many native folk musics in the world and an ever-growing presence of popular music, the restriction to art music may well appear artificial. In comparison with the entire field of music, art music appears ever so narrow to critics who wish to speak of all musics.

My answer to this question (and implicit charge) is that what is at issue here is the definition of music itself: is it all organized sound, or an art created within particular traditions? The prevailing conception of music regards it as any system of organized sound. The philosopher hopes that universal statements might be deduced about music in general, whereas the post-modernist critic would point to a multiplicity of voices heard in many different musics. Here I will simply say that I reject such a conception of music: music is an example of historically contingent activity which acquires its significance and meaning through shared experiences and a common language developed over time. The philosophical understanding of historical contingents such as music must therefore seek an understanding of the particular constitutive traditions, not of all possible constructs. Music is not simply an art of the organization of sound; a philosophy of music so understood would be meaningless. Rather, music is an art created within particular traditions. But these traditions are not simply different voices, as the post-modernist critic would assert: they are deeply imbedded within particular civilizations, of which they are in part constitutive.[3] A musical tradition so understood cannot be displaced from its normative status lightly or easily.

The tradition of Western art music, from the Middle Ages through the twentieth century, may not be stylistically continuous, but it belongs to a continuous artistic enterprise, constantly developing and changing. It belongs to the same civilization as the author and the intended readers: it is our most important musical heritage. And it belongs to much of the rest of the world as well: there are nine orchestras playing Western classical music in Tokyo, and five in Beijing. The appeal of Western art music would appear intrinsic and not merely an accidental fact of history or a case of imperialist hegemony. To make the field of enquiry Western art music is not to assert that there is no other kind of music, but rather to recognize the existence and coherence of a determinate tradition and heritage. As such a tradition and heritage, Western art music surely merits understanding.

This takes us to the second question and the need for a clarification of the subtitle of the book: why 'musical culture' is restricted to the domain of art music. Here it is simply a matter of definition. I employ the word 'culture' in its principal dictionary meaning, its original sense and its most common usage. 'Culture' is the cultivation of the intellectual and moral faculties through the arts and letters. This is the way in which Matthew Arnold used the word in his *Culture and Anarchy* of 1869; the alternative to culture, he argued, is anarchy.[4] On this, I agree completely. Culture is the result of education; the task of education is to lead out of ignorance into knowledge. Thus, if it be objected that the term 'culture' ought to be used in a more modern, anthropological sense to refer to the whole way of life of a people – what used to be called the manners of a people – I would have to respond that we need to retain some word that will allow us to speak of the end product of an education. To be cultured is not just to be learned, although it entails that quality. Rather, the concept of culture also embraces the achievement of a high degree of moral rectitude and the cultivation of taste in the arts. It is a goal that defines the aim of a systematic education of the entire soul.

It is a matter of great irony, therefore, that the contemporary academic preoccupation with 'culture' in its anthropological sense works against this concept of culture as the goal of an education of the intellectual and moral faculties. For to assert that the object of study ought to be the whole way of life of a people is necessarily to call into question the value of a goal of education, which will be achieved empirically with perhaps comparative rarity. Instead, it becomes possible to speak of 'popular culture' as well as 'elite culture', and then the anti-elitist bias of the contemporary academy decides firmly against the validity of the latter. But a 'popular culture' is little likely to lead to significant cultivation of the intellectual and moral faculties, especially in its modern, commercialized forms.[5] Indeed, the term 'popular culture' bears within itself an inherent contradiction if the term 'culture' be understood within its original boundary of meaning. From such confusion will come little understanding.

The anthropological sense of 'culture', however, contains an even greater danger. For, having become the common currency of post-modernist critics of the Western heritage of arts and letters, it has passed into the service of an explicit relativism that denies the existence of intellectual and moral norms. Now, when an anthropologist studies the whole way of life of, say, a tribe, he would certainly say that a tribal culture contains within it such norms. But the concept of a way of life does not itself specify the norms; those remain to be discovered by the researcher. Hence, for the post-modernist sense of 'culture', the absence of norms becomes exactly the attractive feature: one way of life has no intrinsic claim on one's allegiance or judgement in the way that the original understanding of culture did. I would argue, on the contrary, that 'culture' as the cultivation of the intellectual and moral faculties is precisely the concept we need to recover, a term we must not allow to disappear from the language, because it contains within it the norms required for making us civilized human beings. Or rather, it is culture, which, in civilizing humanity, makes us fully human.

Culture in the authentic sense, therefore, requires an education in order to participate in it. At the same time, such culture is shared among those having the appropriate education. Hence, it is possible to speak of 'musical culture' as the sharing in performance of the music which cultivates the intellectual and moral faculties to a high degree. Such culture becomes public, rather than remaining simply private, and so it becomes indeed part of a way of life, although never the whole way of life. But this sense of 'culture' is not invalidated because the segments of a society possessing the requisite education are fewer in number than the entire population, nor is it invalidated by not being shared among all the peoples of the globe. It is a question of intellectual and moral standards within a particular civilization, not of the exclusion of anyone's favourite music. Indeed, the prevailing post-modernist assumption that culture is a means of forging identity, either personal or ethnic, is both socially fragmenting and strikingly at odds with former assumptions. Not so long ago, music was regarded as the universal language, not burdened with the singularities of spoken language. As a result, the various national syles of classical music freely crossed national boundaries, as they still do today. The tribal fallacy has no place in musical culture.

There is a genesis of culture in the original sense of the word, however, and this takes us to the heart of the post-modernist critique of the tradition. That genesis is historical and, for this reason, culture is preserved in the institution of canons. It has always been so: in the ancient world, the works of Homer, and later of Aeschylus, Sophocles, and Euripides, were preserved because they embodied the moral and literary norms the Greek *polis* required. Similarly, long after the Roman Empire fell into ruin, the masterpieces of Cicero, Virgil, Ovid and Seneca were maintained as exemplars of literary and philosophical achievement; they formed the cornerstone of the Renaissance in Western Europe, and through their place in the newly formed secondary schools of the time, they helped to shape the intellectual horizons and artistic imagination of the Western world.[6] Finally, there is a canon of English literature, valid wherever English is spoken: it includes surely, but not solely, Shakespeare, Donne, Milton, Wordsworth, Keats, Shelley, Poe and Tennyson.[7] In music, too, there is a canon, which is simply a fact of life for the musically educated. This book's argument proceeds from the recognition of that fact, rather from a hypothetical position outside the culture aiming at a critique of the canon. Judgements of canonicity are an inevitable part of any culture; indeed the existence of canons would appear to be a necessary condition of civilization. The post-modernist critique of canons is either naïve or disingenuous.

Nevertheless, there is inevitably a debate about the content and extent of the musical canon, which has been particularly acute in the twentieth century because of the conflict in style between classicism and modernism. This book will argue that there is more to this debate than simply a clash of styles in the ordinary course of historical development. Rather, there is a conflict over the nature of order underlying the conflict over the particular stylistic orders in classical and modernist music. I refer to this element as the 'metaphysics of order', but it would be well to offer some clarification on this final aspect of the subtitle of the book. For Aristotle, metaphysics was the science of being as being; it was the branch of philosophy concerned with the nature, not of the things of the visible world, but of the categories by which the world must be understood. As such, the nature of order was central to metaphysics in this sense. Understood as a system of fundamental principles, then, metaphysics is not simply a branch of philosophical inquiry, but the set of core ideas about the nature and order of things; it is in this sense that I employ the term. Although metaphysics as a discipline has passed out of fashion among many in the philosophical community of the twentieth century, ideas about the nature and order of things are unavoidable. The argument of this book is that if there are norms in music, they are necessarily rooted in metaphysical concepts. The question is whether there are indeed musical norms, and whether there ought to be order in music. On this depend all questions of musical canonicity.

A word about sources, finally, is in order. This historical and philosophical enquiry depends on many German and French sources. I have provided citations to readily available English translations of foreign-language sources wherever possible, for one of the great benefits of modern scholarship is the large abundance of translated literature. For more recent sources where there is an accessible edition of collected works, I have provided citations to the original as well as to the translation. For less readily available original sources, however, the reader is referred to the translated text if there is one. For classical or other older philosophical sources, I have followed standard format and provided citations to line number or section number, citing a specific edition only if there is a quotation or if the argument depends on specific wording of the passage.

I would like to thank Professors John Wiley, Stephen Tonsor and Thomas Tentler of the University of Michigan for their encouragement in this project. Through extended conversations with them in the years following the completion of my dissertation, I found the stimulation to embark on a new direction of enquiry altogether. Nevertheless, the arguments presented herein are my own, and I take full responsibility for the views expressed and any deficiencies. I also owe an acknowledgement to my students, who, lacking any prior musical education, often found it difficult to understand the tradition of musical classicism, the claims of modernism and the demands of musical culture; the challenges they posed must be taken seriously by anyone who thinks the art of music worth cultivating. Finally, I would like to thank the anonymous reader at Ashgate Publishing Limited for his careful reading of the manuscript, and judicious criticisms. Most of all, I would like to thank my wife, Linda, for sharing a deep interest in this book's argument, and for reading drafts of the chapters with a critical eye. If this book is at all able to persuade other readers that musical culture matters, and that the nature of order embodied in musical norms matters, then it will be in no small measure due to the contributions of these people to my thinking about a problem which has puzzled me for many years. Accordingly, I hope that this book speaks to

both an academic and a musical audience: it is a book about ideas, for the sake
of the love of music.

Notes

1. See, for example, Donald Mitchell, *The Language of Modern Music*, 2nd edn
   (Philadelphia: University of Pennsylvania Press, 1993), or Laurence Davies, *Paths
   to Modern Music: Aspects of Music from Wagner to the Present Day* (London:
   Barrie and Jenkins, 1971).
2. William W. Austin, for example, took these three as the chief figures of his *Music
   in the 20th Century: From Debussy through Stravinsky* (New York: Norton, 1966).
3. For an explanation and defence of this sense of tradition, see Jaroslav Pelikan, *The
   Vindication of Tradition* (New Haven and London: Yale University Press, 1984).
4. For a modern edition, see Matthew Arnold, *Culture and Anarchy*, ed. J. Dover
   Wilson (Cambridge: Cambridge University Press, 1932), pp. 44–8 on 'culture' as
   the cultivation of harmonious perfection. It is important to note that this was
   standard usage before the twentieth century.
5. For an excellent critique of an important part of modern popular culture, see
   Martha Bayles, *Hole in Our Soul: The Loss of Beauty and Meaning in American
   Popular Music* (New York: The Free Press, 1994). Her argument that popular
   music has been deeply affected by the modernist movement in serious music
   shows the importance of understanding the latter even for this purpose.
6. On this, see Paul Oskar Kristeller, *Renaissance Thought and Its Sources*, ed.
   Michael Mooney (New York: Columbia University Press, 1979).
7. For a lively defence of the concept of a canon in literature, see Harold Bloom, *The
   Western Canon: The Books and School of the Ages* (New York: Riverhead Books,
   1994).

To all with whom I have shared a love of music

Introduction

Western musical culture since the early twentieth century has appeared irremediably bifurcated. On the one hand, there has been the concert repertoire and the operatic canon; these constitute what most people understand by the term 'classical music'. It is perhaps not too much to say that these canonic repertoires appear closed, or at least additions are made to them only with great difficulty and with rare frequency. On the other hand, there has been the musical world of the avant-garde, in which experimentation has taken place often quite radically, and where the search for new ways of self-expression continues apace. If few people outside of the devotees of new music pay it much attention, or if it rarely affects the concert repertoire, that condition seems to alter little about its accepted status as the expression of new music most appropriate to modern times. Indeed, the academic community, with its claim to arbitrate the status of music, appears increasingly committed to the kind of critical approaches to the study of classical music that may well end in a decline of its prestige in the general culture.[1] For it is the new, the absolutely unprecedented, that has been celebrated as the authentic product of musical creativity for over nine decades. The new and the old, therefore, appear in stark contrast as the two poles of musical culture in the modern world.

It is perhaps more appropriate, however, to describe this cultural situation as the existence of two separate musical cultures, one defined by the impulse to preservation and the other by the impulse to innovation. While this dichotomy runs the risk of oversimplification, such a typology is neither unprecedented nor unwarranted. Certainly there are other similar cultural dichotomies: C. P. Snow has described the opposition of the scientific and literary cultures of the twentieth century in such terms.[2] Within the sphere of music, the rival approaches of Arnold Schoenberg and Igor Stravinsky have often been taken as representative of the polarity definitive of modernist approaches, even in spite of the many successful composers who lie outside their realms of direct influence.[3] Thus Schoenberg and his school stand for the most radical direction of musical innovation, while Stravinsky represents the more conservative, yet still modernist, direction. It is as if little else counts.

To be precise, what does not count is the concept of musical creativity that operates within the boundaries of an organic tradition. Modern creativity, indeed, is virtually defined by the rejection of tradition.[4] From this point of view, the concept of a culture defined by the explicit retention of a traditional canon appears intrinsically retrograde and ultimately indefensible. The concept of a canon becomes suspect, the process of its formation reduced to that of the creation and introduction of new works. As a consequence, it is easy to lose sight of the concept of a culture defined by the reception of works, rather than solely by the creation of new works in ever newer styles. Indeed, so imperative does the concept of stylistic innovation appear, that music history, like the history of the arts generally, is conceived in terms of the appearance of new styles. Style, therefore, emerges as the defining mark of creativity.

The dichotomy of innovation and preservation in musical culture may be more radically present today than ever before, but it is not new. Half a century ago, two books defined these poles clearly: Theodore Adorno's *Philosophy of Modern Music* (1948) and Hermann Hesse's *The Glass Bead Game* (1943).[5] It is worth considering their arguments briefly, in order to understand what defines the hostility to preservation in the culture of innovation, and what accounts for the desire to preserve in the culture of tradition. Only in such a way will it be clear what the issues are: that, in fact, there are serious intellectual conflicts underlying the bifurcation of musical culture in the modern world. Although the split is often viewed as a dispute about taste, such a view would be too simple. At issue is nothing less than a metaphysical question masquerading as an artistic and cultural one.

Adorno has been the principal philosophical apologist for the modern musical avant-garde. His defence of the avant-garde rests on the perception that 'What radical music perceives is the untransfigured suffering of man.'[6] Schoenberg's music is for him the archetype of this; it proclaims the universality of loneliness as the essence of the modern condition.[7] Indeed, the task of all art in the modern world must not be the portrayal of some positive resolution of guilt, or an affirmation of transcendence such as traditional art and music sought, but rather the representation of universal self-alienation.[8] It is only in alienation that the individual can continue to exist; hence the only redemptive role any art can play is to display man's estrangement to himself. Adorno sees modern life as meaningless, and modern music as the appropriate expression of that new fact. Hence, 'Modern music sees absolute oblivion as its goal. It is the surviving message of despair from the shipwrecked.'[9] It is this zeal for absolute honesty that produces the criticism of all beauty as an 'illusion' music must now forgo.

Adorno's defence of modernism rests, therefore, on a critique of modern life. A Marxist, he dismisses the taste of 'bourgeois' culture as 'kitsch', and the concert as an 'empty ritual' that must be destroyed.[10] But what distinguishes the twentieth century as modern and therefore requires a critique and a music distinct from earlier times for Adorno is the irredeemable guilt of his own native Germany. As he wrote later: 'There are no words for the noble, the good, the true and the beautiful that have not been violated and turned into their opposite — just as the Nazis could enthuse about the house, its roof resting on pillars, while torture went on in the cellars.'[11] Thus, the massive evil of genocidal totalitarianism seems to Adorno to preclude any artistic representation of goodness, truth, or nobility. Because none of these ideals has been realized in practice, he reaches a radical metaphysical conclusion: they do not exist anymore. Hence, out of a social critique emerges a metaphysical position: there is no goodness or truth or beauty.

The significance of Adorno's position becomes clear in contrasting it with Plato's. For Plato, the good-in-itself was the highest reality, the principle that ordered life to its proper end. The good was a self-subsistent Idea, defined by order and self-sufficiency. Its radiance illuminated all other existents, allowing true knowledge of both the Ideas and of this world of becoming. It made possible the perception of the virtues as lying in the ordering of the soul by reason; thus, it produced the moral and ethical life.[12] Adorno's despairing nihilism reasons from the collapse of the moral life in the modern world to the non-existence of the good as an Idea. In his eyes, all claims for goodness become mere lies. There is nothing capable of ordering life or giving it meaning. The task of music, therefore, becomes the reflection of this metaphysical nihilism instead of the provision of any kind of idealist inspiration.

As a consequence, musical style necessarily embodies a metaphysical representation. For Adorno, the new music of the twentieth century could only be either Twelve-Tone or electronic; the one style precluded was that of tonality, which dominated the 'bourgeois' era from about 1600 to 1900. Yet the negative rejection of tonality conceals an ambivalence of principle: for, on the one hand, the Twelve-Tone Technique has as its aim the composer's total planning of musical materials – the conception of rationality in music for both Adorno and Schoenberg. But, on the other hand, electronic music, with sounds quite outside the traditional consideration of music, also in its own way reveals the composer's total manipulation of materials.[13] In this way, both approaches offer a break with tradition by means of the total control of sound. As has often been argued, however, such control may ultimately converge with the results of chance as far as the auditor is concerned; indeed, Adorno admits the birth of the aleatoric principle in the works of Schoenberg's Twelve-Tone Technique itself.[14] Chaos and control, therefore, are more intimately related than appears possible at first glance. By eliminating recurrent formulae, Schoenberg destroyed musical essence, producing a kind of musical nominalism.[15] In this manner, chaos and control spring from the same impulse and, indeed, become identical at their extremes.

Hence, according to Adorno, modernist musical styles represent the metaphysical nihilism of modern humanity by means of denying the perceptible tonal order characteristic of music during the common practice period. This suggests that the tonal order of the earlier era represented the kind of metaphysical ordering such as Plato describes: an ultimate good toward which all human and cosmic purposes are understood to be directed. For those who embrace Adorno's position, then, the Platonic metaphysic must be rejected, along with the musical style dependent on it.

In contrast to Adorno's metaphysical despair, however, Hermann Hesse gives in his novel, *The Glass Bead Game*, a vision of a culture defined precisely by the attempt to preserve a sense of the good. For him, this is still the hallmark of musical culture in the modern world; music preeminently reflects the instinctive longing of the human soul for an ideal of moral and spiritual goodness. But the metaphors created in the novel are disturbing: for Hesse, too, the modern world risks losing its soul and emptying its culture of the living knowledge of the good.

Hesse's depiction of the imaginary society of Castalia makes the cultivation of music central to the life of the intellectual elite of the educational province. Both scholarship and music appear emancipated from utilitarian purposes; their autonomy is thus a guarantee of their perfection. Yet the imagery is unsettling, for the scholarship Hesse describes consists largely in the discovery of arcane relationships among unrelated cultural artifacts, a history of ideas pursued without genuine historical understanding, and an aestheticism that attempts to make a sacrament out of the quest to perceive the unity underlying all the world's cultures. This kind of scholarship constitutes the essence of the Glass Bead Game. But although one of the glories of the life of the mind, its character supplies its own critique: ultimately, it is only a game.[16] The disillusionment of Joseph Knecht, the Master of the Game, is the novel's indictment of the intellectual sterility of Castalia. His search for a higher good is a search for a nobler life.

The role of music in Castalia, however, fares considerably better. For the musical culture in Castalia was one of its glories, in which there were both active performance and musicological analysis. The contemplative delectation of instrumental music was the supreme aesthetic act. In that sense, the culture was not sterile, for music was not only studied academically, but kept alive as a tradition. It is a metaphor of the place of music in our modern culture, for instrumental music today enjoys pride of place in the tradition of musical performance. Significantly, it was easy enough for Knecht to justify:

> We consider classical music to be the epitome and quintessence of our culture, because it is that culture's clearest, most significant gesture and expression. In this music we possess the heritage of classical antiquity and Christianity, a spirit of serenely cheerful and brave piety, a superbly chivalric morality. For in the final analysis every important cultural gesture comes down to a morality, a model for human behavior concentrated into a gesture.[17]

Here the value of serenity is taken as self-evident. Knecht praises his former music teacher as radiating this quality of soul 'like the light from a star; so much that it was transmitted to all in the form of benevolence, enjoyment of life, good humor, trust, and confidence'. He goes on to say that 'It is the secret of beauty and the real substance of all art.'[18] In particular, it was the substance of the musical traditions which were cultivated in Castalia and were the only source of spiritual pleasure to Knecht.

Yet today such rhetoric is apt to seem hollow. The ascription of a moral effect to music or to any other art sounds implausible, both because such an effect would be highly contingent on the particular works contemplated, but also because any connection between morality and art appears to threaten the autonomy of each. The prevailing assumption today is that the individual is morally sovereign, self-determining outside the minimal legal rules imposed by society.[19] By the same token, art is sovereign within its sphere, with a unique aesthetic value resulting from its autonomy: this is the legacy of Kantian aesthetics.[20] But it is precisely when music or any other art is regarded as an end in itself that it becomes impossible to say whether it has real significance. Hesse's Castalia was founded on contrary premises: the individual was not morally sovereign, and the arts therefore had a deeply moral significance. Nevertheless, the image of Castalian culture is aestheticist, for its intellectual endeavours were pursued as ends in themselves and had no larger purpose. In that sense, the aestheticism of Castalia anticipates that of modern artistic culture.

The most disturbing metaphor in Hesse's image of Castalia, however, is the nature of musical life itself. For the music that was so assiduously cultivated was entirely an older repertoire; Hesse located it as that body of music composed between about 1500 and 1800. It was in this music that the values of tranquillity and order were principally to be found. Of creativity in Castalia there was absolutely none. The intellectual elite could analyse the music of the long distant past, but did not and could not compose music anew. Indeed, creativity in all the arts had been renounced, and in the case of poetry, actually prohibited.[21] The sterility of such a culture is obvious, and it bears an uncanny and unwelcome resemblance to modern culture. For the concert repertoire today is largely determined by a canon of works inherited from the past, although from a rather more recent past than in Hesse's novel. Adorno appears justified in saying that the era of 'bourgeois' culture is irrecoverable; no one dares emulate the works from that era in order to continue that tradition. Therefore, from the point of view of most audiences, all that can be done is to preserve what has come down from the more creative past. There appears to be very little new music judged worthy of reception into the general culture today.

The stylistic divide in modern culture is clearly marked. The music of the canonic repertoire is melodic, is based on a harmonic norm of consonance, and achieves a high degree of tonal coherence through what is generally known as 'functional' harmony. In contrast the music of the avant-garde is founded on a renunciation of melody, consonance and tonal coherence. The classical repertoire is widely performed, but the public has little tolerance for the avant-garde of Schoenberg, Webern, Boulez, Cage and others. Hence, there appear to be only two responses possible: one is to side with the public, after the manner of Hesse; and the second is to agree with Adorno, who rejects the authority of public taste altogether as at once self-satisfied and manipulated by commercialism.[22] But to endorse Hesse's Castalian canon is to commit modern society to an absence of creative endeavour, whereas to take Adorno's position is to condemn the entire canon, and to dismiss any accommodation of public taste as a process that can only produce what Clement Greenberg has called 'kitsch'.[23] Thus, the two sides appear not only mutually antagonistic, but deeply committed to antithetical understandings of music. On the traditionalist side, music becomes an art valued for its supremely pleasurable stylistic qualities, whereas on the modernist side music is valued for the correctness of its intellectual exposition of the hypocrisies of modern society. In this situation, it appears too much to ask which position is true. At this point, we can only ask what the conflict between Adorno's and Hesse's positions might imply for a philosophical understanding of these two divergent musical styles.

Adorno's analysis of modern music makes clear the metaphysical dimension of style. This needs to be taken seriously, in spite of the dismissal of the metaphysical from much of twentieth-century philosophy, for at issue is the nature of order, time and human life's meaningfulness. How these might be related to the technical elements of musical style will be crucial for understanding the present dichotomy of styles. At the same time, Hesse's analysis points to the moral dimension of musical style, which Adorno repudiates. Nonetheless, the ability of music to represent a moral dimension is a crucial part of its metaphysical nature, for what music represents as common to all being must be relevant to specifically human being. Thus, it is necessary to ask of both traditional music and the avant-garde: what are the intellectual foundations of the style? What does the style signify in its representation of nature and human nature? To answer these questions is the task of this book.

In addressing the questions of the fundamental principles and signification of two divergent musical styles, it will be essential to take cognizance of the terms by which these styles were understood at the time of their birth. Most accounts of the aesthetics of classical music focus on the importance of emotional expression; there is no denying its centrality to musical aesthetics from the Baroque through the mid-nineteenth century. Certainly if the self-perception of classical tonality were in fact metaphysical, it would be persuasive to say that music from the common practice period embodies a metaphysical understanding of order. But the relative absence of this perspective seems to make a metaphysical analysis of classical style suspect. By the same token, if the avant-garde actually sought to express the despair Adorno discovers in the style, it could be said to represent the meaninglessness of human existence in a century of genocide and total warfare. But since the style was born in the decade before World War I, Adorno's explanation cannot be taken as accounting for the generative metaphysical or moral significance of the avant-garde. It therefore becomes imperative to ground the inquiry in an historical methodology. This is not to say that the totality of the history of music or of musical aesthetics becomes the goal of recovery, but it is to insist that no understanding of musical styles will be philosophically credible if it is not in the first place historically faithful to the aims of the original understandings. In undertaking such a task, it might be hoped that the sense of despair common to both Hesse's and Adorno's analyses of modern culture could be transcended.

It will be necessary, therefore, to turn to philosophical and other sources which may be unfamiliar to the musician or music historian, or which appear to lie outside the known terrain of the history of composition. Yet the influence of Adorno in the twentieth century ought to testify to the power of philosophical ideas in preparing the ground for the reception of a body of music into the status of a cultural icon. If a similar case could be made for the influence of philosophers in an earlier age, then the relevance of philosophical ideas generally for the history of music ought to be conceded. Recent work in the history of musical aesthetics, indeed, shows promise for a broader construal of the sphere of interest of musicological inquiry. As Carl Dahlhaus observed, the ideas by which music is understood are just as important for understanding the art as the actual notes a composer sets on paper.[24] For music to have embodied a metaphysical view of the world, understanding that view will be possible only on the knowledge of the texts which define it.

To insist on the relevance of philosophical texts, however, is to raise the possibility of serious misunderstanding. For in the Anglo-American philosophical community, the dominant school is that of ordinary language analysis. This approach seeks to understand the nature of things on the basis of customary concepts and ordinary usage of key terms. As a consequence, it is often profoundly ahistorical, indeed, hostile to the notion of historically rooted understanding. If the task is to recover the original essence of either classicism or modernism, however, it will be necessary to take an historical approach, to credit the sources for what light they can shed on cultural phenomena which no longer seem self-evident.[25] To base this inquiry on commonly shared assumptions would be precisely to abdicate responsibility for exploring the assumptions which may be so taken for granted that we cannot be aware of them or be cognizant of their controversial nature. To reject history, therefore, is to risk serious distortion of understanding by allowing the cherished blind spots of a civilization to go unchallenged.

In the case of music, what most seriously needs remedy is the pervasiveness of both an historicist relativism that validates only the present, and a pronounced subjectivism in aesthetic perception. If music, like all the other arts, must be approached with these assumptions, then its insignificance within the context of a larger, shared culture is guaranteed. But it is precisely the aim of modernist aesthetics to deny the concept of a shared culture, to make art a privately autonomous experience. Thus, analytic philosophy and the modernist aesthetic too often join hands to block any re-examination of the adequacy of this view of music.

Both Adorno and Hesse, however, point beyond the realm of the private experience of art to allow that once, at least, a metaphysical or a moral understanding was possible and indeed crucial for the construction of a common culture. This book, therefore, seeks to take seriously the historical positions which underlie the bifurcated musical culture of the modern world. Such a task, however, immediately encounters further obstacles. For are there not suspicions about both metaphysics and a shared ethical life as diminishing the moral agent's autonomous status? Metaphysics in the everyday sense, of course, is already suspect; it suggests the realm of illusory spirituality — although it should be taken seriously as an historical phenomenon whenever it appears as a shaping influence on cultural life. But it is metaphysics in the classical sense that is most suspect: the science of being as being, as Aristotle expressed it, that is, the principles common to all being,[26] appears antiquated in light of the rejection of metaphysics in general by Nietzsche and Heidegger.[27] The twentieth century is deeply nominalist, committed to a denial of universals of all kinds: hence, the universal idea of the good-in-itself, whether conceived along the lines of Plato or Aristotle, appears incomprehensible. When interpretation of art or literature is demanded, then, it becomes reduced to the least common and most obvious denominator: the political. Traditional ideas of beauty, order and ethical content simply make no sense to many today. But to repeat: the price may well be an inability to comprehend either traditional or modernist art; at best, it is to risk a one-sided understanding of art and its significance.

This book, therefore, is an essay in the recovery of the concept of the metaphysical and its historical importance to the musical tradition in both its classicist and its modernist phases. Its method will necessarily be grounded in a respect for historical texts, since it is by texts that traditions are constituted. For music, this is particularly essential, for when music is without words, it is in a sense mute; it does not reveal its secrets on its own. Purely instrumental music is notoriously difficult to interpret definitively; only the presence of a text begins to sweep away the curtains of ambiguity and allow some sense to be made of what is heard. If, following Hanslick's paradigm, we take pure music to be the essence of the art, then music appears essentially ambiguous, devoid of any meaning expressible by words.[28] To make the art of music *sui generis* in this way, however, is to forget both the historical importance of texted music in opera and song, and to neglect the rich resources of contemporaneous philosophical and critical commentary which might reveal a commonly shared context for musical interpretation. The result, in that case, is a puzzle rather than enlightenment.

It will be helpful to consider an illustrative example of the kind of contemporaneous sources available. One of the best arguments for the importance of philosophical aesthetics in the nineteenth century lies in its wide diffusion in works aimed at musicians and music lovers in general. In England, Ernst Pauer's little book, *The Elements of the Beautiful in Music* (1877), provides evidence of the popular dissemination of German idealist aesthetic theory.[29] Based on Ferdinand Hand's *Aesthetik der Tonkunst* (1837), Pauer simplified Hand's philosophy of music and thereby rendered the first significant contribution to musical aesthetics accessible to the general reader in English.[30] Since similar kinds of works had appeared in Germany as well, it will be possible to take Pauer's treatise as an example showing the most important elements of the dominant school of philosophical aesthetics in the nineteenth century. It reveals what was considered important for a layman's understanding of the art.

Pauer conceived of the explanation of music's meaning and significance in terms of beauty – the concept so foreign to the twentieth century. He divided beauty, moreover, into three main types: formal beauty characteristic beauty and ideal beauty. In establishing such a typology, Pauer conceived of beauty as a property of the object of perception, not simply a subjective apprehension on the part of the perceiver. But the three types were moments of beauty, rather than three separable elements. For beauty was a whole: 'A real and perfect work of art results from the union of these three elements or qualities, and not one of them can be dispensed with ... .' One or the other might predominate in a given work, but none could be detached without rendering the work unintelligible and meaningless. The origin of the three moments of beauty lay in life itself, according to Pauer, for they may also be identified as 'a free form, a full and vigorous life, and an ideal animation'.[31] The freedom and vigour of the human spirit, together with its imaginative capacity to conceive the ideal, were the foundation for all creation of the beautiful in art.

It would be possible to trace the constituent parts of Pauer's synthesis to their origins in Kant, Schiller, Hegel, Schelling and Hand, but the important point here is Pauer's hierarchical conception of beauty. Formal beauty is the result of 'order, symmetry, and proportion in a work', but cast in a 'spirit of freedom' so that warmth and a sense of life are preserved.[32] Here, form is not conceived statically, but rather as an image of life itself, rendered in harmonic, rhythmic and melodic motion. Characteristic beauty is precisely what gives musical form its life and energy: following Goethe, he takes it to be 'that which marks or expresses the distinctive qualities of a person or a thing.'[33] This, however, is a matter of expression of feeling; for Pauer as for most nineteenth-century writers, this was what seemed to lie most obviously and uniquely in the aesthetic power of music. For Pauer, as also for many others, this expressive power was given in the language of harmony, mode, key levels and rhythmic figures, although these factors did not completely specify the expression. Ultimately, the perception of the expressiveness and characteristic beauty of a work was largely intuitive.

Even characteristic beauty, however, was not sufficient for the perfect musical work. In common with the Platonic tradition, Pauer expects that intellectual interest will cause enjoyment to reach the highest point, for then 'we seem to be initiated into a kind of mystery, which we are by degrees able to solve, and whose intricacies we can unravel'.[34] This interest is supplied by 'ideal beauty'. For Pauer, this is a matter of the representation of ideas, which exist in the Platonic 'ideal world' and bear the stamp of 'the infinite'.[35] As a consequence of the divergent sources employed, however, Pauer shifts ground constantly in identifying the nature of the ideal. Ideal beauty may occur 'when the soul of the composer reveals itself with the greatest clearness': for the soul inhabits the realm of the infinite, or noumenal, in Kantian metaphysics. Here, the basis for the nineteenth-century biographical approach to musical interpretation becomes clear: it is not simply that music, as an expressive medium, transparently reveals the creator, but rather that the soul itself, the indefinable thing-in-itself for Kant, shines through the musical representation. On the other hand, ideal beauty may occur when purely intellectual ideas cause the soul 'to soar beyond the limits of time and space', as in opera and vocal music. Finally, it may occur when 'feelings are expressed and suggested, through which the distant regions of the infinite announce themselves and appear to us like a halo ...'.[36] Here, Pauer employs the poetic imagery of E. T. A. Hoffmann to speak of the realm of the ideal unarticulated by ideas, but only intimated by feelings of something much greater and more noble than ourselves.[37]

If such prose is difficult to take seriously today, it must nonetheless be understood if the Romantic aesthetic of the nineteenth century is to provide any help in understanding the music of that era. Pauer makes the category of ideal beauty a metaphysical one: that is, beauty becomes a category by which the nature of things in this world, including music, may be understood in objectively ascertainable terms. In particular, it is dependent on the idealist metaphysical tradition extending from Plato to Kant, as different as those two poles of philosophical thought were. But what makes Pauer difficult today is not the confusion of such different conceptions of the ideal or the noumenal realm, but rather the employment of such terminology at all. For it has been characteristic of the twentieth century to subjectivize the concept of the ideal, to deny the philosophical quest for knowledge of essences, to demystify the realm of the noumenal. But the price is a loss of comprehension of the idealist aesthetic and the music it attempted to justify and interpret.

We shall have occasion to return to Pauer and the aesthetic he represents. Here what is important is the structure he erects by which to conceive the relation of the different types of beauty. It is a hierarchical order: form, character, and the ideal constitute an ascending gradation of aesthetic worth. All are kinds of beauty discoverable within a musical work; they possess an ontological reality. But it is the ideal which is the most clearly metaphysical: it suggests the realm of the Platonic Ideas, the Kantian Infinite (as the noumenal realm becomes in Romantic terminology), and Romantic mystery. Music was intelligible only to the extent that it possessed all three degrees of beauty, and it possessed significance only to the extent that it was intelligible on those terms. Beauty was therefore a property of hierarchical ordering, in which the highest degree was the ultimate goal of perception. This is the intellectual framework by which we should approach the musical culture of the nineteenth century.

Yet such idealism no longer convinces, in part because it is no longer understood. If form and expression remain part of the aesthetic vocabulary, they do not possess the same meaning as they did for Pauer. But it is the loss of the intelligibility of the ideal that makes it impossible to understand what provided coherence to the nineteenth-century aesthetic. It does not help that the articulation of the ideal appears so vague in all of the sources, but the twentieth century has rejected the concept of a metaphysical ideal for other reasons as well. This is the realm of beauty Adorno would banish from the modern musical culture; it is also what appears missing in Hesse's account of the ethical serenity of classical music. Ultimately, however, we shall have to take such language seriously if we are to understand the intellectual foundations of the musical tradition inherited from the eighteenth and nineteenth centuries.

It therefore appears that the modern denial of metaphysics and the inability to conceive a shared culture go hand-in-hand. If traditional notions of order and beauty grounded the reception of musical works into the culture of the common practice period, it is also true that the wide sharing of these concepts constituted one of the important conditions for musical creativity. They constituted a common intellectual culture that was able to respond to new works with a critical judgement trained by accepted standards and practice in making judgments. This critical judgement was not simply a matter of rejecting all new works, as too often twentieth-century critics have held it, since the nineteenth century was the time of the very formation of the canonic repertoire. This formation was by means of the acceptance of new works meeting certain standards of form, expressiveness and intellectual significance. Hence, the metaphysical criteria of order and beauty provided ways in which new works could be judged and received into the repertoire.

The bifurcation of musical culture in the twentieth century is the symptom of a deep divide within the larger society. The retention of the classical canon and the quest of the avant-garde for the absolutely new testify to two rival metaphysical visions: the vision of an ideal which orders human life as, indeed, all of nature, and the denial of such an order. Between these, there can be no peace; the concert hall, therefore, becomes the battleground of these rival metaphysical positions. But the existence and nature of order are philosophical questions; they need to be discussed as philosophical issues in order to understand the deepest significance of musical styles. The result may well not persuade anyone to adopt a different musical taste, but it can make clear the issues entailed in both the preservation of the old and the quest for the new.

The study that follows, therefore, seeks to elucidate the mentalities underlying both the culture of classical music and the culture of the avant-garde. It will be a dialectical examination, for the modernist mentality is so taken for granted that it may be difficult to see what is significant about it. Yet the historical existence of alternative ways of conceiving the purposes of human life and musical culture draws attention to the distinguishing characteristics of the modernist view. Thus, much of the exploration of the modernist mentality will take place in the context of the re-examination of classical culture. The specific historical origins of the avant-garde, moreover, cannot assume their fullest significance without a prior understanding of the metaphysics of classicism. At the same time, the significance of classicism does not fully emerge except in contrast to the modernist metaphysical position. Hence, although Part One examines the culture of classicism and Part Two the culture of modernism, both parts rely on the contrast of the two positions to show what is most important in each. The result will be a critical reexamination of each of the two cultures; if the assumptions underlying the classical repertoire no longer convince some in the academy, neither do the assumptions underlying the avant-garde prove immune from criticism. The shared musical culture of Western civilization appears now to be challenged by this situation.

A shared culture, however, is a constituent of the common good of any society; it is the communion in the representation of what gives life dignity and meaning. The post-modernist agenda of denying the necessity or desirability of a shared culture is a political agenda: its radical individualism and subjectivism both reveal and contribute to the disintegration of political culture and civil society. Its thesis that all culture is political is a politicization of culture that, if successful, will destroy not only the shared culture but the possibility of a shared political order as well.[38] But if neither the classicist nor the modernist conception of culture remain credible today, then, it may be necessary to rethink the nature of what gives meaning to human existence before a shared musical life will again make sense. Far from warranting a post-modernist celebration of cultural fragmentation, the challenge posed by the bifurcation of musical life demands a serious reconsideration of the philosophical puzzles and historical developments which have contributed to the appeal of the post-modernist solution in recent years. What follows is an attempt at such a reconsideration.

Notes

1. See, for example, Richard Leppert and Susan McClary, eds, *Music and Society: The Politics of Composition, Performance and Reception* (Cambridge: Cambridge University Press, 1987); and Lawrence Kramer, *Music as Cultural Practice, 1800–1900* (Berkeley: University of California Press, 1990).
2. C. P. Snow, *The Two Cultures; And a Second Look* (Cambridge: Cambridge University Press, 1963).
3. See Theodor W. Adorno, *Philosophie der neuen Musik* (Frankfurt: Europäische Verlagsanstalt, 1958), translated as *Philosophy of Modern Music*, trans. Anne G. Mitchell and Wesley V. Blomster (New York: The Seabury Press, 1973), and Donald Mitchell, *The Language of Modern Music*, 2nd edn (Philadelphia: University of Pennsylvania Press, 1994).
4. On the revolt of the avant-garde, see Renato Poggioli, *The Theory of the Avant-Garde*, trans. Gerald Fitzgerald (Cambridge, MA: Harvard University Press, 1968). On the problem of tradition in the arts, see Paul O. Kristeller, '"Creativity" and "Tradition"', *Journal of the History of Ideas* 44 (1983), pp. 105–13.
5. For Hesse's novel, citations will be to Hermann Hesse, *Das Glasperlenspiel: Versuch einer Lebensbeschreibung des Magister Ludi Joseph Knecht samt Knechts hinterlassenen Schriften*, in *Gesammelte Werke* (Frankfurt am Main: Suhrkamp Verlag, 1970), vol. 9; *The Glass Bead Game (Magister Ludi)*, trans. Richard and Clara Winston (New York: Holt, Rinehart and Winston, 1969).
6. *Philosophie der neuen Musik*, p. 45; *Philosophy of Modern Music*, pp. 41–2.
7. *Philosophie der neuen Musik*, p. 50; *Philosophy of Modern Music*, p. 47.
8. *Philosophie der neuen Musik*, p. 33; *Philosophy of Modern Music*, pp. 27–8.
9. *Philosophie der neuen Musik*, p. 126; *Philosophy of Modern Music*, p. 133.
10. *Philosophie der neuen Musik*, pp. 17–18; *Philosophy of Modern Music*, pp. 9–10.
11. Theodor W. Adorno, *Quasi una Fantasia: Essays on Modern Music*, trans. Rodney Livingstone (London: Verso, 1994), p. 265.
12. See especially Plato, *Republic*, Book VI, 505a–511e.
13. Adorno, *Quasi una Fantasia*, p. 267.
14. Ibid., p. 309.
15. *Philosophie der neuen Musik*, p. 76; *Philosophy of Modern Music*, p. 77.
16. Hesse, *Das Glasperlenspiel*, pp. 99–100, 201; *The Glass Bead Game*, pp. 96–7, 188.
17. *Das Glasperlenspiel*, p. 44; *The Glass Bead Game*, p. 43.
18. *Das Glasperlenspiel*, pp. 346–7; *The Glass Bead Game*, p. 315.
19. The classic statement of this position is John Stuart Mill's essay *On Liberty* (1859). It has not been above criticism; see Gertrude Himmelfarb's Introduction to the Penguin edition (Harmondsworth, 1974).
20. Immanuel Kant specifically excludes the category of the good from aesthetic judgment as being an example of illegitimate 'interest'; the judgement of the beautiful must instead be entirely 'disinterested'. *Kritik der Urteilskraft*, ed. Karl Vorländer (Hamburg: Felix Meiner Verlag, 1990), Part I, Sections 2, 4, pp. 39, 43; *Critique of Judgement*, trans. J. H. Bernard (New York: Macmillan, 1951), pp. 38,

45. The powerful hold of this thesis in the late twentieth century may be judged by Alan Goldman's elegant synthesis, *Aesthetic Value* (Boulder, CO: Westview Press, 1995), esp. pp. 150ff., where he discusses the value of engagement with alternative 'worlds' in works of art.

21. Hesse, *Das Glasperlenspiel*, pp. 110-11; *The Glass Bead Game*, p. 106.

22. *Philosophie der neuen Musik*, p. 15; *Philosophy of Modern Music*, p. 8.

23. Clement Greenberg, 'Avant-Garde and Kitsch', in *Art and Culture: Critical Essays* (Boston: Beacon Press, 1961), pp. 3–21.

24. See Dahlhaus's Preface to the English edition, *Esthetics of Music*, trans. William Austin (Cambridge: Cambridge University Press, 1982), pp. vii–viii. The most thorough recent survey of the history of musical aesthetics is Edward Lippman's *A History of Western Musical Aesthetics* (Lincoln and London: University of Nebraska Press, 1992).

25. Lydia Goehr has pointed to the limitations of analytic philosophy and also recommended taking historical sources seriously in *The Imaginary Museum of Musical Works: An Essay in the Philosophy of Music* (Oxford: Clarendon Press, 1992). Yet her account of the concept of the work places its emergence much later than the historical evidence would warrant, and joins together contradictory aesthetic principles in an attempt to explain the nature of the concept. It will be necessary to re-examine some of the historical material to seek a better account of the aesthetic of the work.

26. Aristotle, *Metaphysics* 1003a21, trans. Richard Hope (1952; Ann Arbor: University of Michigan Press, 1960), p. 61.

27. Martin Heidegger's *Sein und Zeit* (1927) analyses human existence (Dasein) in terms of the subjective psychology of mood, or 'attunement'; it therefore replaces the traditional metaphysical concept of the soul, consisting in powers or faculties, with the moods which make life authentic or inauthentic: see *Being and Time: A Translation of 'Sein und Zeit'*, trans. Joan Stambaugh (Albany: State University of New York Press, 1996), pp. 126ff. Nietzsche rejected the metaphysical being of the good, the true and the beautiful in, for example, the notes published as *Der Wille zur Macht* (1901), translated as *The Will to Power*, trans. Walter Kaufmann and R. J. Hollingdale, ed. Walter Kaufmann (New York: Random House, 1967), Section 804, pp. 423–4. Nietzsche profoundly influenced Heidegger's later philosophy. See Stanley Rosen, *The Question of Being: A Reversal of Heidegger* (New Haven: Yale, 1993), for a reconsideration of this rejection of the most fundamental of philosophical topics.

28. Cf. Eduard Hanslick, *On the Musically Beautiful*, trans. Geoffrey Payzant (Indianapolis: Hackett, 1986), p. 15.

29. 2nd edn (London: Novello, Ewer and Co., 1877).

30. Hand's work, in two volumes, appeared in two editions (Leipzig: Eisenach, 1837 and 1847), and the first part was itself translated into English as *Aesthetics of Musical Art; or, the Beautiful in Music* by W. E. Lawson, 2nd edn (London: W. Reeves, 1880).

31. Pauer, *Elements*, p. 7. The emphasis on life is reminiscent of Hegel's definition of the Idea in terms of life: *The Encyclopaedia Logic*, trans. T. F. Geraets, W. A Suchting, H. S. Harris (Indianapolis: Hackett, 1991), 216, p. 291.

32. Pauer, *Elements*, pp. 9–10.

33. Ibid., p. 19. Cf. Johann Wolfgang von Goethe, *Der Sammler und die Seinigen*, in *Schriften zur Kunst*, Part 1, vol. 33 of *Werke* (Munich: Deutscher Taschenverbund, 1962), p. 199.

34. But Pauer's (and Hand's) source for the concept of ideal beauty is not only Platonic; cf. Friedrich Schiller, *On the Aesthetic Education of Man In a Series of*

Letters, trans. Elizabeth M. Wilkinson and L. A. Willoughby (Oxford: Clarendon Press, 1967), 16th Letter, p. 111.

36. Pauer, *Elements*, p. 38. Cf. *E. T. A. Hoffmann's Musical Writings: Kreisleriana, The Poet and the Composer, Music Criticism*, ed. David Charlton, trans. Martyn Clarke (Cambridge: Cambridge University Press, 1989). *The Poet and the Composer* is one of the most important sources for the Romantic musical aesthetic.

37. See 'The Poet and the Composer' in *E. T. A. Hoffman's Musical Writings*, pp. 188 ff.

38. A comprehensive critique of the theses of post-modernist criticism lies beyond the scope of this book, but it is worth noting that its arguments may be fundamentally challenged: see Pieter C. van den Toorn, *Music, Politics, and the Academy* (Berkeley and London: University of California Press, 1995), who argues that the reduction of music to the political does a disservice to the understanding of music as an art.

PART ONE
The Culture of Classicism

CHAPTER ONE

The Classical Understanding of Tonality

Tonality has traditionally been understood as the foundation of the music composed in the common practice period of the seventeenth, eighteenth and nineteenth centuries. The term embraces everything which appears most distinctive – and to many, most appealing – in the musical style of the period: the prevalence of consonance, rootedness in a tonic key for each work through reliance on functional harmonies, and the integration of melodic or thematic material in different key levels. But tonality in this sense was more than a practice: it was a set of expectations. Above all, therefore, tonality was a normative system.

To seek the intellectual foundations of such a familiar style may seem superfluous. Yet whether the concept of tonality embraces all of the above characteristics, or only the rootedness in a tonic pitch, has become a serious debate. Thus what accounts for the phenomenon of tonality is by no means clear, because what constitutes the core concept is disputed. But the dispute over tonality today arises out of a deeper and longer controversy over its legitimacy. At issue is not just the nature of an historical style, but its claim to normativity. For why, indeed, should consonance, key, functional harmony, and melody have any claim to constitute a privileged style? For critics today, as for the avant-garde earlier in the twentieth century, this is the heart of the issue.

Whereas early theorists of the seventeenth century attempted to make the essential elements of the style dependent on the natural phenomenon of the overtone series, modern theorists of the twentieth century have largely rejected such a claim. At most, the need for a simple tonal unity is recognized, with a plurality of types of tonality; the specific kind of tonality fundamental to the common practice period becomes just one approach among many.[1] But if nature does not ground the details of musical style, then it follows that style is a cultural choice, an arbitrary constellation of parameters which might be chosen quite differently in another historical or social context.

The denial of naturalism, then, leads inevitably to the thesis of historicism, whereby tonality becomes simply one phase in the development of musical organization of sonic materials. This is Adorno's position: tonality was never something created out of natural acoustical facts. Rather, it was part of the attempt to emancipate human nature from physical nature, and thus also to accomplish 'the subjection of nature to human purposes'. As such, it belonged to 'mercantile society, whose dynamics stress totality and demand that the elements of tonality correspond to these dynamics on the most basic level.'[2] On this Marxist view – still important to the post-modernist critique – tonality was an entirely artificial construct arising out of the conditions of bourgeois society. But even without the questionable sociological premise, the sense that any particular tonal organization has a claim to privilege as a result of its intrinsic nature evaporates as a result of historicism.[3] Indeed, it must become impossible to discuss music in terms of a concept of nature. With that, however, the ability to distinguish styles and tastes also becomes impossible: we are left with merely the undifferentiated sonic bath of artificially created sounds. This is to say, then, that how the nature of tonality is understood has everything to do with whether works composed in the style still have a claim on our attention, if not affection. Both the naturalist and the historicist theses appear weak, however, in failing to account for what seems most compelling about tonal music in the specific sense of the common practice period.

Naturalism and historicism re-examined

The weaknesses of both naturalism and historicism bear closer scrutiny. The naturalist thesis may be traced back to the sixteenth century, when Girolamo Fracastoro observed the sympathetic vibration of strings of equal length in the 1540s.[4] Nearly a century later, Marin Mersenne discovered the sympathetic vibration of strings tuned at the octave and at the fifth.[5] Finally, Joseph Sauveur concluded in 1701 that the resonance of a 'fundamental sound' included the intervals of the twelfth and major seventeenth.[6] This was crucial for Jean-Philippe Rameau's explanation of consonance in his *Génération harmonique* of 1737: there, he argued that the overtone series confirmed the ratios of just intonation as natural phenomena arising within the single sound of a vibrating body.[7] Moreover, this single sound contained within it the first five tones of the overtone series – a number he believed to be the limit of what could be heard within such a resonance (see Example 1.1). Hence, on his view, the natural pleasure taken in the major triad, or 'perfect chord', which had been the foundation of his earlier explanation of compositional practice in *The Treatise on Harmony*. Since Rameau's entire concept of key depended on the resolution of a chain of dissonances to a perfect cadence on the tonic, the problem of what actually required dissonance to resolve was critical.[8] With this explanation of a natural need for dissonance to resolve to consonance, the foundations of the new style had at last a firm foundation. Neither simply force of habit nor long tradition of regarding the lowest ratios of string length as desirable was adequate; now the normativity of consonance had a physical justification. But with this solution came also a justification of tonal centredness in the tonic chord, and an explanation of why root movement by fifth was the strongest. The fundamental chord progression, of the dissonant dominant seventh to the consonant tonic, was fully justified (see Example 1.2).

Example 1.1   The overtone series

Example 1.2   Dissonance resolution in the fundamental chord progression

One question that may be raised is whether consonance is adequately defined by the first five tones of the overtone series: is it indeed the limit of what the ear can hear in the resonance of the fundamental? As a definition, it appears little less arbitrary than the older restriction of consonance to the 'simpler' ratios of string length, up to 6:5 as the minor third. Another problem is that Rameau does not fully account for the nature of tonality. In particular the minor triad, the other fundamental consonant chord, is not adequately explained. Rameau argued, mistakenly, that a resonating body also vibrated in modes slower than that of the fundamental sound; hence, the series of lower partials would generate the inverse of the major triad, namely, the minor triad.[9] Hugo Riemann took up this notion at the end of the nineteenth century not only as the foundation for the minor mode, but of the chordal function built on the fourth scale degree as well.[10] But the acoustical error on which this line of thought was based has served to discredit for most modern theorists the founding of any explanation of consonance on the natural phenomenon of the overtone series.

More seriously, perhaps, the naturalist explanation of consonance does not fully address the question of what creates the perception of key across large-scale musical forms. Since key level was already in the Baroque the foundation of musical structure, this is by no means a trivial problem. Rameau simply says that the leading tone creates the sense of key, and recommends that in a longer composition the composer modulate through a variety of keys, 'returning imperceptibly to those keys which are most closely related to the initial key, finishing there in such a way that it appears as if this key had never been left'.[11] In that case, however, one might wonder whether any sense of contrast is really gained by modulation or, alternatively, whether a unified feeling of key could extend across a longer work.

In the nineteenth century, the theorist responsible for contributing the practice of notating chords by Roman numerals, Gottfried Weber, was clearly bothered by this problem: he made it the central focus of his *Theory of Musical Composition.*

> When our ear perceives a succession of tones and harmonies, it naturally endeavors to find amidst this multiplicity and variety an internal connection – a relationship to a common central point ... . The ear everywhere longs to perceive some tone as the principal or central tone, some harmony as a principal harmony, around which the others revolve as accessories around their principal, to wit, around the predominant harmony.[12]

But he cautioned against an attempt to determine definitively how the ear perceives such tonal unity, giving only general laws. He argued a version of Ockham's Razor: the ear explains combinations of tones in the simplest possible way, and once it is accustomed to hearing a particular key as the primary one, does not change its perception of key without sufficient cause. Even so, however, he had to admit exceptions in the form of habits and reminiscences which might determine a completely different perception of key.[13] Thus, Weber recognized the complexity of key feeling in a longer musical work. Indeed, his theory of harmony proves much more fluid than the standard textbook treatment of the classical harmonic language today.

As a corollary, the final element of dissatisfaction with the naturalist theory of tonality must be the almost exclusive concentration on harmony, when it is melody that is the usually predominant object of perceptual attention in tonal music. For Rameau, harmony was the foundation of melody, so that to know the principles governing the harmonic language was to enable the composer to write any melody he chose; the really hard part was to control the harmonic progressions.[14] Among Baroque composer-theorists, Johann Mattheson emphasized melody much more than others. In his *Complete Capellmeister* of 1739, he listed the requirements of a good melody: 'facility' or naturalness, 'clarity' or simplicity of expression, 'flow' without interruptions, 'charm' from generally stepwise motion, and variety in the choice of intervals. Subsequent writers, notably Joseph Riepel and Heinrich Koch in the second half of the eighteenth century, also emphasized melody, especially its role in articulating musical structure.[15] But if the latter two reflect the growing concern with melody typical of the Classical period, it is remarkable that few nineteenth-century theorists continued the interest in melody. Melody was a matter for the composer's personal inspiration, guided by his command of the harmonic language. To the extent, however, that melodic practice was interwoven in practice and perception of tonality, this appears to reduce melody to a strictly subservient role. A naturalist explanation of tonality, then, appears to be of only limited value in accounting for the supremely melodic musical style founded in tonal harmony.

The historicist thesis, however, appears to have the merit of accounting for the development of both musical style and the theoretical justification in one comprehensive system. The composers who have most significantly affected the development of modernist styles in the twentieth century have been proponents of historicism as their justification. Arnold Schoenberg, most famously, argued that tonality had undergone a substantial change over the course of the nineteenth century, going from the case of one tone clearly dominating the succession of chords to a case of 'extended tonality', in which the relation of all the chords to a single tonic became increasingly dubious. From Richard Wagner's chromatic harmonies to Debussy's use of sonorities without chordal function was a short step in his eyes; but as a consequence the commanding power of tonality was gone forever. Moreover, the psychological appeal and sensory comprehensibility of consonance were no longer essential due to the historical developments of musical style: dissonance had become emancipated from the normativity of consonance because of the familiarity of its use.[16] Hence the thesis of historicism led to the corollary of historical evolution from tonality to atonality, and from consonance to dissonance as a norm.

For Schoenberg's contemporaries, the implications of historicism extended even to the progressive use of new tonal materials. Thus, Ferruccio Busoni described the new scales he proposed, resulting in the 'unity of all keys' as a 'kaleidoscopic blending and interchanging of twelve semitones', erasing the difference between major and minor tonalities; but the next step would be the division of the octave into more than twelve semitones.[17] Schoenberg's student, Anton Webern, agreed: since the overtone series was infinite, '[e]ver subtler differentiations can be imagined, and from this point of view there's nothing against attempts at quarter-tone music and the like ...'.[18] Thus the historical evolution from the church modes to the system of major/minor tonality was yielding to the emergence of an era of chromaticism and perhaps even finer intervals. But this is less a theory of tonality than a justification for other systems altogether.

Stravinsky, too, agreed that tonality had passed away, at least in the classic sense of the term. Although he argued for a more clearly perceptible means of organizing musical sonorities than Schoenberg, he also took tonality to be a limiting case of such organization, possessing 'no absolute value.'[19] Thus, compositional practice in the twentieth century, long dominated by the twin examples of Schoenberg and Stravinsky, has distanced itself from a tonality regarded now as outmoded and limited. But the choice of style then either becomes a product of historical necessity, as Schoenberg argued, eliminating the composer's element of choice, or it becomes an arbitrary choice. In Stravinsky's case, the arbitrariness reveals itself in his passage through three distinct styles – the primitive, the neo-classical and the serial – in the search for an authentic voice. In both the primitive and neo-classical phases, however, the conflicting sonorities of polytonality imply an essential ambiguity.

Not surprisingly, the historicist thesis has achieved the status of philosophical orthodoxy. Adorno, as we have seen, echoed the modernist position in his influential *Philosophy of Modern Music*: for him, tonality was a product of the 'bourgeois era'. That era, however, was over; just as the bourgeoisie was being overthrown or was rendering itself obsolete in the twentieth century, so too was tonality overthrown, having become obsolete. If today the political analogy appears suspect, the musical point stands, and is embraced by those who regard tonality as oppressive and its repertoire of works in need of overthrowing. The question of the nature of tonality, therefore, becomes a question of its legitimacy.

Finally, among serious historians of musical ideas, the historicist thesis has also become common currency. Richard Norton has defended the view that there is no natural foundation of tonal organization, but only a culturally determined order which changes over time.[20] Even those who now question the avant-garde rejection of tonality by Schoenberg and his pupils find little sense in tonality beyond a simple tonal unity; the only acoustical foundation of tonal perception, then, is the octave with its implied fifth contained within it.[21] Consequently, any more specific aspect of classical tonality – such as characteristic root movements, chord functions, or scalar patterns – is still seen as culturally imposed, an essentially arbitrary construction of order. But if this order is seen as essentially a socially constructed one, so that music becomes simply a metaphor for the structures of power within society, then the entire point of classical musical aesthetics is dismissed.

As is well known, the dominant account of the aesthetic purpose of music was to represent the passions of the human soul; Rameau was explicit on this point, and so were nineteenth-century theorists such as Gottfried Weber and philosophers such as G. W. F. Hegel and Victor Cousin.[22] Whether individualism is unique to the bourgeoisie and derives from a capitalist mode of production may well be questioned. But the musical expression of the individual and the subjective could be taken as essentially 'bourgeois' only by reading the tonal order itself as a metaphor of capitalist power relations, to the disregard of the aesthetic self-understanding of the practitioners of classical tonality. The Marxist-inspired sociological analysis, therefore, cannot be used to abridge the investigation of the constitution of tonal order. Historicism, like naturalism, also fails to account for what appears most significant about classical tonality.

If Schoenberg was indeed wrong in his dismissal of the continued relevance of tonality for musical audiences in the modern world, nevertheless, the era of classical tonality does appear to be over. Although today minimalist composers write long stretches of music over constant harmonies, and though this may seem to some a return to the practice of tonal centring, it is in fact far removed from the complex and highly ordered language of what is commonly called tonality. Hence we are still in need of an adequate account of the specific order that constituted tonality. This can be procured only by an examination of the original concept of tonality. Whereas both Rameau and Gottfried Weber employed the concept of key, however, and struggled to account for what gave birth to the perception of key in longer compositions, the concept of tonality was itself a nineteenth-century creation, a product indeed of an historicizing view of musical development. Nevertheless, an examination of this concept will show that it was deeply indebted to the naturalist thesis. The relationship of natural factors and historical development in the theory of tonality must therefore be re-evaluated.

The origin of the concept of tonality

The concept of tonality first achieved wide currency in the 1840s through the writings of a Belgian theorist teaching in Paris, François-Joseph Fétis. He rejected all naturalistic means of accounting for the 'science' of harmony, including partials in the overtone series, traditional divisions of string length to produce the integer ratios of just intonation, and consonance within the audible resonance of vibrating bodies. He was particularly concerned to show that melody arose from the same principle as harmony, so that the one would not be merely derivative from the other. Nevertheless, he agreed with the polarity of consonance and dissonance fundamental to Rameau's theory of harmony:

> I saw that among the multitude of combinations composing the harmony of our music, there are two that our musical instinct accepts as existing by themselves ... : the consonant harmony called the perfect chord, which has the character of repose and conclusion, and the dissonant harmony, designated under the name of the chord of the dominant seventh, which determines the inclination, attraction and movement.

These determined the relationships of sounds designated by the term 'tonality'.[23] But in spite of these two chords being as fundamental for Fétis as for Rameau, he understood their dichotomy of consonance and dissonance to be culturally determined, rather than rooted in the natural order. On his view, the plurality of tonal systems among peoples, the variety of church modes, and the rise of tonality in operatic music of the early Baroque undercut any argument for the acoustical basis of tonality.[24] Hence, there are only different relationships among tones, corresponding to particular emotions or sentiments.

Tonality, therefore, was not just one thing for Fétis: it had a history, and that history was part of the concept. He distinguished four stages in the development of tonality. The first was the 'tonalité unitonique' of the church modes, which allowed only one tonic in a piece of music; the predominantly consonant harmonies, conceived intervallically rather than hierarchically, made it impossible to establish a genuine sense of key or to modulate to another. After the solidification of the dominant seventh as an independent sonority, rather than a mere product of voice-leading, it became possible to establish a clear sense of key and to modulate away from it. This was the 'ordre transitonique', which he ascribed to Monteverdi's invention, and which is still thought of as the essential core of the concept of tonality.[25] Following the Baroque, however, this tonal order had undergone further changes, exploiting the duality of the major and minor modes. 'Mozart appears to have been the first who comprehended that there was a new source of expression, and an aggrandizement of the domain of art, in a property of natural dissonant chords modified by substitutions from the minor mode, a property which consists in establishing multiple relations of tonality, that is, the tendencies of the same chord toward different keys.'[26] The result was the 'ordre pluritonique', so called because of the plurality of modulatory possibilities. But because of the expressive properties of the major and minor modes, the history of tonality is not only a narrative of the development of the potential latent within a particular system of tonal relationships. It is also – and this is the crucial point for Fétis – part of the history of human feeling.

This history of emotion becomes much more important in Fétis's analysis of the final stage reached in his day by the evolution of tonality, the 'ordre omnitonique'. He describes the musical style of the 1840s in unmistakably critical terms:

> The enharmonic collectivity of chords substituted from the minor mode, with alteration, and accompanied by a pedal, furnishes the most complete means of indicating a modulation which is not accomplished and that is resolved in the original key. The effect of this harmony is to be identical, taken in isolation, with the natural dissonant chords of another key: the uncertainty over the resolution is therefore the result of the use of the harmonies.[27]

In other words, there was no longer a clarity of harmonic language within one key; all possible chords could be brought within the tonal orbit of one tonic. But this would end by destroying all possibility of modulation, because one key could not be distinguished from another in a piece of music. Thus, he perceived correctly the price that was to be paid for the even more extensive use of chromatic alteration by composers in the second half of the century. Fétis blamed Rossini for what he called the 'degradation' of musical art, accusing him of making melodies too dependent on harmonic modulation for their emotional expression.[28] But this is to suggest that music was being used to express heightened emotional effects which might not be entirely proper.

Fétis saw music as both the culprit and the reflection of broader social trends in this development of its expressive potential. On the one hand, he realized that there was a musical potential within the tonal system that would be fulfilled sooner or later; on the other hand, he had no doubt that 'the frequent employment of the multiple attractions of tonalities would have the very grave inconvenience of exciting incessantly the nervous emotions'. Music, therefore, would have an inherently social effect, making the exaggerated emotions of the contemporary opera house more prevalent in the world outside the stage. Yet he also saw music as the reflection of that society, which was already in a state of nervous excitement. There was far too much of an addiction to 'the sensation of surprise' for Fétis; he lamented the 'satiety of simple emotions' as 'one of the maladies of the human species'.[29] The character of simplicity and purity was his ideal, therefore, in both human feeling and musical style. In this sense, the history of tonality was already a history of its decay.

It is clear that in spite of his relativizing argument, Fétis absolutizes the value of the Baroque *ordre transitonique*. Even the musical brilliance and elegance of Mozart effected a falling away from the ideal standard of the purity of key perception. The existence of a hidden normativity within Fétis's historicist conception of tonality raises, therefore, a question regarding the origin of his norms. For if it should turn out that his ideals have a sufficient philosophical justification, then his argument for historical or cultural relativism would turn out to be contradicted by his own premise. In that case the historicist argument against the intrinsic nature of musical normativity might also be seriously weakened.

The ideal of character to which Fétis subscribed, however, is easily identifiable and, to the extent that it had a long philosophical pedigree, it surely has a claim to attention. It is essentially a Stoic ideal: Seneca, for example, makes tranquillity the essence of happiness, and the simple life the means to achieve it.[30] But much the same ideal can be found as well in religious faiths; peace, for St Paul, is one of the fruits of the Holy Spirit (Gal. 5:22). Among nineteenth-century philosophers, both Hegel and Cousin endorse the ideal of tranquillity of soul as the highest aspiration of human character.[31] Passion, on this traditional view, is to be conquered as an enemy of the soul's tranquillity; it is a disturbance of the soul, rather than something to be sought for its stimulation. This is the view of Fétis, and is opposed precisely to the sense of passion which has come to dominate the conception of character in the modern world.

Alasdair MacIntyre has pointed to the degree to which the modern conception of the personality is determined by what he calls 'emotivism'.[32]

Philosophical expressions of this are easy to find: MacIntyre points to G. E. Moore's *Principia Ethica* (1903) as one of the most influential statements of it in the English language, but Heidegger's *Being and Time* (1927) could also be adduced as the leading statement in continental philosophy, as it describes the phenomenological perception of human existence in terms of its moods, or states of 'attunement'.[33] Through the enormous influence of Heidegger's Existentialism on twentieth-century thought and, indeed, way of life (one thinks especially of the student revolts of the 1960s), the emotivist culture has been established in the modern West. Thus, while Moore provides a theoretical justification of self-indulgence, it is not necessary to establish this as even the archetypical expression of emotivism. Emotivism may fairly be regarded as the character type of modernity. Attempts, then, to reclaim the role of the passions against what some regard as the exaggerated claims of reason betray the wisdom of the classical idea: Robert Solomon's index of the passions, for example, includes thirteen which are unambiguously positive, twenty-four which are negative, and two which might be regarded as ambiguous.[34] Although the capacity to feel the negative emotions at appropriate times is essential to a well-formed human character, the interesting point is that so many of the passions are negative. They are indeed disturbances of the soul. To celebrate the passions as constituting the meaning or fulfilment of life, therefore, is not without risk.

In the classical conception of the ethical life, however, happiness was considered the goal of the life of virtue; in Aristotelian terms, *eudaimonia* was the aim of moral and intellectual excellence.[35] It therefore makes a great difference whether happiness is conceived in terms of tranquillity or in terms of passion or excitement. In the former case, the ideal is one of stability, so that the virtues and duties of moral life come to fulfilment in a state of satisfaction with the achievement of excellence. In the latter case, however, excitement and passion cannot be permanently sustained by any single achievement; hence, they require ever new objects of attraction by means of endless activity, and always with the risk of amoral actions. Reconceiving passion and excitement as happiness turns the moral world upside down, for any sense of satisfaction must be rejected as contrary to the quest for excitement. But if satisfaction is the only genuine motivation of the moral life, then there would be no motivation to pursue ethical excellence or to fulfil moral obligations in an ethic of excitement. The rejection of happiness as tranquillity of soul, therefore, is fraught with moral consequences. To the extent that this argument can serve to ground an ideal of human feeling, the norm of character seen in Fétis appears justifiable, however at odds it might have been with trends in his day or beliefs generally held today.

This means, however, that the musical norm corresponding to the ideal of tranquillity of soul cannot be dismissed out of hand. The normativity hidden within Fétis's conception of tonality betrays the historicist framework in which he presents it. In fact, the very terms he employs suggest the true nature of his tonal norm: the stages of the evolution of tonality are 'orders' of tonality: tonality is fundamentally an order. If it possesses no natural basis, then, what accounts for the nature of its order?

The concept of tonality is founded irreducibly on the polarity of consonance and dissonance. This is true for Fétis as much as for Rameau. But whereas Rameau defined consonance first in terms of certain traditional numerical ratios, and later in terms of the natural resonance of vibrating bodies, Fétis denies the validity of all such attempts. Consonances are simply what please the ear: the perfect consonances of the octave and fifth, and the imperfect consonances of the thirds and sixths. So far, this is unexceptional. He departs from traditional presentations, however, in considering the perfect fourth a 'mixed consonance' and the augmented fourth or diminished fifth '*consonances appellatives*' – that is, consonances which name the key.[36] Always before, these were treated as dissonances, but Fétis brings them over to the side of pleasing tonal relations, while still recognizing their ambiguous harmonic character. His list of dissonances, then, retains the seconds and sevenths, together with other augmented and diminished intervals as they are used to lead to a melodic resolution. The effect, however, is to blur the distinction between consonance and dissonance sufficiently to make the categories appear arbitrary.

Nevertheless, the harmonic categories of consonance and dissonance are crucial to Fétis's attempt to derive both melody and harmony from the same set of relations, to see them both as belonging to the phenomenon of tonality. For melody, the fundamental concept is that of the scale, which consists of tones of repose, tones of attraction and neutral tones (see Example 1.3). The tonic, the fourth and the fifth are the only tones of repose, while the leading tone (*la note sensible*) is the definitive note of attraction. The third and sixth notes of the scale lack a conclusive character, but they define the mode. This analysis of the scale is derived, however, from the analysis of the attractiveness of the harmonic intervals above the tonic. Considering the interval of the fourth a consonance allows him to justify the fourth scale degree as a tone of repose. Since a major or minor triad can be built on it, as on the tonic or the dominant scale degree, the result is a consistent account of the fundamental opposition built into tonality, the difference between attraction and repose. Hence, he defines modern tonality as residing 'in the attractions of certain intervals to the intervals of repose, and in the connection

Repose   Active   Neutral   Repose   Repose   Neutral   Active   Repose

Example 1.3   Active and passive tones of the scale

of these latter with others which, although deprived of the character of attraction, have however that of conclusion'.[37] The dynamic of attraction to the tonic defines the nature of the tonal order for Fétis.

The important point here is that it is what may be called a teleological order: it is defined by its capacity for directed tonal motion toward an immanent goal. As such, the naturalness or lack thereof matters very little; what does matter is the internal consistency and clarity of perception of the directedness embedded within the harmonic and melodic language. Hence, the language can develop historically, as Fétis described, and still remain comprehensible as a kind of tonality. Yet there will be clear limits to that development, as he insisted. For if the perception of the distinctness of keys is seriously eroded, then modulation becomes impossible; and if the fundamental distinction between consonance and dissonance is denied to the listener, then the entire dialectic of tension and repose disappears, including that of the harmonic language of classical tonality. A teleological order depends, at the very least, on clear sonic polarities and more subtle contrasts.

Since such contrasts are precisely what the twentieth-century avant-garde has sought to deny, it is worth considering the arguments against their natural origin, together with what acoustical foundations there might really be, in order to understand better the nature of the tonal order. In particular, it will become clear why a mere tonal unity is not a sufficient account of the concept of tonality, but rather that an account of the normativity of consonance, functional harmony and return to the original key is required. To what extent the teleological nature of tonality was understood during the common practice period will be crucial for establishing the credibility of this interpretation of classical musical style.

The teleological order of tonality

Traditionally, the contrast between consonance and dissonance has been the foundation of the teleological order of tonality, essential to the directedness inherent in the resolution of the latter to the former. Schoenberg and his pupils, however, conceived consonance and dissonance not as polar opposites, but as qualities arranged along a scale of degrees of complexity. For Schoenberg, this was fundamentally a matter of the degree of comprehensibility, arising from the position of an interval as it appears in the overtone series; he had argued in his *Harmonielehre* of 1911 'that dissonant tones appear later among the overtones, for which reason the ear is less intimately acquainted with them'. Hence, the so-called dissonances were simply 'more remote consonances', and the greater the familiarity with them, the more the 'difficulty of comprehension' would be removed.[38] Since he perceived this to have been the process at work over the course of the nineteenth century, it seemed to him that it could be continued in the twentieth century, and that what he called 'the emancipation of the dissonance' could make the comprehensibility of dissonance exactly equivalent to that of consonance. It has been argued persuasively that this is simply impossible from a perceptual and psychological point of view.[39] But the important point here is Schoenberg's claim that dissonances are just tones that appear later in the overtone series, so that there is no essential difference between consonance and dissonance.

As we have seen, Anton Webern carried the argument even further, claiming that because the overtone series is in principle infinite, historical progress in musical perception is also potentially infinite. Thus, tonality had yielded to chromaticism, as the consonances at the bottom of the series and the diatonic intervals of the third octave finally were replaced by the prevailing use of the chromatic intervals of the fourth and higher octaves in both linear and harmonic constructions. Yet Webern also insisted that 'we must understand that consonance and dissonance are not essentially different – that there is no essential difference between them, only one of degree'.[40] Chromaticism and dissonance were explained by the same principle: the natural phenomenon of the higher reaches of the overtone series. They were not essentially different from the diatonic, consonant intervals, yet at the same time they had definitively replaced them.

What is significant here is the marriage of naturalism and historicism in a way that undermines the claims of each in the argument. On the one hand, there is a clear doctrine of historical development, and on the other, a firm foundation in the natural phenomenon of the overtone series, which had heretofore always been used to justify the essential distinction between consonance and dissonance. Now, either the overtone series is or is not the foundation of intervallic perception; one cannot have it both ways. Against the claim for the determining nature of the overtone series is the apparent arbitrariness of limiting the perception of consonance to the first five intervals of the series; the same criticism can be made of the older, but equivalent formulation of the Pythagorean division of the vibrating string, in which the consonances are taken to be the first five integer ratios and their octave complements. In that case, however, there ought not be any reason for one particular historical development. But if the overtone series is the source of perception of clear intervallic distinctions, then an infinite historical development of appreciation for 'more complex', that is, dissonant intervals in the series would appear questionable. The issue might well not be one simply of comprehensibility.

Both the naturalist and the historicist accounts of tonality, therefore, appear weak. If naturalism appears arbitrary in its definition of consonance and insufficient in its explanation of tonality, historicism turns out to rely on a naturalist explanation, in sometimes self-contradictory ways. The attempt to define what gives pleasure to the ear by means of either a historicist or a natural perception of resonance appears, therefore, to fail on the prevailing points of view today. There is, however, a legitimate acoustical explanation of the perception of musical intervals. It was discovered by the great nineteenth-century physicist, Hermann Helmholtz, but its essential principle had been realized even in the Renaissance. This is the true union of natural principles and historicist discovery.

After Fracastoro had observed the sympathetic vibration of strings, concluding that sound was transmitted by air waves, Giovanni Battista Benedetti hypothesized that consonances were generated 'through a certain equalizing of the percussions or through the equal concurrence of air waves, or their cotermination'.[41] This was in 1563; Mersenne repeated the explanation in 1636, arguing that the frequent reinforcement of the vibrations of the lower tone was the source of the pleasure taken in consonance: 'because pleasure comes from union; that is why one says that love unites hearts and the affections, and that resemblance is the cause of love ...'.[42] The consonances, therefore, could be arranged in a hierarchy, but there would be a considerable gap between the consonances and the dissonances based on a calculation of the reinforcement of vibrations: there would not be a simple continuum such as the overtone series suggested to Schoenberg. But the essential point is that the principle of a physical basis for consonance lying in the reinforcement of waveforms was realized very early. The numerical ratios of Pythagorean tuning, and later of just intonation (expressed also in the overtone series), were simply the shorter way of representing the concept of differences readily perceived by the ear.

It was Helmholtz, however, who finally explained the phenomenon of consonance and dissonance completely in 1862. Since resonating bodies vibrate in the upper partials simultaneously with their fundamental tone (which he was the first to realize accounted for timbre), it followed that the harmoniousness of an interval was a function of the 'beats' produced by the upper partials interacting together: the fewer beats, the more consonant the interval.[43] The more dissonant the interval, the more beats, and the more complex the wave form will appear if the sum of the constituent wave forms is plotted on a graph. The closer a wave approximates the smooth curve of a single, pure pitch, the more consonant it will be perceived to be. Hence there is good reason for saying that there is a perceivable difference between consonance and dissonance; while both qualities may exhibit a continuum, it cannot be argued that they merge imperceptibly into one another. There simply is not the ambiguity that Schoenberg and others have claimed.

Helmholtz's work, therefore, corroborates the ratios of just intonation, but also explains why Fétis's objections to a natural explanation do not require the complete abandonment of naturalism. The issue of the consonance of the perfect fourth and the diminished fifth is in fact settled by a natural explanation, as indeed their ratios according to just intonation already imply:

4:3 in the former case possesses precisely the same kind of 'simplicity' as a perfect fifth (3:2), and even 15:11 in the latter case should sound complex, rather than clashing, for example, in the manner of minor second (11:10). Moreover, except for the octave, slight deviations in temperament will not materially affect the perception of the beats produced by the upper partials.[44] Rameau, too, had argued that the ear would hear intervals in different temperaments as approximating the pure sound of just intonation.[45] The traditional mathematical explanation was therefore not as ungrounded as it has appeared to modern critics. There is a real acoustical difference between consonance and dissonance, which the tradition of musical perception since the Renaissance has recognized. Moreover, it is clear why dissonance has – until the twentieth century – been thought to require resolution: a dissonant interval is not just more complex than a consonance; rather, it is in some sense painful to the ear because there really are clashes in the partials of the sounding tones. If twentieth-century composers have often sought a higher and more constant level of pain than the tradition allowed, audiences have in general not accepted the perceptual burden; the relative simplicity and purity of consonant intervals makes consonance intrinsically normative.

If consonance is normative, however, it must predominate and be the goal of tonal motion. Dissonance, therefore, must be treated judiciously as requiring resolution. The traditional rules of part-writing guaranteed that dissonance would not threaten coherence, but would rather generate a sense of tonal directedness toward consonance. Thus, neither the traditions of part-writing nor the judgement of public taste can be dismissed out of hand. The normativity of consonance was crucial for the development of the harmonic language of the common practice period.

The second element in the system of tonality, then, was precisely the harmonic language, generally conceived since Hugo Riemann as functional harmony. But this concept of chordal function was in fact a long time emerging as a theoretical construct. Whereas dissonance had been understood in a consistent way from the Renaissance through the mid-nineteenth century, the harmonic language was much more evolutionary. It therefore poses a greater problem for understanding the teleological nature of tonality, for it appears more purely historical and thus accidental. Nevertheless, if we pay attention to the ways in which theorists actually described the harmonic language, it will be clear that there was equally a natural basis for it as for consonance. However much the language evolved, it remained within the potential defined by the acoustical nature of sound, the emergence of atonality being a denial of this rather than an historical extension.

The cadential pattern of the dominant chord moving to the tonic was already in use in the fifteenth century. Although it was later strengthened by the addition of a dissonant seventh, first in suspensions and later as an independent sonority, it appears in Renaissance practice as defined by root movement.[46] Rameau, however, was the first to define the concept of a chord progression.[47] His notion of a 'fundamental bass' consisting of the roots of chords enabled him to classify progressions by root movement. Movement by a fifth was the strongest, movement by a third was the next strongest, and movement by a second weak and therefore reserved for deceptive cadences or other situations requiring 'licence'.[48] The tonic chord was 'perfect' because it was consonant; all other chords were normally dissonant and also normally moved down a fifth in their roots. Thus the dominant (in his terminology, the 'dominant-tonic') was the seventh chord built on the fifth scale degree, and all the other chords were simply 'dominants', being seventh chords on the other scale degrees.[49] This dual reliance on root movement and dissonance resolution is what obscures the question of priority in determining the nature of harmonic progression: which was truly primary in impelling the harmony forward?

The importance of dissonance resolution to the Baroque sense of harmonic progression is heard clearly in the chains of suspensions in the music of Corelli, most familiarly (see Example 1.4 where each dissonance is marked with '×'). It underscores the centrality of the distinction between consonance and dissonance for the evolution of the tonal system. But it does make the nature of that system ambiguous. Rameau himself emphasized both dissonance resolution and root movement in forming the final cadence. Regarding the former, he says: 'If each of these sounds bore a perfect chord, the mind, not desiring anything more after such a chord, would be uncertain upon which of these two sounds to rest. Dissonance seems needed here in order that its harshness should make the listener desire the rest which follows.'[50] Elsewhere, however, he is explicit about the constitutive nature of root movement: 'If the perfect chord of a note is preceded by the seventh chord of a note a fifth above, then the dominant, which ordinarily bears a perfect chord and which bears a seventh without destroying its fundamental in any way, must also be preceded by the seventh chord of the note a fifth above it.'[51] Here, then, is the recognition of a basic chord progression (ii–V–I in modern notation) that subsists by root movement, to which dissonance resolution adds the sense of impulsion toward the tonic triad. There was indeed, therefore, an incipient notion of harmonic directedness dependent upon root movement to establish a key.

Rameau's own caution that music filled with dissonances is not very agreeable confirms this yet more definitively, however: unremitting dissonance, even if every voice resolved properly and propelled the music forward harmonically, was hardly acceptable.[52] Over a century later, Wagner's *Tristan und Isolde* remained the exception that proved the rule; whatever its expressive purposes, dissonance always possessed intelligibility due to its musical function. Moreover, for Rameau dissonances needed in general to be prepared by consonances, and should resolve to consonances,[53] so that the

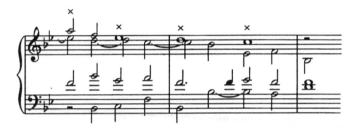

Example 1.4   Dissonance resolution as tonal impulsion in Baroque music: Arcangelo
Corelli, Concerto Grosso in B-flat Major, Op. 6, No. 5, 3rd movement

element of dissonance could hardly be said to predominate. Finally, since
modulation could establish temporary tonics, it was by no means the case that
Rameau's theory required endless dissonance. Root movement, then, was the
more fundamental element in creating harmonic directedness.

By the nineteenth century, Gottfried Weber could identify the 'essential'
harmonies of a key as those chords built on the tonic, the dominant and the
subdominant scale degrees; chords built on other scale degrees were
'accessory' harmonies.[54] Thus there was a clear sense of chordal hierarchy, a
sense recognized by Fétis as well.[55] But there is little sense in either Weber or
Fétis of there being one fundamental chord progression outside of the
cadential movement from dominant to tonic. Indeed, Weber's discussion of
harmonic progressions is revealing: he lists all the possible progressions,
merely finding some stronger than others.[56] Instead, both theorists discuss a
great complexity of chord progressions, reflecting a more fluid harmonic
language that by this time relied on secondary dominants for emphasis and for
modulation. In that context, then, root movement by fifth was extremely
important. The sense of harmonic directedness, therefore, was now dependent
on a chord's hierarchical relation to the tonic and on the use of secondary
dominants. The recognition of this state of affairs was facilitated by Weber's
invention of labelling chords with Roman numerals.

The hierarchy was nevertheless still defined by the relation of a fifth
symmetrically around the tonic. Thus, the constitutive element in both the
Baroque and the Classical-Romantic conception of the harmonic language was
rooted in the first interval after the octave in the overtone series: there is an

acoustical foundation for the most important root movements and the primary harmonies of a key. Although the subsequent theory of Hugo Riemann was considerably more complex, and based on erroneous assumptions about the nature of 'undertones', his development of a theory of harmony that could account for all diatonic and altered chords within a basic framework of three chordal functions was a recognition of the importance of harmonic directedness.[57] Based on the same three functions of tonic, subdominant and dominant, it elevated a natural hierarchy into a fully developed teleology.

The development and refinement of a teleological understanding of the harmonic language of tonality went hand-in-hand with the evolution of compositional practice. Riemann's theory of functional harmony, therefore, reflects the complexity of late nineteenth-century harmonic usage, which continued to develop along the lines indicated already by Fétis. But the important point here is that ever since Rameau, there had been a realization that there was more to the nature of tonal directedness than simply dissonance resolution. There was an authentic sense of the directedness of harmonic motion, the potential of which was gradually realized over the course of the next century and a half. The common practice period, therefore, really was defined by a unified conception of tonality. Fétis's argument, that the history of music exhibits simply shifting phases of the broad construct called 'tonality', misses a crucial distinction. The *ordre unitonique* of the Renaissance, which he defined by the pan-consonant harmonies resulting from strict rules regarding voice-leading and dissonance control, differs fundamentally from the *ordre transitonique* that resulted from the use of the dominant seventh as an independent sonority requiring both harmonic and dissonance resolution. The subsequent orders of tonality, then, fall within the orbit of the development of the intrinsic potential of the major/minor system of the *ordre transitonique*; they do not differ in their essence from the foundation of the common practice period.

Nevertheless, Fétis's distinctions between the phases of development within the common practice period are valuable for raising the question of the role of modulation within larger works. For the *ordre transitonique* was distinguished by modulation to different key levels; the *ordre pluritonique* by modulation through enharmonic equivalents to keys borrowed from the parallel major or minor; and the *ordre omnitonique* by the extensive use of altered chords to create a whole range of temporary tonics. Nevertheless, as we have seen, what creates key perception is somewhat of a problem for the theory of music: whether the modulations are to closely related keys, as in the Baroque, or to keys far removed from the original tonic, how the original key may be heard as the point of return at the end of a piece is by no means a straightforward matter. Rameau's and Weber's equivocations reflect, therefore, a real dilemma in the theory of classical tonality. Why is key perception so important if in fact it is often rather ambiguous and perhaps even undermined by modulation? A closely related question emerges, then: why is modulation so important to the sense of musical structure in tonal music? These are matters of the large-scale teleology of tonal music.

Key perception, modulation and the creation of the tonal order

Key perception arises in the first instance in the tonal context created by a melody or theme harmonized with chords drawn from those related functionally to the tonic. Yet it is not simply the harmonization which implies a tonic, but the melody itself; for both the composer and the listener, the melody may indeed take priority over the harmony in determining the perception of key. Thus the relation between melody and tonality becomes an important, if often neglected, part of music theory.

Like the theory of tonal harmony, the qualities defining good melodic writing also partake of a teleological order. Fétis was correct in seeing the need to integrate melody and harmony into a single theory; his account of the scale as composed of both tones of repose and tones of attraction means that melodies will be perceived in terms of the tonal tension between active and passive tones. That is, the active tones, defined in terms of their inherent dissonance with respect to the tonic, will be perceived to demand resolution, whether or not they are actually dissonances with respect to the underlying harmony. This is far more successful in accounting for how melodies actually work than the theory common today, which sees the tonic as simply providing the most frequently heard note, or the note metrically most emphasized in the melody.[58] Examples 1.5 and 1.6 show melodic occurrences of the tonic heard as points of resolution marked with an arrow, and harmonic occurrences of the tonic chord marked with an asterisk. In these examples from Bach's *Magnificat* and Verdi's *Requiem* – widely separated in period and style – the tonic is far from being the most frequent tone, and in Verdi's case, it is the dominant which is actually the predominating tone. Thus the tonic need not be the most frequent pitch, but it does need to be the pitch heard as the goal toward which the entire melody moves as the result of the need for resolutions of active tones and of the supporting harmony.

In this century, Deryck Cooke has been the most prominent representative of the point that Fétis made in the nineteenth century; his account of the natural tendencies of all twelve notes of the chromatic scale in the context of a major or minor key completes the analysis given by Fétis.[59] But essentially it remains true that active tones resolve downward to the next passive tone, except for the leading tone, which resolves upward to the tonic. Yet Cooke's resulting theory of musical expressiveness has not in general been well received, nor has his naturalist account of the tonal tensions of the scale. As a consequence, the understanding of the value of melody has remained

Example 1.5   Johann Sebastian Bach, *Magnificat* in D Major, BMV 243, 2nd movement, 'Et exultavit', mm. 1–12

impoverished in the twentieth century, its teleological nature obscured by the prevailing scepticism regarding all natural ordering. But melody turns out to be of vital importance in establishing the sense that key level matters, and in creating the perception of a tonic at a local level.

If key perception is crucial to the teleology of melody, however, it becomes imperative to face the questions raised by Gottfried Weber's account of the ambiguities created by modulation: how could a sense of tonality be maintained in spite of large-scale digressions, and why would modulation be necessary at all? Rameau's answer to the latter question had been the traditional argument for variety: just as dissonance adds needed spice to a composition, so does the use of a number of different key levels. As he put it,

Example 1.6   Giuseppe Verdi, *Requiem*, 2nd movement, 'Lachrymosa dies illa', mm. 1–10

'the ear does not respond with pleasure to a key which is heard too often'.[60] Precisely because each temporary tonic could be emphasized compellingly, however, it was possible to use key level as the principal means of structural articulation; its role in this regard is too well known to require elaboration here.[61] Nevertheless, a complex musical structure with great variety in key levels might render key perception ambiguous.

What is taken for granted by all theorists, however, is the reason for seeking not just tonal digression, but return to the tonic. If Gottfried Weber was right in recognizing the complexity of key perception, then it should be no surprise to find that as pieces grew longer and more complex in their key structure in the nineteenth century, the emphasis given the return of the tonic also grew proportionately. For example, Mozart often made the return of the tonic at the recapitulation of his sonata forms a matter of subtlety: as in Example 1.7, the retransition to the recapitulation in the finale of the 'Jupiter' Symphony, there is neither a difference in dynamic level nor a break in the melodic flow to correspond to the cadence re-establishing the tonic key and the opening theme. In contrast, Beethoven and Carl Maria von Weber emphasized the recapitulation through dynamic level, motive elimination and cadential harmonic tension: they left no doubt that the tonic had returned along with the first theme, as illustrated in Example 1.8, the retransition to the recapitulation in Weber's Overture to *Oberon*. Later nineteenth-century composers also made the return of the tonic a genuine point of arrival. Only such a return could erase the potential ambiguity of key perception.

Example 1.7   Wolfgang Amadeus Mozart, Symphony No. 41 in C Major, 4th movement, mm. 220–28

Modulation appears, therefore (at least in later practice), as not just a technique for ensuring tonal contrast, but as a way of setting up a directed order at the largest scale of musical structure. This means that tonality must be understood as teleologically ordered from the most local dimension of a dissonant interval or harmony requiring resolution, through entire melodies and their underlying chord progressions, to the return of the tonic key at the end of a piece. In fact, the importance of the return as the goal accounts for why the initial presentation of the tonic key is often so brief in both Baroque and Classical music. It is the final presentation that requires emphasis. In particular the emphasis on the tonic in the recapitulation of a sonata form establishes the teleological nature of what otherwise might appear to be simply a formulaic musical structure.

Thus, the tonal order must be understood as thoroughly teleological in all

Example 1.8   Carl Maria von Weber, Overture to *Oberon*, mm. 158–66

its dimensions. Even the polarity of the major and minor modes reveals an element of this kind of directedness. It is present in the reluctance of Baroque composers, for instance, to end a movement in a minor key: the Picardy third reflects the sense that the minor mode is itself a construct requiring resolution. Something of the same perception accounts for the larger-scale resolutions of minor keys to major keys in multimovement symphonic works of the nineteenth century; from Beethoven to Mahler, the general sense of minor keys as expressing pain and suffering was not allowed, except in rare instances, to remain the final emotional outlook of a work. Thus, the major mode was regarded as the normative mode, just as consonance was the normative kind of interval.

The comprehensive nature of teleology in the system of tonality makes its foundation, therefore, a crucial principle for its sense of legitimacy and significance. As we have seen, there is a natural foundation of the tonal system as the necessary condition for the historical development of its potential. The difference between consonance and dissonance is a real, acoustical difference, not simply a culturally created one. 'What pleases the ear' is to some extent susceptible of cultural modelling and historical evolution, but the fundamental categories are given by the nature of the waveforms themselves. So, too, with the system of functional harmony: root movement by fifth has its natural origin in the relation perceived in the first intervals of the overtone series; the complexity of the entire system of chord relations is, however, an historical realization of the potential only latent within a range of options defined by the major/minor polarity. Finally, the modulatory possibilities are a function of the system of chord relations, but what is allowed as lying within the range of the intelligible will be dependent on what has already achieved a level of cultural currency. The larger the scale of the order, then, the more culturally and historically conditioned it will be. But the natural foundation can never be forgotten completely, or rejected out of hand, without the loss of the intelligibility of the tonal construct as a whole.

Thus, when modern theorists and philosophers of music claim that tonality was neither historically nor logically necessary, this statement is only half the truth. For although there are certainly elements of historical contingency in the exploitation of stylistic possibilities, there is nonetheless a logical necessity founded on the acoustical facts of the overtone series: consonance will be perceived as intrinsically normative, yielding a normative goal of the return of the tonic triad. In this regard, Schoenberg's attempt to relativize musical perception by construing the overtone series as a simple continuum fails to understand the true significance of the series as a ground for the comprehension of consonance and dissonance. The intervals between tones in the series arise as the fundamental and non-continuous distinction between consonance and dissonance. Hence, it is necessary to recognize that there are both naturalist and historicist elements in the cultural phenomenon of tonality. Only their complementary combination can do justice to the stylistic achievement of the common practice period.

It is the natural elements of tonality, moreover, which give it the crucial immanently goal-directed quality it displays. For without the natural foundation of consonance and of chord function in root movement, there would be no inherently persuasive normativity built into the system. Here we see why the denial of the naturalist thesis is so important to its critics and to the avant-garde: naturalism alone grounds a genuine norm. The aim of the avant-garde has been to deny the authority of existing norms, and the only way to do that is to attack the concept of the natural origin of normativity. Yet its critics have an important point: to claim too much for the natural order is to overstate the case. Tonality is not simply an expression of the nature of things;

it is, especially in the higher reaches of its complexity, a culturally created and historically evolved system of perception. Whether one regards it as out of date, or as the pinnacle of musical achievement, makes little difference, however, for the necessity to understand it for what it is. Hence, the important result of this inquiry so far is that tonality is a teleologically ordered system of tonal relations, having a natural foundation that provides an immanently defined set of norms, and a potential for a culturally constructed set of relationships of considerable complexity.

Nevertheless, this conclusion raises further questions. If tonality is to be regarded as an immanently teleological order, why was that kind of order so important? What did it signify? If neither naturalism nor historicism alone uniquely justifies the legitimacy of the tonal order, then it becomes clear that such legitimacy as it once possessed must have rested on other grounds. To enter into the realm of the legitimacy of musical norms, however, is to leave the realm of music theory and approach that of aesthetics. But if musical norms appear today difficult to justify, it seems impossible to recognize any authoritative grounding of aesthetic norms. It is for this reason that the controversy over the nature of tonality is the shadow of the larger controversy over its legitimacy. Order, however, is a metaphysical concept, so that the question of the legitimacy of the tonal order is ultimately a question of the significance of order in a metaphysical sense. It therefore becomes necessary, if we are to understand the significance of classical tonality, to consider the broader question of what kinds of order musical systems represent.

Notes

1. This is the position taken by William Thomson in his *Schoenberg's Error* (Philadelphia: University of Pennsylvania Press, 1991), p. 82; Roger Scruton recognizes the historic importance of 'triadic tonality', but places it among other possibilities as well in his *Aesthetics of Music* (Oxford: Oxford University Press, 1997), pp. 272–81.

2. Theodor W. Adorno, *Philosophie der neuen Musik* (Frankfurt am Main: Europäischer Verlagsanstalt, 1958), pp. 65, 18; *Philosophy of Modern Music*, trans. Anne G. Mitchell and Wesley V. Blomster (New York: Seabury Press, 1973), pp. 64, 11.

3. This has become the standard textbook view; cf. Otto Karolyi, *Introducing Music* (London: Penguin, 1965), p. 62.

4. On Fracastoro, see Claude V. Palisca, *Humanism in Italian Renaissance Musical Thought* (New Haven: Yale University Press, 1985), pp. 255–7.

5. Mersenne's observation can be found in his *Harmonie universelle, contenant la théorie et la pratique de la musique*, 2 vols, facsimile edited by François Lesure (1636; Paris: Centre national de la recherche scientifique, 1963), vol. 2, p. 52.

6. See Deborah Hayes, 'Rameau's theory of harmonic generation; an annotated translation and commentary of *Génération harmonique* by Jean-Philippe Rameau' (Stanford University: PhD dissertation, 1968), pp. 286–7.

7. Ibid., p. 77.
8. Jean-Philippe Rameau, *Treatise on Harmony*, trans. Philip Gossett (New York: Dover Publications, 1971), Book III, Chs 26–7, pp. 284–8. For a facsimile edition of the 1722 original, see *Traité de l'harmonie réduite à ses principes naturels* (New York: Broude Brothers, 1965).
9. Hayes, 'Rameau's Theory of Harmonic Generation', pp. 32, 64.
10. For Riemann's derivation of the minor triad and the *Unterklang* or inverse sonority functioning as a subdominant, see his *Harmony Simplified; or The Theory of the Tonal Functions of Chords*, trans. H. Bewerunge (London: Augener, [n.d.]), pp. 3, 8.
11. Rameau, *Treatise on Harmony*, Book III, Ch. 23, p. 268.
12. Gottfried Weber, *Theory of Musical Composition*, trans. James F. Warner, 2 vols (Boston: Wilkins, Carter and Co., 1846), vol. 1. pp. 254–5. This is a translation of Weber's *Versuch einer geordneten Theorie der Tonsetzkunst*, 3rd edn, 4 vols (Mainz: Schott, 1830). The first edition appeared in 1818.
13. *Theory of Musical Composition*, vol. 1, pp. 336–48.
14. Rameau, *Treatise on Harmony*, Book II, Ch. 19, pp. 152–4.
15. Johann Mattheson, *Der vollkommene Capellmeister*, trans. Ernest C. Harriss (Ann Arbor: UMI Research Press, 1981), pp. 300ff. Mattheson is discussed in Joel Lester, *Compositional Theory in the Eighteenth Century* (Cambridge, MA: Harvard University Press, 1992), p. 163; on Riepel and Koch, see pp. 261–7 and 285–7. Riepel's major work was the *Anfangsgrunde zur musikalischen Setzkunst* (1752–68); Koch's treatise was the *Versuch einer Anleitung zur Composition* (1782–93).
16. Arnold Schoenberg, 'Composition with Twelve Tones (I)', in *Style and Idea: Selected Writings*, ed. Leonard Stein, trans. Leo Black, rev. edn (Berkeley: University of California Press, 1984), pp. 216–17.
17. Busoni, 'Sketch of a New Esthetic of Music,' trans. Th. Baker (1911), in *Three Classics in the Aesthetic of Music* (New York: Dover Publications, 1962), p. 93.
18. Anton Webern, *The Path to the New Music*, ed. Willi Reich, trans. Leo Black (1963; London: Universal Edition, 1975), p. 15.
19. Igor Stravinsky, *Poetics of Music in the Form of Six Lessons*, trans. Arthur Knodel and Ingolf Dahl (1942; Cambridge, MA: Harvard University Press, 1970), pp. 35–6.
20. Richard Norton, *Tonality in Western Culture: A Critical and Historical Perspective* (University Park, PA: Pennsylvania State University Press, 1984), pp. 37, 59–60.
21. Thomson, *Schoenberg's Error*, p. 66.
22. See Rameau, *Treatise on Harmony*, Book II, Chs 20, 23, pp. 154–6, 163–4; Weber, *Theory of Musical Composition*, vol. 1, p. 18; Hegel, *Vorlesungen über die Ästhetik*, ed. E. Moldenhauer and K. Michel, *Werke in zwanzig Bänden* (Frankfurt am Main: Suhrkamp Verlag, 1970), vol. 15, pp. 148ff.; *Aesthetics: Lectures on Fine Art*, trans. T. M. Knox, 2 vols. (Oxford: Clarendon Press, 1975), vol. 2, pp. 901ff.; Victor Cousin, *Lectures on the True, the Beautiful and the Good*, trans. O. W. Wight (1854; New York: Appleton, 1875), pp. 173–5.
23. François-Joseph Fétis, *Traité complet de la théorie et de la pratique de l'harmonie, contenant la doctrine de la science et de l'art*, 4th edn (Paris: Brandus, 1849), p. iii; all translations of Fétis are the author's. For the prior history of the concept of 'tonality', dating back to 1810, see Ian Bent, ed., *Music Theory in the Age of Romanticism* (Cambridge: Cambridge University Press, 1996), pp. 37ff.
24. Fétis, *Traité complet*, p. xi.

25. Ibid., pp. 165–6.
26. Ibid., p. 177.
27. Ibid., p. 195.
28. Ibid., pp. 199–200. It would be a mistake, of course, to take Fétis too literally on the nature of tonal practice in the second half of the century. In fact, it is only beginning to attract careful attention; see *The Second Practice of Nineteenth-Century Tonality*, ed. William Kinderman and Harald Krebs (Lincoln: University of Nebraska Press, 1996), in which the essays argue for the maintenance of tonal contrast and directionality.
29. Fétis, *Traité complet*, pp. 200 and 183, respectively for these arguments.
30. Seneca, 'On Tranquillity of Mind', in *Dialogues and Letters*, ed. and trans. C. D. N. Costa (London: Penguin, 1997), p. 33.
31. Hegel, *Werke*, vol. 13, pp. 207–8; *Aesthetics*, vol. l, pp. 157; Cousin, *The True, the Beautiful and the Good*, p. 152, follows Plato, *Symposium*, pp. 210a–212a, in ascribing to the ideal of beauty-in-itself the character of simplicity and purity.
32. Alasdair MacIntyre, *After Virtue*, 2nd edn (Notre Dame: University of Notre Dame Press, 1984), pp. 11ff.
33. Martin Heidegger, *Being and Time: A Translation of 'Sein und Zeit'*, trans. Joan Stambaugh (Albany: State University of New York Press, 1996), p. 126.
34. Robert C. Solomon, *The Passions: Emotions and the Meaning of Life* (Indianapolis: Hackett, 1993), pp. 223ff. His index of the emotions is not intended to be exhaustive, but it is indicative of a general truth about our emotional lives: it is easier to feel discontent than it is to be happy.
35. Aristotle, *The Nichomachean Ethics*, Book I, Section 7, 1097a–1098a, trans. and ed. David Ross (Oxford: Oxford University Press, 1925), pp. 11–12. On the relation between happiness and the ethical life generally in classical thought, see Julia Annas, *The Morality of Happiness* (New York: Oxford University Press, 1993).
36. Fétis, *Traité complet*, pp. 7–8.
37. Ibid., p. 21.
38. As Schoenberg argued in his essay, 'Composition with Twelve Tones (I)' from 1941, in *Style and Idea*, pp. 216–17.
39. Thomson, *Schoenberg's Error*, p. 69.
40. Webern, *The Path to the New Music*, p. 16.
41. Quoted in Palisca, *Humanism in Italian Renaissance Musical Thought*, p. 258.
42. Mersenne, *Harmonie universelle*, vol. 2, p. 51 (author's translation).
43. Hermann L. F. Helmholtz, *On the Sensations of Tone as a Physiological Basis for the Theory of Music*, trans. Alexander J. Ellis, 2nd edn (1885; reprinted New York: Dover, 1954), pp. 184ff.
44. Ibid., pp. 199–200. The imperfect consonances will be more forgiving than the perfect fifth or fourth.
45. Rameau, *Treatise on Harmony*, Book I, Ch. 5, p. 32.
46. On this see Carl Dahlhaus, *Studies on the Origin of Harmonic Tonality*, trans. Robert O. Gjerdingen (Princeton: Princeton University Press, 1990), pp. 122ff.
47. Lester, *Compositional Theory in the Eighteenth Century*, pp. 8, 31ff.
48. Rameau, *Theory of Harmony*, Book II, Ch. 1, pp. 60–61.
49. Ibid., Book II, Ch. 9, p. 83.
50. Ibid., Book II, Ch. 1, p. 62.
51. Ibid., Book II, Ch. 21, p. 158.
52. Ibid., Book II, Ch. 9, p. 87.
53. Ibid., Book II, Ch. 16, pp. 118 ff.
54. Weber, *Theory of Musical Composition*, vol. 1, p. 259.

55. Fétis, *Traité complet*, p. 23.
56. Weber, *Theory of Musical Composition*, vol. 2, pp. 407–90.
57. Riemann, *Harmony Simplified*.
58. Cf. Thomson, *Schoenberg's Error*, p. 120.
59. Deryck Cooke, *The Language of Music* (Oxford: Oxford University Press, 1959), summary on pp. 89–90.
60. Rameau, *Theory of Harmony*, p. 268.
61. On this, see Charles Rosen, *The Classical Style* (New York: Norton, 1972), p. 33 on sonata form, and p. 51 on musical form in general.

CHAPTER TWO

Harmony, Order and the Good

The justification of the art of music is cast for the modern world in terms of the concept of aesthetic value. The legitimacy, significance and potential for meaning of music are all made to rest within modern philosophy on this notion of a peculiar value attached to artistic effort, which has largely replaced the older account of beauty as the end of art. Philosophical accounts of the aesthetic value of music have generally focused during the last century on either emotional expressiveness or the perception and appreciation of formal qualities. For much of the twentieth century, the formalist account predominated, composers themselves often endorsing the formalist view. Both Paul Hindemith and Igor Stravinsky articulated such a doctrine as most suited to the neo-classicism of their own music, but even Arnold Schoenberg appeared to concur in the period after his development of the Twelve-Tone Method.[1] Among philosophers, Suzanne Langer most notably argued that music is an 'unconsummated symbol', that is, a symbol lacking a clear referent. At most, it reflected in its motion the pattern of life; the essence of music was simply the motion of tonal forms.[2] This itself recalls Eduard Hanslick's definition of music as 'tonally moving forms', which on his view could not express any emotion or represent anything outside the tones themselves.[3] The formalist aesthetic of music appears ideally suited to the supremacy of purely instrumental music in the concert hall.

More generally, however, philosophical aesthetics has emphasized the autonomy of art and the uniqueness of the 'aesthetic experience'.[4] On this view, the contemplation of form is held to be the sole end of art, in which 'appreciation' consists largely in understanding the formal relationships.[5] For music specifically, most philosophers have rejected any idea of intrinsic meaning; its essence is held to lie rather in the disposition of the tones themselves, having purposiveness only in the sense of existing for our contemplation.[6] The formalist perspective, then, became characteristic of most textbook approaches to the understanding of music. At its core lies the concept of aesthetic value of the experience of a work of art, which had its origin in the philosophy of John Dewey.

Dewey's concept of the aesthetic experience makes the enjoyment of the person beholding a work of art central. 'An object is peculiarly and dominantly esthetic, yielding the enjoyment characteristic of esthetic perception, when the factors that determine anything which can be called an experience are lifted high above the threshold of perception and are made manifest for their own sake.'[7] Indeed, for Dewey, a work of art just is the experience, rather than some object, its aesthetic value made a function of the expression found in it. In the case of music, that experience resides in the listener's perception of motion, so that the expression remains abstract.[8] The value of this experience, however, has no objective existence, and thus it cannot be ascribed, in the case of music, to the objective presence of an expressive content. Thus it is the listener who must construct whatever meaning he finds in the musical experience.

Today, the tide has turned, with a renewed emphasis on the ways in which music can affect the emotional response of the listener.[9] The contemporary debate on the nature and aesthetic value of music reflects a reversal of the course of the nineteenth-century debate, in which the theory of expressiveness, widely held in the first half of the century, yielded to the incisive arguments of Hanslick's formalism after the 1850s. Yet there is a crucial difference between today's version of expressivism and the nineteenth-century varieties, which tended to emphasize the objective presence of emotion in a musical language. For following Dewey, the modern concept of aesthetic value makes value reside in the experience of the art itself. This means, however, that the aesthetic value of expression in music will remain a subjectivist value; the traditional doctrines of emotional expression in music have not been restored.[10] Thus the subjective pleasure in emotional response to music has largely replaced the elements of form as the source of aesthetic value.

In common with the subjectivism of aesthetic value, analytic philosophers today tend to look to the listener to impose on the music whatever emotional content seems appropriate. Jerrold Levinson, for example, interprets Mendelssohn's *Hebrides Overture* as expressive of hope, without any grounding in the hermeneutical principles current in the nineteenth century.[11] Other aestheticians disbar metaphorical representation of emotion in music, which would be intelligible by means of conventions governing tonal relationships.[12] But by neglecting historical conventions governing expression or representation in music, such an approach makes the listener in effect imagine the emotion experienced, projecting his own feeling onto the music.[13] The prevailing subjectivism of analytic musical aesthetics springs, however, not from a dogmatic rejection of an external world, but rather from the inevitable failure to find within musical concepts themselves the means of their interpretation. It is the consequence of the neglect of historical and intellectual contexts for music.

The sympathy which music is powerfully able to awaken springs, then, on this new view, from the congruence of music generally with the emotional life, rather from any specific correspondences between particular stylistic features and immutable aspects of human nature, or between specific elements of a musical-emotional language and particular states of feeling. The result is to weaken the concept of aesthetic value yet further, for there is nothing universal about such a private experience of musical feeling: it cannot be said to possess a value persuasive to anyone else. Thus in comparison with the nineteenth-century conceptions of musical expressiveness, which Hanslick thought weak and unpersuasive, the twentieth-century version appears weaker still.

The questions raised at the end of the last chapter, however, do not ask about the subjective value of all music, or even of tonal music in the traditional sense. Rather, the questions concerned the importance a particular kind of directed order once had, what it signified and what legitimated its norms, providing what might be called an 'objective value'. These questions address metaphysical issues: for order is an ontological category, and its nature and purpose are properly metaphysical questions. Although the rise of tonality certainly was associated with the revival of ancient doctrines of musical expressiveness, the answer to the question of objective value lies neither with expression nor form considered in themselves. It is instead the ability of tonality's teleological order to function as a metaphor of the larger order of reality that becomes important. Thus music will be in its own way a search for and representation of truth. In that case, however, the question of taste as an appreciation of style is far from being subjectively determined as a matter of aesthetic value. Rather, taste in music becomes a question of the musical apprehension of the nature of things. The normativity of tonality, then, will turn out to rest on something deeper than either natural principles of tone or historical development of style. Its legitimacy will be bound up with the significance of order in itself.

Harmony and the nature of the good in classical philosophy

Directed order, in the Western philosophical tradition, has always been associated with the category of goodness. We say that an action is good if it is done for a clear purpose, and that purpose is good; if it is an appropriate means to the end and is good in its own right; and if what the action brings into existence is in fact good. All three conditions must be met: we do not judge an action to be good if it has a wrong purpose, even if from a bad end some good might result on occasion; nor do we judge an action to be good if it fails on its own account to have an essential quality of rightness; nor do we judge an action to be good if, in spite of good intentions, it brings into being a worse state of affairs than before. To say all this is to speak very generally, and certainly it does not establish the nature of the moral good. But it does establish the teleological character of moral action.

The musical order of tonality, therefore, is not altogether dissimilar to what is already familiar from everyday life and common assumptions: it too has the character of directed order. The connection between order and goodness, however, needs to be drawn much more carefully to establish the metaphysical significance of tonal music. To do so we shall need to return to the philosophical tradition that supplied the context for the creation of Western

music. What was known by educated people in previous centuries is often in
need of recovery and restatement today in order to understand the assumptions
which, precisely because they were so much shared in common, were not in
need of explicit statement. The historical links between philosophy and music,
therefore, are crucial for understanding the normativity of the kinds of order
classical music possesses. The modern quest for understanding a subjectivist
aesthetic value arises only because the historical quest for knowing the good
has been abandoned.

To understand the nature of the good, however, is the most important task
of philosophy; indeed, it is the totality of the philosophical quest for wisdom.
It also appears elusive: Plato refers to the Idea of the good-in-itself in his
Republic, yet ultimately leaves it undescribed. It is like the sun, in that it gives
birth to the perception of other things, but, also like the sun, it is not something
that can be looked at directly.[14] This apparent unknowability leads some, like
Iris Murdoch, to argue that the good cannot be known in its essence, just as
theologians argue that God cannot be known in His essence in this life.[15] It also
leads easily to the modern nihilist conviction that the good does not exist at all
if it cannot be known: for how are we to decide if it is not simply an invention
of the human mind for purposes of making life bearable, or concealing the
truth that there is nothing really objectively given for which to live? Thus,
Platonism, on this view, may lead ineluctably to nihilism.

Nevertheless, Plato was not as reluctant to analyse the good as his latter-
day critics and defenders both assert. The way in which he connects goodness
with order is crucial for understanding the metaphysical significance of music.
In the *Philebus*, he has Socrates address specifically what constitutes the good
in a debate with Protarchus, who seeks to defend the position that pleasure is
the ultimate good. Such hedonism is easily defeated, however, for at the very
least memory and the exercise of reason must enter into the human good if
pleasure itself will be remembered as being good. Socrates goes far beyond
this, however, to rank the elements comprising the good; many of the elements
actually receive their justification elsewhere in Plato's corpus, rather than in
the *Philebus*. It is therefore worth paying close attention to this ranking of the
elements of the good, since it summarizes the most important metaphysical
claims of Plato's philosophy.

Socrates begins his final summary by arguing that beauty, proportion and
truth are good and constitute goodness, so that the first element of the good
consists above all in 'measure, moderation, fitness, and all which is to be
considered similar to these'.[16] Here the concept of moderation refers to *tò
métrion*, what is measured, linked to the first item listed, *métron*. Fitness,
however, refers to [*tò*] *kairion*, what is of time – to which Socrates alluded
earlier in referring to 'a by no means feeble cause which orders and arranges
years and seasons and months' – that is, the wisdom and intellect of God.[17] In
the *Timaeus*, Plato makes a similar point more fully: the Maker of the universe

took such delight in it that he determined to make it yet more like its eternal pattern, to make it a 'moving image of eternity' since it could not be itself eternal and unchanging. Thus, 'when he ordered the heavens he made in that which we call time an eternal moving image of the eternity which remains for ever at one'. This time consists, then, of the cycles of days and nights, the months and the years.[18] It is clearly intended here to be good, because the divine father who made the world in his delight modelled time on the eternal living pattern as closely as the nature of the created world would allow. The cyclical order of time, therefore, is among the highest elements of the good in the *Philebus* because the cosmos itself is as close to eternity as is possible. Elsewhere, Plato specifically identifies goodness and order in his description of the state of affairs before the creation of time: 'God, therefore, wishing that all things should be good … and finding the visible universe in a state not of rest but of inharmonious and disorderly motion, reduced it to order from disorder, as he judged that order was in every way better.'[19] Here, then, is the justification for the position taken at the end of the *Philebus*. Measure itself, measured order, and the specific order of time are the highest elements comprising the good.

The second rank Socrates cites is 'proportion, beauty, perfection, sufficiency and all that belongs to that class'.[20] Here again attention to the Greek text illuminates an otherwise obscure list: proportion is '*tò symmetrion*', as what is harmoniously proportioned or balanced; beauty is '*[tò] kalòn*', which always had rich connotations in ancient Greek extending from physical beauty to moral perfection of character; and sufficiency is a translation of '*tò téleon*', as what has completeness. Clearly here Plato is attempting to capture the sense of harmonious wholeness as an essential component of the good. This wholeness may be dependent on a concept of measure for the balance of proportions it exhibits, but the point is that such balance is more than a mere measured correctness. Hence the emphasis on completeness and on beauty.

Beauty for Plato, however, must be understood within the context of the *Symposium*. There, in the famous ascent passage, Diotima describes the degrees and kinds of beauty which awaken love. One begins by loving beautiful bodies, progressing to the love of beauty in souls: this is the ethical dimension central to the Greek concept. Then one graduates to the contemplation of 'the beautiful as appearing in our observances and our laws', followed by the beauty of all knowledge. At this point a person is ready to contemplate the beautiful-in-itself, which can only be described poetically: it is everlasting, unchanging, indivisible, existing 'ever in singularity of form independent by itself'. Hence Diotima concludes: 'In that state of life above all others, my dear Socrates, … a man finds it truly worth while to live, as he contemplates essential beauty.'[21] Beauty-in-itself, then, is what gives purpose to life: it is the *telos*, or goal, of human existence. Its contemplation is the completion of life.

With the concepts of measured order, harmonious wholeness and unchanging perfection, Plato has established the nature of the good. The further elements of the human good, intuitive reason and practical reason (*nous kai phronesis*) express the dimension of the human activities of soul necessary to realize the good. So, too, are the branches of learning, and the pure pleasures that accompany desires for all these elements of the good: they are not to be overlooked in the ranking of the components of the good. But it is order and harmonious wholeness with which we shall be concerned here. These are the principles of the good which will hold true for all particular human characteristics, activities and institutions described as good. It is therefore worth exploring their implications for music.

The concept of harmony has obvious potential for allowing music to be understood as an art of the good and the beautiful. Indeed, the oldest account of music's metaphysical significance recognized precisely this dimension: this was the doctrine of the Music of the Spheres. In the form enunciated by the sixth-century Boethius, the music of the universe was the highest kind of music, serving as a model for the music or harmony of the human soul and hence also for the instrumental music humans create for their pleasure. Boethius describes the music of the universe as consisting 'in the combining of the elements and the variety of the seasons which are observed in the heavens', but he also interprets the cosmic motion of the heavenly bodies, which produced the seasons, as producing a literally sounding, yet inaudible harmony: for 'How indeed could the swift mechanism of the sky move silently in its course?'[22] This congruence between sounding music and the harmonious relationship of all the parts forming the cosmos was the powerful explanatory factor in the doctrine of the Music of the Spheres. It was a doctrine that maintained its hold over the imagination of musical theorists through the Renaissance. Yet to the modern mind, it hardly seems satisfactory, for if taken literally, it must be absurd in the post-Copernican universe.

Attention to Boethius's sources, however, suggests that it was the concept of harmony as a metaphysical dimension common to all being, rather than the cosmic sounds, which were the most important element of the doctrine. The origins of the doctrine can also be traced back to Plato, who describes the order of the universe in Book X of the *Republic* in terms associated with music. Here, however, the cosmic spheres themselves make no sound; rather, the heavenly bodies revolve around the earth as whorls attached to a spindle, eight concentric rims of various sizes and speeds of revolution. 'Each of the spindle's circles acted as the vehicle for a Siren. Each Siren, as she stood on one of the circles, sounded a single note, and all eight notes together made a single harmonious sound.'[23] In addition, the Fates sang their songs of the past, present and future: the songs of the Fates and the Sirens together constituted the music of the universe. This heavenly music, then, is an expression of the measured order of the universe, but it is a sound that must be created by living, divine beings, just as human music, the expression of the passions and states of human character, must be created by living, mortal beings. Thus, the largest significance of music lay in its reflection of the intrinsic beauty of the heavens, and of the order of time created by the motions of the heavenly bodies. The subsequent development of the doctrine of the Music of the Spheres made these points more explicit.

Although Plato had described the motions of the heavenly bodies in terms of mathematical ratios in the *Timaeus*, he did not suggest that these motions themselves created any sounds, much less specifically musical ones. That suggestion originated with Cicero, who modelled his *Republic* on that of Plato, including a description of a vision of heaven in 'The Dream of Scipio' in the last book of the *Republic*. Here he describes a sound, 'so loud and agreeable', which pervades the heavens and causes wonder and astonishment to Scipio the Younger as he contemplates what his elder relation, Africanus, shows him in heaven. The concept serves two purposes. First, humanly created music imitates this heavenly music, so that musicians have the possibility of returning to this place, just as the pursuit of other heavenly activities earns others the possibility.[24] But the larger purpose is to provide an intimation of the delights of heaven, so that Africanus can urge his relation to contemplate the heavenly regions instead of the transitory fame and glory of earthly kingdoms. Heaven is the reward of virtue, and thus the harmony of the soul will find its reward in the delights of the musical harmony of the cosmos.

Cicero, then, interprets the notion of harmony far more literally – in a sounding, musical sense – than Plato. Yet the intent is never simply to render the motion of the sun, moon and planets sensuously perceptible in a crude way, but rather to make the abstract concept of metaphysical harmony intelligible through the metaphor of music. For, of course, the music of the spheres cannot be heard, ostensibly because human ears are always filled with it, and so grow accustomed to what would otherwise cause deafness. But this is weak, and Cicero's explanation does not have to convince in order for the metaphor to work. Boethius repeats the argument for a literally sounding, yet inaudible harmony, but also returns to the more basic Platonic emphasis on the order of time produced by the heavenly motion, as well as the harmony of the constituent elements of the cosmos: 'Now unless a certain harmony united the differences and contrary powers of the four elements, how could they form a single body and mechanism? But all this diversity produces the variety of seasons and fruits, and thereby makes the year a unity.'[25] As for Plato, then, the metaphysical concept of harmony was what made a thing intelligible; in this case, the year becomes a perceivable unity through harmony. But, more specifically, the order of the seasons in a year was defined by the heavenly motions; the seasons and their fruits are what we mortals really perceive as cosmic order. Hence, the concept of a providential order of time is what the doctrine of the music of the spheres ultimately signifies. This is to say, however, that humanly created music attains its significance precisely in imitating the harmony of the motion underlying the cyclic order of time. Unlike Langer's theory of an unconsummated symbol, the ancient doctrine saw a clear referent of music in the cosmic order.[26]

With the ancient doctrine of the Music of the Spheres clarified in this manner, it becomes possible to see why Boethius linked it with what he called 'human music', or the harmony of the soul, in explaining the significance of 'instrumental music', that is, music created for a purpose. For by the harmony of the soul he meant the joining together of the parts of the soul – the rational and the irrational – and the parts of the body together with the mutual adaptation of the soul and body to form one being; this is to suggest that the parts of the soul can in fact be adapted to each other. Thus, instrumental music possessed its power over the soul because its order corresponded to the soul's own order or harmony. The character of music was critical in affecting the soul: a stern mind, for example, 'either finds joy in the more stirring modes or is aroused by them'.[27] All three kinds of music, then, possessed a common essence of harmony or order, and their integration into one system made instrumental music both a reflection of the order and beauty of the world and an expression of the order and character of the soul. There was no separation between the metaphysical and the ethical significance of music: the expressive potential of music arose out of a metaphysical ground.

But this is precisely the ordering of the soul that Plato and Aristotle counted as the essence of virtue, in which reason regulates the irrational impulses of the soul so that a harmonious order in character and conduct is maintained. This, in turn accounts for their statements of the Doctrine of Ethos: humanly created music was capable of expressing not only the passions of the soul, but states of character as well. Aristotle, for example, is explicit on this: 'Rhythm and melody supply imitations of anger and gentleness, and also of courage and temperance, and of all the qualities contrary to these, and of the other qualities of character, which hardly fall short of the actual affections, as we know from our own experience, for in listening to such strains our souls undergo a change.'[28] Now, anger is a passion, but courage and temperance are two of the cardinal virtues. Thus, although post-Renaissance doctrines of musical expression have tended to emphasize the expression of emotion or passion, the ancient Doctrine of Ethos was broader in scope. Music expressed far more permanent states of character, and in representing the harmony of virtue or the disharmony of vice, it also created in the listener the same state of character.

It is possible to say, therefore, that the Doctrine of Ethos did not suffer from some of the objections raised against many of the post-Renaissance versions of the concept of musical expressiveness. Not only was there a fairly consistent ascription of certain affects to the modes of ancient Greek music; there was a sense of genuine universality about the human soul. That is, the soul had a clear structure, and that structure was a harmonious order. This concept of the soul as an ordered whole, then, provided a foundation for the concept of virtue as the proper harmonious ordering of its elements; the nature of the soul grounded the ethical ideal. There was no risk of the subjectivism seen in many recent twentieth-century accounts of musical aesthetics, nor was there a divorce between ethics and aesthetics such as Hanslick's formalism rested upon. If the weakness of nineteenth-century expressivist theories of musical aesthetics was their excessive concern with passion or emotion instead of character, at least they perceived a genuine link between the art of music and the experience of life. Since Hanslick, that link has been severed, so that making a metaphysical argument regarding the significance of tonal music intelligible is difficult.

Nevertheless, we have seen that the concept of harmonious balance in an ordered whole made sense to the ancient world. It continued to be accepted through the Middle Ages and the Renaissance, although by the time of Zarlino the Music of the Spheres was difficult to defend in its classical form.[29] When John Dryden penned his 'Song for St. Cecilia's Day' in 1687, the 'heavenly harmony' from which the universe began was now the 'tuneful voice' of God. Although it called 'a harmony' into existence, that universal harmony became what others have called 'the Great Chain of Being': as Dryden expresses it, 'The diapason closing full in Man.'[30] But Dryden's main concern in the poem is the power of music to express human passions; only at the end, in the trumpets of the Last Judgement, does the music from God assume a more cosmic purpose in bringing the world to an end.

It is therefore possible to see that classical conceptions of music provided concrete illustrations of Plato's assignment of harmony, measure and time to the good. Harmonious order was good, because it was part of the Idea of the good, and it was seen most clearly in the cyclic order of time defined by the motion of the heavenly bodies. Thus, in spite of the fact that the world is subject to change and corruption, it was nonetheless a good world on Plato's view, because it was an orderly, harmonious whole made by a divine Maker who had his eye on the eternal Forms which served as archetypes for everything in the world. The order in the visible world that constituted its goodness or beauty was a reflection of a more perfect order of Forms, and was manifested not only in the orderly motion of the heavenly bodies and the time they create, but also in the constitution of matter and the hierarchy of beings comprising the cosmos. The cosmos was in every way an ordered world, a single, beautiful and excellent whole. Humanly created music imitated this kind of order, not as a real imitation of specific heavenly sounds, but in the general sense that both music and the cosmos rested on the same foundation of mathematical intelligibility. The harmony ancient writers discovered in music was not, of course, a consonance of vertical sonorities, but melodic intelligibility arising from determinate scales defined by the modes. Thus, musical harmony was capable of reflecting all kinds of true harmony, from the cosmos to the human soul. In this way, musical order itself partook of the nature of the good.

Music and the goodness of teleological order

Nevertheless, if we ask what the concept of order entails in a deeper metaphysical sense, attention to the classical philosophical tradition shows that it covered more than just the concepts of harmony, measure, or perfect wholeness. Something else was required, and it will turn out to be vital for understanding the specific musical order of tonality. In particular, attention to Aristotelian metaphysics reveals the crucial role played by the concept of a *telos*, or immanent goal, which functions to order a whole in a more specific way. The analogy with the role of the tonic in tonality will be implicitly evident already.

Aristotle's analysis of the relation between an ordered whole and its good makes the distinction between order as simple harmony among the parts and order as centring on the final end. As he states in the *Metaphysics*, regarding whether the good is something separate from the order of an army, for example: 'For an army's good lies both in its order and in its commander, more expecially in the latter; for he is not the result of the order, but it results from him.'[31] Thus, the source of an order, although part of the whole, just as the commander is a part of the army, is yet distinct from the order it produces; and all the other parts of the whole have their order not simply in being in harmony among themselves, but in serving the end that commands them. Following Aristotle, Thomas Aquinas also distinguished carefully between the sense of the good as an end and the quality of goodness that derives from being conducive to an end; the latter requires both harmony among the parts and their ordination to the final end.[32] Thus, teleological ordering is a further development of the concept of order beyond that of harmony or consonance of the parts.

Aristotle insists that this kind of ordering is pervasive, that, in particular, the world itself manifests it most clearly. 'The world is not such that a thing is unrelated to another, but it is always a definite something. For all things are ordered together around a common center .... This is the sort of principle that governs the nature of anything.'[33] Hence, he concludes that the world can have only one principal unmoved Mover as the source of the ordering of motion in the cosmos. It is of the utmost importance that this Mover be good, for it must impart motion through desire and intelligibility only, or it will be moved and therefore not be the ultimate source: there can not be an infinite regress of movers. It awakens desire by being good, and fulfils the intellect by being intelligible.[34] This, however, is Aristotle's argument for the existence of a divine Mind, for only the life of the mind possesses the necessary self-sufficiency required for it to be unmoved by anything outside of itself. Thus, the divine Mind attains its perfection through the contemplation of its own thoughts, and by those thoughts inspires the love of the intelligible that motivates all the other minds and moves all the other bodies in the cosmos. The final good of the cosmos, in other words, must be both an immanent part of the cosmic order, yet a transcendent source of that order as its inspiration and motivation.

Since Plato, too, held that the Idea of the good was a goal that ordered all knowledge and inspired the pursuit of true knowledge, it is apparent that the classical philosophical tradition understood the concept of a teleological order as vital to the concept of order itself. In spite of disagreement over the nature of the *telos* as an Idea or a divine Intelligence, only some type of transcendence could provide the authoritative source of order. This is crucial for recognizing the metaphorical capacity of tonality as an order of metaphysical signification.

The Platonic-Aristotelian concept of teleological order may be understood as the general intellectual background undergirding the creation of the musical tradition of Western culture. In particular, it should be understood as the broadest philosophical context for the emergence of tonality, since Aristotelianism was maintained in the Scholastic tradition of Thomas Aquinas, and Platonism was revived both during the Renaissance and at the beginning of the Romantic era in the nineteenth century. The directedness toward the tonic so characteristic of tonality has a clear intelligibility according to the classical model of teleological order: it entails much more than the concept of harmony or consonance, the kind of measured order Plato emphasized as one of the chief components of the good. Rather, the way in which the good itself orders all of existence and knowledge becomes the most important kind of order. Thus, tonality may be said to have the inherent potential of being regarded as a metaphor of teleological order. That is, it can represent the nature of the cosmos, the goodness of all existence in the world.

At the same time, it is possible to see from our consideration of the classical formulations of the teleological concept why modern philosophy has largely discounted its importance, in spite of the intuitive appeal it might have for explaining the nature of the moral life. Here it is not so much the apparent emptiness of the Idea of the good in Plato's formulation that is important, for Aristotle had long ago criticized Plato's doctrine of Ideas on that account.[35] Instead, it is the Aristotelian concept of the necessity of final ends that proves problematic. Modern science developed as a critique of Aristotelian science precisely because the importation of final causes into physics and biology generated absurdities. Descartes, in particular, rejected the role of final causes in scientific understanding, a view that triumphed by the end of the seventeenth century.[36] Yet for the modern world, the threat posed by Aristotelianism is of a different order altogether, for even holding the realm of science apart from teleology, the concept apparently leads ineluctably to the necessity of admitting divine governance of the world. For a critic such as Adorno, who denies the existence of goodness in the world altogether, there is no argument to be made for either an immanent or a transcendent source of order as the highest good. Since tonality appears inseparable from its metaphorical potential as the representation of teleological order in general, it follows that tonality must be exhausted: there is nothing, on this point of view, for the metaphor to represent. Tonality is dead, then, because the concept of ordering toward a highest good is dead.

Nevertheless, whether Adorno is right or not regarding the possibility of goodness in the world, our examination of the differences between Plato's and Aristotle's accounts of order and the good raises an important question within the context of classical metaphysics itself, which is of no small importance for understanding the nature of the good. For in answer to the question 'What is the good?' Plato provides a list of elements, including measured order, perfection and harmonious balance, as well as intellect (*nous*) and practical reason. Aristotle, on the other hand, identifies intellect (*nous*) as the highest good, which stands at the head of all teleological order in the world: it becomes the object of both cosmic and human contemplation. The intellectual difficulty here is not the apparent discrepancy within the ranking of *nous* in the good, but the question of what constitutes the goodness of the *telos* itself: is it order, or is it intellect? When the question is transposed into the terms of Christian theology, as it was in the adoption of Aristotelian philosophy in the work of St Thomas Aquinas, the question indeed becomes critical: what accounts for the goodness of God? Is God good because of what He does, or is He good because of who He is? If the former, then is there not a standard of goodness outside of God? But if the latter, is not goodness identical with power, so that God's might becomes right? These are significant theological questions in their own right. But the answer to the question of whether tonality can be a metaphor of metaphysical goodness will depend precisely on the nature of the ultimate *telos*.

The answer suggested by both St Augustine and St Thomas in the context of Christian philosophy, however, avoids the above dilemma in a way that is also crucial for grounding an understanding of the significance of all teleological order. In countering the Manichean argument against the goodness of material existence, St Augustine insisted that goodness was fundamentally identical with being: although a created being's moral goodness might be increased or diminished, 'it is necessary, if the being is to continue, that some good remain to constitute the being'.[37] Thus, existence per se is good. St Thomas explains it more distinctly: 'Goodness and being are really the same, and differ only in idea ... . But goodness presents the aspect of desirableness, which being does not present.'[38] But since all rational beings desire their own continuance, the desirableness of existence in itself must be ackowledged.

Thus, whether one follows St Thomas in conceiving of God as the pure act of existing, or a more classical account of God as divine mind or intellect, the result will be to see God as the highest good. In either case, then, there will be no standard of goodness outside of God, nor any derivation of goodness from an assertion of divine power. The goodness of the *telos*, God's goodness, will be identical with His existence. This means that the teleological order Christians understand God to create as the object of human perception must be an order of goodness precisely because all existence is good in itself. But the metaphorical significance of tonality, then, points not in the first instance to the aspect of divine ordering of the world, but to the goodness of all being as being. Adorno's critique of tonality completely misses this dimension of the goodness of existence.

We may still ask, however, what constitutes the being of goodness in general, since it now appears to be a quality of desirableness inherent in existence and not simply an attribute of God or a quality bestowed out of God's power. Here, again, the philosophical tradition provides an answer that is useful for understanding the metaphorical potential of music. Plato, as we have seen, described the highest beauty as being that which exists always in singularity or simplicity, perfect and immutable. Aristotle also described the unmoved Mover as eternal, immutable and 'without parts and indivisible'.[39] Thus, the perfect goodness of the highest good lay in its absolute simplicity or unity of being. But this concept could be extended to the goodness of all being; as Boethius argued: 'You know, then, that everything that is remains and subsists just so long as it is one, but perishes and dissolves immediately it ceases to be one?' Hence, he concludes that 'unity and goodness are identical'.[40] With this, St Thomas agreed: composite beings have no being if they are not united to form a whole.[41] Hence, the goodness of existence, which is the foundation of any further argument for the goodness of a harmonious or a teleological order, resides in the unity of being.

A conception of music that emphasizes the necessity of tonal unity, therefore, understands the absolutely minimal condition of the existence of a musical work as a perceptible whole. But it also, then, understands the minimal metaphorical level at which music with an identifiable tonal centre functions: it represents the unity of existence that is constitutive of the goodness of all being. That is, music with tonal unity, such as that of the Middle Ages as well as the forms of tonality from the common practice period, can be understood as a metaphor of the goodness of existence per se.

Our retracing of the paths of traditional metaphysics, however, also makes it clear why a mere tonal unity does not suffice as a description of the nature of tonality. For tonality as we have described it includes more levels of order and therefore more levels of metaphorical potential: it is founded on the measured order of consonance and the specifically teleological order of functional harmony in a bipolar major/minor system. The order of consonance, however, is seen historically in the music of the Renaissance: fittingly, one might add, given the recovery of Plato which was a critical part of the Italian intellectual revival. But it, too, is only a necessary, not a sufficient condition of tonality, and it can serve as a metaphor only of the goodness of the particular kind of measured order of which it partakes. The full sense of tonality, embodied in the stages marked by Fétis as the *ordre transitonique*, the *ordre pluritonique* and even the *ordre omnitonique*, answers to the teleological order described most fully in the Aristotelian metaphysical tradition. One may say, therefore, that tonality in this sense may become the metaphor of the ordering of all existence to the highest good. It attains its true metaphysical significance, however, in becoming more than a symbol reflecting the universal character of being. It is rather both an expression of, and a participation in, the true order of being.

Philosophical and historical questions

If the argument for a metaphysical significance of the order of tonality is persuasive as a consequence of its being grounded in the categories developed in the Western philosophical tradition, there nevertheless arise a number of troubling questions for this analysis. First, as already suggested, it may appear to make an acceptance of tonality dependent on a particular religious view of the world as subject to some form of divine governance. If so, would not only the style of tonality itself for contemporary composers, but also the works inherited from the common practice period, become a matter of controversy? Indeed, this is already happening; so that the philosophical argument which might seem most promising for providing insight into the significance of classical music may seem to end in undermining its relevance to many people. What in an earlier age would have been the largest argument for its universality, therefore, might well confine it to the margins of modern society.

Second, although the essay in seeking a metaphysical understanding of tonality rests on a valid hermeneutical principle, namely the general relevance of Platonism and Aristotelianism to Western culture, it raises the question of a more specific link between these received ideas and the thought that was current during the common practice period. The historian may well ask how much of this composers knew, how much critics knew, how much, indeed, audiences knew. These are legitimate questions, although for the most part they lie beyond the scope of this book to answer. Nevertheless, it is imperative to consider at least briefly how much the metaphysics of teleological order we have sketched was actually the conception of music current during the period when tonality was the reigning principle of musical style.

Finally, the historical associations sketched above raise a more specific question: why was tonality so late in developing? Medieval polyphony did not define consonance as the norm for vertical sonorities except at cadences, and there was no sense of necessity in root movements or harmonic function. Only in the Renaissance did consonance become the constant norm of vertical sonorities, so that dissonance disappeared except as an occasional aspect of voice-leading or as, later, an expressive device. Simultaneously, the development of the dominant-tonic cadence begins then to suggest the authority of root movement by a fifth, but only in this limited way. Hence, although there was throughout these centuries a sense of the necessity of tonal unity, there was little that resembled what the system of tonality ultimately became. Yet if tonality is in even a partial sense a naturally occurring order, one might think it would not have been so long in being discovered.

Particularly, moreover, if tonality embodies an Aristotelian understanding of the order of being, it would seem a rather late flowering for a style rooted in the philosophical school that dominated the High Middle Ages. Why, indeed, should polyphonic music have had to evolve through the increasingly complex stages of order to reach the style that was most fully representative of a teleologically conceived cosmos? Some factor in the development of musical style remains unaccounted for here, in spite of the intuitive persuasiveness of teleology as the object of the metaphorical potential of tonality. For the remainder of this chapter, we shall address these questions briefly as a way of pointing to what remains to be considered more deeply in the next two chapters.

For the first question, regarding the potential decline of interest in a style of music tied too closely to a metaphysical understanding of the world, the question really ought to be whether this way of understanding the world is justified. Aristotle argues that there cannot be an infinite regress of ends without removing the concept of end altogether. But in that case, rationality itself is destroyed along with the good: 'Rationality, at least, is incompatible with such an infinite series; for the reasonable man always acts for the sake of something, and this serves as a limit ... .'[42] Thus, if there is not a highest good, reason will have nothing to attain and will disappear. Precisely this has happened, however, in the modern world.

As Friedrich Nietzsche argued, existence itself becomes meaningless when one cannot believe in any 'highest values', or posit 'a beyond or an in-itself of things that might be "divine" or morality incarnate'.[43] If the good or God could not be justified, then faith in reason would also be without warrant in Nietzsche's eyes. But his argument gives the lie to itself: for it is reasoned, and this fact indicates that it is not reason that is the real problem for modernity, but what it leads to: goodness, virtue and the requirements of morality recognized as authoritative over the individual. For Nietzsche, morality was 'only a sign-language of the emotions', and values were not authoritative by virtue of reason, but created by the will to power.[44] This was not the innocuous exercise of an exhuberant will, however, for Nietzsche makes it clear that 'to a being such as "we are" other beings have to be subordinate by their nature, and sacrifice themselves to us'.[45] For this reason, there was an inevitable political and social dimension, 'in which the will of philosophical men of power and artist-tyrants will be made to endure for millennia ...'.[46] Nietzsche's prophecy of nihilism thus becomes its own call for fulfilment in an amoral politics of tyranny.

It is not necessary to rehearse here the whole history of Existentialist philosophy and its close connection with totalitarian politics in the twentieth century to see that Nietzsche represents a common type of modern man. But it is a type that surely a reasonable person ought to reject. Hence, it may not be so easy to dismiss Aristotle's point about the necessity of a *telos* for human rationality, or to read his whole metaphysical argument as justifying an acknowledgement of a highest good in the form of a divine mind. As regards whether this ties tonal music too closely to a particular conception of reality, certainly there are eminently reasonable philosophers who make just such a claim: Roger Scruton, for one, argues that music cannot flourish without a climate of religious belief, and urges a revival of tonality of some sort in order to restore modern musical culture to some measure of health.[47] But if the argument so far here carries any weight, the issue for tonality as a principle of style is not perhaps such a full-fledged revival of a religious world-view, as an acknowledgement of a specific metaphysical understanding of reality. For what tonality signifies is the nature of the whole order of being, in which existence is perceived as good in itself, and all being is conceived as ordered toward a final end. Human life, then, will have meaning to the extent that the highest use of the intellect is taken to be the contemplation of the harmonious order of all existence and the providential design evident in that order. At the level of style, tonality signifies no more than that.

For the second question, however, regarding the degree to which our argument for the metaphysical metaphor of tonality reflects the self-understanding of the culture that produced it, the answer will at least initially appear unsatisfactory. For strikingly few philosophers or theorists attempted to connect any of the arts with metaphysical principles during the eighteenth and nineteenth centuries. The most notable exception was Friedrich Schelling (1775–1854). Schelling's *Philosophy of Art*, consisting of lectures given at the University of Jena in 1802–03, makes the most concerted attempt to read the philosophy of art in genuinely Platonist terms. For Schelling, art attained its importance because it was the means by which the Platonic Ideas of the Good and the True became realized as the Beautiful.[48] Hence, art is 'the representation of the forms of things as they are in themselves', that is, of the Platonic archetypes of all things.[49] This is to say, however, that art is the most important means of human cognition of the nature of reality. It possesses, therefore, the highest metaphysical significance. Schelling makes music a special case of what is true for art in general.

For Schelling, music is the art that makes its own unity the symbol of all real unity of being, which is the foundation of the cognition of goodness. Whereas for all theorists and most philosophers, however, the unity of music has been perceived to lie in the scalar or harmonic dimensions, Schelling makes the rhythm the central means by which unity is created in the multiplicity of tones. He dismisses the expressive nature of the tonal materials as strictly secondary, arguing that it is only the ordering in time which makes the tones comprehensible and therefore capable of having expressive meaning at all. Rhythm, therefore, is what creates specifically musical meaning, as opposed to any additional layer of expressive meaning. It is the transformation of mere tones into a sequence with the character of necessity, 'whereby the whole is no longer subjected to time but rather possesses time within itself'. That is, music's symbolism of time is not an external one, but rather an internal reflection of the essence of time: its metaphysical representation arises from its bearing the essence of time within itself. This is a claim made plausible, however, by Schelling's understanding of rhythm as more than just the metrical pattern of beats; it includes the rhythm of the phrasing in forming the larger structures defining a musical work.[50] This larger understanding of rhythm is crucial to the metaphorical capacity of the art of music.

Thus, to speak more concretely, the cyclic nature of time according to Plato's account is captured in the cyclicity of the metrical pattern itself, while the regularity of the phrasing in building up the larger structure unfolds its pattern in the same way that the years add up to form a lifetime. The fundamental order of music, then, is not harmonic at all, but temporal. This has the merit of locating the capacity of metaphysical representation in the same kind of order that the ancient doctrine of the Music of the Spheres adduced to demonstrate the orderliness of the world. Schelling makes this point explicitly, in what would otherwise be an embarrassingly naïve repetition of the ancient doctrine. For he takes the cosmic bodies to represent in some measure 'the eternal things or ideas', so that 'the forms of music as the forms of ideas viewed concretely are also the forms of the being and life of the cosmic bodies as such; hence, music is nothing other than the perceived rhythm and the harmony of the visible universe itself'.[51] Schelling's neo-Platonic understanding of the relation of the cosmos to the world of Ideas, however, does not detract from the larger truth that time, as created by the motions of the heavenly bodies, is a measurable order, and music, as a temporal art, participates (in its traditional forms) in the same kind of metrical order. The focus on rhythm, therefore, provides the most appropriate analogy with the temporal order of the cosmos.

Schelling's contemporary, G. W. F. Hegel, also emphasized the matter of rhythm to some extent. In his *Aesthetics*, he recognized that music cannot be reduced to just the tonal materials a composer employs in a work. Rather, tones must be ordered temporally as well as harmonically and melodically.

The temporal ordering consists in the regular pattern of accented and unaccented beats, so that the passing of time in music is not indeterminate or incomprehensible. But Hegel's emphasis here is on the listener's perception, rather than the order itself: the regular repetition of accents creates a uniformity across time 'in which self-consciousness finds itself again as a unity'.[52] Thus, the unity of musical metre corresponds to the unity of the self in time, and indeed helps to raise the unity of the self to self-consciousness. This differs from Langer's much less specific conception of musical motion as symbolic of life; it also differs significantly from Schelling's genuinely metaphysical point, which sees all of existence as ordered by time, embodied and presented in the rhythmic element of music.

In making the rhythm of music the foundation of its metaphor of order, Schelling does not neglect the other aspects of musical order, however. He recognizes the unity of music's tonal materials in what he calls (after an older usage) 'modulation': 'modulation is the art of maintaining the identity of the one tone that is the predominating one within the whole of a musical work ... .' But this is to speak very generally of what appears to be a simple tonal unity, such as had obtained in music since the Middle Ages. Schelling has little to say regarding the 'artificial method of guiding song and harmony through several tones by means of so-called modulation and cadences, and of finally returning to the main tone', an aspect of musical art that is entirely 'modern'.[53] Thus, to the rhythmic unity of a musical work, he adds its tonal or harmonic unity, without, however, analysing the peculiarly directed quality of the musical style rooted in tonality. This remains true as well even in his discussion of the third unity of music, melody. In spite of recognizing the expressive nature of the harmonic language and the element of imagination in melody,[54] he misses the crucial role played by particular forms of harmonic and melodic ordering. This has remained the serious omission in most philosophies of music ever since.

Nevertheless, if Schelling and the prior philosophical tradition were right in arguing for the metaphysical significance of music in at least a general sense, then the question of whether the specific order of tonality can be regarded as a natural phenomenon is not trivial. The question with which we began in the last chapter becomes crucial to the capacity of music to bear metaphysical meanings. For if tonality be merely historically contingent, a culturally relative phenomenon, then so is its construction of order. In that case, it is open to the same kind of objections that Adorno and others raise: it can present no universal significance as the representation of the way the world really is. If, on the other hand, it is in large part, or even only in some measure, a natural phenomenon, then its construction of order reflects the nature of reality in general. In that case, it will correspond to the goodness we perceive in the world and, indeed, demand of the world. The truth of our perception of the goodness of order will be represented in the music that is composed and performed in our culture; this truth will be guaranteed by the truth of tonality as a natural phenomenon. As we have seen, the latter appears to be the case. It is therefore not a substantial weakness in the argument that so few philosophers during the common practice period of music focused on the metaphysical dimension of the art. The theoretical account of music as a natural phenomenon provided the crucial grounding for metaphysical categories.

Tonality, however, allowed music to develop highly expressive capacities because of its teleological character, and the aspect of musical expression was what most philosophies of music addressed. We noted at the beginning of this chapter how twentieth-century theories of musical expression frequently produce a subjectivist account of a listener's reading emotion into the music. The tonal order, however, was able to ground objective accounts of emotional expression, precisely because of its intrinsic order. Expression in music depends on clear contrasts; consonance and dissonance were thus the earliest available, providing obvious metaphors of pleasure and pain to late Renaissance composers. With the crystallization of the major and minor modes and the development of a clearly articulated system of keys, musical expression had both more contrasts and more subtle nuances at its disposal. From Rameau and Mattheson in the eighteenth century, through Schubart and many others in the nineteenth century, the objectivity of musical perception was codified into a language of emotional expression.[55] But simply to emphasize the expressive elements as constituting a kind of vocabulary would be to miss an important dimension: the ability of tonal music to represent dynamic emotional states. For it is not just that dissonance is a metaphor for pain, or minor keys a metaphor for sorrow, but rather that for the most part these states of negative emotion were indeed expected to resolve in a piece of music. As Hegel recognized, the longing for resolution and the achievement of reconciliation were fundamental to musical art.[56] The metaphysical goodness of the tonal *telos*, therefore, becomes the emotional *telos* of resolution of pain and suffering.

The historical development of the capacity of tonality to represent a teleological metaphysic remains, however, a matter of curiosity. Earlier music had reflected the conception of a metrical ordering of existence through the rhythmic element, but a teleological ordering of existence only weakly through the harmonic element. Long before the sense of even a pan-consonant *ordre unitonique* had emerged, regular cadences resolved sometimes pungent dissonances into perfect consonances, emphasizing the reciting tone and final of the mode: this is evident in the use of the double leading-tone cadences in the French Ars Nova of the fourteenth century. But the introduction of a cadence requiring only a single leading tone, seen first in the work of Guillaume Dufay in the fifteenth-century Burgundian School, represented an advance in the complexity of the tonal ordering by permitting a clear sense of directedness toward the cadential point. As Example 2.1 shows, the double leading-tone cadence in fact evades the directionality inherent in what is now called the leading tone by resolving it downward before returning to the tonic; only the dominant tone of the scale receives an upward resolution from a raised subdominant. The new means of emphasizing the final of the mode required raising the seventh tone of the scale in the Dorian and Mixolydian modes, thus beginning the process that eventually led to the crystallization of the major/minor system.[57] Thus, Renaissance music, though largely consonant in sonority after the time of Josquin des Prez and lacking a sense of directed harmonic motion except at cadential points, did possess a certain degree of teleological ordering. In this, it conformed to the Christian theological understanding of the *telos* of human existence.

Double leading-tone cadence (14th century)

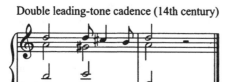

Single leading-tone cadence (15th century)

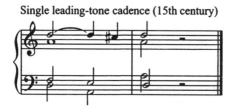

Example 2.1   Cadential figures of the fourteenth and fifteenth centuries

The emphasis on consonance and on the unity of the final tone of the mode, however, reflects far more convincingly two more basic philosophical points: that unity is the essence of the goodness of existence per se, and that the cyclic conception of time was the foundation of metrical order and therefore also of consonance in Western music. Consequently, only the development of secular music at the end of the Renaissance, with its demands of the faithful expression of the sense of the vocal text, led to an unambiguously teleological conception of harmony and melody as possessing the contrasts and nuances necessary for the perception of complex emotional states and the resolution of pain and suffering. The dramatic narrative of opera, in particular, drove the development of the musical language to the tonality of the *ordre transitonique*.

Thus the late emergence of tonality, compared with the medieval renewal of teleological metaphysics, becomes understandable.

It would surely be the greatest of ironies, however, if the reflection of an Aristotelian metaphysic compatible with Christian theology could find its truest expression only in the field of secular music, and at a time when it was being challenged by developments in the new science. Although Aristotelianism remained important in the Counter-Reformation, it would seem remarkable if such a teleological metaphysic were associated with the rise of tonality. Hence the historical question remains without an entirely satisfactory answer: Why was the teleological ordering of music so late coming into existence? Or was there perhaps a more specific, more recently emergent concept which it embodied and represented metaphorically? The historical irony, therefore, compels a deeper examination of the history of the concept of order during the common practice period.

Notes

1. Paul Hindemith, *A Composer's World* (New York: Doubleday, 1961), pp. 37–47; Igor Stravinsky, *Poetics of Music in the Form of Six Lessons*, trans. Arthur Knodel and Ingolf Dahl (Cambridge, MA: Harvard University Press, 1942), p. 77. Also Arnold Schoenberg, 'New Music, Outmoded Music, Style and Idea' (1946), in *Style and Idea: Selected Writings of Arnold Schoenberg*, ed. Leonard Stein, trans. Leo Black (1975; Berkeley: University of California Press, 1984), p. 123, where he defines the idea of a piece in terms of the restoration of balance to the state of unrest created by the tensions between multiple tones. The idea of a piece, then, is purely musical.
2. Suzanne K. Langer, *Feeling and Form: A Theory of Art Developed from 'Philosophy in a New Key'* (New York: Scribner's, 1953), pp. 31; 107–10. Cf. *Philosophy in a New Key: A Study in the Symbolism of Reason, Rite, and Art*, 3rd edn (Cambridge, MA: Harvard University Press, 1957), pp. 204–45 on music.
3. Eduard Hanslick, *On the Musically Beautiful*, trans. Geoffrey Payzant (Indianapolis: Hackett, 1986), p. 29; 11.
4. As in Jerome Stolnitz, 'The Aesthetic Attitude', in *Introductory Readings in Aesthetics*, ed. John Hospers (New York: Free Press, 1969), pp. 17–27; William Tolhurst, 'Toward an Aesthetic Account of the Nature of Art', *Journal of Aesthetics and Art Criticism* 42 (1984), pp. 261–9.
5. See for example Harold Osborne, *Aesthetics and Art Theory: An Historical Introduction* (New York: Dutton, 1970), pp. 293ff.; Monroe Beardsley, *Aesthetics: Problems in the Philosophy of Criticism*, 2nd edn (Indianapolis: Hackett, 1981).
6. See for example Beardsley, *Aesthetics*, p. 338, for a strong defence of formalism in music. The description of the formal elements became the goal of music appreciation textbooks: see, for instance, Joseph Machlis and Kristine Forney, *The Enjoyment of Music*, 6th edn (New York: Norton, 1990).
7. John Dewey, *Art as Experience* (1934; New York: Berkley, 1980), p. 57.
8. Ibid., p. 208.
9. The influential document in this shift was Peter Kivy's *The Corded Shell:*

Reflections on Musical Expression (Princeton: Princeton University Press, 1980).

10. Malcom Budd, *Values of Art: Pictures, Poetry and Music* (London: Penguin, 1995), pp. 147–52; and Aaron Ridley, *Music, Value and the Passions* (Ithaca: Cornell University Press, 1995). The current theory of the auditor's imagination of emotion in response to the music further subjectivizes the aesthetic experience in the absence of particular conventions of particular musical traditions being known.

11. Jerrold Levinson, *Music, Art, and Metaphysics: Essays in Philosophical Aesthetics* (Ithaca: Cornell University Press, 1990), especially the last chapter, 'Hope in "The Hebrides"'.

12. Stephen Davies adopts a behaviourist approach to emotional expression in his *Musical Meaning and Expression* (Ithaca: Cornell University Press, 1994), pp. 223–8; the result is also a projection of the listener's own interpretation.

13. See Roger Scruton's essay, 'Understanding Music', in *The Aesthetic Understanding* (London: Methuen, 1983), pp. 77ff.; also Roger Scruton's *The Aesthetics of Music* (Oxford: Clarendon Press, 1997), esp. pp. 343ff.

14. *Republic*, Book VI, 508e; Book VII, pp. 514a–517e.

15. Iris Murdoch, *The Sovereignty of Good* (1970; London: Routledge and Kegan Paul, 1985).

16. *Philebus* 66a, trans. Harold N. Fowler in Plato, *Statesman, Philebus, Ion*, Loeb Classical Library, vol. 164 (Cambridge, MA: Harvard University Press, 1925), pp. 393–5.

17. *Philebus* 30c, in ibid., p. 267.

18. Plato, *Timaeus* 37, in *Timaeus and Critias*, trans. Desmond Lee, rev. edn (London: Penguin, 1977), p. 51.

19. *Timaeus* 30a, in ibid., p. 42.

20. *Philebus* 66b, p. 395.

21. *Symposium* 210c–211d, trans. W. R. M. Lamb in Plato, *Lysis, Symposium, Gorgias*, Loeb Classical Library, vol. 166 (Cambridge, MA: Harvard University Press, 1925), pp. 203–7.

22. Cited from Boethius's text of the *De institutione musica*, I, Section 2, as given in Oliver Strunk, ed., *Source Readings in Music History* (New York: Norton, 1950), p. 84.

23. Plato, *Republic*, Book X, 617b, trans. Robin Waterfield (Oxford: Oxford University Press, 1993), p. 375.

24. Marcus Tullius Cicero, *The Republic*, Book VI, Section 18, in *De re Publica, De legibus*, trans. C. W. Keyes, Loeb Classical Library, vol. 213 (Cambridge, MA: Harvard University Press, 1928), pp. 271–3.

25. Boethius, *De institutione musica*, I, Section 2, in Strunk, *Source Readings*, p. 84. It is therefore vitally important to distinguish the metaphysical concept of harmony in the world from the literal idea of a sounding cosmic harmony or specific cosmological ratios in the traditional doctrine; for a popular account of the latter, which however fails to establish a connection with musical practice, see Jamie James, *The Music of the Spheres: Music, Science, and the Natural Order of the Universe* (New York: Grove Press, 1993).

26. Langer sees music as having 'the semblance of organic movement', an undivided, unconsummated symbol of the subjective experience of time: *Feeling and Form*, pp. 110, 126.

27. Ibid., p. 80.

28. Aristotle, *The Politics*, Book VIII, Section 5, 1340a, trans. Benjamin Jowett, ed. Stephen Everson (Cambridge: Cambridge University Press, 1988), p. 191. Cf. Plato, *Republic*, Book III, 398c–400c, on the characteristics of modes and

rhythms, and which are suitable and which are not.

29. See Claude V. Palisca, *Humanism in Italian Renaissance Musical Thought* (New Haven: Yale University Press, 1985), pp. 163ff., for the history of the doctrine.

30. On this concept, see Arthur O. Lovejoy, *The Great Chain of Being: A Study of the History of an Idea* (1936; Cambridge, MA: Harvard University Press, 1964). The scale of being to which Dryden refers was important also to Plato's account of the harmony of creation in the *Timaeus* 50, 92. The text of John Dryden's poem may be found in *Six Centuries of Great Poetry*, ed. Robert Penn Warren and Albert Erskine (New York: Dell Publishing, 1955), pp. 280–81.

31. Aristotle, *Metaphysics* 1075a, trans. Richard Hope (1952; Ann Arbor: University of Michigan Press, 1960), p. 267.

32. St Thomas Aquinas, *De Veritate* XXI, 1; see *An Introduction to the Metaphysics of St Thomas Aquinas*, texts edited and translated by James F. Anderson (Washington, DC: Regnery Gateway, 1953), p. 78.

33. Aristotle, *Metaphysics* 1075a, p. 267.

34. *Metaphysics* 1072a–b, pp. 258–60.

35. Cf. *The Nichomachean Ethics*, Book I, Section 6, 1096a–1097a.

36. In the Fifth Discourse of the *Discourse on Method*, Descartes describes his hypothesis that the world could be sufficiently explained as having come into existence by God's creation of matter in chaos, together with the physical laws of nature; to this would have to be added God's creation of rational souls: see René Descartes, *Discourse on Method and the Meditations*, trans. F. E. Sutcliffe (Harmondsworth: Penguin, 1968), pp. 62–3.

37. St Augustine, *The Enchiridion on Faith, Hope and Love*, trans. J. F. Shaw, ed. Henry Paolucci (Chicago: Regnery Gateway, 1961), Section 12, p. 12.

38. *Summa Theologica*, 5 vols, trans. Fathers of the English Dominican Province (1948; reprinted Westminster, MD: Christian Classics, 1981), Part I, Q.5, art.1, p. 23.

39. Aristotle, *Metaphysics* 1073a, p. 260.

40. Ancius Boethius, *The Consolation of Philosophy*, trans. V. E. Watts (London: Penguin, 1969), Book III, Section 11, p. 105.

41. St Thomas Aquinas, *Summa Theologica*, Part I, Q.11, art.1.

42. Aristotle, *Metaphysics* 994b, p. 38.

43. Friedrich Nietzsche, *Der Wille zur Macht: Versuch einer Umwertung aller Werte*, ed. Peter Gast and Elisabeth Förster-Nietzsche, in Section 3, *Sämtliche Werke in zwölf Bänden* (Stuttgart: Alfred Kröner Verlag, 1964), vol. 9, p. 10; *The Will to Power*, trans. Walter Kaufmann and R. J. Hollingdale (New York: Vintage Books, 1968), p. 9.

44. Friedrich Nietzsche, *Jenseits von Gut und Böse*, Sections 187, 260, in *Sämtliche Werke in zwölf Bänden* (Stuttgart: Alfred Kröner Verlag, 1964), vol. 7, pp. 95–6, 201–2; *Beyond Good and Evil*, trans. R. J. Hollingdale, ed. Michael Tanner, rev. edn (1973; London: Penguin, 1990), pp. 110, 195.

45. *Jenseits von Gut und Böse*, Section 265, *Werke*, vol. 7, p. 212; *Beyond Good and Evil*, p. 204.

46. *Der Wille zur Macht*, Section 960, *Werke*, vol. 9, pp. 640–41; *The Will to Power*, p. 504. On the political implications, see Bruce Detweiler, *Nietzsche and the Politics of Aristocratic Radicalism* (Chicago: University of Chicago Press, 1990).

47. *The Aesthetics of Music*, especially pp. 458ff.

48. F. W. J. Schelling, *Die Philosophie der Kunst*, ed. M. Schröter, *Werke* (Munich: C.H. Beck and R. Oldenbourg, 1959), vol. 3, pp. 377ff., Section 20; *The Philosophy of Art*, trans. and ed. Douglas W. Stott (Minneapolis: University of Minnesota Press, 1989), p. 31. The lectures comprising this work were published

in Schelling's *Sämtliche Werke*, ed. Karl F. A. Schelling, 1859. Nevertheless, Schelling's personal influence was great through his contacts with the Jena Romantics, including Friedrich and August Wilhelm Schlegel. The composer, Carl Maria von Weber, was introduced to Schelling's writings after 1807: see Weber, *Kunstansichten: Ausgewählte Schriften* (Wilhelmshaven: Heinrichshofen's Verlag, 1978), p. 14. In the first half of the nineteenth century, lectures were often more influential than published writings. In Schelling's case, his exaltation of the arts as the representation of truth, goodness, and beauty was the significant contribution to Romanticism.

49.   Schelling, *Philosophy of Art*, Section 24, p. 32.
50.   Ibid., Section 79, pp.109–11. Note that this is more specific than the mere sense of organic movement found by Langer to be the significance of music: it is time, not life, that music presents.
51.   Ibid., Section 83, p. 116.
52.   G. W. F. Hegel, *Vorlesungen über die Ästhetik*, in *Werke in zwanzig Bänden* (Frankfurt am Main: Suhrkamp Verlag, 1970), vol. 15, p. 166; *Aesthetics: Lectures on Fine Art*, trans. T. M. Knox, 2 vols (Oxford: Clarendon Press, 1975), p. 915.
53.   Schelling, *Philosophy of Art*, Section 80, pp. 111–12.
54.   Ibid., Section 81, p. 112.
55.   See Jean-Philippe Rameau, *Treatise on Harmony*, trans. Philip Gossett (1722; New York: Dover Publications, 1971), Book II, Chs 20, 23, 24, pp. 154–6, 163–6 on expressive properties of music; also Christian F. D. Schubart, *Ideen zu einer Ästhetik der Tonkunst* (1806; Leipzig: Reclam, 1977), pp. 284–7 for the expression of key characteristics. For a history of the latter element, see Rita Steblin, *A History of Key Characteristics in the Eighteenth and Early Nineteenth Centuries* (Ann Arbor: UMI Research Press, 1983).
56.   Hegel, *Werke*, vol. 15, pp. 197–8; *Aesthetics*, p. 939.
57.   For a clear survey of the development of Renaissance style, see Howard M. Brown, *Music in the Renaissance* (Englewood Cliffs, NJ: Prentice-Hall, 1976).

CHAPTER THREE

Tonality and the Metaphysics of Temporal Order

The concept of time is, as we have seen, one of the most concrete examples of the abstract metaphysical concept of order. The Platonist conception of time is cyclical, seeing in the endless repetitions of the motions of the heavenly bodies, and therefore also of the days, months and seasons, the moving image of eternity itself. It is an example of metrical order, of the consonance and harmony of the parts which form a well-ordered whole. In this regard, ancient philosophers such as Boethius, and the Romantic philosopher, Schelling, found it to be the model for musical order: for the measured order of the scale of a mode, in the case of Boethius, and for the metrical organization of rhythm, in the case of Schelling. But Schelling's point was that music as an art is in some sense an imitation of the order of time, not simply of the abstract metaphysical concept of order. Hence, the concept of time emerges as the most concrete context for understanding the metaphorical significance of music.

In the twentieth century, Adorno, too, has recognized this. He finds Schoenberg's music, especially in his later style, disjointed, consisting of shocks and contrasts, so that there is no musical unity or continuity. As such, it accomplishes the negation of time, so that he concludes: 'Late Schoenberg shares with jazz – and moreover with Stravinsky – the dissociation of musical time. Music formulates a design of the world, which – for better or for worse – no longer recognizes history.'[1] This is a profound insight; it holds true for much of even more recent avant-garde music and, if we regard atonality from the point of view of Boethius, for Schoenberg's early Expressionist works as well. For the lack of a modal scalar pattern and of a harmonically consonant order would seem to undermine the entire capacity of this new music to function as a metaphor of harmonious order and consonance, including the cyclic order of time. Moreover, the fragmentation of rhythmic regularity in both Schoenberg and Stravinsky destroys the perception of cyclicity itself. Therefore, since modern music negates time in these ways, it is not only the case that music's metaphorical capacity is eroded; it helps also to change the way in which modern society conceives of time itself. Time for the modern world risks becoming fragmented and senseless, so that even the earlier, Platonist conception of time will not make sense as a context of human life. In this way, time as it is ordinarily perceived becomes a philosophical problem.

Adorno, however, focuses not on the demise of the cyclic concept of time arising from the ancient doctrine of the Music of the Spheres, but rather on the modern absence of a sense of history. The negation of historicity points, then, to another dimension of time altogether: the aspect of linearity which was so important before the twentieth century. Indeed, a linear conception of time is absolutely essential to the sense that there is a history to be discovered in spite of the underlying cyclicity of the seasons and years. Hence, one of the distinguishing features of Western civilization has been its strong sense of historical continuity from ancient times to the present, achieved through the practice of historical writing. It was not only the nineteenth century that cultivated the historical record: both Thucydides in ancient Greece and the historical books of the Hebrew Bible offer examples of linear narrative. Nevertheless, only in the eighteenth and nineteenth centuries did there emerge a practice of historical writing which found in modern history the kind of purposiveness found originally in the Biblical narrative – although now secular rather than divine in purpose. If this has indeed been abandoned in the twentieth century, it would mark a profound change in the temporal consciousness in Western civilization. If such a change were embodied in modern music, it would be the reflection of a broader cultural shift.

Taking music seriously as a metaphor of the concept of time, then, means that it is necessary to understand the modern view of time in order to understand what is at stake in the musical metaphor. The difference between traditional and modernist concepts of time is not just the contrast between continuity and discontinuity, but rather the contrast in the potential for time and existence itself to be regarded as good. The result for music is a choice between a tonal order that is metaphorical of goodness and an avant-garde that at least implicitly denies such goodness.

The modern concept of time

The modern attitude toward time has been most thoroughly articulated by Martin Heidegger. First in his 1924 lectures on *The Concept of Time*, and then in his magisterial *Being and Time* of 1927, Heidegger developed the rejection of history, tradition and linearity that we have seen already in abbreviated form in Adorno's remarks. But since Heidegger gives so much fuller an account of the modern attitude, it will be helpful to consider his arguments at some length in order to establish the character of modernism as a phenomenon. It will then be possible to understand why the modern concept of time seeks to foreclose the question of the origin of the goodness of existence.

In the 1924 lecture, Heidegger states emphatically, 'Time itself is meaningless'; by this he seeks to exclude the possibility of a coherent narrative of life, an argument he makes at length in *Being and Time*.[2] Instead, Heidegger argues for a disconnected multiplicity of times: past, present and future, but finds that it is only the future which lends authenticity to human existence (Dasein). In particular, the present – the moment in which we live –

is what we measure by the clock; it is the result of trying to objectify time. But then Dasein loses its authenticity, indeed loses time itself. For living with a 'watch in hand' makes life seem busy, filled with the ordinary and 'everyday' activities which rob life of both personal identity and the sense of futuricity that he finds essential to that identity.[3] The striking thing about Heidegger's argument, however, is the hostility to measure, even in the classical sense of the times of the day. All cyclicity becomes suspect as a kind of measure, and measure is perceived as that which robs life of its authenticity. Hence, the present, which he takes to be the product of such a measure, can only be illusory. Together with measured order, it must be rejected.

What, however, of the past? For Heidegger, the past is the source of the dread of death. On the one hand, this is essential: facing the prospect of death is the defining experience of human existence, making possible the authenticity of Dasein. Death becomes associated with the past, then, because the origin of the self in non-existence lies in the past. Hence, for Heidegger, the past is just death itself, the source of dread and anxiety. Although in *Being and Time*, he makes the modality of the past entirely derivative from the future, in the earlier lecture, there is another sense: the past rather defines 'the authentic "how" of my Dasein', that is, the authenticity of how one faces death.[4] But this authenticity of existence is precisely the mood of dread. Thus, the past has no dignity or joy to lend to life; it must be perceived as the temporal representation of nothingness. Although it cannot be rejected as illusory like the present, it cannot be affirmed either.[5] It establishes the existential problem for Dasein.

Dasein can attain its authenticity, therefore, only in the future. Dasein 'runs ahead' – looks forward – to its potentialities by facing the possibility of death in recalling the past. But only in anticipating its future possibilities can human existence overcome the burden of necessity and facticity imposed by the dead weight of the past. Hence, Heidegger claims that 'the fundamental phenomenon of time is the future'. What he calls 'being futural' breaks down all the 'idle talk', busyness and restlessness which condemn a person to 'the bad present of the everyday'; this mode of existence alone can give meaning to life.[6] But the future is ultimately just that which the past holds up to Dasein: non-existence, death, Nothingness. Thus, in spite of the claim that 'Being futural gives time', Heidegger's sense of the future is always overshadowed by the dread of death. His concept of time devalues the future as much as it does the present and the past. Life appears intrinsically meaningless because time itself is a projection of Nothing into Nothingness.

Nevertheless, Heidegger's focus on the future as the exclusive modality of time possessing worth was typical of the intellectual and artistic culture of the 1920s. Already the Futurists had taken up the position of hostility to the cultural legacy of the past, calling for the destruction of museums, aesthetic idealism and rationality itself. In the *Futurist Manifesto* of 1908, Marinetti had regarded the museum as a cemetery, equating the past with death just as effectively as Heidegger was to do with more philosophical sophistication: 'To admire an old picture is to pour our sentiment into a funeral urn instead of hurling it forth in violent gushes of action and productiveness.'[7] Here is the avant-garde rejection of tradition as a foundation for creativity; only the absolutely new will have any merit for the new, modern age. But the significant point here is that a changed conception of time emerges clearly as a corollary: if the past is to be cast off, and if the present matters only in its subservience to the goals of the future, the teleological direction of time is truncated. Time's arrow points forward, but it is rootless and without substance. Time itself, and not only the artistic and philosophical products of the modern age, will no longer be endowed with a ground of permanence. In Heidegger's language, futurity depends on resoluteness of the will, not on the object of willing.[8] But if it is resoluteness which guarantees authenticity, then there will be no moral restraint on willing. The result is a philosophy, like the Futurist Movement itself, which can consort with fascism and not feel the prick of conscience.

The avant-garde in music has been defined by the same dynamic concept of time. As Schoenberg wrote in his 1946 essay, 'New Music, Outmoded Music, Style and Idea', new music 'differs in all essentials from previously composed music'. It always presents something new which has never been presented or expressed before; he takes this to be the mark of all new music in every age.[9] But this is to extend the thesis about time's futuricity even farther than we have yet seen. For it is one thing to say that the modern age is characterized by a new sense of time, an orientation toward the future instead of the past, but it is another to claim that in fact this is true of all ages in the past, as well as the modern present. From our perspective, however, it should be clear that not all ages have in fact shared the same sense of time: if the modern age is defined by its futuricity, this stands in complete contrast to the cyclicity which dominated the ancient world. Nevertheless, it is this futuricity which fragments time in the modern world, for without a capacity for embracing the present and the past, there will be no possibility of temporal continuity. More specifically, the exclusive preoccupation with newness and the future prevents the association between measured harmony in the cycles of time and the goodness Platonic writers asserted as intrinsic to order in general and the cosmos in particular.

It would appear, however, that the futurist conception of time might be construed as in fact teleological, but in a different way from that of previous traditions. The concern with creating something new certainly raises a question regarding the difference between this kind of goal-directedness and the teleology of the order of tonality. Perhaps the New Music, as Schoenberg implies, has a new future as its aim. Nevertheless, if Adorno is correct in sensing that Schoenberg's music dissolves time, then the question of the meaningfulness of that future, and indeed of time itself, becomes problematic. The possibility of a futurist *telos* without the context of a larger meaning of time would appear self-contradictory.

The modern view of time explicitly finds life meaningless, precisely because it removes the past from view. This is evident in Nietzsche who, like Heidegger, makes the anticipation of the future the fundamental aspect of human existence, yet rejects the positing of definite goals. 'Becoming must be explained without recourse to final intentions; becoming must appear justified at every moment ... ; the present must absolutely not be justified by reference to a future, nor the past by reference to the present.'[10] Here the denial of the concept of the good as an object of final intention becomes crucial to the denial of a definite end in willing. As a consequence, the process of becoming is what is to be pursued for its own sake. In that case, however, it is not just the present and the past which will appear devalued; the future as well loses any real importance. To that extent, the modern concept of time devalues time itself. The goodness of time, therefore, turns out to be identical with the goodness of existence.

The influence exercised by Nietzsche over the avant-garde, as over Heidegger and much of twentieth-century philosophy, was critical for shaping the history of the arts in that century. Expressionism as an artistic movement was largely inspired by Nietzsche, and especially the publication of *The Will to Power*.[11] Composers, too, were deeply affected; Schoenberg in particular planned a symphony on the subject of overcoming Nietzschean nihilism in the years after writing *Pierrot lunaire* (1912). Although he did not write the projected symphony, his original plans nevertheless indicate how seriously he took the appearance of nihilism – a subject to which we will return in Chapter 7. Thus, Adorno appears right to argue that there is a fundamental shift in the concept of time in the modern avant-garde.

The question remains, however, as to what precisely was rejected. For the primary object of Nietzsche's attack was not a concept of time in itself, but rather the notion of a goal of becoming that was a transcendent end or metaphysical good. For him, the idea that a *telos* located outside the human self, in God or eternity, was what would have to be given up in order to address the origin of nihilism.[12] That is, any idea of a metaphysical good, such as we have explored in the previous chapter, devalued time and existence in his eyes. But although the classical philosophers had framed their arguments for the ultimate good in terms of an eternal order of being, it is the Christian concept of the relation between God and creation which provides the strongest account of a teleological conception of time. Nietzsche's primary object of criticism was precisely the religious hypostasis of God as the *telos* of human life. Thus, the questions arise: What is the foundation of the perceived goodness of time in any sense? What accounts for the perception of value in the temporal order defined by classical tonality? How does this understanding of temporality differ from the modern with its emphasis on futuricity? Only if we can answer these questions will it be possible to understand the difference between traditional musical culture and the avant-garde.

Traditional concepts of time

The modern concept of time is defined by its anticipation of the future and its hostility to the past; the present, therefore, has value only insofar as it is a moment oriented toward the future. The uniqueness of this may be understood not only in contrast to the classical sense of the cyclicity of time, but indeed to the respect for the past evident in classical writings and transmitted through them as the common intellectual culture of our civilization. Seneca, for example, praised the past as sacred, 'removed from Fortune's sway'. Being able to recall all the days past at will allows one to relish precious memories and to relive the activities which have made life meaningful; this is how life, indeed, acquires meaning.[13] Seneca is just as emphatic as Heidegger in condemning the restless, preoccupied, busy person who has no time to live in a genuine sense. But his prescription is diametrically opposed to Heidegger's: to cherish the past, rather than to reject it in favour of an as yet unlived future. St Augustine, too, esteemed the memory of the past as fundamental, for it makes possible all perception of the self, all imagination, future expectation, and feeling of emotions. Thus, to speak truly, the memory is the mind.[14] In contrast again to Heidegger, who seeks the authentic self in the act of willing the future, St Augustine finds the self rooted in the very memory of the past that Heidegger and the modern world reject. In fact, Plato makes much the same point in the *Philebus*, where Socrates argues that the power of memory is crucial even for recognizing whether one is feeling pleasure or pain.[15]

According to the classical model, then, it is precisely a sense of the past which gives value to life. For Christianity, however, eternal life with God is the goal of human existence on earth, and this raises a question in spite of St Augustine's respect for memory. Although time lies outside of eternity according to the standard account given by St Augustine, nonetheless, the believer's experience of time comes to an end with the beatific vision in heaven.[16] Thus, Milton could write, describing the commonplace understanding of a personified time, 'Fly envious Time, till thou run out thy race /... For when as each thing bad thou hast entombed, / And last of all, thy greedy self consumed, / Then long Eternity shall greet our bliss / With an individual kiss ...'.[17] Heaven is conceived as the overcoming of all evil, death, and contingency, so that it indeed is a triumph over created time. As such, it provides the goal of human existence; it orders time teleologically.

The crucial question is whether this view of the perfection of heaven devalues the nature of time as we live it, or endows it with an order of goodness. Nietzsche insists on the former; if heaven is good, this world must be taken as evil. The theological tradition, however, does not support that view. St Augustine, for example, insists repeatedly that everything God made is good, although not unchangeably good, or it would have no being at all. Considered as a whole, the ensemble is indeed 'very good', because the 'ensemble constitutes the universe in all its wonderful order and beauty'.[18] But since time itself is an aspect of the created world, its goodness must follow as well. Thus, in common with the rest of the classical world, St Augustine finds the universe to be orderly, beautiful and good.[19] The order of time is an indispensable part of this goodness.

Yet, significantly, time itself presents puzzles in St Augustine's view. It appears divided into past, present and future, the modalities we have examined thus far in both the modern and the ancient accounts. Only the present, however, is existent, he argues, for the past has ceased to be, and the future does not yet exist. On the other hand, the present has its being only in passing away, so that 'we cannot rightly say that time is, except by reason of its impending state of not being'.[20] But any period of time we call 'the present' is immediately divisible into hours and minutes, so that the present reduces to only an instant. Thus, we are compelled to admit that the present, which is the only point of time that exists, has no duration at all – a result that would seem to deny its existence, and time's existence, altogether. St Augustine has recognized, then, the potential reduction of time to meaninglessness inherent in focusing on the modalities of time; Heidegger's version of nihilism and his attempt to resolve it in the resoluteness of a Nietzschean will appear to be one possible outcome of any conception of time in terms of its linearity. It is of the greatest importance, however, that St Augustine resolves the apparent paradox of the non-existence of time, thereby escaping the meaninglessness of a present defined by its singularity.

St Augustine rejects the cyclical concept of time in Plato's account, denying that the motions of the heavenly bodies constitute time or even a means of measuring time. He accepts the linearity of time as divided into past, present and future, however, in only a limited sense.[21] Instead, time exists and is measured entirely in human thought. The faculty of memory makes possible the retention of past events in the mind, and this retention constitutes the past; the mind also, however, makes possible the anticipation of the future, based on judgements, so that all our perception of time depends on mental recollection and measure.[22] Thus, to speak truly, only the present exists – but in mental attention, not as a momentary instant. What we call the past, present, and future, then, are best described in terms of memory, direct perception and expectation: as mental acts of attention taking place in the present.[23] This is a psychological conception of time not far removed, indeed, from Heidegger's own subjective phenomenology – but with a very different result. For St Augustine, the subjective perception of time yields a validation of the present, and therefore, a high estimation of the goodness of all of time and existence.

Christian theology succeeds, therefore, in recognizing the worth of time as it is lived and perceived in this world. All three modalities of time – past, present and future – turn out to be essential to the perception of the goodness of human existence. The present is the time in which life is lived, the past recalled and the future anticipated: it, therefore, must be accounted as the most valued modality of created time. The past, however, is the foundation of existence, the source of personal identity, as well as the locus of authoritative revelation in history. It, too, has a value which cannot be negated. Finally, of the future it may be said that without the hope of eternal life, the Christian would have no ground for hope at all in this world; there would be little indeed for which to live. In that way, then, the teleological ordering of time on the Christian account yields a conception of the goodness of all the modalities of time. Nietzsche is simply wrong in his understanding of human psychology: it is eternity alone which gives profound hope and bestows goodness on this life.

In spite of human sin and temporal suffering, therefore, Christian theology recognizes the goodness of this life in a deeper way than had classical philosophy. For Plato had not had a temporal past or future grounded in eternity in his concept of time, so that the sense of continuity in human life was restricted to a cyclically recurring present. Yet the goodness of the days and seasons has proven indeed to be an important constituent of the perception of the goodness of existence. Both the classical and the Christian conceptions of time, therefore, emphasize necessary elements in the goodness of human existence: the one cyclical, the other linear, both perceive the present as of fundamental importance. Hence, when the value of the present is denied, as it has been by modernism generally, the goodness of existence disappears altogether. Then humanity is left with hatred of the past and dread of the future: this is the experience of time in Heidegger, and the root of the endless restlessness and revolt against the norms of tradition in the avant-garde of the twentieth century. Adorno was right to perceive that Schoenberg's music, like modernity in general, dissolved time itself; what emerges from this is the dissolution of the goodness of existence. As we shall see in Part Two, this becomes crucial to understanding the avant-garde.

If we seek, however, the temporal foundation of classical music, the Christian conception of time emerges as the far more important context in comparison with any generalized Aristotelian teleology. The Christian teleology places created time and its subjective apprehension in the metaphysical framework of the beatific vision of God as the ultimate good. In contrast to Plato's concept of an original beatific vision remembered in this life, Christianity anticipates the vision as futural with regard to this life, but eternal once attained in the next. Within this life, then, time is perceived as linear, embracing a distinct past, present and future. But it is the past which is emphasized as the foundation of that linearity; it is the locus of divine revelation, the proof of transcendence that lends its goodness to present existence. Within this framework of a dual evidence of transcendent order, the present attains its unique value, in spite of its necessarily momentary nature. The goodness of the order of time, therefore, is a direct function of its divine *telos*. In contrast to the modern conception, which truncates the modality of time by dismissing the past and making the present merely transitory, the traditional Christian understanding allows all the modalities of time as essential to its teleological nature. It would make sense, then, for classical tonality to arise within the context of Christian culture, rather than in either the pagan world or the modern, and to have its significance in the reflection of this temporal order. The theology of transcendence is the foundation of the goodness of time for the Christian world.

Yet there is still an historical irony. The Renaissance *ordre unitonique* may be perceived as reflecting the value of the present in the perspective of eternity according to traditional Christian theology. Yet tonality fully developed as the *ordre transitonique* did not arise until Christian culture had been substantially modified by the Renaissance humanist revival of classical antiquity, and it did not achieve its full potential until the Enlightenment began to chip away at many of the theological tenets. In spite of the teleological correspondence with a theological world-view, tonality appears associated indisputably with secularity, especially in its close ties to opera and to secular music generally. Such a link not only fails to corroborate the hypothesis of a religious significance of tonality; it suggests that tonality could develop fully only when that significance waned in influence. To understand this, it is necessary to turn, therefore, to the specific philosophical systems which can help to make sense of the relation between time and the world.

The post-Renaissance order of time

The history of philosophy since the Renaissance has been dominated by the problems posed by the developments of science. This has affected the concept of time no less than other aspects of life. But since time is a specific instance of the metaphysical concept of order, it is therefore the case that the changes in world-view created by modern science affect the way in which order in general is conceived. Such scientific changes, however, rarely affect other areas of thought deterministically; rather, the essence of philosophical reflection is debate. It would be surprising, therefore, if in fact the concepts of time and order were not in some measure significant philosophical problems for the modern world. A brief consideration of the problem of order in general will demonstrate the point and provide the context for understanding the emergence of a new concept of time in the seventeenth and eighteenth centuries.

The Copernican revolution is usually taken as the defining event in the development of the new science. But when Copernicus overthrew the Ptolemaic cosmology in the sixteenth century, he did not replace the authority of Plato's conception of order. Plato's account of the order of the cosmos in the *Timaeus* is a mathematical one, and that view of the world continued to inspire the work of Johannes Kepler in his discovery of the laws of planetary motion at the beginning of the seventeenth century. Thus, in one important sense, modern science is the fulfilment of the Pythagorean dream of understanding the world through number. Yet in another sense, it accomplished a revolution in the ancient concept of order, for although Plato's account of the order of the cosmos was mathematical in principle, it was also visible and simple in nature. Now the true order was mathematical in form, immanent in Nature, invisible and abstract. It consisted in the laws of Nature, rather than simple diagrams and ratios.[24] Nature itself, then, becomes hypostasized as an abstract being, replacing the cosmos of the ancient world's understanding of the context of human life.

This is a problem, however, for the Christian teleological understanding of the relation between God and His created world. For the new mathematics could demonstrate the harmony of the world's order, but not its teleological ordination toward God as the final end. Hence, the great mathematicians of the seventeenth century – Descartes, Pascal, Newton and Leibniz – were all concerned to show that the new concepts of mathematical order supported rather than contradicted the traditional understanding of God's relation to the world. The solutions varied: Descartes removed final ends from his conception of Nature but still understood God as the First Efficient Cause, whereas Pascal had to separate the Christian faith from science altogether, denying the traditional arguments for the existence of God as inferred from the created order.[25] Only Leibniz took up the challenge of trying to integrate final ends into the order of Nature that was now understood mathematically, thus attempting to preserve the teleological ordering of the world toward God.[26] The way in which he accomplished this established much of the view of the world that dominated Western thought between the late seventeeenth and the late nineteenth centuries. It was crucial for establishing a conception of teleological order that corresponds closely to that found in the musical practice of tonality.

Gottfried Wilhelm von Leibniz is best known as the philosopher of optimism, most often today through the satire of Voltaire's Dr Pangloss in *Candide*. Yet Leibniz's optimism does not differ fundamentally from that of St Augustine: it was a serious attempt to consider the problem of evil in a world that a good God had created. St Augustine had insisted, with Genesis 1:31, that this world is 'very good', and Leibniz agreed. This is the optimal world that

God could have created: Leibniz's argument on this point is in agreement with the tradition. God creates with the purpose of communicating Himself; hence, He communicates His goodness and His perfection.[27] But since 'all that God does ... is harmonious to perfection', the goodness of His creation consists in perfect harmony.[28] This is the cornerstone of Leibnizian philosophy; he was convinced of the 'Pre-established Harmony of all things amongst themselves, of that between nature and grace, between the decrees of God and our actions foreseen, between all parts of matter, and even between the future and the past ... .'[29] Thus, the union of the body and the soul, and the correspondence between the perception of nature and the actual operation of nature could be explained in terms of the Pre-established Harmony as well.[30] This did not mean he closed his eyes to evil and suffering; what he called metaphysical evil was the consequence of the operation of general laws and did not reflect on the merit of individuals who suffered. Sin, however, was individual, and was possible because of the freedom of will in man that was a vital part of the created order.[31] Evil, therefore, was not an indictment of the goodness of God, but an inevitable part of the harmony of the world God had created. The overall order of the world still had to be counted as good because it was harmonious.

What distinguishes Leibnizian optimism, however, from earlier answers to the problem of evil is the even more intrinsically teleological nature of order as Leibniz conceives it. Not only is man ordained to God as his final end, but God has created the entire world purposively; God is therefore the final cause of all creation. Hence, Leibniz defends the concept of final causes as relevant to a scientific understanding of the world. It is in human affairs, however, that the purposiveness of existence is most evident: this is found in the concept of progress. 'As the climax of the universal beauty and perfection of God's works, it must also be recognized that the total universe is engaged in a perpetual and spontaneous progress, so that it always advances toward greater culture.'[32] Thus, the idea of progress, although sometimes held to be a consequence of the secularization of the doctrine of salvation, was in fact for Leibniz a direct extension of the concept of a teleological ordering of the world according to God's purposes.[33] But whereas earlier writers had considered the world as an ordered whole because of the harmony of its motion, Leibniz now held time itself to be ordered in an infinite progress. He therefore transformed the traditional concept of the world as an order of being into, remarkably, an order of becoming.

This does not, however, simply add an element of directedness onto the principle of harmony, as indeed the traditional theological conception of ordination to the beatific vision does for the order of human existence. Rather, it immanentizes the teleological ordination toward completion and perfection, so that, although it is grounded in the transcendent perfection of God, the end is taken into the order of creation, to be realized in time itself. This introduces far more complexity into the account of order, so that complexity becomes vital to the world's beauty and goodness and perfection. For Leibniz, perfection consists in 'the greatest possible variety, together with the greatest possible order'.[34] The metaphysical goodness of being, therefore, is a product not only of ordination to God and of harmony among the parts of the world, but also of the complexity of the parts ordered toward a realization of perfection in time. It is this understanding of order which lies at the heart of the Baroque development of tonality.

Leibniz himself provides only the briefest remarks concerning music. 'Music charms us, although its beauty consists only in the harmonies of numbers and in the counting (of which we are unconscious but which nevertheless the soul does make) of the beats or vibrations of sounding bodies ... .'[35] Here Leibniz simply identifies sensual charm with mathematical harmony. Hence, it is certainly not the case that the system of major/minor tonality developed as the result of the influence of Leibnizian metaphysics, nor even that Leibniz recognized the particular character of musical order in his lifetime. But he did share in a concept of order common to the seventeenth and eighteenth centuries, and especially to musical theorists who sought to ground music in the laws of nature.

Therefore, we must search elsewhere for a correspondence between the new metaphysics of teleological perfection and the teleological order embodied in tonality. First, Leibniz does provide a solid link between the apparently Aristotelian conception of teleology in tonality and the general philosophical currents of the seventeenth century, for in general Leibniz framed his metaphysical rebuttal of Descartes in an attempt to revive the basic categories of Aristotle's thought. Thus, we can say that both Leibnizian philosophy and the new system of tonality reflect a similar conception of order, in which the transcendent *telos* was taken to be thoroughly immanent within the system of order, somewhat after the manner of Aristotle's divine Mind that dwelt within the cosmos. Second, however, there was a deliberate search to accommodate the greatest amount of complexity within the framework of a teleological order. In this sense, then, tonality corresponds to the philosophy of optimism and may be taken as a metaphor of the greatest possible goodness of being.

We have already seen that Rameau identified variety in itself as a legitimate reason for dissonance and modulation to different key levels. Why variety should have been taken as self-evidently desirable, however, remained mysterious. Leibniz, however, provides an answer: it is not just variety, but the greatest possible variety in the context of the greatest possible order which constitutes perfection according to the Baroque understanding. Since this order, in both cases, is teleological, both dissonance and key levels must be used in a way that accomplishes their resolution to their appropriate goals. Hence, dissonance assumed a much more vital role in Baroque music than it possessed in the Renaissance. In both cases, dissonance was required to resolve, but by the end of the seventeenth century, its resolution to consonance was used to propel the music forward both melodically and harmonically to the tonic; it was no longer simply incidental to a largely consonant sonority. Thus, Baroque music required the complexity of dissonance in order to complete the gradation of sonority for the perfection of the entire tonal system. In a similar way, the use of modulation as a principle for articulating large-scale musical structures introduced a level of complexity that had been completely impossible in modal polyphony, making the return to the tonic key the perceptible goal of musical form itself. Thus, the formal qualities of tonal music correspond exactly to the metaphysical goodness of being as it was defined by Leibniz.

The significance of this correspondence, which is analogical and not explicit in our sources, emerges from our earlier consideration of the nature of musical metaphors of order. Music represents what it is: in this case, it is a complex, teleological order in which the goal of tonal motion is contained within the system. Moreover, the natural foundations of consonance and root movement which theorists sought and found during this period made music a part of the natural order in a far deeper way than it had been possible to say of the earlier modal order. Thus, it was not necessary for music to be self-consciously a symbol of the world, or an explicit metaphor for understanding the world as it had been according to the ancient doctrine of the Music of the Spheres. Rather, for Leibniz and his contemporaries, music was part of the natural world, arising from its laws and therefore comprehensible by reason. But the tonal order, for that very reason, partook of the same beauty and goodness as the larger world. On this, Leibniz could sound thoroughly traditional: 'Order, proportions, harmony delight us; painting and music are samples of these: God is all order; he always keeps truth of proportions, he makes universal harmony; all beauty is an effusion of his rays.'[36] Thus, Leibniz affirms the largest points of the traditional understanding of order; harmony, complexity and ordination to a knowable final end are the marks of goodness and beauty. They characterize both the order of the world and the order of tonal music, so that a musical work becomes a reflection of perfection itself, a Leibnizian monad reflecting the whole.

What appears, then, as the emergence of the system of tonality at the moment when the influence of humanism began to erode the theological dimension of traditional culture turns out to be a misapprehension of the relation between musical and philosophical developments. For if it is Leibniz's understanding of metaphysical order which underlies the Baroque development of tonality, then the metaphysical order in question is thoroughly theological in nature. Far from tonality's origins in operatic music representing the secularization of culture, it must be taken as the product of an immanentizing impulse whereby the transcendent goal becomes part of the knowable world. Certainly Baroque and Classical *opera seria* in general celebrated the victory of good over evil and, through the convention of the *deus ex machina*, made the action of the classical gods a clear metaphor of divine providence according to the Christian understanding of the term.[37] But if the gods appeared on stage as beings known in this world to resolve the action of the opera, and doing so moreover in the tonic key, then the concept of an immanent teleology in both music and metaphysics makes sense of these cultural conventions. In this way, tonality became a metaphor of a generally acknowledged providential order. Leibniz's optimism is the culture of Baroque opera and the metaphysical foundation of the order of tonality.

If we understand Leibnizian optimism as the foundation of Enlightenment culture, whatever other intellectual currents which later came to question or to ridicule its more naïve expressions, then we are in a position to understand why tonality emerged when it did. The congruence of a musical style with a doctrine of the immanent realization of perfection affected both the stories told in opera and the creation of instrumental forms of music. For the striking fact about symphonic and chamber music in the Classical period, especially, is their optimism: few works are in minor keys, and when Beethoven does begin a work in minor, it ends triumphantly in major – as in his Fifth and Ninth Symphonies. The expressive character of tonal music, which arises precisely from the twin sources of the major/minor polarity and its teleological nature, is therefore put in the service of a higher metaphysical purpose.

Our analysis of the concept of time has revealed that this is not to be seen as just an expression of faith in ultimate justice, but rather an actual perception of divine providence *in* this world. As Schiller's Ode to Joy states, joy is a 'beautiful spark of the gods', but it commands 'the firm decrees/In eternal Nature'. Although Beethoven omits the fourth stanza from his setting, it is crucial to Schiller's poem: Joy 'coaxes flowers out of their buds./The sun out of the firmament'; Beethoven simply allows that 'All beings drink joy/At Nature's bosom'.[38] Thus, the Almighty Father, of whom the poem speaks and whom the symphony depicts in its most religious tones, is known by the immanent principle of joy; joy is the force behind the laws of Nature. The same principle which ought to animate humanity, and indeed unite humanity in one brotherhood, is also the principle of energy in the universe. It is fitting that Beethoven, at the end of the Enlightenment, desired to set this text to music. Its immanent teleology was to inspire the greatest symphonic work of the Classical era.

The concept of time in nineteenth-century Idealism

With Schiller, however, we enter the world of German Idealism, where we find the most systematic and most influential expression of the teleological conception of time. We have already encountered Friedrich Schelling's Platonic idealism as one attempt to make sense of the world in terms of an order which reflects a higher order in the realm of the Platonic Ideas. But in general, it can be said that one of the principal motivations of Idealist philosophy was to find a way to reconcile the natural and the human realms, which modern science threatened to sunder. The completion of Leibnizian optimism, then, lies pre-eminently in the philosophy of Hegel. Here there is an immanent teleology of progress of the same kind as in Leibniz. It occurs within the context of the larger purpose of uniting logic, Nature and Spirit as the progressively more active manifestations of the Idea, or truth.[39] In this way truth itself becomes historicized. For our purposes, it will be helpful to consider Hegel's philosophy of human time as the origin of the nineteenth century's conception of progress as an immanent teleology. The correspondence with the kind of order represented in the orders of tonality Fétis distinguished, then, will make our understanding of the metaphorical potential of tonality complete.

Hegel is famous for conceiving the achievements of philosophy in his own day as the culmination of historical development. This kind of self-satisfaction, when pardoned, is taken to be the product of an approach that seeks to overcome the errors of the past. Yet Hegel sees all history, and especially the history of philosophy, rather as a matter of a continuously developing tradition, preserving what the spirit has achieved in the past and adding to it, 'swelling like a mighty river', so that the insight of reason is indeed the growing revelation of the universal spirit of reason.[40] As an attempt to recover from earlier one-sidedness in the debates over transcendence and immanence of the spirit of reason, for example, Hegel could legitimately point to the success of the dialectical method as an example of the progressive realization of rational understanding. The achievements of the past are, for Hegel, not so much errors as essential attempts, necessarily partial, to understand the nature of things. Progress, therefore, is not continuous on this view, but it is cumulative.

On the other hand, it is often difficult, in retrospect, to see history as culminating in the Hegelian enterprise: neither did philosophical speculation come to an end, nor did Hegel himself prove unambiguous in his legacy. But it is Hegel's conceptualization of history in terms of its religious and political dimensions which is of importance here. The Spirit, as the Spirit of God, reveals itself in progressively more inward forms, developing from the intimations of the spiritual in primitive societies to the polytheistic representations of Greco-Roman classicism, and culminating in the union of the divine and the human in the Incarnation of Christ. On the other hand, the political aspect of this development corresponds to the liberation of the individual spirit, so that the sense of personal freedom grows proportionately.

In primitive societies, only the ruler is free, whereas in the classical polis, the body of citizens becomes free; only in the modern world, under the influence of Chrisitianity, does liberty become universal. Thus, the development of the divine Spirit is simultaneously the growth of the individual human spirit: Hegel's concept of historical time is explicitly progressive.[41] Such progress unites spirituality and liberty in individuality.

The important point in Hegel's conception of historical progress, however, is precisely what appears most problematic from both a philosophical and a theological point of view. For his doctrine of progress makes the realization of complete philosophical self-consciousness the moment of perfection immanent in historical time. Thus, the infinite progress in Leibniz becomes an apparently finite development in Hegel – and therefore more troubling. By the same token, Hegel's doctrine of the divine Spirit's self-revelation being identical with the spirit of humanity's liberation appears to equate the divine and the human in a strikingly heterodox way.[42] Yet the result is to make the moment of divine perfection not only knowable, but present to all. Hence, the *telos* of divine-human history is thoroughly immanent: it is located within history itself, indeed within the immediate present of Hegel's day. As a result, the teleological conception of time which we found in Leibniz was accorded even more weight in Hegel's historicism. The truth of his claim is surely disputable, but the self-confidence it engendered in the nineteenth century is not. It became the dominant conception for much of the nineteenth century. It is little wonder, then, that Romantic music reflects such an immanent sense of teleology.

Fétis conceived of the music of his day, what we now call the Romantic era, as the *ordre omnitonique*. Fétis's point was critical: there seemed to be no true differentiation of keys because of the frequent use of enharmonically altered chords. Nevertheless modulation was crucial to musical form in the Classical and Romantic periods; its control was the achievement of sonata form and the reason for its prevalence. Precisely because there was more ambiguity within a key, there was often greater contrast in modulation to more distantly related keys. Thus the tonic was firmly embedded in Romantic music as a clearly perceptible goal of tonal motion. If we see in that practice an analogue of the immanent *telos* such as Hegel describes as the perfection found within historical time, it is surely not stretching the point to regard music in the common practice period as, in the largest sense, a metaphor of the conception of time. The expressive character of music, especially during the nineteenth century, must be understood, then, as arising in relation to the knowable ideal of perfection that the fullness of time reveals. Hence, the kind of longing for an ideal heard in so much Romantic music is not simply the longing for a tonic. It is, above all, the palpable yearning for resolution in a key that represents perfection. This is the hallmark of Romantic style, the result of an ideal held as a completely immanent *telos*. But it is in the genre of the symphony that the most important manifestation of this teleology is found: for in taking over Beethoven's emphasis on the triumphant attainment of the ideal in the finale movements, the nineteenth-century symphonists affirmed the prevailing belief in the possibility of the realization of the ideal.

The tonal metaphor of temporality

It is therefore possible to see the emergence and growth of the musical practice of tonality as a corollary of the emergence and growth of a particular kind of temporal order. The immanently conceived *telos* of a progressively realized ideal was fundamental both to the concept of time in the eighteenth and nineteenth centuries and to the concept of a teleological tonal order. It is not the case, to emphasize the point made earlier, that any particular philosopher provided the impetus for the musical development, or that tonality represents in a literal fashion the concept of time. The musical order, however, is a metaphor of the metaphysical, because it is a specific kind of order, interpretable in the same terms as order in general for all being. Thus, tonality represents a particular conception of the goodness of order, one rooted in the complex notion of a transcendent *telos* perceptible immanently in the world.

But it is the order of time, in particular, to which the art of music belongs, and which it represents most directly. The existence of a prevailing doctrine of temporal progress toward the realization of an ideal of perfection, then, makes such an immanent teleology in the temporal order the implicit referent of musical metaphor. Although there is always the emotionally expressive dimension to tonal music as well, the argument here is that this should be regarded as subordinate to metaphysical significance. As we have seen, the idealism of philosophical exponents such as Ernst Pauer, Friedrich Schelling and others, makes this point explicitly. In the case of Pauer, who popularized the tradition of German Idealism as a way of explaining the significance of the musical tradition in the second half of the nineteenth century, this provides persuasive evidence that the metaphysical import of tonal music really was regarded by the musically informed as the highest context for the art.

The association of tonality with the particular concept of a progressive time, however, raises anew the question of Adorno's thesis that tonality is exhausted in the modern world. Whether that thesis makes sense in isolation from the metaphorical capacity of the style will depend on one's view of the history of style and the necessity of not repeating what has already been done; the historical evidence for both of those criteria remains ambiguous. But if tonality is associated with either Leibnizian optimism or Hegelian historicism, then the conclusion is likely to be far more damaging to any possibility of continuing or restoring the practice of tonality. For if the relevance of the style depends on acceptance of a doctrine of progress, then surely Adorno is right to perceive this as impossible after all that has happened in the twentieth century. And if the relevance of tonality would depend on acceptance of Hegel's doctrine of the immanence of the divine in the workings of the World-Spirit, then even the works inherited from the traditional canon might appear doomed – whether on Adorno's Marxist critique, or through a Nietzschean scepticism, or even in orthodox Christianity. At least it would be necessary to vindicate some of the more controversial aspects of the Hegelian relation between ideals and their manifestation in the world.

Nevertheless, Adorno is surely correct to draw a link between the perception of goodness in the world and belief in the ideal: one of the traditional arguments for the existence of God proceeds from the perception of a providential ordering in the world to the positing of a Creator. His argument, that ideals do not exist if they are not found anywhere in the world, is not, however, entirely logical, for an ideal does not cease to exist simply because particular manifestations or representations of it cease. But this conclusion would be a necessary consequence of Hegel's identification of the divine and the human spirit. If, however, the transcendence of God and the finitude of humanity are kept separate, Adorno's despairing attack on any representation of goodness in an evil world loses its point. Yet it is admittedly difficult to believe in the good, or in God, if there be no goodness perceivable in the world.

Hegel's larger point, therefore, provides a valuable insight into human perception of the Ideal: there must be some concrete evidence of it, some particular example identifiable as good at a point in history, if the Idea of the good is to make sense to people. It is only the location of the Ideal in the present or future that becomes problematic in the modern world. Works of art, literature and music, however, function to keep alive the representations of the good inherited from the past. Thus, it is Hegel's progressivist historicism which necessarily becomes Adorno's nihilism today, unless it can be corrected by other varieties of philosophical idealism. But this means that if tonality can be conceived in broader idealist terms, then it too may continue to possess a degree of relevance as an expression of a knowable ideal. As we have seen, this is in fact the case. In its most general metaphor, tonality represents the good of a teleologically conceived order; this is the significance of the preservation of the canon of classical music in modern culture. But this is to point to the necessity of considering the museum of musical works, its aesthetic, and the contemporary attack on the concept of the work if we are to understand the growing rift between the culture of preservation and the culture of innovation in the modern world. What requires answering is how the order of time that is human existence might be perceived as good, even without subscribing to a doctrine of historical progress.

Notes

1. Theodor W. Adorno, *Philosophie der neuen Musik* (Frankfurt am Main: Europäischer Verlagsanstalt, 1958), p. 61; *Philosophy of Modern Music*, trans. Anne G. Mitchell and Wesley V. Blomster (New York: Seabury Press, 1973), p. 60.
2. Martin Heidegger, *The Concept of Time*, trans. and ed. William McNeill (Oxford and Cambridge, MA: Blackwell, 1992), p. 21; cf. *Being and Time: A Translation of 'Sein und Zeit'*, trans. Joan Stambaugh (Albany: State University of New York Press, 1996), p. 5.
3. Heidegger, *The Concept of Time*, pp. 15–17; cf. *Being and Time*, pp. 302, 379–80.
4. Heidegger, *The Concept of Time*, pp. 11–12; cf. *Being and Time*, pp. 299–300.
5. Hans Jonas remarks upon the negativity of the past, as well as the striking absence of a genuine present in *Being and Time*, in the Epilogue to *The Gnostic Religion: The Message of an Alien God and the Beginnings of Christianity*, 2nd edn (Boston: Beacon Press, 1963), p. 336. Jonas is surely correct in seeing this as essentially a gnostic attitude reborn.
6. *The Concept of Time*, p. 14; cf. *Being and Time*, p. 391.
7. Originally published in *Le Figaro* (February 20, 1909); trans. Joshua C. Taylor, in Herschel B. Chipp, ed., *Theories of Modern Art: A Source Book by Artists and Critics* (Berkeley: University of California Press, 1968), p. 287.
8. *Being and Time*, p. 273.
9. In Arnold Schoenberg, *Style and Idea: Selected Writings*, ed. Leonard Stein, trans. Leo Black (1975; Berkeley: University of California Press, 1984), p. 114.
10. Friedrich Nietzsche, *Der Wille zur Macht: Versuch einer Umwertung aller Werte*, Section 708, in *Sämtliche Werke in zwölf Bänden* (Stuttgart: Alfred Kröner Verlag, 1964), vol. 9, pp. 478–9; *The Will to Power*, trans. Walter Kaufmann and R. J. Hollingdale (New York: Vintage Books, 1968), p. 377.
11. Donald E. Gordon, *Expressionism: Art and Idea* (New Haven: Yale University Press, 1987), pp. 11–19.
12. *Der Wille Zur Macht*, Section 20, *Werke*, vol. 9, pp. 19–20; *The Will to Power*, pp. 16–17.
13. Lucius Annaeus Seneca, 'On the Shortness of Life,' *Dialogues and Letters*, trans. C. D. N. Costa (London: Penguin, 1997), p. 70.
14. St Augustine, *Confessions*, trans. R. S. Pine-Coffin (Harmondsworth: Penguin, 1961), Book X, Sections 8–17, pp. 214–23.
15. Plato, *Philebus* 21c.
16. *Confessions*, Book XII, Section 12, pp. 288–9. Cf. *The City of God*, Book VI, Section 6.
17. John Milton, 'On Time', text in *Six Centuries of Great Poetry*, ed. Robert Penn Warren and Albert Erskine (New York: Dell Publishing, 1955), pp. 241–2.
18. St Augustine, *The Enchiridion on Faith, Hope, and Love*, trans. J. F. Shaw, ed. Henry Paolucci (Chicago: Regnery Gateway, 1961), Section 10, pp. 10–11. Cf. Gen.1.
19. See also St Augustine, *On Free Choice of the Will*, trans. Thomas Williams (Indianapolis: Hackett, 1993), Book. III, Section 5, pp. 79, 82, where the order and dignity of the heavens are explicitly affirmed.
20. *Confessions*, Book XI, Section 14, p. 264.
21. *Confessions*, Book XI, Section 23, p. 271; Book XI, Section 27, p. 276.
22. *Confessions*, Book XI, Section 18, p. 267; Book XI, Section 28, p. 277.
23. *Confessions*, Book XI, Section 20, p. 269.

24. See R. G. Collingwood, *The Idea of Nature* (Oxford: Clarendon Press, 1945), pp. 101–2.

25. Cf. Etienne Gilson, *God and Philosophy* (New Haven: Yale University Press, 1941), pp. 74ff., for a perceptive discussion of the problem of understanding God in modern philosophy.

26. Gottfried Wilhelm von Leibniz, 'Critical Remarks Concerning Descartes' Principles', in *Monadology and Other Philosophical Essays*, trans. Paul and Anne M. Schrecker (Indianapolis: Bobs-Merrill, 1965), Section 28, pp. 30–31.

27. St Thomas Aquinas, *Summa Theologica*, Part I, q. 44, art. 4.

28. Leibniz, *Theodicy: Essays on the Goodness of God, the Freedom of Man, and the Origin of Evil*, trans. E. M. Huggard, ed. Austin Farrer (La Salle, IL: Open Court, 1985), Section 74, p. 162.

29. Ibid., Section 62, p. 157.

30. Leibniz, 'Monadology', *Monadology and Other Essays*, Sections 56–61, pp. 156–8.

31. Leibniz, *Theodicy*, Sections 19, 147, 241, 284, pp. 135, 216, 276, 300.

32. Leibniz, 'On the Ultimate Origination of the Universe', in *Monadology and Other Essays*, p. 93.

33. Cf. J. B. Bury, *The Idea of Progress: An Inquiry into Its Origins and Growth* (London: Macmillan, 1920). Hans Blumenberg argues the point of the rise of the concept of progress through human reason as the consequence of the growth of a doctrine of the absolute transcendence of divine grace: *The Legitimacy of the Modern Age*, trans. Robert M. Wallace (Cambridge, MA: MIT Press, 1983), p. 137. This is more subtle than Karl Löwith's thesis of a concern for the philosophy of history and the doctrine of progress as the results of secularization in his *Meaning in History: The Theological Implications of the Philosophy of History* (Chicago: University of Chicago Press, 1949), but one that still needs modification when considering the Enlightenment and the subsequent rise of Idealism.

34. Leibniz, 'Monadology', Section 58, *Monadology and Other Essays*, p. 157.

35. Quoted in *Music and Aesthetics in the Eighteenth and Early-Nineteenth Centuries*, ed. Peter le Huray and James Day (Cambridge: Cambridge University Press, 1981), p. 15.

36. Leibniz, *Theodicy*, Preface, p. 51.

37. See, for example, Gluck's *Iphigénie en Aulide*, which begins and ends in C major, the final chorus being a celebration of Diana's mercy in sparing the life of Iphigenia. This is a much more merciful ending than either Euripides' or Racine's version of the story: opera departs even farther than neo-classical spoken drama from pagan classicism.

38. Friedrich Schiller, 'An die Freude', *Gedichte, Erzählungen*, ed. Dieter Schmidt, in *Schiller's Werke* (Frankfurt am Main: Insel Verlag, 1966), vol. 3, pp. 53–4 (author's translation).

39. See Hegel's *Encyclopaedia of the Philosophical Sciences* (1830), especially Part Two, *Philosophy of Nature*, trans. A. V. Miller (Oxford: Clarendon Press, 1970), Section 258, on time and its relation to eternity. Hegel affirms traditional conceptions of the eternity of transcendent universals, even as they inform the temporal processes of all becoming.

40. Hegel, *Introduction to the Lectures on the History of Philosophy*, trans. T. M. Knox and A. V. Miller (Oxford: Clarendon Press, 1985), p. 10.

41. The most important texts for understanding Hegel's concept of historical development are: *Vorlesungen über die Philosophie der Geschichte*, ed. H. Glockner, *Sämtliche Werke in zwanzig Bänden* (Stuttgart: Frommans Verlag,

1928), vol. 11; *The Philosophy of History*, trans. J. Sibree (New York: Dover Publications, 1956), esp. pp. 102–10; *Lectures on the Philosophy of Religion,* trans. R. F. Brown, P. C. Hodgson and J. M. Stewart, 3 vols (Berkeley: University of California Press, 1984–87); and the *Aesthetics: Lectures of Fine Art*, trans. T. M. Knox (Oxford: Clarendon Press, 1975): see *Werke in zwanzig Bänden*, ed. E. Moldenhauer and K. Michel (Frankfurt am Main: Suhrkamp Verlag, 1969), vols 13, 14, 16, 17. On Hegel's historicism, see Stephen Houlgate, *Freedom, Truth and History: An Introduction to Hegel's Philosophy* (London: Routledge, 1991), pp. 5–40.

42.   On the origins of this, see Cyril O'Regan, *The Heterodox Hegel* (Albany: State University of New York Press, 1994).

CHAPTER FOUR

Narrative, Temporality and the Aesthetic of the Work

The concept of the musical work has come under increasing scrutiny in recent years. Critics have found it a historically limited concept, outmoded in the modern world, and indeed artistically limiting to the extent that its preservation as a norm for musical creativity appears to preclude exploration of alternatives.[1] Such a critique, however, like so many other revaluations of traditional concepts in musical aesthetics, is indebted to the work of Adorno. Already in *The Philosophy of Modern Music*, he had written that the concert of works displayed in performance is an 'empty ritual' which 'must be destroyed'.[2] For him, it will be recalled, the only alternative to the avant-garde was 'kitsch', and therefore even the works inherited from the past have fallen into the latter category. To preserve them is to make the concert hall a museum, which is to elevate the creativity of the past to an illegitimate status as a norm for the future.[3] Thus, the culture of preservation, such as we saw Hesse describing, is to be rejected. But this is not simple hostility to the past or its aesthetic; it is rooted in a recognition that the modern avant-garde no longer composes 'works'. Schoenberg and Webern had so condensed the musical form and expression in their compositions as to disrupt the status of these as works; their brevity deprived them of the authoritative status enjoyed by, say, a Beethoven symphony or a Verdi opera. This was not purely a musical development: the real problem lay 'in a social condition which reflects nothing binding and affirmative enough to guarantee the internal harmony of the work sufficient unto itself'.[4] This is to say, however, that without an ideal there cannot be a concept of an artistic work.

It becomes imperative, therefore, to return to the concept of the ideal as a metaphysical construct in the philosophy of the nineteenth century. We began the effort to recover the metaphysical understanding of classical tonality with the example of Ernst Pauer's popularization of idealist aesthetics, *The Elements of the Beautiful in Music*. Pauer's book articulated a hierarchy of kinds of beauty, from the formal to the characteristic to the ideal. It was the concept of the ideal which proved the most difficult, being at once suggestive of the transcendent, yet also ill-defined and ambiguous. If sense is to be made of the concept of the musical work, however, the concept of the ideal must be clarified. If, as further argued, classical tonality serves as a metaphor not only of teleological order in general, but of the temporal ordering toward an ideal in particular, then the connection with the metaphysics of temporal order must be made explicit. Since the concept of the musical work is usually taken to reside in its hypostasizing the composer's emotional expression,[5] an understanding of the work as the embodiment of a genuine ideal would substantially alter the modern critique. It may not be possible to resurrect the relevance of aesthetic idealism to the twenty-first century, but it should be possible to understand the integrity of the earlier aesthetic. At issue is the ability to understand tonal music as a narrative of progress toward an ideal.

Idealist musical aesthetics reconsidered

It will be helpful to return to Pauer's little treatise on musical beauty briefly. Pauer illustrated his conception of the three types of beauty by considering the art of painting. A simple portrait might have, for example, the beauty of form in its representation of a person without having any of the other types of beauty. A painting of subjects in action might exhibit characteristic beauty by showing the people as vigorous, exhibiting their personalities through characteristic actions. But if a painter would show his subjects 'as genii or angelic spirits, as denizens of a higher world', then they would be 'idealized'.[6] Moreover, if there is allegory or symbolism present, then the representation of ideas dominates the painting; in such a manner, the music of Bach, Handel, Haydn, Mozart and Beethoven possessed ideal beauty according to Pauer. It was precisely this kind of beauty, however, which constituted the unique vocation of music, in contrast to the more mimetic arts: for 'it firmly seizes the life of the human soul with its sorrows and joys; and, subjecting these feelings to the idea of the beautiful, represents by sounds the expressions of individual truth, and, as it were, the presentiment of an infinite life'.[7] Thus, the task of music was always to rise above the mere expression of emotion in order to present ideas through allegory or musical symbolism, and to suggest the possibility of a spiritual life unbounded by the limitations of physical existence. Two aspects of the ideal stand out, therefore: spiritual transcendence, and the centrality of allegory and symbolism. But the emphasis on allegory suggests the importance of musical narrative to the idealist aesthetic.

If we turn to Pauer's original source of inspiration, the elements of the ideal become more clear as they were articulated earlier in the nineteenth century. Ferdinand Hand's *Aesthetik der Tonkunst* (1837) was the first independently subsisting philosophy of music in the nineteenth century; it established the art as a proper object of enquiry in its own right. Although usually dismissed today as too verbose and a work of synthesis rather than of real originality,[8] Hand's work was an influential document in the history of aesthetics. Indeed, Hanslick's treatise, *On the Musically Beautiful*, would have been inconceivable without the earlier work, and Hanslick pays Hand the compliment of citing several passages which he found particularly objectionable.[9] Here, it is precisely the synthetic quality which makes Hand important for understanding the idealist aesthetic: by fusing Kant, Schiller, Hegel and Schelling into one system applied to music, Hand made possible a broadly based aesthetic which would recognize the role played by form, expression and ideas in music. He was able to avoid, therefore, the one-sidedness that characterized both Kantian formalism and Romantic expressivism, both of which have continued to characterize musical aesthetics in the modernist period. The key to being able to embrace these two opposing positions, however, was the concept of the ideal, which transcended the elements of form and expression, and at the same time ordered them as their ultimate *telos*. As an aesthetic of teleological order, it was perfectly suited to describing the aims of tonal music of the nineteenth century.

Like Pauer, Hand described ideal beauty as the appearance of the Infinite or the Idea. He was more explicit than Pauer, however, in identifying the ideal with the general or the universal: when the particular in characteristic beauty is portrayed as a general truth, 'the ideal raises us into the sphere of the general and seeks to grasp the high meaning of ideas immediately in images, which devolve on a symbolic representation. This symbolic significance is precisely the property of ideal beauty.'[10] Thus, the emotional content of characteristic beauty achieves its significance only by pointing symbolically to the realm of the universal. Indeed, for Hand, the more inexpressible is the meaning of music, the closer it is to the ideal.[11] In this way, instrumental music in particular often suggested the realm of the Infinite. This is often misunderstood, however, for it makes it appear as if vagueness is the essence of the ideal – precisely the problem with which we began in our original confrontation with nineteenth-century idealism.

Hand's own analysis of instrumental works, however, points in another direction. He takes Beethoven's Fifth Symphony as the quintessential example of ideal beauty, beginning a process that has ever since recognized the paradigmatic nature of this particular work. He describes the first movement as earnest and imposing, 'which a held-back, almost hellish fire animates'. Here there is no reference to a programme or to a biographical interpretation; the character of the music itself suffices to suggest images by which to understand it. The second movement links the opposing qualities of the gentle and the austere into one apprehension of characteristic beauty; expressiveness, therefore, is cultivated precisely through such contrasts. Conflating the Scherzo with the Finale, Hand describes the effect as being 'where an ideal region welcomes us. It is a gloomy realm of the spirit-world, where ... unrest appears not to end until the resting point, where with rich fulness and majesty ... a spiritual life overflows, as if it would give up hope of embracing a human heart.'[12] This means that the Finale establishes the spiritual transcendence of the work. The symphony, therefore, can be understood only in terms of its narrative structure. The expressivity of the music raises the general states of feeling to the status of universals of the human condition; this is one element of the ideal.

But the second, more important, element is the narrative itself, as the contrasts of the first three movements give way to the triumphant Finale. Once Hand has discussed the language of musical expression and the categories of the ideal, he is able to speak more concretely of the 'transfiguration', the 'victory of the spirit', and the 'rising to the Infinite' in the Finale.[13] This is what raises the listener to the realm of the ideal in the fullest sense, so that the work becomes a revelation of the ideal both as a spiritual allegory and as the resolution of the emotional conflicts embodied in the previous movements. Indeed, this is the way in which most listeners would probably describe the experience of the Fifth Symphony, but without the extra philosophical baggage of 'the ideal'. Nevertheless, the concept of the ideal is crucial for distinguishing the narrative aspect of the symphony as a whole from the merely expressive dimensions of specific themes and particular movements. The kind of analysis Hand provides for Beethoven's most famous work can easily be extended to many other symphonic works from the nineteenth century which conform to the same essential paradigm of being narratives of triumph: for example, Brahms's First Symphony, Tchaikovsky's Fourth, Mahler's First, and explicitly the triumph of life over death in Mahler's Second. But the concept of the ideal is crucial for understanding the nature of such narratives: the finales are triumphs specifically of the ideal.

Hand concretizes the concept of ideal beauty by distinguishing among several different kinds: the great, the noble, the splendid, the marvellous, and the sublime, as well as the idealized emotional states of joy, melancholy and seriousness.[14] Thus expressivity, once raised to an intellectual level by the distinctness of musical character possible in classical tonality, provided the content of the ideal. Indeed, he provides an exhaustive elaboration of these and other categories of ideal beauty. But the most important category for Hand was 'the sentimental'. This was the essence of the Romantic style; it was the suggestion of the ideal through feeling that was the decisive element. As he explained it: 'Earthly bliss in relief and woe constitutes the character and the goal of sentimental feeling; this, however, can only be yearned for, not achieved.'[15] As the fundamental character of Romantic music, we recognize immediately the type of sentimental ideal in the music of Chopin, for example; Hand himself cites the music of Spohr. What is important here is the location of the ideal in specifically earthly bliss: not a transcendent ideal, it is nonetheless not something that can be grasped or achieved definitively in this life. If such bliss once existed, it cannot be recaptured; it can only be remembered and lamented. It therefore remains elusive, yet fully imaginable, as in so many art songs from Beethoven's *An die ferne Geliebte*, Schubert's *Die schöne Müllerin*, and Schumann's *Dichterliebe*, to Mahler's *Lieder eines fahrenden Gesellen*. The sentimental, indeed, is the essence of the art song in the nineteenth century.

The concept of the sentimental, however, once again underscores the centrality of narrative. For in a state of woe we anticipate and yearn for a resolution in earthly bliss, rather than in an unperceivable heavenly reward. It is therefore an intrinsically teleological feeling, in which the goal is thoroughly immanent. The ambiguous character of the *telos* corresponds precisely to the character of time in the Leibnizian formulation: time has an immanent, yet never-completed goal, just like the earthly bliss that cannot be achieved. Hence, the capacity to express this is the peculiar property of tonality, whose *telos* is also immanent in any given work. In instrumental music, however, the narrative does reach its completion in the arrival at the tonic key, often in a representation of the character of triumph. Thus, there is truth in the Romantic conviction that instrumental music was the most expressive of the ideal: not because the ideal was vague or ill-defined, but because of the very nature of tonality and the conventions governing large-scale musical forms. Symphonic music in particular moved beyond the sentimental to an affirmation of the ideal itself.

The concept of the ideal, therefore, turns out not to be so difficult to grasp as nineteenth-century philosophical language often makes it appear. Earthly bliss is easy to imagine, but difficult to realize. But music portrays just such a realization, so that the general becomes concrete. This is, indeed, the importance of the art, of all art, on the idealist view: it makes the ideal perceptible, so that it does not remain merely abstract, an imaginary figment of the intellect. Once again, then, we return to the question that Adorno raised for us at the outset: is such belief in the ideal possible in our ravaged world?

Before accepting Adorno's negative answer, it would be well to reflect upon the consequences of its rejection. It is one thing to say, with Adorno, that the ideal no longer exists in the modern world; it is quite another to have to give up conceiving an ideal and yearning for it. In such a condition, would there be any reason to seek recovery from what Adorno calls the shipwreck of the twentieth century? Without a vision of something better, surely there would be no reason to seek to transform the world, no hope that there might yet be something better. Indeed, without an ideal, what reason is there to go on living? Not all ages will be as openly sentimental as the nineteenth century, but to eliminate the category of yearning for bliss altogether will be to condemn any society to emotional petrification in despair.

The concept of the ideal, therefore, deserves to be taken seriously in its historical realizations, whether or not it seems possible to regain a belief in the relevance of it today. It is currently fashionable to regard music as a journey through musical space.[16] If we recognize the historical importance of idealism, however, it will be possible to understand tonal music as the narrative ordered by the ideal, rather than just a journey through musical space. Hence, a consideration of the most important articulation of nineteenth-century idealism, the aesthetic of G. W. F. Hegel, is crucial for establishing the nature of the ideal and the narrative order of tonal music.

Narrativity and the Ideal

We have already encountered Hegel's general conception of the ideal as the state of tranquillity, understood in terms not just of the emotional life, but more deeply in terms of character. His own argument for this rests on the infinitude of the human spirit 'when it actually comprehends its universality and raises to universality the ends it sets before itself ...'.[17] As we have seen, however, it is possible to give a more persuasive argument from contradiction; the weight of the philosophical tradition argues in favour of there being just such an ideal of character. What is of more significance, then, is Hegel's argument for this ideal of character as 'the Ideal' of artistic representation. This is more controversial, since it might be supposed – and commonly is in the twentieth century – that art can represent anything. But, for Hegel, the very nature of art as the sensuous representation of the intellectual realm means that art presents the essence, or Concept of life: that is, the ideal of character. This is a purification of what will be seen in ordinary life, for 'art brings into this harmony with its true Concept what is contaminated in other existents by chance and externality', and this is the Ideal as an artistic concept.[18]

Hegel distinguishes among several manifestations of the ideal of character and their corresponding artistic Ideals. In particular, the classical Ideal is one of 'serene peace and bliss', while the romantic, that is, Christian, Ideal is 'a joy in submission, a bliss in grief and rapture in suffering, even a delight in agony'.[19] It is the romantic Ideal which is of the greater interest here, because it accounts for the ideal of character for the entire Christian era, of which the nineteenth century was only the most recent part. This conception of the Ideal is a dialectic one: it recognizes the existence of conflict between spirit and the flesh, between intellect and the ways of the world. Yet it also insists on the resolution of such conflict in submission to God's will and in the blissful acceptance of grief. These attitudes have their model in Christ Himself; they work to inspire the particularly romantic forms of heroism found in medieval tales of chivalry, for example.[20] But they also may be seen as standing behind the 'romantic' forms of tragedy found in Shakespeare (such as Hamlet's acceptance of death while attempting to avenge his own father's death) and in Goethe (such as Egmont's courageously sacrificial death for the triumph of Dutch liberty). Thus, the romantic Ideal differs fundamentally from the classical, which Hegel regards as marked by absolute serenity, but which works itself out often enough in tragedies as an acceptance of the demands placed on the individual by sometimes contradictory duties.[21] In the romantic model, in contrast, the resolution entails overcoming the external opposition of injustice. In both, then, there is an acceptance of death, but the tragic conflicts arise from different sources.

Hegel's analysis of classical tragedy may be challenged in many of its details. His paradigm is his understanding of *Antigone* as the story of the conflict between the duties owed to the state and the duties owed to the gods of the dead and to the family.[22] Yet the conflict is perhaps not so finely balanced as Hegel attempts to show: Creon becomes a tyrant in his zeal to defend the city's integrity, so that Sophocles' play is at least as much a study in the illegitimacy of arbitrary edicts as of the legitimate demands of the state. Antigone accepts her death sentence in terms of her obedience to the higher duty owed to the gods, for neither Zeus nor Justice could ordain what Creon has ordered.[23] Nevertheless, Hegel's point regarding the serenity of classical tragedy is borne out by Antigone's dignified courage in defying Creon's interdict of her brother's burial as well as her acceptance of the death sentence with a sense of hope and honour. So, too, had Oedipus accepted responsibility for the horror of his crimes. Thus, while Antigone herself may be better understood as manifesting the Greek sense of heroic idealism, the character of classical tragedy indeed emphasizes the tragic figure's acceptance of responsibility, rather than the overcoming of external injustice.

At the same time, the Hegelian understanding of romantic tragedy must be similarly deepened. Hegel regards the twin aspects of submission and suffering as most characteristic of tragedy in the Christian era, but there is an even more important element to Christianity's understanding of the role of suffering in the narrative of life: that is the necessity of contrition in coming to repentance and seeking divine forgiveness. This is the aspect most visible in nineteenth-century opera, where the narrative is genuinely tragic, in contrast to the stories of redemption from suffering characteristic of eighteenth-century *opera seria*. For nineteenth-century serious opera, the action moves from sin to repentance and divine forgiveness, in spite of the ultimately tragic nature of the suffering it entails. Wagner's *Tannhäuser* and Gounod's *Faust* are two of the most famous examples, but they are typical for their time. Even a study in the ambiguity of sin and love such as Verdi's *La Traviata* depends on the movement toward repentance and reconciliation on the part of all the major characters – Violetta, Alfredo and Germont. Thus, there is both an ideal of action and an ideal of character in the romantic sense of the tragic, as Hegel recognizes. These concepts within 'the Ideal' are of the most crucial importance in making sense of the submission in repentance which was characteristic of Romantic opera.

The discussion of dramatic examples of the Ideal makes the conceptual relation of narrative and the Ideal clear. For Hegel, the Ideal always implies a narrative, and especially so for the romantic form. The existence of external conflicts requires both an internal and an external resolution. He is explicit on this point in the case of music. Music is the expression of feelings and of states of character, to be sure, in both sacred and secular genres.[24] But he counsels a restraint on the expression of emotion on essentially classical grounds: emotions should not be unbridled, but should recognize 'an abiding peace and freedom'. In the most beautiful music, therefore, there is a 'reconciliation with self', so that if there is grief expressed, 'it is assuaged at once'.[25] But this is to assert the necessity of musical narrative of the emotions, with the Ideal of tranquillity as the specific *telos* of tonal and emotional progress. Hence, it is no surprise to find Hegel most convincing in his account of sacred music, opera and art song, for all of these have a more or less explicit potential for narrative. The challenge will be to extend the concept of narrative to instrumental music in a systematic way. What matters here, however, is the association of the Hegelian Ideal with musical narrative: the Ideal establishes a teleological order in the emotional content of music which corresponds to the teleological ordering of time in the system of tonality itself.

Hegel allows us to see, therefore, that at the level of style there is a close correlation between tonality as a musical system and its expressive capacity. Tonality developed into an effective expressive system precisely because of its teleological nature: there was an expectation of the resolution of pain and suffering, which was reflected in the resolution to consonance at the local level, and in the resolution to the tonic key, usually in the major mode, at the largest level of a movement or a whole work. Thus, tonality was not teleological just in the narrowly musical sense, but rather more deeply in its narrative use of expressive metaphors. It is this capacity for narrative which is both the striking characteristic of tonality and the most difficult to understand today. For it might be objected that often it is apparent that operatic arias, for example, and even programme music exhibit some sort of tension between their narrative content and purely musical demands; even conceding a narrative element to large-scale instrumental genres would not remove the purely formal demands these require. The complexity of opera, the lyric nature of art song and the symmetry of individual instrumental musical forms all threaten to undermine the connection between musical elements and the capacity for narrative. Thus narrativity seems suspect if taken too literally.

The principal difficulty the concept of musical narrative poses in the modern age, however, is of a different order. For nothing seems more antithetical to modernity than the positing of coherence in a story. Heidegger, once again, is explicit: 'The first philosophical step in understanding the problem of being consists in ... not "telling" a story, that is, not determining beings as beings by tracing them back in their origins to another being ... .'[26] This is to say that the meaning of a person's existence cannot be found by relating a story of the family and its origins, for example, in the manner of nineteenth-century novels, or of tracing the influence of others' ideas and values on the formation of one's own character. The authentic person will create himself and all his own ideas and values, becoming, as it were, his own god. Indeed, Heidegger employs language normally reserved for the divine to describe human existence (Dasein): its essence lies in existence.[27] On such a view, the temporality of human nature consists not in a narrative of past origins and determinative events, but rather in the projection onto the future of the resoluteness of the will.[28] But the model, then, is not narrative at all, but the plan or the projection. Moreover, in spite of Heidegger's forceful critique of instrumental reason, such planning requires precisely the exercise of instrumentality.

If the rejection of narrative is characteristic of modernism, however, the hostility of Adorno and others to the concept of the work becomes understandable. It is not only, then, a question of whether there is something affirmative enough, or substantially long enough, to constitute a standard symphonic genre, for example. More deeply, it is a question of whether there can be any narrative structure to sustain a sequence of different musical ideas. The disappearance of contrasting sonorities in Schoenberg's Expressionist pieces, and the concomitant shortening of the musical expression to the point of vanishing brevity in the orchestral pieces of Webern are only the technical aspects of a larger reorientation of artistic purposes. What Heidegger suggests is the possibility that the crisis of the work is precisely the crisis of narrative in general.

Yet the rejection of narrative is not without a price. Life cannot, in fact, be totally constructed by the autonomous individual. Indeed, it becomes meaningless just to the extent that the individual attempts to emancipate himself from the context of family, friends and the larger community in order to pursue aims unrelated to the needs of others. Heidegger's existentialism is not a solution, but instead the creation of a problem which has suffused the culture of the modern West. His greatest influence has come since the 1960s, and the legacy has been to make the search for autonomous authenticity into the norm of character and personality. It is not too much to suggest, however, that the result has been the normalization of a kind of anti-social pathology. To what extent the avant-garde shares in this remains to be seen; here we take Heidegger as symptomatic of general trends in modernity, rather than as bearing a direct relation to any particular musical development or aesthetic theory. Nevertheless, philosophy often reveals explicitly what is only implicit in the contemporary arts, and to that extent his work may offer important clues about the nature of modernism generally.

If it is true, therefore, that life cannot be self-constructed according to our own designs, it is clear why life makes sense only to the extent that it can be understood as a narrative. As Alasdair MacIntyre argues, life is always at least to some extent teleological, or must appear so in retrospect. Moreover, we can understand life only by relating our experience to stories already familiar to us: fairy tales, biblical stories, mythology, history.[29] One might well add to this list classic works of literature – and music. Such familiar stories have a *telos*, and it is one that affirms a moral framework in which others count as providing the constitutive context of human life. This helps to clarify the nature of the *telos* of real life: it is a sense of the whole that can be understood only in retrospect. The ancient Greek proverb, 'count no man happy till he dies, free of pain at last',[30] reflects the sense of the wholeness of a life which must be considered before ascribing happiness, or well-being, as its goal. Thus, to comprehend life as a narrative toward wholeness is what it means to find the meaning of life. The twentieth-century rejection of this provides an important insight into both the nature of aesthetic modernism and the social prevalence of personal maladjustment.

As Adorno understood, it is precisely the lack of integrity, of internal harmony in the social condition of modern humanity, which finds its reflection in the lack of an internal harmony sufficient to maintain the concept of a musical work. The experience of tyranny (one might add, of both Right and Left) and the experience of social fragmentation in the post-war free world have so disrupted the perception of the social subsistence of wholeness and harmony that little remains to serve as a model for the arts. But Adorno's Marxist critique misses the larger point: there will be no sense of the integrity of the social community without an understanding of what creates a meaningful individual life. That means that if the teleology of individual existence requires an account of how one is constituted by one's family, friendships and local ties, rather than by one's self-projected achievements, then this understanding must precede any attempt to reconstitute the social order. For there must be a clear notion of what order it is that matters; if it should turn out to be local rather than national, personal rather than economic, largely given rather than voluntary, then the Marxist critique of modern society would have little to offer. But the kind of society which would seem to hold the greatest promise of a restoration of integrity, therefore, would turn out to look much like the kind of society nurtured before the advent of either modern capitalism or socialism.[31] This is the social world out of which classical tonality emerged, and which the musical narratives describe. Whether such a social order could be reinvented remains extremely doubtful.

In this situation, the arts assume, contrary to Adorno's argument, an even greater importance than they might otherwise have. Mikhail Bakhtin has argued that, in the realm of literature, time must be represented in concrete terms, that it must find its embodiment, as it were, in a kind of space, what he calls a 'chronotope'. Thus, the different kinds of narratives in the genre of the novel, for example, require different kinds of spatial representations of time.[32] The argument can be extended, however: if the temporal order which grants life meaning has any hope of being perceived, then it must be through a concrete embodiment. If this will not be in the social reality of contemporary life, then it can be established only through the artistic representation of time.

Hence the continued importance of both music and the novel as forms of art in the modern world; hence, too, the necessity of preservation of the acknowledged masterpieces when the modern world itself cannot provide viable models of teleological order for life. What tonal music does, specifically, is to provide a model of teleological order that is both temporal and of metaphysical significance, and, through its capacity for emotional expressivity, metaphorical of the narrative of a life that reaches its completion in the integrity of a whole. This is what the aesthetic of idealism attempted to express in making life the content of the art of music and the ideal of character the Ideal of art. Precisely the wholeness of such a life constitutes the wholeness of the work of music.

Musical narratives of the temporality of the Ideal

To speak in these general terms remains within the boundaries of musical aesthetics as a philosophical discipline. Yet there are clear limits to such an approach: it is only possible to account for the practice of tonality at the level of style. To say that the narrativity of the ideal requires a temporally immanent *telos*, and that this explains the uniquely teleological characteristics of tonal practice, summarizes what has been of necessity a lengthy reconstruction of a view now largely forgotten and often discredited. But the aesthetic of the work, which is the natural result of an emphasis on the teleology of the whole, suggests that a closer examination of specific kinds of works might serve to make the argument more concrete and persuasive. In particular, if narrativity lies at the heart of tonal music, then it will be necessary to speak more concretely about the kinds of narrative the different genres of music can represent. For otherwise, if the concept of narrative remained at the level merely of the return of the tonic after a modulatory digression, then the entire metaphorical potential of tonality will have been trivialized. What must be recalled is always the inherent expressivity of tonality, so that the expressive potential is never divorced from the narrative framework. But this can be understood only with respect to individual works; philosophy necessarily yields to the practice of critical perception if it has any value. Indeed, the idealist aesthetic in the nineteenth century served to ground a critical practice that was of vital importance to the reception of new works. Here, however, what is of importance is not the reception of new works, but the necessity of understanding the received ones properly, and of understanding the reasons for their survival in the culture of preservation in the twentieth century. Several examples follow, therefore, in which the concept of temporal narrative will emerge with respect to individual works in three different genres: opera, art song and the symphony.

If tonality makes possible the representation of the narrative unity of life in music, it is easy to see the relevance of tonality to opera – indeed why, historically, it was opera that helped to provide the context for the emergence of tonal practice. Moreover, it is easy to understand the connection between the temporality of the ideal and the Baroque and Classical practice of providing happy endings to subjects which were tragic in classical mythology, such as the story of Orpheus and Eurydice. For *opera seria* could not afford to end tragically if the progress toward an ideal were the goal of operatic representation. Again, the optimism of the eighteenth century must be understood not as a trivial matter of naïve hope, but rather as a profoundly metaphysical expectation that time itself will bring the *telos* of human existence into being, in spite of pain and suffering. Hence, even in Mozart's masterpieces, there are such genuinely optimistic endings: certainly in the *opera seria*, *La Clemenza di Tito*, which celebrates the mercy of the Roman Emperor, but also in the much more well-known *Die Zauberflöte*. Only *Don Giovanni* approaches the tragic, in the sense of Don Giovanni's death, but even here we understand his condemnation to hell as an act of divine justice, and therefore an accomplishment of the ideal in a metaphysical retribution. In this context, then, the Classical practice of giving operas a clear tonic key, announced in the overture, is understandable as a reflection of the narrative unity of life they represent: C major in the case of *La Clemenza di Tito*, E-flat major in the case of *Die Zauberflöte*. The tonal integration of the overture and finale, therefore, is the musical representation of the ideal, not simply a return to the tonic at the end as a purely formal device.

It is the nineteenth-century repertoire, oddly enough, which poses the greater problem for understanding the relevance of the idealist aesthetic to opera. For serious opera turned to the genuinely tragic for subject matter, and the unity of key so crucial to the Classical repertoire broke down after mid-century. The tragic nature of opera, then, suggests itself as the origin of the breakdown of tonal practice; the heightened emotionality of the genre which Fétis noted in Rossini becomes even more pronounced among later composers as a consequence of the emphasis on a deeper pathos as time fails to produce the ideal as a state of earthly bliss. But this is to admit that, at least in eighteenth-century terms, progress has ceased to be the doctrine defining the temporal order: the ideal is no longer the immanent *telos* of operatic action. In general, Romantic nineteenth-century opera has neither the heroism of a Hamlet or an Egmont, nor the narrative of recognition of an unrealized crime or character flaw after the manner of an Oedipus. Thus, it becomes necessary to search more deeply for an understanding of the nature of the relation between tragedy and the temporality of the ideal.

What nineteenth-century opera provides, however, is a deeper conception of the ideal. No longer considered simply as a state of bliss, it becomes the state of redemption from sin. In that sense, the ideal remains the goal of operatic action; temporality has its *telos*, but it is no longer completed fully in this life. In Wagner's *Tannhäuser*, for example, the conflict within Tannhäuser's heart between the sinful love of Venus and the virtuous love for Elisabeth is resolved in favour of the latter, although only through the death of Elisabeth and at the cost of Tannhäuser's own perishing. The Wagnerian theme of redemption through love must be understood, therefore, rather as redemption through death: for without Elisabeth's dying, Tannhäuser would never have been stricken enough in conscience to forsake the temptation of the Venusberg. Only by praying to Elisabeth in heaven is the sinner's soul cured; the blooming of the staff confirms the divine grace the Chorus of Pilgrims proclaims. Thus the opera presents an ideal: it is the redemption from sin, but now this redemption is understood as transcendent in origin and realization. But the tonal unity characteristic of Classical opera disappears: what matters is the expressivity of the keys, as in the use of the bright key of E major for the love of Venus and the use of the comparatively darker E-flat major for the holy love of Elisabeth; the overture and the Venusberg music open in E major, while the final scene of Act III closes in E-flat major.[33] The polarity of keys is heard as a contrast between the wildly passionate and the noble or holy. Tonality in this expressive sense thus remains vital to the inner structure of the opera. It is only the tonal unity of the opera that declines with the advent of the turn to the tragic.

A similar process and dramatic theme can be found in Verdi's *La Traviata*. Again, individual numbers manifest clear rootedness in keys, but the opera as a whole lacks one key that could be called a tonic for the entire work. The nature of the tragedy, however, is remarkably similar, though the gender roles are reversed: only Alfredo's love accomplishes the redemption from the sin that has stained Violetta's life. Although Violetta dies, her previous sacrifice of her own love for Alfredo has been her ennobling action. The reconciliation between her, Alfredo and Germont in Act III establishes a bond of mutual forgiveness which is the earthly ideal corresponding to the Wagnerian redemption from sin.[34] Thus, by comparison, Verdi's opera centres on a more explicitly immanent ideal as the goal of the narrative. The fact that it is inseparable from the tragedy does not remove its character as the ideal, but only emphasizes its imperative nature. Thus, once again, the idealist aesthetic helps to make sense of an opera that otherwise might well appear, as it did to contemporary critics, to be something sordid in subject and merely sentimental in pathos.[35] Love, in this opera as in *Tannhäuser*, is essentially self-sacrifice. This is the ideal of character corresponding to the ideal of the redemption from sin.

French opera as well demonstrates a similar understanding of the ideal. Charles Gounod's *Faust*, as one of the best known of mid-nineteenth-century operas, serves as an example. The apotheosis of Marguérite at the end is the transcendent *telos* of the opera; prepared in a rising sequence of keys, from G major to A major, to B major, as she glimpses the sight of the 'radiant angels' in heaven, the passage resolves in C major, the key of purity and grace and rejoicing. Thus, while C major has been used in this way only once before in the opera – at the close of the Cathedral scene, when the Chorus reaches the conclusion of the *Dies irae* in singing of divine grace rather than of retribution – it becomes nevertheless the clear key of resolution for the entire action of the opera.[36] Marguérite's forgiveness is proclaimed by the angelic choir, and even Faust's forgiveness is hinted at in the stage directions, which call for Mephistopheles to be barred by the shining sword of the Archangel Michael. Thus, the metaphysical conflict between good and evil in this life is resolved not only transcendentally, but also immanently: Faust's redemption from his compact with the devil becomes a subsidiary part of the resolution of the opera. Divine forgiveness, therefore, is here the ideal, as in *Tannhäuser*, and it is crucial that it be accomplished through the sacrificial death of the character most innocent and pure. That is, Marguérite's acceptance of death as just punishment for her transgressions is vital for her own redemption from sin; it also brings Faust to a state of humility for the first time. In learning to pray to God, he breaks the power of Mephistopheles. Sacrifice and humility, therefore, remain the ideal of character here as well as in Wagner and Verdi.

It should be clear, then, that the mere change from the optimism of a happy ending to the genuinely tragic endings of nineteenth-century opera does not alter the possibility of opera being considered a narrative of the ideal of forgiveness, or as exhibiting the ideal of character understood as self-sacrifice. The narrative of tragic opera affirms these aspects of the idealist aesthetic just as surely as the convention of the happy ending affirmed the virtues of Mozart's Tito or Tamino in the eighteenth century. The *telos* of redemption in nineteenth-century opera, however, acquires a transcendent dimension that was often missing in eighteenth-century opera, so that temporality is marked by both an immanent and a transcendent teleological character. In this way, tragedy affirms the existence of an ideal of both character and action as the goal of its narrative.

If the temporality of the ideal is present, after all, in the larger genre of opera, the art song appears to present difficulties in precisely the opposite direction. For as a fundamentally lyric genre, the setting to music of lyric poetry may not present an explicit narrative of action. Ballads and song cycles constitute important exceptions: Schubert's *Die schöne Müllerin*, Schumann's *Dichterliebe* and Mahler's *Lieder eines fahrenden Gesellen* tell stories which determine the deployment of musical means of expression. Nevertheless, the lyric poem does not in general aim to tell a story; as Hegel puts it, lyric poetry is the form of the poet's feelings and ideas, 'the spirit's own subjective disposition', such as possesses a universal validity.[37] But if subjectivity universalized is the essence of lyric poetry, it would seem especially difficult to construe this as a species of narrative, whether standing alone or set to music. Moreover, the emphasis of much nineteenth-century poetry is clearly on the sentimental, and even in the examples of song cycles cited above, the narrative is neither tragic in a classical sense nor redemptive as in nineteenth-century opera. Instead, the cycles proceed to the projected death of the poetic hero as the end of his sorrow over the loss of his love: love is here sentimentalized within the context of overwhelming sorrow.

Just as in the case of tragic opera, however, such a narrative reveals an implicit grounding in an ideal. For in life lies the impossible ideal of love, whilst in death lies surcease of sorrow. In the penultimate song from Schubert's cycle, 'Der Müller und der Bach', the Miller looks forward to death (in G minor) as the time when 'the angels / Close one's eyes, / And sob and sing / The soul to rest'. The Brook, into which he is prepared to cast himself, however, promises (in G major) that 'when love / Is released from pain, / A little star, a new one, / Twinkles in heaven'.[38] Similarly for Schumann's treatment of Heinrich Heine's poems, the poetic hero wishes to cast his love and pain into a gigantic coffin: and the musical setting turns from an initial key of C-sharp minor to D-flat major in the piano postlude, reflecting the release from pain not expressed in Heine's poem. Finally, Mahler's poetic hero leaves the scene of his beloved's now married life, saying goodbye in the key of E minor; the key shifts to an ambiguous alternation of C major and minor for his journey. As he finds a linden tree under which to sleep – in at least a metaphor of death – he finds peace for the first time in the pastoral key of F major – although the orchestra concludes the music with an abrupt turn to the tonic minor.[39] Thus within the sentimentalized world of the art song, death is the ideal of peace as the surcease of sorrow, and love is the ideal of bliss only dreamt of, but not realized by the poetic hero.

It is no accident that the art song most often focuses on the loss of love as the essential and universal feeling. Within an individual song, not part of a cycle, this loss depends for its intelligibility on a sentimentalized ideal. Gustav Mahler's setting of 'Nicht Wiedersehen!' from *Des Knaben Wunderhorn* illustrates the purity of sorrow as an expressive device. In the first part of the song, the speaker says goodbye to his beloved, expecting to see her again the next summer; but when he returns, he finds her buried in her grave three days before, her 'mourning and weeping' having brought her to her death. The second part of the poem, then, consists in the confrontation with death: he goes to her grave to say goodbye, once again, calling to her 'Until she answers me!' – and commanding her to open her grave. The poem ends with the greatest pathos: 'You hear no little bell ringing, / You hear no little bird calling, / You see neither sun nor moon!'[40] But such sentimental pathos is clearly not an invention of the Romantic era, for this text comes from German folklore, as collected by Achim von Arnim and Clemens Brentano at the beginning of the nineteenth century (1806–08). This is proof of its authenticity as a universally possible human feeling.

Mahler's music underscores the sentimental nature of the poem. The tonic key is B minor; the cadences in the minor keys emphasize the Neapolitan sixth, adding to the sense of darkness that pervades the poem. When the young man returns to enquire after his sweetheart, there is a brief turn to the subdominant chord of D minor (G minor), as the flattened sixth chord which leads back to the dominant, F-sharp major. The news of his sweetheart's death is given in B minor, and again, there is a turn to the subdominant function in D minor upon the resolution of the young man to seek her grave. But when he implores her to open her grave, and reflects that she will hear no more bells or birds, nor see sun or moon, the key shifts to B major, as shown in Example 4.1. This is a surprising modulation, with an essentially ambiguous significance: at the moment of highest anguish, the mode is now major. It may be seen as a reflection of the innocence of death: removed from the sorrows of the world which brought her to her death, the young woman has found peace at last. It is the young man who, when he must say goodbye once again in the final four measures, returns to B minor: the sorrow of loss is on this side of the grave. Thus, musically, the setting establishes a contrast between the ideal of peace and the pathos of loss. But the ideal of peace, heard in such ironic contrast to death, is also understood as a sentimental reflection of what has been lost: bells, birds, sun and moon – all that marks off time in the beauty of this world, she will experience no more.

In this way, the song escapes the risk of submersion in unmitigated sorrow, to which the poem itself points, and ascends to a suggestion of an ideal of bliss. The ideal, however, is simultaneously a hope and a remembrance, and as a condition of earthly existence, it will never more be attained. Hence, the passage in B major concludes with a diminished seventh chord (measure 162) before returning to B minor. The art song, therefore, although it lacks a strong narrative element, requires the presence of at least the hope of a release from suffering and the remembrance of a love worth mourning. Such a narrative of hope and memory is an implicit condition of poetic and musical significance.

The ideal of love, therefore, is confirmed in its loss; the remembrance of love becomes the only experience of the ideal. Sentimentality would appear to be the necessary condition for feeling the worth of another human being. But such a narrative enclosed within a lyric poem that is essentially a cry of the heart means that narrative is still intimately linked with the lyric. It is just that its narrative remains implicit as an unstated condition of poetic and musical significance. Ferdinand Hand was correct in recognizing that the category of the sentimental in fact revealed the ideal as its essential vision – if not in love, at least in relief from sorrow as the earthly bliss in the midst of woe.

Example 4.1   Gustav Mahler, 'Nicht Wiedersehen!', mm. 41–64

Example 4.1   continued

Example 4.1   concluded

If opera and the art song turn out to have such clear connections between narrativity and the ideal, in spite of the difficulties they initially presented, instrumental music is notoriously more difficult to accommodate in the model of narrativity required by the idealist aesthetic. At the same time, paradoxically, it becomes tempting to superimpose a narrative structure on at least some of the standard works as a means of comprehending their aesthetic value, a move which was popular in the nineteenth century but which philosophers of music now largely reject.[41] The question of what or who has triumphed in the case of music without a poetic voice does not prevent the average listener from acceding to this long-standing interpretive device. The kind of characterization of the movements offered in programme notes and orchestral commentaries relies heavily on the suggestion of a sequence of expressive moods in the various movements of a work to convey the 'story' unfolding in the symphony as a whole. Even in the symphonies of Brahms, which Hanslick celebrated as admirably suited to his formalist aesthetic, we find exactly the kind of Romantic expression adapted to the framework of the Classical symphony: thus, a recent guide to the First Symphony can remark upon the 'upwardly striving' melody of the introduction to the first movement, and the sometimes 'darker, more despairing character' of quieter moments in the allegro. In like manner, the second movement becomes 'serene', and the Allegro non troppo of the Finale concludes with 'the triumphant statement of the chorale' from that movement's introduction.[42] Here, again, is the evidence of the necessity of the concept of narrative to give the purely instrumental work some intelligibility.

Yet the issues raised by Hanslick are real: in particular, the requirements of musical form do not appear to support a narrative interpretation within individual movements. Rather, the symmetry of sonata-allegro form, scherzo and trio, and so forth, appears to impose a static quality on the abstract musical narrative of digression from the tonic and the ultimate return to the original key. A closer consideration of Brahms's First Symphony, however, will reveal the extent to which – even in the case of a composer approved for his strictness of form – the expressive potential of tonality is capable of yielding a narrative of expression in the context of symmetrical musical forms.

In the first movement's introduction, the opening theme is not simply an upwardly striving chromatic line; it is also harmonized by a descending chromatic line in the first two measures and a pedal on the tonic (C), shown in Example 4.2(a). The result is a series of dissonances, which achieve their resolution only at the dominant chord at the beginning of the ninth measure. Now, this combination of dissonance and chromaticism is itself an expressive device, known since the Renaissance: dissonance connotes emotional pain, and chromaticism the intensity of a feeling of instability. Read in this way, the introduction to the first movement establishes an emotional atmosphere of intense pain in the key of C minor, recalling the key of Beethoven's Fifth, a work which has been understood since the nineteenth century as expressive of great unhappiness at fate.[43] The main theme of the allegro, then, is notable for its continuation of the rising chromatic figure in the bassoons, violas and violoncelli, as the counterpoint to the main arpeggiated theme in the violins: see Example 4.2(b). This is followed by a second phrase constituting a melodic dissonance of a falling diminished seventh, as in Example 4.2(c), before closing with the inversion of the chromatic figure. Thus, a more sustained analysis of the musical content in terms of the traditional elements of musical expression suggests the possibility of a genuine reading of the emotional content of this work.

Such emotional content, however, establishes the possibility of narrative. Within the first movement, the second theme extablishes a contrast in character to the extent that it is quieter and more lyrical, but its reliance on the

a)   First movement, mm. 1–3

b)   First movement, mm. 42–6

c)   First movement, mm. 51–7

Example 4.2   Johannes Brahms, Symphony No. 1 in C Minor, Op. 68, 1st and 4th
            movements

d)   First movement, mm. 130–34

e)   Fourth movement, mm. 407–13

Example 4.2   concluded

melodic interval of the falling diminished fifth (Example 4.2(d)) suggests that the element of dissonance has only been muted somewhat from the diminished seventh in the first theme. Similarly, the closing theme's use of the same interval to propel its upward ascent, in combination with the inversion of the opening theme of the allegro, makes the expressive character of the whole movement unified: it is surely intended to be heard as the musical representation of intense pain and suffering. Each main section – the exposition, development and recapitulation – builds to its highest dynamic level just before yielding to the cadence which resolves the tension. This sequence of tension and release, therefore, reaches an end only in the coda (Meno allegro), but the movement as a whole has a unified expressive content. The superimposition of this emotional content over the musical narrative of the re-establishment of the tonic key of C minor in the recapitulation creates a narrative of emotional instability resolving to an uncompromising statement of pain and suffering.

With this analysis, the triumphant character of the Finale's Allegro non troppo in C major becomes more apparent. In contrast with the intense anguish of the first movement, the passion of the second, and pathos of the introductory Adagio in C minor, the main theme of the Allegro is played first with the character of quiet joy, and then (at the animato) with the character of genuine triumph. The resemblance of the first theme of the Allegro to the *Ode to Joy* theme of Beethoven's Ninth Symphony is well known, but it should not be overlooked that just such references could be counted on to convey, by association, all the meaning with which the original was invested. Thus, the emotional narrative of Brahms's First Symphony emerges from an acquaintance with the expressive conventions of nineteenth-century symphonic literature. The ideal as bliss and triumph over grief is the immanent *telos* of this symphony, as of so many others. Perhaps for this reason, the chorale in the coda assumes, with its overtly religious character, the nature of a beatific vision of the ideal (see Example 4.2(e)). The narrative of the symphony is not simply one of triumph over grief or suffering, but one of the emergence of a vision of the ideal out of earthly woe. Instrumental music, even in its purest form, is indeed capable of representing the ideal and conveying a narrative of its realization.

Narrative, therefore, is the essence of the concept of the musical work. It is insufficient to assert that mere expressiveness suffices to establish the work concept; there must be some immanent or transcendent ideal toward which the music moves. Moreover, this ideal requires a teleological ordering of time: the narrative is a narrative of human life, not of abstract metaphysical states. Hence, tonality, which establishes an intrinsic metaphor of temporality in both its harmonic and rhythmic dimensions, is the essential stylistic means by which the narrative of a teleologically ordered temporality is realized. We see, therefore, that if there is hostility to the concept of the work, it must have its origin in a hostility to ideals in general. The issue is not whether there is historical progress visible in the world today, as Adorno attempted to argue, but rather whether a person's life makes sense.

The aesthetic of idealism was grounded in the belief that human existence is meaningful, and that it is ordered by a larger good. Such a good is defined by the ideal of character conceived as the nobility of heroism, sacrifice and virtue, and by the ideal of happiness conceived as tranquillity, and consisting in a life lived in the context of others as well as in the contemplation of some kind of transcendent vision of ideal goodness. To believe in such a complex good requires acknowledging both the capacity for genuine nobility and human sinfulness with its need for forgiveness. Far from being prevented by the existence of sin, then, the knowledge of the ideal depends upon its recognition, for otherwise it would be necessary to take the flawed world we see as the necessary embodiment of the good-in-itself. But this will not do.

It would appear, therefore, that the modernist rejection of the possibility of ideals is rooted more deeply than Adorno's perception of irredeemable evil. Since in fact the avant-garde arose well before Adorno found the twentieth century locked in depravity, it is time to examine its origins more closely.

Doing so will permit us to understand the mentality that despairs of the good and the ideal while at the same time appearing to reject their relevance to human life. Much of the character of the modernist mentality has already emerged in the course of our examination of the culture of preservation of classical music. Nevertheless, the discrepancy between Adorno's apology for the avant-garde and the historical emergence of the movement suggests that the culture of modernism must be understood in terms of its original motives and not simply in terms of its Marxist-inspired reception. Just as the culture of classicism has turned out to be considerably more sophisticated in its theoretical underpinnings than its critics have recognized, so too it may well be the case that the culture of modernism is more complicated than its apologists recognize. If that proves to be the case, it will once again become a legitimate question to ask if the contemporary bifurcation of musical culture is truly an inevitable product of the modern world, or if there might be a better way of conceiving the role of serious music in modern society.

Notes

1. Cf. Lydia Goehr, *The Imaginary Museum of Musical Works: An Essay in the Philosophy of Music* (Oxford: Clarendon Press, 1992), pp. 80, 260–73. Richard Leppert and Susan McClary are more explicit in their motivation to receive 'the musics of marginalized peoples on the same methodological footing as the music of the European canon': Leppert and McClary, eds, *Music and Society: The Politics of Composition, Performance and Reception* (Cambridge: Cambridge University Press, 1987), p. xviii.
2. Theodor W. Adorno, *Philosophie der neuen Musik* (Frankfurt am Main: Europäische Verlagsanstalt, 1958), p. 17; *Philosophy of Modern Music*, trans. Anne G. Mitchell and Wesley V. Blomster (New York: Seabury Press, 1973), pp. 9–10.
3. Adorno, *Philosophie der neuen Musik*, p. 36; *Philosophy of Modern Music*, p. 32.
4. Adorno, *Philosophie der neuen Musik*, p. 41; *Philosophy of Modern Music*, p. 37.
5. Goehr, *The Imaginary Museum of Musical Works*, p. 242.
6. Ernst Pauer, *The Elements of the Beautiful in Music*, 2nd edn (London: Novell, Ewer, and Co., 1877), p. 39.
7. Ibid., p. 45.
8. Carl Dahlhaus, *The Idea of Absolute Music*, trans. Roger Lustig (Chicago: University of Chicago Press, 1989), p. 15; most writers ignore Hand completely.
9. Eduard Hanslick, *On the Musically Beautiful*, trans. Geoffrey Payzant (Indianapolis: Hackett, 1986), p. 90.
10. Ferdinand Hand, *Aesthetik der Tonkunst*, 2nd edn, 2 vols (Leipzig: Eisenach, 1847), vol. 1, p. 272 (author's translation).
11. Ibid., vol. 1, p. 274.
12. Ibid., vol. 1, pp. 273–4.
13. Ibid., vol. 2, pp. 426–7.
14. Ibid., vol. 1, p. 279.
15. Ibid., vol. 1, pp. 314–15.
16. As Scruton does, *The Aesthetics of Music* (Oxford: Clarendon Press, 1997),

p. 270.

17. Hegel, *Vorlesungen über die Ästhetik*, in *Werke in zwanzig Bänden*, ed. E. Moldenhauer and K. M. Michel (Frankfurt am Main: Suhrkamp Verlag, 1970), vol. 13, p. 205; *Aesthetics: Lectures on Fine Art*, 2 vols, trans. T. M. Knox (Oxford: Clarendon Press, 1975), p. 155 (pagination continuous in the two volumes).

18. *Werke*, vol. 13, pp. 205–6; *Aesthetics*, p. 155.

19. *Werke*, vol. 13, pp. 208–9; *Aesthetics*, pp. 157–8.

20. *Werke*, vol. 14, p. 169ff.; *Aesthetics*, pp. 552ff.

21. Hegel's analysis of the Greek concept of the tragic is found in *Aesthetics*, p. 1198; the romantic tragedy, pp. 1223–4; see *Werke*, vol. 15, pp. 525–6, 556–7.

22. *Werke*, vol. 15, p. 549; *Aesthetics*, pp. 1217–18.

23. Sophocles, *Antigone*, lines 499–502. See Sophocles, *The Three Theban Plays: Antigone, Oedipus the King, Oedipus at Colonus*, trans. Robert Fagles, ed. Bernard Knox (New York: Viking Penguin, and London: Allen Lane, 1982), p. 82.

24. Hegel, *Werke*, vol. 15, pp. 205–8; *Aesthetics*, pp. 946–7.

25. *Werke*, vol. 15, pp. 197–8; *Aesthetics*, p. 939.

26. Martin Heidegger, *Being and Time: A Translation of 'Sein und Zeit'*, trans. Joan Stambaugh (Albany: State University of New York Press, 1996), p. 5.

27. Ibid., pp. 274, 293 (*inter alia*).

28. Ibid., p. 300.

29. Alasdair MacIntyre, *After Virtue*, 2nd edn (Notre Dame: University of Notre Dame Press, 1984), p. 216.

30. The last line (1684) of Sophocles' *Oedipus the King*, spoken by the Chorus: *The Three Theban Plays*, p. 251.

31. Cf. Michael Sandel, *Liberalism and the Limits of Justice* (Cambridge: Cambridge University Press, 1982), for a defence of the communitarian thesis. Also MacIntyre, *After Virtue*, p. 220.

32. Mikhail M. Bakhtin, *The Dialogic Imagination*, trans. and ed. Michael Holquist and Caryl Emerson (Austin: University of Texas Press, 1981), p. 250.

33. The score is published as Richard Wagner, *Tannhäuser in Full Score* (New York: Dover Publications, 1984).

34. The libretto is available in dual Italian–English text as Giuseppe Verdi, *La Traviata*, trans. Edmund Tracey (London: John Calder, and New York: Riverrun Press, 1981).

35. As did Paul Scudo in his review of *La Traviata*: 'Revue musicale', *Revue des deux mondes* (1856), 6, p. 929.

36. The vocal score is available as Charles Gounod, *Faust: A Lyric Drama in Five Acts with English and French Text* (Miami, FL: Belwin, Inc., [n.d.]).

37. Hegel, *Werke*, vol. 15, p. 415; *Aesthetics*, p. 1111.

38. Measures 20–41, author's translation: the score is published in Franz Schubert, *Complete Song Cycles: Die schöne Müllerin, Die Winterreise, Schwanengesang*, ed. Eusebius Mandyczewski (New York: Dover Publications, 1970), pp. 1–53.

39. The score is published in Gustav Mahler, *Songs of a Wayfarer and Kindertotenlieder in Full Score* (New York: Dover Publications, 1990), pp. 1–57.

40. Measures 48–61, author's translation: the score is published in Gustav Mahler, *Des Knaben Wunderhorn and the Rückert Lieder for Voice and Piano* (Mineola, NY: Dover Publications, 1999), pp. 63–6.

41. Peter Kivy, *Music Alone: Philosophical Reflections of the Purely Musical Experience* (Ithaca and London: Cornell University Press, 1990), p. 200. Not coincidentally, however, Kivy also cannot find any purpose in purely

instrumental music beyond enjoyment (p. 95), nor any explanation for calling any particular work 'profound' (p. 216).

42. Donald Ellman, 'The Symphony in Nineteenth-Century Germany', in *A Guide to the Symphony*, ed. Robert Layton (Oxford: Oxford University Press, 1995), pp. 148–9.

43. C. F. D. Schubart assigned to the key the expression of unrequited love: *Ideen zu einer Ästhetik der Tonkunst* (1806; Leipzig: Reclam, 1977), p. 284 – not perhaps irrelevant for either composer.

PART TWO

The Culture of Modernism

CHAPTER FIVE

Music and the Nature of Modernism

If Hermann Hesse's novel, *The Glass Bead Game*, serves as a metaphor for the dominance of a musical culture of preservation in the twentieth century, the other great novel of twentieth-century musical life, Thomas Mann's *Doctor Faustus*, supplies a metaphor for understanding the decline of a flourishing, creative musical culture. In the fictional character of Adrian Leverkühn, Mann gives the reader a fused portrait of two men whose work has indeed shaped twentieth-century intellectual and musical life: Friedrich Nietzsche and Arnold Schoenberg. That is, he takes the musical achievements of Schoenberg – the development of atonality and then the Twelve-Tone Method – and associates these with the nihilism of Nietzsche. Mann thus produces an image of the modernist mentality that becomes more than a representation of two of its leading creators; he captures what has become a pervasive characteristic of modern society: the inability to love. In doing so, he makes Leverkühn's personality and music into a disturbing counterpoint of lovelessness to accompany the agonies of two world wars.

Mann employs the legend of Faust to supply the central image of the novel: Leverkühn's bargain with the devil, which recalls Faust's exchange of his soul for the pursuit of his desires. But the novel's image of a contract with the devil, in which Leverkühn loses his soul as the price of earthly fame, is not the explanatory principle of the loss of the ability to love. For Leverkühn had long before rejected the nobler feelings such as love, together with the ideas of beauty and goodness – of all, that is, which could serve as objects of love. In this way, Mann's novel helps to explain the domination of artistic culture by modernism as the result of a psychological and intellectual process. Indeed, the metaphor suggests that the culture of musical modernism would have to be seen as the product of widely shared beliefs and ways of perceiving and feeling, in which the inability to love renders the ideas of beauty and goodness moot. To understand the origins and nature and avant-garde, then, would be to understand modernity itself.

It may be tempting to take Mann's thesis as merely a literary stance. But one of the striking characteristics of twentieth-century intellectual culture has been the prevailing hostility to Romanticism as a style expressive of ordinary feelings. This is particularly evident in the musical realm: Igor Stravinsky's remark, 'Do we not, in truth, ask the impossible of music when we expect it to express feelings, to translate dramatic situations, even to imitate nature?' speaks not only of the attitude among the Neo-Classicists, but for most of the schools of composition.[1] Even Arnold Schoenberg, whose own work contributed so much to the rejection of Romanticism, felt compelled to add to his explanation of Expressionism as 'the representation of inner processes' the following attack on the general attitude in 1928: 'But I must not say that loudly, for all that is despised today as romantic.'[2] As he understood it, the Age of Romanticism died in November 1918; there was no arguing for a continuity of aesthetic principles after World War I.

To be more specific, however: nothing has been feared so much in the twentieth century as sentimentality, the expression of emotional idealism rooted in a vision of happiness or love. This has been true not only for composers, but for philosophers and critics as well. Sentimentality itself is suspect, its musical and literary representations seen as false and pretentious.[3] The accompanying reduction of supremely appealing, melodically expressive music to the category of 'kitsch' constitutes a refusal of legitimacy to all sentimental music. Hence, Theodor Adorno despised the 'saccharined religion' of Gounod's *Ave Maria*: 'Its basic gesture is supplication in pious self-abandonment. The soul delivers itself into the hands of the Almighty with uplifted skirt.'[4] For Adorno, the issue was not the abuse of Bach's Prelude in C Major; it was the obvious display of emotion that offended. Thus, the category of the sentimental becomes linked with banality and kitsch, as if the essence of bad art were the outward display of any emotional state, but particularly of any longing for an ideal. But if this rejection of the sentimental is the defining affective paradigm for the twentieth century, it becomes clear that what is at stake is a whole way of feeling, a way of framing life both conceptually and emotionally. To reject the category of the sentimental, then, is to reject any emotional attachment to a conception of the ideal. The embarrassment with which subjects of love and idealism are generally regarded today is the legacy of nearly a century of rejection by the intellectual and cultural elites.

The psychology of modernism

We have already seen that for Adorno the suspicion of the sentimental springs from his conviction that there are no ideals of truth, goodness or beauty. For Schoenberg as well, beauty became irrelevant for musical composition. In his *Harmonielehre* of 1911, he poured scorn on theorists who would attempt to derive musical rules from aesthetic judgements about the musically beautiful.

> These judgments, 'beautiful' or 'not beautiful,' are entirely gratuitous excursions into aesthetics and have nothing to do with the logic of the whole. Parallel fifths sound bad (why?). This passing note sounds harsh (why?). There are no such things as ninth chords, or they sound harsh (why?). Where in the system can we find logically, mutually consistent answers to these three 'why's? In the sense of beauty? What is that?[5]

Both in his aesthetic and in the aural experience of his music, Schoenberg's rejection of beauty defines the modernist impulse.

It is the modernist rejection of beauty and the expression of noble feelings that demands explanation. In Thomas Mann's novel, Adrian Leverkühn also rejects the sentimental, when the narrator, Serenus Zeitblom, criticizes a dogmatic approach to musical composition as excessively rationalist: 'In any case not sentimental' is the response. But this is not only because Leverkühn approves rigid laws governing music; it is also because he does not consider love to govern music. For love is not for him the strongest human emotion. Instead, he regards interest as stronger, which the narrator, Serenus Zeitblom, redefines as 'a love from which the animal warmth has been withdrawn'.[6] Leverkühn agrees, and in doing so admits to the psychological factor lying behind the rejection of love and sentimentality: his intellect – and his pride in his intellectuality – are so overweening that there is no tempering of his spirit by feelings. As Zeitblom observes later, 'Natures such as Adrian's have not much "soul". It is a fact ... that the proudest intellectuality stands in the most immediate relation of all to the animal, to naked instinct ... .'[7] For Mann, the future creator of a completely prescriptive method for musical composition with twelve-tone rows was ruled by a dual motive, intellectuality and naked desire. Leverkühn's soul was bifurcated, leaving no middle range for sentiment to mediate the two extremes.

Yet if Mann depicts the modern soul as abandoning the traditional Platonic, tripartite image of intellect, emotion and desire in order to show the importance of emotion, he does not depict the psychology of his model with accuracy. For Schoenberg may have suppressed the more tender feelings of which he had once been capable, but the result was not to enlarge the role of 'naked instinct'. What is important instead is the peril of a strict dualism of spirit and flesh, mind and matter. For this would indeed leave no room for ordinary emotions, with the result an inability to understand the nature of love in any terms other than lust.[8] Certainly this describes the trend in modern culture since Mann's writing of the novel, however little it applied to Schoenberg, his model for Leverkühn. But the modern hatred of sentimentality is the consequence of such a reduction of emotion to desire.

There are implications, moreover, for the way the intellect itself is understood according to Leverkühn's position. For in identifying interest as the strongest emotion, he named a kind of desire that can be grasped and measured easily by the intellect. The use of the intellect in reasoning, then, becomes a matter of weighing the strength of desires and the advantages of particular interests. It is a purely utilitarian, instrumental reasoning that results from making interest the paramount emotion; this describes the prevailing conception of reason in the twentieth century.[9] Not only has utilitarianism been the predominant ethic, but the conception of human nature has been generally that of a bundle of desires, the merits of which must be adjudicated and the means of achievement decided upon with at best a consideration of a criterion of universality.[10] This, however, as Alasdair MacIntyre has argued so successfully, is a diminished conception of practical reason compared with older philosophical traditions. For on the modern conception, there is no weighing of the demands of virtue, no judgement of the proper ordering among the goods constituting the good life, no recognition of the vital role that passions must play in the virtuous life, and no genuine sympathy with those whom our actions may affect.[11] It is as much to say that the concept of practical or moral reason has been eliminated, for when interest suffices to determine the choices to be made, there is in fact no moral judgement involved. Thus Leverkühn's rejection of the supremacy of love among the emotions entails as well the rejection of practical reason and the relegation of the intellect to a purely instrumental role. The primacy of reason itself is thereby substantially curtailed.

The narrator's definition of interest as 'a love from which the animal warmth has been withdrawn' is also revealing, however, of another important constituent of the modern mentality. Leverkühn's utilitarianism necessarily yields a subjectivist view of reality: all external claims upon the self will be measured against the perception of self-interest. The result is a denial of the possibility of defining the good objectively as a universally encompassing, self-sufficient final end. There can be no ontologically existent Idea of the good, no God with a transcendent claim upon man: this is the meaning of the pact the devil bestows on the composer. But in fact the devil draws the subjectivist conclusion explicitly for Adrian:

> Your tendency, my friend, to inquire after the objective, the so-called truth, to question as worthless the subjective, pure experience: that is truly petty bourgeois, you ought to overcome it. As you see me, so I exist to you. What serves it to ask whether I really am? Is not 'really' what works, is not truth experience and feeling?[12]

The self's feeling of power inevitably becomes the only reality once the good is rejected as an objective category: this was the realization of Nietzsche, and the devil preaches it in the novel with clear-sighted consistency.[13]

Less obviously, perhaps, but no less truly, the narrator's conception of love is just as subjectivist as Leverkühn's. If interest is 'a love from which the animal warmth has been withdrawn', then the implication is that love with the animal warmth remaining to it will still be a love of self, as lust. The result is that the novel accurately portrays the central dilemma of twentieth-century psychology: whether lust or interest be considered the stronger, both yield the doctrine of the supremacy of the self, in which desire in one form or another dominates the soul.[14] This is what Alasdair MacIntrye has remarked upon as the emotivist self of the twentieth century. But what Thomas Mann portrays is a self defined by emotions of a particular type: species of desires, but not the nobler emotions of the love of beauty and goodness. Just as reason was truncated, the emotions too become attenuated by the focus on the self's interests and desires.

Thomas Mann therefore explains Leverkühn's rejection of beauty by locating the reasons in the consequences of the prevailing conceptions of human nature and morality in the twentieth century. Leverkühn's repudiation of beauty was of a piece with his scorn of sentiment: although he could praise the musical construction and feeling of triumph in Beethoven's Leonore Overture No. 3, for example, he felt compelled to add, 'I do not like to call it beautiful, the word "beauty" has always been half offensive to me, it has such a silly face, and people feel wanton and corrupt when they say it.'[15] This remark of Leverkühn's echoes not only Schoenberg's position, but as we have seen the general attitude of intellectuals in the twentieth century. The reason is certainly larger than the influence of one man. For when neither an objectively existing order of goods nor the claims of other people are acknowledged as constituents of reality or of the self, the self comes to be defined by its desires alone, without the moderating influence of either practical reason or the ordinary human emotions. It will be inevitable, then, to measure the attainment of success by subjective standards, that is, by the strength of the naked desires themselves. For such a self, there is little need of what Zeitblom called 'the beautifying, veiling, ennobling' work of the soul in creating poetry to clothe desire or interest.[16] In particular, a conception of the self in terms of desire alone leaves no reason for either a poetry or a music expressive of love. The rejection of an objectively definable goodness outside the self leaves no beauty to love.

It is fair to ask, however, if Mann was justified in his perception of the character of musical modernism. For it is one thing to point to the lovelessness of totalitarian regimes, or even to produce a psychological portrait of a philosopher or composer as a means of depicting the character of modern society. But it would be quite another matter to claim that the music itself represents or expresses in some manner the same lovelessness. The closest that Mann comes in the novel is a reference to Schoenberg's Twelve-Tone Method, which is described as an invention of Leverkühn's. This new rationalism of method threatened to dissolve both freedom and the faculty of reason altogether: 'The rationalism you call for has a good deal of superstition about it ... . Contrary to what you say, your system seems to me more calculated to dissolve human reason in magic.' Leverkühn acknowledges that 'reason and magic may meet and become one ... in belief in the stars, in numbers ... .'[17] But this is to say that an apparent rationalism such as governed Schoenberg's music may indeed dissolve into irrationalism, leaving music entirely outside the realm of subjective choice. The question remains whether this accounts for the character of lovelessness and nihilism attributed to Schoenberg's music, and by extension to musical modernism in general.

As we have seen, Adorno took as the two representative types of modernist music the two principal composers of the twentieth century, Schoenberg and Igor Stravinsky. In order to understand the essential nature of musical modernism first-hand, it will be fruitful to examine the two most famous and influential works of these composers, the works which appear most characteristic of the modernist enterprise: Schoenberg's *Pierrot lunaire* and Stravinsky's *Le Sacre du printemps*. The first had its premiere in 1912, the second in 1913; together, they articulated the two poles of modernism and reveal the nature of the revolt against beauty. In shaping the course of the twentieth century, these works reveal as well the collapse of love as the motive of human life. The rise of an emotivist self defined by its desires, on the one hand, and by primitive instincts on the other, serves to define the twin poles of the modernist mentality.

Schoenberg and the emotivist self

The centrality of desire for the emotivist self is seen most clearly in Schoenberg's most successful atonal work, *Pierrot lunaire*, Op. 21. This work was greeted with some acclaim by critics upon its premiere in Berlin in 1912, so that of all of Schoenberg's atonal works, it has achieved the status of a work that defines musical modernism.[18] In fact, however, it is one of the few major works Schoenberg managed to complete after his break with tonality in 1908. This makes *Pierrot lunaire* all the more important for understanding the essence of modernism. Too often it is seen simply as one more expression of Schoenberg's personal troubles, in this case, his rejection as a composer.[19] Yet the origin of the work cannot be reduced to the autobiographical element as neatly as many of his other Expressionist works, such as *Erwartung* or *Die glückliche Hand*, for the twenty-one poems comprising its text were drawn from a set of fifty by the Belgian Symbolist poet, Albert Giraud. Giraud's *Pierrot lunaire* appeared in 1884; it was translated into German by Otto Erich Hartleben, a poet in August Strindberg's circle in Berlin, in 1893.[20] Thus the poetry already had a wide public reception. Schoenberg chose twenty-one of the poems, and reorganized their sequence so that the coherence of the symbolism would be clearer than in the original. A close analysis of the text will show that the poetry attests to the impossibility of creating beauty when the moral order of a culture has been destroyed by the emotivist self's intoxication with desire. Schoenberg's setting, therefore, will emerge as a fitting reflection of the thesis of the cycle.

There are two main characters and a central symbol in Schoenberg's setting of *Pierrot lunaire*. The cycle is narrated by a poet who despairs of his own creativity and seeks inspiration however he can find it; he, rather than Pierrot, is the principal subject of the cycle. The 'moonstruck' Pierrot, however, is the alter ego of the poet, a grotesque incarnation of the traditional *commedia dell'arte* clown to whom the poet turns for inspiration. Pierrot's surreal experiences are a transformation of the poet's desires and despair. But it is the moon that looms over both the poet and Pierrot, dominating the cycle through its symbolism of desire and despair. The moon, therefore, emerges as the key to understanding the work.

Schoenberg's setting of the twenty-one poems is divided into three parts: on the title page of the score, he indicated 'Dreimal sieben Gedichte aus Albert Girauds Pierrot lunaire.'[21] Schoenberg's interest in numerology has been noted by several interpreters, and some have seen even this choice of three times the 'perfect' number seven as evidence of influence by numerology.[22] Yet the grouping of the poems into three parts of seven each does serve to create a structure giving the work a clear meaning. In the first part, the poet dominates, his desires and despair finding reflection in the symbol of the moon. In the second part, he turns to Pierrot for inspiration, praying to him for a return of the gift of laughter. But Pierrot's escapades are hardly amusing: he robs graves, offers his heart dripping with blood as a figurative sacrifice for humanity, and imagines his own execution. In the third part, Pierrot's further adventures do at last bring the poet some measure of release from his despair. Yet it is only a subjective recovery, for the conditions symbolized by the moon remain the underlying reality for the modern world. The image of the moon, then, demands careful examination.

The poet-narrator's emotional odyssey takes place in the context of the moon's symbolism of tormenting desire. In the first poem, 'Mondestrunken', the moonlight is described as 'this holy drink' with which the poet intoxicates himself: it is 'The wine that one drinks with one's eyes'. But this is so because the flood of moonlight awakens desire: 'Desires, dreadful and sweet,/Swim across the flood without number!' The nature of his desire begins to be suggested in the second poem, 'Columbine', in which the poet wishes to pluck the petals off one of 'The pale blossoms of moonlight' falling upon his beloved's brown hair. The fourth poem, however, finally makes explicit the association of the moon with femininity: 'Eine blasse Wäscherin' describes the moon as 'the mild maid of heaven' who 'stretches naked, silver-white arms/ Below in the flood'. But the image of the moon as a female figure dates back to Luna in Roman mythology, where she was associated with Diana in Greek myth, the goddess of chastity.[23] This traditional symbolism will prove vital for understanding *Pierrot lunaire*.

The erotic nature of the poet's own desires emerges clearly in the next poem, 'Valse de Chopin': 'The harmonies of wild desire disturb/The icy dream of despair – /As a pale drop of blood/Colors the lips of a consumptive.' The poet's despair is a sickness unto death – to borrow Kierkegaard's phrase – of which his 'wild desire' for feminine love is an integral part. This is the poetic counterpart to Leverkühn's animal instinct in Thomas Mann's novel.

The ideal of a chaste love, however, is dead in the modern world. The next poem, 'Madonna', depicts a wounded and bleeding *Mater dolorosa* representing the death of all hope: 'In thy wasted-away hands / Thou holdest thy Son's body, / To show him to all mankind – / Therefore the glance of men shuns thee, / Thee, O Mother of all sorrows'. Men, that is, shun the highest feminine example of chaste and holy love in Christianity because they wish to avoid the sight of her crucified Son. Rejecting salvation, they reject all moral ideals. This is confirmed in the seventh poem, which closes the first part of the cycle; 'Der kranke Mond' – 'The Sick Moon' – brings together the earlier symbolism of the feminine in the moon with the image of the death of love from the previous poem. This is possible because of the traditional association of the moon with the Virgin Mary as well as with Diana-Luna.[24] The origin of the poet's despair is therefore explained in the death of belief in moral ideals:

> Thou gloomily death-sick moon,
> There on heaven's black cushion,
> Thy appearance, so feverishly colossal,
> Enchants me like a strange melody.
>
> Thou diest of insatiable love-sorrow,
> Of yearning, deeply stifled,
> Thou gloomily death-sick moon,
> There on heaven's black cushion.
>
> The lover, who in sensual orgy
> Thoughtlessly sneaks to the beloved,
> Is amused by thy play of moonbeams –
> Thy pale, torture-born blood,
> Thou gloomily death-sick moon.

The chaste moon, like the poet, is sick unto death, yearning for a love that can never be found. Lust, not love, is the highest reality for modern man.

With this as the central theme of the cycle, it is easy to understand the appeal of Giraud's poetry and the relative critical success of Schoenberg's setting. Lust, moral decay and nihilistic despair were themes typical of Symbolist poetry at the end of the nineteenth century.[25] This reflected a widespread moral collapse, in which the rejection of virtue and the moral ideals of chastity and fidelity frequently led to the psychological disintegration of those most eager to embrace the new antinomian freedom.[26] For that reason, Schoenberg's cycle of songs explores an objective condition of a historical cultural milieu. But the moral crisis of the *fin de siècle* was part of the emergence of the culture of modernism: hence the importance of *Pierrot lunaire* for musical modernism in particular.

It becomes critical, then, to examine what happens to the poet's sense of despair in the face of the 'insatiable love-sorrow' that is the consequence of the death of moral ideals and the reduction of the self to instinctual desire. The second part of the cycle begins with a poem in which the night is portrayed as 'Dark, black, giant moths' which, having 'murdered the brilliance of the sun', now descend 'Upon the human hearts below'. Thus the night becomes the symbol of total despair for the poet. In the following poem, the poet then prays to Pierrot for relief from this despair, and the remainder of the cycle relates Pierrot's adventures for the inspiration of the poet. They are macabre adventures, however: in an ironic contrast with the traditional figure of the clown, Pierrot's escapades produce horror rather than laughter. First, in 'Raub', he is shown robbing graves; in 'Rote Messe', he celebrates a Mass at which he offers his own heart as the holy sacrifice. Far from elevating the role of the poet, as this is sometimes seen, it (like the preceding poem) blasphemes the sanctity of the holy.

It should be no surprise, then, to find Pierrot's hanging to appear imminent in the following poem, 'Galgenlied', and to hear Pierrot dreaming of his execution in 'Enthauptung', where the moon appears as 'the shining Turkish sword'. Images of blood and death pervade these four poems, suggesting that death is the inevitable end of despair produced by the death of love as an idea. The second third of the cycle ends with 'Die Kreuze', in which the poet compares his verses to holy crosses, and himself to one crucified. But neither the poet's death nor Pierrot's priestly self-sacrifice earlier brings any expectation of salvation: the poet on his cross of verses is simply beset by a 'fluttering ghostly swarm of vultures'. Poetry is the poet's death, the record of his tormenting despair.

The poems that follow in the final third of the cycle contain some of the most bizarre imagery yet. It might be tempting to dismiss much of this imagery as imaginative symbolism that Giraud could not quite control, except that Schoenberg shows its integral relation to Pierrot's yearning for 'his native heaven' with which the last section begins: it will define the 'modern sentimental' mentality of Pierrot, in opposition to traditional sentimentality as the yearning for an ideal. There are images of sadistic cruelty in 'Gemeinheit!' ('Meanness!') and 'Serenade'; in the former, Pierrot bores into the head of his fellow mime, Cassander, and inserts a pipe with which to smoke, while in the latter, he draws a giant viola bow across the bald head of Cassander. On the other hand, 'Parody' offers a last image of love in a loveless world: an old duenna loves Pierrot 'with sorrow', but 'The moon, the angry mocker', shines on her without compassion. In the following poem, 'Der Mondfleck' ('Moonstain'), Pierrot angrily tries to expunge the image of the moon wherever it falls on him: for him as for the poet in the first part of the cycle, the moon is a source of misery and torment. But that confirms the import of the symbolism throughout the circle: it is not the poet's personal despair that is the subject here, but rather the threat of the objective world because of the destruction of the ideal of love. Without that ideal, there can be only cruelty, torment and anger. These, then, constitute the character of the 'modern sentimental' feeling.

Schoenberg's cycle ends with the coming of day and Pierrot's return to his homeland, Bergamo. The poet's words suggest the recovery of a measure of tranquillity in the final song, which is usually taken at face value:

> A lucky wish for joy makes me cheerful,
> Which I long despised:
> O old scent out of fairy-tale time,
> Intoxicate again my senses!
>
> I disclosed all my displeasure;
> Out of my sun-framed window
> I look freely on the good world
> And dream out in blessed distance ...
> O old scent – out of fairy-tale time![27]

Yet the text is revealing: the poet's cheerfulness is as subjectivist as his despair that was caused by wild desire; it is his wish for joy that makes him cheerful. Only a return to 'fairy-tale time' could produce the poet's recovery of hope. Thus the despair of the preceding poems is the authentic voice of modern feeling.

Schoenberg's musical setting accordingly avoids any of the stylistic manifestations of objective goodness and beauty. As in his other Expressionist works, the music is relentlessly dissonant, atonal and unmelodic, although there is more motivic treatment of the material than in *Erwartung*, for example. Yet the leaps of large melodic intervals, seen in both the accompaniment and vocal lines in Example 5.1(a), constitute melodic dissonances which act to destroy the coherence of the melody or counterpoint. In this way Schoenberg's music for *Pierrot lunaire* illustrates the rejection of the elements most crucial for the metaphysical significance of tonal music, those which defined music as the metaphor of the goodness of being. Thus atonality becomes intelligible philosophically as a revolt against the unity and harmony of being.

But there is a further radicalization of the tonal disintegration begun in 1907 in the use of *Sprechstimme* for much of the vocal line. In this cross between singing and speaking, the voice begins on the note indicated in the score and then immediately glides to the next pitch. The result is that in a passage employing this technique, there is no pitch stability for even the duration of a note-value: the most fundamental element of music, the clarity of pitch level, is now dissolved.[28] Hence the ontological condition of music is denied: the revolt against beauty, seen theoretically in the *Harmonielehre*, becomes a revolt against being itself. Thus the poet's apparent recovery of some degree of tranquillity at the end of the cycle is not matched by a corresponding recovery of musical order. As Example 5.1(b) shows, the accompaniment suddenly reduces to thirds and triads, but without affirming any tonal centre. Moreover, the voice remains in *Sprechstimme*, so that even the one consonant triad formed with the accompaniment (marked with an asterisk in the example) is evaded. This brief reappearance of consonance in

a) No. 7, 'Der kranke Mond', mm. 1–6

Example 5.1   Arnold Schoenberg, *Pierrot lunaire*, Op. 21, Nos 7 and 21

b)   No. 21, 'O alter Duft', last 5 measures

Example 5.1   concluded

the entire cycle remains only a theoretical point, not an aural experience for the listener.

Pierrot lunaire, therefore, is a work that does more than express the pain and torment of characters who suffer from the moral and spiritual decay of the modern world. It is, more deeply, a representation of the disorder of the world itself, proclaiming and accepting the loss of chastity, holiness, love and beauty. There is no sentimentality in the music because there is no ideal, no Idea of the good, to order life or to inspire love. There can only be consuming desire, despair and death as the consequences of the emotivist self in its loss of an ordered world.

Stravinsky and the nihilism of sacrifice

The understanding of life found in *Pierrot lunaire* is not limited to Schoenberg, however: many composers have shared it. Nihilism is the essence of modernism for both Schoenberg's most famous work and the society out of which it sprang. A similar nihilism lies at the heart of a second work that defined musical modernism contemporaneously with *Pierrot lunaire*, but that has had a much greater public acceptance as a modern classic: Igor Stravinsky's *Le Sacre du printemps* (1913). Like *Pierrot lunaire*, it is characterized by the utter absence of sentimentality in both its subject matter and its music. As Stravinsky's summary of the action of the ballet makes clear, the dance in honour of spring, the first part of the ballet, ends in a sacrifice that accomplishes no true purpose. The second part, 'The Great Sacrifice,' is described thus:

> All night the virgins hold mysterious games, walking in circles. One of the virgins is consecrated as the victim and is twice pointed to by fate, being caught twice in the perpetual dance. The virgins honor her, the chosen one, with a marital dance. They invoke the ancestors and entrust the chosen one to the old wise men. She sacrifices herself in the presence of the old men in the great holy dance, the great sacrifice.[29]

Innocence here becomes a warrant for death; it ceases to be an ideal to be preserved.

The sacrifice of a young and innocent girl in the midst of a celebration of the renewal of life is usually interpreted as a fertility rite, a primitive propitiation of a pagan god of spring. Stravinsky's own retrospective account of the origin of the ballet adds a motive for the sacrifice not present in the original libretto: 'I saw in imagination a solemn pagan rite: sage elders, seated in a circle, watched a young girl dance herself to death. They were sacrificing her to propitiate the god of spring.'[30] But there is no warrant for this in the libretto; on this Adorno agrees.[31] The choice of the particular victim from among a group of virgins is arbitrary and fatalistic, and her death is presented as an inevitable accompaniment to regeneration rather than as a means to accomplishing that end. For that reason, Stravinsky's original title for the ballet, *The Victim*, seems indeed to capture more of the substance of the plot than the final title of *The Rite of Spring*.[32] The ballet might better be regarded as a celebration of death in the midst of life.

Le Sacre thus belongs to the cult of primitivism. The rituals of pagan Russia possessed an attraction as a contrast to the refinement of modern society; Sergei Prokofiev's *Scythian Suite* is another example of musical primitivism. But what underlay the evocation of the primitive was the glorification of brutality; brutality was an assault on civilized values that often found its inspiration in the writings of Friedrich Nietzsche. The violence of Nietzsche's *Will to Power* was the hammer directed against the received traditions of civilization, the alternative to what was perceived as nihilism. Indeed, the aim of apocalyptic regeneration through violence was the common theme of many writers and artists: Georges Sorel and Oskar Kokoschka are among the most famous.[33] In this way violence and brutality became part of the modernist culture of nihilism.

The plot structure and musical form of *Le Sacre* bear out this nihilistic theme of primitive violence. The ballet is organized into two parts, 'A Kiss of the Earth', and 'The Exalted Sacrifice'.[34] Each part opens with an introduction evocative of nature through the employment of lyrical melodies; nature is thus contrasted with the more rhythmic violence of the human world. The dramatic tension in Part I arises from the contrast between the young girls and the young men: the girls celebrate the coming of spring in their dances, alternating with the more violent rituals of the men. The young men dance first a Ritual of Abduction and then The Game of the Rival Towns, in which violence is explicitly the theme: the first a simulated kidnapping of one of the girls, the second a simulated battle. Into this dichotomy is inserted the entrance of the Oldest and Wisest One, who kisses the Earth in a gesture of ritual love. This leads to the Dance of the Acquisition of the Earth to close Part I. The entrance of the Oldest and Wisest One is a static procession, but the Finale partakes of the brutal rhythmic character of the Young Men's dances: rhythm thus appears as the male musical principle, lyricism the female. Part I closes, therefore, with the victory of the male over the female, but with the full participation on stage of the female dancers.

Part II is much simpler in structure. The action begins with the Mystic Circle of the Young Girls, repeating the lyrical melody of the Introduction to Part II. But the Naming and Honoring of the Chosen One, where the sacrificial victim is identified by the fate of the dance itself, is a return to the rhythmic principle, even though the dancers are young women: the victim will be sacrificed to the satisfaction of the old men. The Evocation of the Ancestors, like the Procession of the Sage in Part I, is harmonically and rhythmically static: it prepares the way for the Ritual Performance of the Elders as the Forefathers of Mankind. This is a lyrical movement, in a Lento tempo; it reflects the majesty of the elders. The Final dance, the Sacrificial Dance of the Chosen One, is marked by a return to the rhythmic male principle: the young woman dances herself to death, and is held up in the arms of the old men at the end. Again, then, there is the victory of the male over the female, with the full participation of the female dancers.

Le Sacre du printemps, therefore, is a darkly sexual ballet. But the ritualized abduction in Part I leads not to rape, but to death in Part II. If, in the highly charged erotic atmosphere of Wagner's *Tristan und Isolde*, love and death were inextricably linked, here the former is completely subordinated to the latter. In nineteenth-century Romanticism, love might never be requited, but it could be longed for, and death understood as the only condition for its fulfilment. In the new world of the twentieth century, love itself is banished, and death becomes a substitute for, rather than a fulfilment of love. The significance of *Le Sacre* lay precisely in bringing this shift in the role of sexual love to the forefront of public attention in Paris, the musical capital of the world at that time.

If Stravinsky's ballet was a celebration of primitive barbarity, then its success in the concert hall must be the astonishing aspect of its history. This is especially so, given the controversy it engendered upon the premiere of the ballet in May of 1913. While some doubts have recently been expressed about the nature and extent of that controversy – possibly even to the point of suspecting that a substantial part of it was staged by Stravinsky's supporters – it nevertheless remains true that the ballet itself has rarely been performed.[35] In contrast, the orchestral score achieved a place in the concert repertoire very quickly; already in 1914, its place was established. Yet the reasons for this divergence are not far to find: the score contains enough folksong melodies from Russian chant to appeal to the ear, in spite of the brutality of its rhythms and the dissonance of its harmonic language.[36] The ballet, in contrast, is visually jarring: Nijinsky choreographed it so that the dancers' movements were jerky or stomping, their pose defined by the toes pointing inward and their knees bent. Both the dancers on the stage and the critics of the time complained of the lack of visual beauty in the principal art-form devoted to the exhibition of living beauty.[37]

The subject of the ballet notwithstanding, then, the music of *Le Sacre* has become thoroughly familiar to audiences in the years since the initial *succès de scandale*. The melodic phrases – fragmentary, to be sure – help listeners feel that they are at least on the edge of a familiar approach to music. Nevertheless, the ballet is most famous for its irregular accents, changing metres and relentlessly driving rhythms, which function to create the atmosphere of primitive vitality. Yet it is precisely the violent disintegration of metrical order which affords the key to understanding the significance of the music, for it is more profound than simply a violation of predictability. Rather, as Hegel and Schelling understood, metrical regularity is the principal necessary condition of the individual's participation in the temporal order of being; regular beats are what establish the significance of music as a reflection of the kind of harmonic motion exhibited in the cosmos itself.[38] Hence a denial of metric regularity is a denial of the temporal order of being, just as atonality is a denial of the intrinsic unity and natural harmony of being. What Schoenberg accomplished in the latter way, Stravinsky pursued in the former: for both, music in the modern world had to spring from a revolt against being.

Although the rhythm is the most radical element of the musical style of *Le Sacre*, it is not surprising that other elements exhibit a similar disintegration of order. The work is in fact highly dissonant, although the dissonant harmonies have the reputation of being more tame than in Schoenberg's music, largely because of their static nature. Yet, for instance, the opening of 'The Augurs of Spring' employs a dissonant chord consisting of A-flat, F-flat, G, B-flat, C-flat, D-flat and E-flat, repeated in eighth notes (quavers) for eight measures. This is, in effect, a bitonal chord, F-flat major against an E-flat seventh. Or again, the 'Sacrificial Dance' that closes Part II opens with a chord consisting of E-flat, B-flat, D, F-sharp, A and C: a bitonal construction of E-flat and a D-seventh. Triadic construction, therefore, is not completely abjured, but the tonal implications are denied by the sharply dissonant adjacent chords, which create tone clusters rather than two or more tonalities. Finally, there are significantly melodic moments, but they are highly fragmented, so that the order of linear continuity is broken. Stravinsky had seen Schoenberg's Three Piano Pieces, Op. 11 (1911) before composing *Le Sacre*; what he absorbed from them was a sense of how far it might be possible to push the limits of tonal disintegration.[39] The debt Stravinsky owed Schoenberg, although largely unacknowledged, was profound.

The cumulative effect of all the ways in which Stravinsky's music exhibits a revolt against order cannot be described in terms of stylistic categories alone. Rather, the lack of an image of goodness and love in the action of the ballet is reflected in music that lacks all sentimental feeling. As Adorno observes, *Le Sacre* is mournful, but not out of pity for the victim who dances herself to death; it is instead 'the outcry of creatural incarceration'.[40] It becomes an indictment of existence itself. Thus *Le Sacre du printemps* reveals no less than Schoenberg's music the decisive characteristics of the modern mentality. The inability to feel love, which Thomas Mann identified as the emotional core of modernism, is the inevitable result of the rejection of the ideals of goodness and beauty. But as the ballet demonstrates vividly, to deny the Idea of the good is to deny the dignity and even the continued existence of human beings: the revolt against being has existential as well as musical consequences. The inability to love will become the inability to feel pity for one's fellow human beings.

The new mentality and modern musical culture

We have seen that the musical tradition which was forged from the Renaissance through the nineteenth century culminated not only in a common practice of functional tonality and a canonic repertoire that preserved the most laudable achievements of that practice, but also a coherent aesthetic that accounted for the significance of that practice and that repertoire. This aesthetic recognized the aim of the art of music as the representation of the order of human life, in which emotional expression was central but nevertheless subordinated to the sense of the larger metaphysical goodness of existence. By the beginning of the nineteenth century, this aim was codified in the concept of beauty, so that the order and expressiveness of beauty were linked explicitly with the Platonic Ideas of the good and the true.

In contrast to the twentieth-century mentality, the Idea of the good provided a crucial substantive object of love in the nineteenth century, even when a belief in God might not always have been sustained. Beauty therefore still had real meaning: it was closely connected with the realm of the ideal. Hence the sentimental, as we have seen, was a vital category of feeling, linking the realm of formal or material beauty with that of ideal beauty, or as Ferdinand Hand described it, yearning for earthly bliss in the midst of woe. The rejection of the sentimental has been characteristic not just of Schoenberg, Leverkühn's prototype, but of twentieth-century culture in general; it is a denial of the possibility of even yearning for earthly bliss. Such bliss is an ideal, a vision of beauty, without which human life has little real hope. To reject beauty and sentimentality, therefore, is to leave life bereft of love, hope, or any perception of worth. The devil's curse on Leverkühn – 'Thy life shall be cold, therefore thou shalt love no human being'[41] – becomes a curse pronounced upon an entire culture. As in Mann's novel, the curse is already prepared thoroughly by the intellectual rejection of anything besides self-interest or desire as a motivation of human choice.

These considerations point to why Thomas Mann chose to combine the figures of Friedrich Nietzsche and Arnold Schoenberg in the character of Adrian Leverkühn. It was not simply that these two men have been among the most prominent influences on twentieth-century culture, nor that Schoenberg was influenced by Nietzsche to a considerable extent. Rather, Mann must have recognized the deep affinity of Nietzsche's nihilism and Schoenberg's rejection of beauty in his music. He suggests that both positions sprang from the same roots: the denial of the good, reason and morality, in the context of a total subjectivism. Seen in this light, these two figures become parallel products of a culture as much as the twin creators of modernist culture. Thus, Nietzsche's nihilist denial of the good and Schoenberg's rejection of aural beauty emerge as related phenomena, two sides of the same historical process. The denial of an ultimate good has as its corollary the rejection of beauty as the perceptible being of goodness.

If Schoenberg and Nietzsche are understood as parallel products of modern culture, however, rather than just as the principal architects of modernism, then it becomes possible to comprehend how they achieved their wide influence among intellectuals. For Schoenberg in particular, this is a great problem, for if his music lacks the beauty of the common practice tradition and the sensual appeal of the less radical composers of the twentieth century – such as Prokofiev and Shostakovich – then how did his ideas about music, from the emancipation of dissonance in atonality to the Twelve-Tone Method, come to have wide acceptance among both critics and composers? What accounts for the resonance of such theories in the face of evident aural ugliness, which one would think repellent? The analysis suggested by Thomas Mann's novel suggests an answer: his theories and his music have corresponded to the intrinsically nihilist nature of modern utilitarian and subjectivist culture. Thus, if Schoenberg stands as the best representative of artistic modernism, it was Friedrich Nietzsche who most clearly articulated the nature of modern nihilism. In this way the musical tradition and theoretical edifice that had been constructed so painstakingly over the course of four centuries came to an abrupt end during the first decade of the twentieth.

The nihilism of Friedrich Nietzsche, the emotivism of Arnold Schoenberg and the primitivism of Igor Stravinsky combined to raise a challenge to the traditional musical order. The sense that the old moral order was dead was common to both Schoenberg and Stravinsky, just as Nietzsche had proclaimed it a generation before. But it was not just the moral order that appeared no longer to exist; there was no ideal of goodness left to celebrate – and this, to emphasize, well before the outbreak of World War I and the coming of the horrors that were to mark the twentieth century. Thus Thomas Mann appears justified in portraying the new musical style of Leverkühn-Schoenberg as born out of the inability to love. But this should not be interpreted as a judgement upon the personality of Schoenberg; instead, it emerges as a judgement against the whole of modernist musical culture. Indeed, it becomes a judgement against the defining characteristics of modern society.

The rejection of the expression of love and other noble feelings, as Mann portrays it, answered to a widely held belief that the human psyche is simply the sum of its desires together with the pleasures and pains attendant upon desire. To see oneself as caught between two opposite principles – pleasure and pain – is not only to leave out the principle of love, but to deny the existence of an ultimate good: it is the essence of nihilism. It is also an implacable psychological dualism; from that to a yearning for an occult solution is but a short step, which may account for Schoenberg's reputed interest in numerology, the reason that dissolves in magic according to Mann's narrator. But the disturbing implication is that the success of the revolt against beauty becomes intelligible in light of the dominant conceptions of being and human nature in modern society.

The place of *Le Sacre du printemps* in modernist musical culture also testifies to the extent of the nihilist mentality in modern society. That Stravinsky appears more conservative than Schoenberg, as Adorno recognized, does not alter his influential role in the emergence of musical modernism, for in taking the extremely dissonant style of Schoenberg and making it palatable for concert audiences, he helped to make acceptable what Schoenberg could not with his more atonal approach. Yet the significance of

Stravinsky's style – in both its dissonance and its rhythmic violence – not only celebrates the world of the primitive, but denies the rule of a civilizing ideal of goodness able either to motivate love or to give an ennobling purpose to death. Life, therefore, becomes meaningless: *Le Sacre* becomes the twentieth-century's archetypical essay in nihilism.

Stravinsky, however, was not alone in idolizing the violence of primitive peoples: Béla Bartók's *Allegro barbaro* of 1911 captures much of the same spirit as *Le Sacre*, and Bartók's interest in Magyar folk music was motivated in part by a desire to find an alternative to the modes of expression of traditional tonality.[42] Moreover, his pantomime, *The Miraculous Mandarin*, although conceived as a protest against the violence of World War I and completed only in 1919, portrays violence as the inevitable consequence of modern life; it is, therefore, an equally nihilist work.[43] This is not surprising, in light of Bartók's enthusiasm for Nietzsche, dating back to at least 1908.[44] The nihilism shared by Bartók and Stravinsky in this crucial period, therefore, helps to account for the influence of Schoenberg's music on them. For like Stravinsky, Bartók knew Schoenberg's Piano Pieces, Op. 11.[45] In both cases, the example of complete atonality was to have a long-lasting effect that thoroughly transformed the style of composers who remained generally more accessible than Schoenberg himself.

It is necessary, therefore, to understand Schoenberg more carefully as the originator of the particular traits of musical modernism. We can point to the pervasive intellectual influence of Nietzsche, the climate of nihilism created by modern utilitarianism, and the rise of an emotivist conception of the self as essential elements in the modernist culture. But for the origin of the specific musical traits understood as central to the modernist style – the denial of tonality, consonance and melodic character – all lines point back to Schoenberg as the originator of the most radical and at the same time the most influential approach to music in the twentieth century. To understand what was distinctive about Schoenberg will be to understand what lies at the heart of twentieth-century modernism in music. This task will require placing Schoenberg in a larger intellectual context than is normally recognized as relevant for composers.

Notes

1. Igor Stravinsky, *Poetics of Music: In the Form of Six Lessons*, trans. Arthur Knodel and Ingolf Dahl (Cambridge, MA: Harvard University Press, 1970), p. 77.
2. Arnold Schoenberg, 'Breslau Lecture on *Die glückliche Hand*', in *Arnold Schoenberg, Wassily Kandinsky: Letters, Pictures and Documents*, ed. Jelena Hahl-Koch, trans. John C. Crawford (London: Faber and Faber, 1984), pp. 105–6.
3. Cf. Mark Jefferson, 'What's Wrong With Sentimentality', *Mind* 92 (1983), pp.

519–29; most recently, Roger Scruton, *The Aesthetics of Music* (Oxford: Clarendon Press, 1997), pp. 485–8. The sentimentality Scruton attacks, however, appears far removed from the authentic definition provided by Hand. Jefferson argues that sentimentality rests on a false fiction of innocence that in turn brutalizes the potential threats to the object of sentimental devotion. This, however, is guilt by association: the real quarrel appears to be with the existence of an ideal at all. The philosopher Robert C. Solomon is almost alone in defending sentimentality; see his article, 'On Kitsch and Sentimentality', *Journal of Aesthetics and Art Criticism* 49 (1991), pp. 2–13

4. Theodor Adorno, *Quasi una fantasia: Essays on Modern Music*, trans. Rodney Livingstone (London: Verso, 1994), p. 37.

5. Arnold Schoenberg, *Theory of Harmony*, trans. Roy E. Carter (Berkeley: University of California Press, 1978), p. 10.

6. Thomas Mann, *Doktor Faustus: Das Leben des deutschen Tonsetzers Adrian Leverkühn erzählt von einem Freunde*, in *Gesammelte Werke in zwölf Bänden* (Oldenburg: S. Fischer Verlag, 1960), vol. 6, p. 96; *Doctor Faustus: The Life of the German Composer Adrian Leverkühn as Told by a Friend*, trans. H. T. Lowe-Porter (1948; New York: Vintage Books, 1971), pp. 68–9.

7. *Werke*, vol. 6, p. 197; *Doctor Faustus*, p. 147.

8. *Werke*, vol. 6, pp. 249–50; *Doctor Faustus*, pp. 187–8. If this does not describe Schoenberg with precision, it is nevertheless fundamental to the modernist mentality. Rudiger Safranski applies Mann's analysis to the philosopher who was to be so important for the Symbolists and Expressionists, Arthur Schopenhauer: see his *Schopenhauer and the Wild Years of Philosophy*, trans. Ewald Osers (Cambridge, MA: Harvard University Press, 1989), p. 138. The dualism Mann noted – of pure intellect and animal instinct – divides the artistic avant-garde as a whole in the twentieth century, leaving sentimentality out of the repertoire of human emotions.

9. The limited conception of reason which has been characteristic of the twentieth century has multiple origins. The utilitarianism of Jeremy Bentham and John Stuart Mill is one obvious source; Mill's attempt in his *Utilitarianism* of 1861 to posit a special feeling of social unity is both inconsistent and unsuccessful in avoiding a reduction of reason to a calculus of pleasures and pains. But René Descartes had already banished moral judgement from the purview of reason in his *Discourse on Method* (1637); his reason could only be mathematical or technical for the utility of making ourselves 'masters and possessors of nature': *Discourse on Method and the Meditations*, trans F. E. Sutcliffe (Harmondsworth: Penguin, 1968), Sixth Discourse, p. 78. This is emphasized by David Roochnik, *The Tragedy of Reason: Toward a Platonic Conception of Logos* (New York and London: Routledge, 1990), pp. 64–76. The difference between the ancient concept of practical reason and the modern notion of instrumental reason is explored by Charles Taylor, *Sources of the Self: The Making of the Modern Identity* (Cambridge, MA: Harvard University Press, 1989), pp. 86ff. Finally, on the nature of reason as the articulation of judgements concerning goods, see Alasdair MacIntyre, *Whose Justice? Which Rationality?* (Notre Dame: University of Notre Dame Press, 1988).

10. For a thorough critique of the deontological self, see Michael J. Sandel, *Liberalism and the Limits of Justice* (Cambridge: Cambridge University Press, 1982).

11. Alasdair MacIntyre, *After Virtue: A Study in Moral Theory*, 2nd edn (Notre Dame: University of Notre Dame Press, 1984) is the best historical and philosophical account of the defects of the modern moral temper. See also Taylor,

Sources of the Self, esp. pp. 53ff.

12. Mann, *Werke*, vol. 6, p. 323; *Doctor Faustus*, p. 242. That the conversation occurs during a dream only emphasizes the now indeterminate status of the 'real'.

13. Nietzsche's reduction of human nature to a 'will to power' is familiar, but he himself draws the emotivist conclusion: 'The noble type of man feels *himself* to be the determiner of values ... .' *Jenseits von Gut und Böse*, Section 260, in *Sämtliche Werke in zwölf Bänden*, (Stuttgart: Alfred Kröner Verlag, 1964), vol. 7, pp. 201–2; *Beyond Good and Evil: Prelude to a Philosphy of the Future*, trans. R. J. Hollingdale, ed. Michael Tanner (1973; London: Penguin, 1990), p. 195 (italics in the original, but note the verb 'feels').

14. See MacIntyre, *After Virtue*, especially pp. 6–35 on modern emotivism; and Taylor, *Sources of the Self*, pp. 53ff. on the problem of modern subjectivism.

15. Mann, *Werke*, vol. 6, pp. 108; *Doctor Faustus*, pp. 78–9.

16. *Werke*, vol. 6, p. 197; *Doctor Faustus*, p. 147.

17. *Werke* vol. 6, p. 258; *Doctor Faustus*, pp. 193–4.

18. William Austin testifies that *Pierrot lunaire* first established Schoenberg's international reputation: *Music in the Twentieth Century: From Debussy through Stravinsky* (New York: Norton, 1966), p. 195. For a collection of reviews, see Arnold Schoenberg, *Dossier de Presse de Pierrot lunaire*, ed. François Lesure (Geneva: Editions Minkoff, 1985). The work was the result of a commission from an actress, Albertine Zehme; there is no ground for concluding, however, that the poetic text does not reflect Schoenberg's aesthetic aims or fundamental outlook, as John C. Crawford and Dorothy L. Crawford assert in their *Expressionism in Twentieth-Century Music* (Bloomington: Indiana University Press, 1993), p. 86.

19. This is how Carl E. Schorske understands *Pierrot lunaire* in his *Fin-de-siècle Vienna: Politics and Culture* (New York: Vintage Books, 1981), pp. 355–7. On the other hand, Colin C. Sterne emphasizes the artist's search for inspiration as the essential subject of the work in his book, *Arnold Schoenberg, The Composer as Numerologist* (Lewiston, New York: Edwin Mellen Press, 1993), pp. 60–61. Most musicological discussions, however, do not take the text seriously: William Austin comments on the musical style at length without considering the import of the text in his *Music in the Twentieth Century*, pp. 195–211. Joan Peyser limits her analysis of the textual content to the remark: 'This Pierrot presents many apparently psychotic features whose significance was being brought to light by psychoanalytic psychology': *The New Music: The Sense Behind the Sound* (New York: Delacorte Press, 1971), p. 32. Crawford and Crawford simply take the poems to 'reflect the idea of art-for-art's sake – an attitude antithetical to expressionism' – and therefore evidently, not worth discussing: *Expressionism*, p. 86. Alan P. Lessem, however, does take the text seriously enough to devote several pages to dismissing its 'surface' quality of decadent aestheticism, arguing instead for the poems being an ironic commentary on *fin-de-siècle* decadence: *Music and Text in the Works of Arnold Schoenberg* (Ann Arbor: UMI Research Press, 1979), pp. 124–6. There are, however, good reasons for taking both the symbolism of the poetry and Schoenberg's appropriation of it seriously – rather than ironically – as a description of the modern world.

20. Albert Giraud, *Pierrot lunaire*, trans. Otto Erich Hartleben (Berlin: Verlag deutscher Phantasten, 1893).

21. In the discussion that follows, all poetic and musical quotations will be drawn from the piano reduction of *Pierrot lunaire*, made by Erwin Stein (Vienna: Universal Edition, [1984]). The texts of the poems are given on pp. 1–2. All translations are the author's.

22. Colin C. Sterne makes a convincing case for numerological influence in his

Arnold Schoenberg, The Composer as Numerologist, pp. 57–119: he sees pitches, note values, and all other musical parameters as informed by such occultism. This is consistent with the numerological superstition that is already well known: Joan Peyser remarks upon it in *The New Music*, pp. 10–11.

23. See James Hall, *Dictionary of Subjects and Symbols in Art*, rev. edn (New York: Harper and Row, 1979), p. 196.

24. Hall, *Dictionary of Subjects and Symbols*, p. 213.

25. Stephane Mallarmé's 'L'Après-midi d'un Faune' is one of the best known examples of Symbolist poetry today: though based on classical mythology, it is a poem of erotic memories or dreams. But the poetry of Paul Verlaine is more typical of much Symbolism: filled with despair over the decadence of the age and the meaninglessness of life, it expresses a pain that even the poet cannot identify precisely. In 'Il pleure dans mon coeur', Verlaine concludes: 'It is far the worst pain/not to know why,/without love or disdain,/my heart has such pain'. *French Symbolist Poetry*, trans. C. F. MacIntyre (Berkeley and London: University of California Press, 1958), p. 31.

26. The link between sexual promiscuity and psychological disintegration is apparent from many accounts of Bohemian life at the turn of the twentieth century. In his consideration of the literary circle surrounding August Strindberg in Berlin during the 1890s, Evert Sprinchorn documents the sexual obsessions and failed marriages of the poet Richard Dehmel, the minor novelist Stanislaw Przybyszewski, the painter Edvard Munch, as well as Strindberg himself: see his introduction to *Strindberg's Inferno, Alone and Other Writings*, trans. E. Sprinchorn (Garden City, New York: Doubleday, 1968), pp. 10ff.

27. It should be noted that this is not the last poem in Giraud's original cycle; it is No. 35.

28. That *Sprechstimme* was conceived as an explicitly expressive device is made clear in Schoenberg's diary for 1912: see Crawford and Crawford, *Expressionism*, pp. 86–7.

29. Quoted in Modris Eksteins, *Rites of Spring: The Great War and the Birth of the Modern Age* (Boston: Houghton Mifflin, 1989), pp. 9–10.

30. Igor Stravinsky, *An Autobiography* (1936; London: Calder and Boyars, 1975), p. 31. This element of propitiation is usually emphasized by concert guides and programme notes, since it makes the work more palatable by presenting the girl's death as purposive: see, for example, Arthur Jacobs, *Lend Me Your Ears: A Guide to Orchestral Music – From Vivaldi to Bernstein* (1987; New York: Avon Books, 1990), p. 327.

31. Theodor W. Adorno, *Philosophie der neuen Musik* (Frankfurt am Main: Europäischer Verlagsanstalt, 1958), p. 136; *Philosophy of Modern Music*, trans. Anne G Mitchell and Wesley V. Blomster (New York: Seabury Press, 1973), pp. 145–6.

32. Stravinsky's own words from an interview the day after the first performance confirm this: he sought 'to express the sublime uprising of the universal harvest'. Vera Stravinsky and Robert Craft, *Stravinsky in Pictures and Documents* (New York: Simon and Schuster, 1978), pp. 524–6. Here the emphasis on renewal makes death or sacrifice unnecessary. Eksteins agrees: see his *Rites of Spring*, p. 39.

33. For a discussion of Sorel and his *Reflections on Violence* (1908), see H. Stuart Hughes, *Consciousness and Society: The Reorientation of European Social Thought 1890–1930*, rev. edn (New York: Vintage Books, 1977), pp. 161–82; on the influence of Nietzsche in Expressionism, see Donald E. Gordon, *Expressionism: Art and Idea* (New Haven and London: Yale University Press,

1987), pp. 14–24.

34. The translations used here are given in Igor Stravinsky, *The Rite of Spring in Full Score* (New York: Dover Publications, 1989), reflecting Stravinsky's own preferences.

35. On the inconsistencies among the accounts of the premiere, see Ecksteins, *Rites of Spring*, pp. 10–16.

36. Adorno notes that the use of ostinato also helps to create a cohesive force to overcome the prevalence of dissonance: *Philosophie der neuen Musik*, p. 142; *Philosophy of Modern Music*, p. 152.

37. Ecksteins, *Rites of Spring*, p. 51.

38. Friedrich Wilhelm Joseph Schelling, *The Philosophy of Art*, ed. and trans. Douglas W. Stott (Minneapolis: University of Minnesota Press, 1989), Section 83, p. 117; Georg Wilhelm Freidrich Hegel, *Vorlesungen über die Ästhetik*, ed. E. Moldenhauer and K. Michel, *Werke in zwanzig Bänden* (Frankfurt am Main: Suhrkamp Verlag, 1970), vol. 15, pp. 165–70; *Aesthetics: Lectures on Fine Art*, 2 vols, trans T. M. Knox (Oxford: Clarendon Press, 1975), vol. 2, pp. 915–18.

39. Crawford and Crawford, *Expressionism*, p. 172. Stravinsky also heard *Pierrot lunaire* in rehearsal in Berlin in 1912, and he praised the 'musical imagination' of the work and the 'whole contrapuntal and polyphonic structure': Austin, *Music in the Twentieth Century*, pp. 263–4.

40. *Philosophie der neuen Musik*, pp. 148–9; *Philosophy of Modern Music*, p. 159.

41. Mann, *Werke*, vol. 6, p. 332; *Doctor Faustus*, p. 249.

42. Crawford and Crawford, *Expressionism*, p. 186.

43. Ibid., p. 189.

44. Ibid., p. 181.

45. Ibid., p. 186.

CHAPTER SIX

The New Music and the Influence of Theosophy

However much the bounds of tonality had been stretched by chromatic harmony in the nineteenth century, it was the proclamation of a 'New Music' by Arnold Schoenberg and his school that created a musical avant-garde radically divorced from the tradition. The initial form the New Music took was defined by the Expressionist style Schoenberg developed between 1908 and 1915. The works he composed in this period were characterized by what he called 'the emancipation of dissonance' from the necessity of resolving to consonance, and by the break from tonality altogether. Both of these factors affected the nature of his melodic writing as well, so that the tonal coherence of melodic lines was denied. In addition, many of the works were deliberately athematic, with even the repetition of motivic ideas avoided. Thus every aspect of style was a radical rupture with the past, even Schoenberg's own past practice. It was a rejection of everything that had been expected in music.

As we have seen, however, it was also explicitly a revolt against beauty.[1] The idea of beauty, however, once had had a definition, which when applied to music was capable of giving answers justifying the practices of tonal melodic and harmonic writing. Even the increasing subjectivism of aesthetic judgement at the end of the nineteenth century does not account for the rejection of the concept of beauty, for Schoenberg had already passed judgement on the efforts of music theorists: 'To hell with all these theories, if they always serve only to block the evolution of art and if their positive achievement consists in nothing more than helping those who will compose badly anyway to learn it quickly.'[2] Schoenberg's position therefore involved a rejection of both theoretical and aesthetic systems. Neither beauty nor law had any place in music for Schoenberg now.

He repeated this point more emphatically later in the *Harmonielehre*, in the chapter on non-harmonic tones. There he provided examples of dissonant chords in Bach and Mozart, which he claimed no aesthetician should allow, but which in fact arose from passing tones and neighbour tones in a manner consistent with standard eighteenth-century practice; Schoenberg's musical citations obscured the actual voice-leading.[3] From this he concluded that these were examples of 'ugliness' at the very heart of the traditional repertoire. 'But if it is really ugly, then who is right? The aesthetician or the artist? History leaves no doubt whatsoever about it, that he is right who will always be right: he who creates, even when it is ugly.' The artist did not need the concept of beauty: 'To him integrity is enough. To him it is enough to have expressed himself. To have said what had to be said; according to the laws of his nature.'[4] Thus integrity or truthfulness replaced the idea of beauty for Schoenberg: the composer had only to express himself honestly. What this means, therefore, becomes the problem.

The problem of musical Expressionism

Expressionism has generally been understood as a style founded on emotional self-expression.[5] The doctrine of self-expression has become so deeply ingrained in the artistic and musical ideology of the twentieth century that it is difficult to question it, or to imagine that there might be alternative aesthetic theories. Yet the genesis of this ideology in Schoenberg's writings suggests two pertinent questions: why was it essential to reject beauty, and what precisely did self-expression mean? To join them together: why did self-expression necessarily (on Schoenberg's view) entail the rejection of beauty? For Beethoven certainly 'expressed' his view of the world in his Ninth Symphony, and romantic composers from Schumann to Mahler put their deepest feelings into their music. But such expression was always tempered by the aim of representing beauty. Thus, for instance, Hegel's claim that music was the language of 'subjective inwardness' was subsidiary to the larger purpose of art as the representation of the ideal of personality.[6] Why were they able to do this in accordance with the idea of beauty, whereas suddenly at the beginning of the twentieth century, Schoenberg was not able to accept the relevance of beauty or any other criterion except 'truthfulness'? Why, in more musical terms, was it suddenly necessary for music to be dissonant, atonal and unmelodic in order to be truthful? These are questions that have never been answered satisfactorily, for they depend on seeing Schoenberg's compositional choices as deliberate rather than as a product of historical necessity, as he attempted to portray them.

As is now known, however, Schoenberg underwent a deep personal crisis during the years 1907 and 1908 as a result of his wife's affair with the painter Richard Gerstl. The nature of his crisis was long concealed: Schoenberg and his wife, Mathilde, had befriended a young Expressionist painter, Richard Gerstl, who was occupying quarters in their apartment when he ran off with Mathilde. She subsequently returned, but Gerstl committed suicide, so that Schoenberg suffered both a cruel betrayal and the loss of a close friend. He himself contemplated suicide, and never completely recovered the affection he had felt for his wife as a result of her betrayal.[7] It was the turning point in the development of his musical style.

That Schoenberg's modernism was the result of a turning point in his compositional practice, however, runs counter to one of the essential tenets of the avant-garde. As we have seen in Chapter 1, Schoenberg himself argued for the historical necessity of the 'emancipation of dissonance' after the freer treatment of dissonance by Wagner, Strauss, Mussorgsky, Debussy and others; his student, Anton Webern, later echoed the argument.[8] But the coincidence of Schoenberg's personal crisis and psychological trauma in 1908 with the first experiments with atonality cannot be discounted, however much the atonal style had been prepared by other composers' increased use of dissonance or his own increasing chromaticism since *Verklärte Nacht* of 1899. Thus the claims of historical inevitability with which both Schoenberg and Webern later justified the decisive break with tonality must be viewed as a mask concealing the actual impetus. In fact, this personal crisis was more than the impetus for the break with tonality: it was the inspiration and the essential content for much of the atonal music composed by Schoenberg between 1907 and 1912.

Certainly Schoenberg's own aesthetic before 1908 was not one of self-expression. The string sextet, *Verklärte Nacht*, Op. 3, was composed after a poem by the Symbolist poet, Richard Dehmel; it is a paean to an adulterous love that will 'transfigure' the child of a woman's loveless marriage.[9] Although the work appears uncannily prophetic in retrospect, it was composed two years before he married Mathilde. Schoenberg's music follows the poem closely, expressing both the woman's anguish and her lover's tenderness. Beginning in D minor and ending in D major, the work employs the traditional means of representing redemption from suffering. The tonalities are clear, as in Example 6.1(a), where the main theme is in D minor; the exception is one passage of extreme chromaticism ('Lebhaft bewegt', mm. 132–68), corresponding to the woman's moment of self-accusation. Nevertheless, even in this case, the motivic patterns are treated sequentially, and the harmonies are intelligible as consisting largely of diminished and half-diminished seventh chords, as shown in Example 6.1(b). The two measures shown in the latter case begin with an E-flat seventh chord and resolve on a G-six-four, that is, on the second inversion of the major subdominant; thus, in spite of diminished chords in the second half of each measure, the overall tonal impulsion lies within the borrowed harmonies of D minor. The other large works of the early years are similarly expressive of a programme or a text, rather than of Schoenberg's private life and, for all of their harmonic and contrapuntal complexities, are tonal with passages of exquisite beauty. The tone poem *Pelleas und Melisande*, Op. 5, and the sections of the *Gurrelieder* that were completed before 1908 demonstrate Schoenberg's commitment to the traditional, Romantic aesthetic.

Schoenberg first abandoned tonality altogether in the last movement of the String Quartet No. 2, Op. 10, composed in 1907 in the midst of his troubles. This movement was the setting of Stefan George's poem, 'Entrückung' (Release), describing death as a release from life and the return to a heavenly sphere:

a)   mm. 34–8

b)   mm. 138–9

Example 6.1   Arnold Schoenberg, *Verklärte Nacht*, Op. 4

I am dissolving in tones, circling, weaving,
Of baseless thanks and unnamed praise,
Resigning myself contentedly to the great Breath. ...
The earth trembles whitely and pliantly like whey.
I climb over enormous gorges.
I feel like I swim above the highest clouds
In a sea of crystalline brilliance –
I am a spark only of holy fire,
I am a resounding only of the holy voice. [10]

This is set to music which completely abandons a key signature and avoids any clear tonic (see Example 6.2). Here, if fidelity to the text were Schoenberg's aesthetic principle, it would be possible to understand atonality as the musical representation of the first line: 'I am dissolving in tones, circling, weaving.' But if Schoenberg were simply expressing his own sense of despair as he contemplated suicide, then atonality would have to be regarded as the accidental innovation suitable as the musical language of suicidal depression. Neither case, however, would appear important enough to support his claim to have discovered the historically necessary evolution of tonality into the next stage of the emancipation of dissonance, which has come to be called atonality. Nor, indeed, would Schoenberg's achievement have become so influential historically.

What should be noted above all is George's vision of death in this poem. For him, death meant the dissolution of the personality, so that there could be no real hope for the bliss of the soul after death. The great Breath or Spirit would absorb the soul; the spark of life would rejoin the larger heavenly flame; the individual's voice would become simply part of the divine voice. But the extinction of the personality through absorption into the divine is not an orthodox understanding of eternal life or the resurrection of the body in the Judeo-Christian tradition; it is rather a gnostic doctrine. [11] It is far from a consoling view: for it is the metaphysical guarantee of despair in the face of death. As we shall see, this becomes paradigmatic for understanding Schoenberg's musical creativity from this point forward.

With this understanding of the metaphysical nature of the text's teaching, however, there is little distinction between the principles of self-expression and the expression of the text in the Second String Quartet. Certainly there appears to be no tension between the two principles in the other large vocal works of Schoenberg's Expressionist period. In these, the texts themselves reflect Schoenberg's own psychological trauma. Thus, for example, in the *Fifteen Poems from 'Das Buch der hängenden Garten'*, Op. 15 (composed in 1908–09), Schoenberg took Stefan George's poetic description of the loss of love as a metaphor of his own life, reflecting that total loss in music now devoid of consonance and a tonal centre, and therefore lacking in coherent melody as well. [12]

The opera *Erwartung*, Op. 17 (also composed in 1909), similarly reflects

Example 6.2   Arnold Schoenberg, String Quartet No. 2, Op. 10, 4th movement, voice
and violin lines

the composer's own anxiety, even though it was composed to a libretto supplied by Marie Papenheim. In this ambiguous work, a woman anxiously looks for her lover, only to find him murdered – or perhaps only to find that she has murdered him. Although the librettist based her work on her own interest in pathological psychology, she wrote the text upon Schoenberg's request, and it is difficult not to see in it a close resemblance to his own psychic dissolution, or his own metaphorical 'murder' at the hands of his wife.[13] The music for the opera carried the dissolution of melody inherent in atonality to its furthest limits: Schoenberg avoided all motivic repetition as much as possible.[14] Consistent dissonance, the denial of a tonal centre, and the rejection of melody were the musical means of representing extreme psychic disorder. In this respect, Schoenberg was faithful to the logic of the traditional musical language, while rejecting the aesthetic of beauty and musical order.

Again, however, for these atonal works to be given the decisive historical status they have been afforded compels them to be regarded as transcending the purely personal. The intended public nature of musical performance makes an implicit claim for the universality of the truth of their expression. The texts, then, must be taken as describing the human condition itself, not merely Schoenberg's, and the music the nature of order in general. But this is precisely what proves troubling.

In his next work, *Die glückliche Hand*, Op. 18, Schoenberg united the principles of self-expression and fidelity to the text by writing the libretto himself. The initial sketches for the libretto to this strange and abbreviated opera were begun in the year of his crisis, 1908, but he did not begin work on the score until 1910; the music was completed only in 1913.[15] There is little action in the opera, but every detail is a transparent rendering of Schoenberg's position as the victim of his wife's adulterous affair. It opens with an anonymous Man in the grips of a hideous monster and the Chorus gently chastizing him for dreaming of worldly fulfilment. In the next scene, the Man sees a beautiful young Woman and seeks her love, but loses her to a Gentleman. The third scene finds the Man in a ravine in a wilderness, from which he ascends to a grotto. There he takes a hammer to a piece of gold, and smashing it, produces a jewel-studded diadem. Just then, however, the Woman reappears, her dress torn, followed by the Gentleman, who holds a part of her dress. The scene ends with the Man in utter despair, pleading for the vision of the Woman to stay with him. The final scene returns to the setting of the opening: the hideous monster once again has the Man in its clutches, and the Chorus lectures him. 'Did you have to live again what you so often lived? Can you never renounce? Never at last resign yourself? ... You seek to lay hold of what will only slip from you when you grasp it ... . You poor fool!'[16] The lesson Schoenberg drew from his experience is clear: there is no use in loving, nor any point in dreaming beautiful visions. Just as the diadem the Man had created had to be forfeited, beauty in Woman was not his to possess. For

Schoenberg, there was no beauty left to express in music; see Example 6.3 for the use of far sharper dissonances than we have seen in the earlier works. In particular, the reliance on minor seconds and major sevenths in the harmonies, together with the avoidance of any tonal centre, destroys any sense of aural beauty or order.

Given this unity between personal life and musical composition, the question of why self-expression seemed necessarily to entail the rejection of beauty may well appear to have a sufficient explanation in Schoenberg's personal affairs. In the works composed after 1907, he found or created a text reflecting his own perception of the lack of beauty in the world, and the music he wrote expressed that lack of beauty. Yet this is not an adequate explanation of Expressionism, for only the imperious demands of the doctrine of artistic self-expression could justify overriding the traditional aim of representing beauty and goodness, to which he had earlier subscribed. Moreover, as we have seen in *Pierrot lunaire*, the text chosen for that work reflected a general dissolution of moral bonds at the turn of the century; clearly it resonated with Schoenberg's own situation, but at the same time it transcended it. But to say that Expressionism was simply the product of a nervous breakdown would be to trivialize the emergence of atonality and to deny its predominant historical influence in the twentieth century. Other Expressionist composers and artists also suffered similar psychological difficulties – notably Kandinsky, Webern and Bartók.[17] But although such emotional instability is a striking feature of the first generation of the avant-garde, it does not suffice to explain specific stylistic choices. A better explanation of Expressionism must be sought.

Schoenberg's practice of uniting autobiographical expression and expression of a text is called into question, moreover, by his own remarks. For at the height of his Expressionist period, he denied all responsibility of music to an objective world outside the self – including fidelity to a text in vocal music. In an essay written for Wassily Kandinsky's almanac, *Der blaue Reiter* (1912), Schoenberg explicitly denied that he sought to represent the sense of the text, claiming that it was not only unnecessary but undesirable to do so. Rather than the text being expressed in the music, the music would reveal the personality of the composer directly.

> With compositions based on poetry the exactness of rendering the action is as irrelevant to its artistic value as the resemblance to the model is for a portrait. A hundred years later no one will be able to check the likeness, but the artistic effect will always remain. This effect will exist not because a real man, the man apparently depicted, appeals to us ... but because the artist appeals to us, the person who expressed himself here and who must be recognized in the portrait in a higher degree of reality.[18]

But this is to take the nineteenth-century interpretive doctrine of expressiveness, by which a composer was believed to express his character in his musical style, and transform it into a compositional programme, thus

Example 6.3   Arnold Schoenberg, *Die glückliche Hand*, Op. 18, final scene

Example 6.3   continued

Example 6.3   concluded

making his doctrine of self-expression a repudiation of responsibility to an objective world outside the self. In the previous century a composer's music was still faithful to a text within the expressive parameters of tonality; henceforth, fidelity to an objective model would be 'irrelevant'.

Moreover, from the perspective of the traditional understanding of the art of portraiture, this is an astonishing inversion of artistic value. Alberti, the Renaissance artist and theorist, had said that painting 'represents the dead to the living many centuries later, so that they are recognized by spectators with pleasure and deep admiration for the the artist'.[19] The admiration for the artist was dependent on the recognition of the person depicted, that is, on the perception of the artist's skill in capturing another person's character – not of the artist's self-expression. But Schoenberg not only denied this traditional aim of representational art; he praised the move toward abstract art by Wassily Kandinsky and Oskar Kokoschka, for whom 'the external object is hardly more ... than a stimulus to improvise in color and form and to express themselves as only the composer expressed himself previously'.[20] If these remarks are taken seriously, however, they cast doubt on the meaning of even the doctrine of self-expression, for such abstract improvisation would appear to reveal little recognizable about the artist.

Schoenberg's later efforts to define his artistic intentions during the period between 1908 and 1914 only add to the mystery of the meaning of the doctrine of self-expression for him. In a lecture delivered on the occasion of the 1928 Breslau production of *Die glückliche Hand*, he admitted that 'it is a certain pessimism which I was compelled to give form to at that time: "Fateful Hand, which tries to grasp that which can only slip away from you, if you hold it."'[21] But there was little discussion of music in the lecture, aside from a defence of the necessity of changes in style. Instead, he focused on a peculiar aspect of the opera, the great attention he demanded be paid to the lighting effects. The libretto is quite specific in calling for changes in the colour illuminating the set and the individual characters. The third scene, for instance, begins with a grey-green light, followed by yellow-green and blue-violet. As the man approaches one of the grottos, its light changes 'rather quickly from dark-violet to brown, red, blue and green, and then to a bright, delicate yellow (citrus-yellow)'.[22] In the lecture, Schoenberg called this 'making music with the media of the stage', so that colours as well as tones should create some sort of 'musical' effect.[23] Such synaesthetic theory was not unprecedented; Baudelaire, and later the Symbolist poets, had posited 'correspondences' between tones and colours, and more recently Scriabin had experimented with it in his tone poem, *Prometheus*, Op. 60 (1910).[24] Schoenberg's explanation, however, raises serious questions about the adequacy of emotional expression as a description of his artistic intentions in his opera.

Schoenberg sought to bring the media of the stage 'into relationship with each other according to deeper laws than the laws of the material ...'. Yet, he conceded,

> It would be completely arbitrary if one were, for example, to construct a scale of mime, or a rhythm of light. Naturally, such an endeavor could only be risked by someone who could trust his feeling for form and could say to himself that however the thoughts to be represented might be constituted, he was sure of being able to think them; however the feelings to be expressed might revolt others, he was sure he could order them. If one had this self-confidence, however, one could serenely abandon oneself to one's imagination, without theories.[25]

The emphasis on order and form in this passage would seem familiar if applied to music in the traditional manner, for musical rhythm and tonality depend on naturally perceptible relationships. Here, however, Schoenberg finds that a true analogue in the media of the stage would be arbitrary. But an order that is arbitrary is no order; it lacks the minimum condition of a perceptible form.[26]

Thus the passage does not articulate a traditional aesthetic. On the other hand, Schoenberg also denied the Expressionist aesthetic: 'This kind of art, I don't know why, has been called expressionist: it has never expressed more than was in it!' Rather, he preferred the label, 'art of the representation of inner processes'.[27] This peculiar phrase obscures Schoenberg's meaning, for thoughts and feelings are now replaced by 'inner processes' as the content of art. The result is to leave the nature of the new music suddenly open to question.

It is not clear, therefore, what the doctrine of self-expression meant to Schoenberg. In one breath, he admits the potentially repulsive nature of the feelings expressed, so that once again we see the rejection of the beautiful. In the next breath, however, he seems to deny any kind of emotional content extrinsic to the work. The latter may be regarded as a disingenuous mask of the now obviously autobiographical nature of Die glückliche Hand, but the term he preferred to describe his artistic aims, 'the representation of inner processes', then becomes all the more puzzling. In combination with the denial of fidelity to the text in his essay for Der blaue Reiter, these remarks of Schoenberg would seem to make it impossible to identify what the feelings or the 'inner processes' might be in any musical work. Schoenberg's aesthetic appears to approach meaninglessness.

Wassily Kandinsky, however, used much the same language in his essay, 'On Stage Composition', which he printed as an introduction to his play, 'The Yellow Sound', in Der blaue Reiter. Recognizing that each art is completely different in its method, he claimed that all the arts share the same final goal, knowledge, which 'is reached through delicate vibrations of the human soul'.[28] The goal, then, is an 'undefinable and still distinct spiritual action (vibration)', and 'when the artist finds the appropriate means, it is a material form of his soul's vibration, which he is forced to express'.[29] The representation of the soul's 'vibrations' was the foundation of Kandinsky's own synaesthetic theory – as in the title of the play – for the material media of tones, colours, and words could all equally express 'vibrational' states of the soul. He called these states 'the inner sound'.[30] The similarity to Schoenberg's 'inner processes' is clear.

Kandinsky drew several conclusions from the primacy of the the concept of an 'inner sound'. First, the 'external appearance of each element' in an artistic work ceased to matter; second, the more coherent the external appearance, the more the 'inner effect' would be weakened. 'External irregularities' – disharmonies in more traditional language – would therefore actually help to create a feeling of 'internal unity'.[31] Finally, from this dualism of 'inner sound' and external appearance, Kandinsky came to the 'practical discoveries' of using 'the inner sound of only one element' in a multimedia work, of eliminating the plot in a play and external unity in general, and allowing 'inner unity' to create 'an endless series of methods that earlier could not exist'.[32] It need hardly be pointed out that this programme involves the rejection of rational intelligibility altogether. Not only is the inner knowledge that he seeks through art indefinable; the severing of all connection between 'inner unity' and outward form means that such unity cannot be rationally perceivable.

Kandinsky's expressionist aesthetic, therefore, rested on an extremely peculiar understanding of human nature, perception and reality in general: this is the basis of his abstract art. Such art expressed an indefinable 'inner unity'. But if we recall that Schoenberg praised Kandinsky's abstract improvisations in colour and form in his essay for *Der blaue Reiter*, then the parallels between their views become much more significant. In fact, they had become good friends no later than January of 1911, so that the sympathy of their views calls for a closer examination.[33] Kandinsky's aesthetic of the visual arts helps to explicate the otherwise cryptic remarks of Schoenberg on music; their complementary conceptions of Expressionism reveal the underlying source of the latter's doctrine of the representation of inner processes. The concept of a new music, then, will become intelligible in terms larger than the merely autobiographical.

Artistic concepts in Kandinsky and Schoenberg

Kandinsky had praised Schoenberg's music already in his most famous theoretical work, *Concerning the Spiritual in Art* of 1911. 'His music leads us into a realm where musical experience is a matter not of the ear but of the soul alone – and from this point begins the music of the future.'[34] In this treatise, however, Kandinsky was much more specific about the nature of the soul's inner states, which the artist should try to express. Contrasting two principles of expression, the external and the internal, Kandinsky claimed:

> After the period of materialist effort, which held the soul in check until it was shaken off as evil, the soul is emerging, purged by trials and sufferings. Shapeless emotions such as fear, joy, grief, etc., which belonged to this time of effort, will no longer greatly attract the artist. He will endeavor to awake subtler emotions, as yet unnamed. Living himself a complicated and comparatively subtle life, his work will give to those observers capable of feeling them lofty emotion beyond the reach of words.[35]

But emotions that lie 'beyond the reach of words' must be non-rational feelings; he looked to such feelings, then, to rescue the soul from its more 'materialist' emotions, such as fear, joy and grief. These more common emotions are definable because they have specific objects and are awakened by definite causes. One fears something, or feels joyous because of some event, or grieves the loss of someone beloved. For that reason, they are always in some measure rational feelings.[36] Kandinsky, however, rejected them, preferring instead indefinable and unnamed emotions for artistic expression. By definition, these must be difficult to understand.

He was able, nevertheless, to give examples of these 'loftier' kinds of feelings in the Symbolist poetry and Impressionist music of the *fin de siècle*. The characters in Maeterlinck's dramas 'are not people of past times as are the heroes in Shakespeare. They are merely souls lost in the clouds, threatened by them with death eternally menaced by some invisible and sombre power.'[37] The sense of gloom, confusion and utter terror at the unknown seemed to Kandinsky to herald a new age of feeling. Similarly, he praised the music of Maeterlinck's contemporary, Claude Debussy, who had made an opera of Maeterlinck's *Pelléas et Mélisande*, for in his music, 'one hears the suffering and tortured nerves of the present time.'[38] He could have said the same of Schoenberg's music.

These examples illustrate the kind of unnamed and indefinable emotions Kandinsky expected to provide spiritual regeneration. Gloom, confusion, terror at the unknown, and tortured nerves are all emotional states lacking a definite object. Indeed, these are psychopathological, and it is not surprising to note that Kandinsky, like Schoenberg, had suffered intense psychological distress over a marriage that was coming apart – in 1907.[39] Yet, as in the case of Schoenberg, it would be an unfair trivialization of his aesthetic to perceive its essence as lying solely in the psychological traumas of its creator. When Kandinsky praised Symbolist poetry for causing the soul to experience 'an emotion which has no relation to any definite object',[40] the anti-rationalism of his aesthetic must be taken seriously. For Kandinsky, like Schoenberg, defined the pure life of the soul in terms of emotions that were not tied to the material world. For both men, this was 'the spiritual' in art.[41]

The reality of unnamed emotions without objects or material causes was what Kandinsky meant by his repeated insistence on 'internal truth' or 'inner meaning'.[42] The artist who possessed an 'inner need' had an emotional insight that required expression in a way as compelling as a claim of rational truth or knowledge, but it was not a rational truth. This language is strikingly similar to Schoenberg's claim in the *Harmonielehre* of the same year, that integrity or truthfulness is enough for the composer, whose own internal laws were to replace those of an externally imposed concept of beauty.[43] Hence truth appeared now in opposition to beauty in Schoenberg's formulation. Kandinsky, however, did not pose the dichotomy of inner and outer as a conflict between truth and the idea of beauty: he made a distinction rather between 'inner beauty' and 'outer beauty', in which '[t]o those who are not accustomed to it the inner beauty appears as ugliness because humanity in general inclines to the outer and knows nothing of the inner'.[44] Yet even here there is a radical dichotomy between inner and outer that replaces the traditional neo-Platonic concept of an inner beauty that informs and manifests itself by outwardly harmonious order. Kandinsky's 'inner beauty' excludes outward harmony precisely because the latter is rational and sensually perceptible. The inner is alone worthwhile because it is the world of non-sensuous emotions.

Kandinsky, however, was much more specific than Schoenberg regarding the aesthetic implications of such 'inner meanings' for art. Because the 'loftier' emotions lack objects, so too will their artistic depiction. Hence, unnamed emotions required abstract art, that is, art without the representation of objects.[45] For Kandinsky, forms and colours in themselves possessed an emotional content which could be perceived by a viewer. 'The forms, movement, and colours which we borrow from nature must produce no outward effect nor be associated with external objects. The more obvious is the separation from nature, the more likely is the inner meaning to be pure and unhampered.'[46] Abstract art, then, was the logically necessary consequence of his commitment to the fundamentally irrational emotions.

The parallels with Schoenberg's music are striking. Schoenberg described his music as the 'art of the representation of inner processes', so that his emphasis on self-expression at the expense of fidelity to the text becomes intelligible in light of Kandinsky's theories. Certainly the kinds of objectless emotions Schoenberg expressed in his music after 1908 resemble those Kandinsky praised: terror at the unknown, anxiety, confusion, despair. Although these feelings have names, they are not ordinary emotions. Finally, the musical means whereby such emotions were expressed – the atonal, unremittingly dissonant and unmelodic musical language – make Schoenberg's music sound as abstract as Kandinsky's Expressionist paintings look: there is no coherence created by recognizable musical events any more than the paintings embody coherent, rationally perceivable meanings through identifiable objects. For both Schoenberg and Kandinsky, the sacrifice of external beauty and order to an indefinable 'inner' unity, truth, knowledge, or process was vital for the regeneration of art. What lay at the heart of their shared Expressionist aesthetic, therefore, was not only a commitment to the representation of utterly irrational and pathological emotions. Rather, both men understood such emotions as the highest expression of the human spirit. In their view, it was the task of the arts to revive the capacity for people to feel these irrational emotions as a matter of spiritual renewal.

Kandinsky's more explicit theories thus help us to understand Schoenberg's otherwise puzzling doctrine of self-expression. The self that found expression in music consisted entirely of non-rational, objectless emotions, which were given embodiment in the music directly. There they created an 'inner' unity not dependent on external tonal ordering. Indeed, tonal ordering would diminish this inner unity; the rejection of the concept of beauty was a necessary step to the achievement of this elusive, non-rational quality. There are other aspects of Schoenberg's works in this period, however, that even more compellingly demand a reading in terms of Kandinsky's aesthetic. The synaesthetic use of colour in *Die glückliche Hand* is one of them, and the invention of 'tone-colour melody' (*Klangfarbenmelodie*) in the Five Pieces for Orchestra, Op. 16 (1909) is another. The two concepts are closely related and appear to parallel Kandinsky's emphasis on colour as the primary means of emotional expression. The similarities, moreover, suggest a common origin and provide a vital clue for understanding their deeply irrational views of human nature and artistic expression.

As we have seen, the visual aspect of colour was important to Schoenberg in *Die glückliche Hand*, where the stage directions specify the colours illuminating the set and the individual characters. The libretto also specifies the colours of the curtains, the clothes, and the elements of the set. Schoenberg himself placed great emphasis on the coloured lighting as an integral part of the opera: in a letter to Ernst Legal, General Director of the Kroll Opera in Berlin (14 April 1930), he insisted on 'the use of colored lights. Strong lights are needed, and good colors'.[47] That this was his first demand shows the importance he attached to it. In the lecture for the Breslau production in 1928, he explained his synaesthetic doctrine in terms reminiscent of Kandinsky:

> In reality, tones, if viewed clearly and prosaically, are nothing but a particular kind of vibrations of the air. As such they indeed make some sort of impression on the affected sense organ, the ear. By being joined with each other in a special way, they bring about certain artistic and, if I may be permitted the expression, certain spiritual impressions. Now since this capability is certainly not present in tones alone, it should be possible, under certain conditions, to bring about such effects with other media ... .[48]

Colour, therefore, was as expressive as musical tones. Moreover, Schoenberg used the telling phrase, 'spiritual impressions', to convey the idea of emotional effect. In both the expressiveness of colour and the way of phrasing the doctrine, Schoenberg recalls the teachings of Wassily Kandinsky.

Kandinsky, however, was explicit in his 1911 treatise concerning the emotional qualities inherent in colours. In his view, these qualities made colour intrinsically expressive, and necessarily aroused the embodied emotion in the viewer. Professing not to be sure whether colours acquired their expressive effect by traditional associations or somehow more directly, he nevertheless cited precedents for the expressive theory of colour in Goethe, Delacroix and more recently the Symbolists.[49] Certainly some of his expressive characteristics of colours are traditional, or at least understandable because of natural associations: blue as heavenly, green as restful ('the colour of summer'), white as the colour of purity, and black as the colour of grief and death. What is distinctive in this treatment, however, is the reduction of traditionally objective symbols to merely emotional expression: for instance, blue as the symbol of heaven yields a statement that 'the ultimate feeling it creates is one of rest'.[50] Thus, everything in the external world is reinterpreted in terms of the emotions aroused. It is not surprising, then, that the meanings of many other colours seem arbitrary: for instance, orange as the colour of confidence, violet as the colour of sadness, light red as the colour of strength and triumph.[51] Kandinsky's characterization of colours provides the key to unlock the mystery of Schoenberg's use of colour in *Die glückliche Hand.*

At the height of the action in the third scene, after the Man has made the diadem, he stands on the stage while a wind crescendos around him. Accompanying the wind is a 'light-crescendo', in which the changes of colour correspond to the Man's gestures. He looks at his hand in reddish light; 'his eyes grow excited' to dirty green light; he becomes obviously angry with blood-red light; and finally the storm ceases with a bright, yellow light. The Woman then emerges to a mild blue light.[52] According to Kandinsky, red in general expresses 'a determined and powerful intensity'; dirty green conveys the effect of 'violent raving lunacy'; and yellow has 'a material parallel in the human energy which assails every obstacle blindly'.[53] Thus, the light-crescendo is used to establish the Man's character and feelings in the moment between his production of the diadem (which had been greeted with hostility by the workers in the grotto) and the emergence of the Woman with her dress in disarray and in the company of the Gentleman. Interpreted according to Kandinsky's scheme, we understand the Man (representing Schoenberg) as determined and powerful in his creative life, but yielding to raving madness and anger before recovering the 'energy which assails every obstacle blindly'. The heavenly Woman, unfortunately, is lost to him forever. While not all of Schoenberg's uses of colour in the opera correspond so closely with Kandinsky's descriptions, this scene would be completely unintelligible without the key provided by Kandinsky.

With such a view of the expressive nature of colour, then, it is little surprise that Schoenberg would assert a similarly expressive use of tone colour. The idea of tone-colour melody was first employed in the third movement of the Five Pieces for Orchestra, Op. 16 (1909). Like the vocal works of this period, the Five Pieces were related to the crisis of the year before. The first movement is entitled 'Vorgefühle' (Forebodings), and the second 'Vergangenes' (The Past). Once again, the style is atonal and highly dissonant, conveying the anxiety and emotional pain of Schoenberg's private life. The third movement, however, is curiously static, consisting almost entirely of overlapping dissonant chords played by different groups of instruments. It was later entitled 'Summer Morning by a Lake: Colours', but this was a retrospective attempt to conjure an Impressionistic account of tone-colour melody. But Schoenberg was never much interested in the pure description of nature; the heart of his Expressionist aesthetic was the need to represent indefinable subjective feelings. This movement, then, demands an interpretation of the original title, 'Chord-Colours'.[54]

The third movement may best be understood in the context of the rest of the work as an autobiographical representation of his moment of crisis. The fourth movement's title, 'Peripetie', signifies a tragic reversal of fortune; containing both violent and lyrical music, this movement clearly corresponds to the shattering events of 1907–08 in the composer's life. The fifth movement, 'The Obbligato Recitative', combines tone-colour melody with a more active rhythmic interest. Imitating a Viennese waltz transformed into an atonal idiom without melodic formulas, it functions as a bitter commentary on life.[55] The crucial third movement, therefore, in which tone-colour melody appears in its purest form, is situated as a moment of suspension between the contemplation of the past in the second movement and the loss of tranquillity in the moment of crisis in the fourth. In the analogy with visual colours, it presents a shifting tableau of emotions discernible solely in the timbres employed in the orchestra: see Example 6.4 for the alternation between woodwinds and French horns (with English horn) at the opening of the movement as an illustration of the principle. Yet without a key to unlock the meanings of those timbres, the emotions remain undefinable.

Schoenberg gave a theoretical justification of tone-colour melody in his *Harmonielehre* two years later. Pitch, tone colour and volume were the three components of a musical tone, which he then argued reduced to two: tone colour and volume: 'I think the tone becomes perceptible by virtue of tone color, of which one dimension is pitch. Tone color is, thus, the main topic, pitch a subdivision.'[56] Taken at face value, this is astonishing neglect of even an elementary knowledge of physics. Nevertheless, Schoenberg went on to posit the possibility of progressions of tone colours analogous to the patterns of pitches that constituted ordinary melodies. That he did so at the end of the chapter on 'Chords With Six or More Tones' is revealing: such complex harmonies entailed substantial dissonances which undercut tonal coherence. Melody in the ordinary sense was precluded, therefore, so that tone-colour melodies might indeed appear as comparable entities.

Schoenberg, however, concluded the chapter with telling phrases as he advocated tone-colour melody as the future direction of the art of music. 'I firmly believe it is capable of heightening in an unprecedented manner the sensory, intellectual, and spiritual pleasures offered by art.' Believing that 'it will bring us closer to the illusory stuff of our dreams', he closed with oddly rapturous words: 'Tone color melodies! How acute the senses that would be able to perceive them! How high the development of spirit that could find pleasure in such subtle things!'[57] The use of 'spirit' and 'spiritual' affords the vital clue: they are the same words as in Kandinsky's vocabulary, where they are connected in a similar way with subtlety. Schoenberg, therefore, evidently regarded tone-colour melody as another expressive device comparable to visual colour in its ability to effect a direct communication of abstract, objectless emotions from the composer to the appropriately attuned listener.

The origin of such peculiar ideas thus becomes a pressing question. It is

Example 6.4   Arnold Schoenberg, Five Pieces for Orchestra, Op. 16, 3rd movement

Example 6.4   concluded

unlikely that Schoenberg knew Kandinsky before 1911, yet tone-colour melodies had been used in the Five Pieces for Orchestra in 1909. Moreover, the emphasis on visual colour in *Die glückliche Hand* also bears an early date, for the libretto was begun in 1908 and completed in 1910; only then did Schoenberg turn to writing the music. But Kandinsky's own interest in the expressive properties of colour also dates from 1908, long before he knew Schoenberg. It is therefore reasonable to suppose that they were influenced by the same source, and that their artistic friendship was nourished by their pre-existing, common interest.[58] Here lies the key to understanding the origin of Schoenberg's musical doctrines during the period of his decisive break with tonality.

The theosophical origins of Expressionism

The origin of both Kandinsky's theory of colour and concept of the spiritual is well established.[59] The theosophical writings of Madame Blavatsky, Annie Besant, Charles Leadbeater and Rudolf Steiner were vital influences on Kandinsky's thinking beginning in 1908.[60] This was the year after his own period of psychological distress; introduced to theosophy by a student, he perhaps turned to the theosophists for help in coping with his own psychological problems. He attended lectures given by Steiner in Berlin and had other opportunities in Munich, so that even though he did not formally join the Theosophical Society in Germany, he was nevertheless deeply imbued with the theosophists' teachings and endorsed their understanding of the human soul and spiritual reality.[61] But 1908 was a significant year in the history of theosophy in Germany in any event, for both Leadbeater's *Man Visible and Invisible* and Besant and Leadbeater's *Thought-Forms* were translated into German in that year.[62] These books provided systematic expositions of the associations of colours and shapes with emotions, a source of much of Kandinsky's own artistic practice in his abstract paintings.[63] Rudolf Steiner had also described the 'spiritual' meanings of colours in his *Theosophy* of 1904 and in other writings.[64] These efforts purported to find the meaning of colours vital for perceiving the spiritual nature of a person's soul. Thus, there was a large body of theoretical literature to guide artists – and composers – interested in the emotional significance of colour and its implications for synaesthesia in the arts.

Since the assignment of meanings to colours is essentially arbitrary, it is not surprising that Kandinsky occasionally departed from his sources in creating his own theory. Nevertheless, the consistency among Kandinsky, his sources and Schoenberg's usage is striking. Table 6.1 identifies the meanings of colours according to Leadbeater, Steiner and Kandinsky, together with the use of colour by Schoenberg in *Die glückliche Hand*.[65]

Table 6.1   Use of colours in Leadbeater, Steiner, Kandinsky and Schoenberg

	Leadbeater	Steiner	Kandinsky	Schoenberg's use
Violet		Nobility	Sadness	Goblet (ii)
Blue	Religious	Devotion	Heavenly	Woman (iii)
Green	Ingenuity	Adaptability	Restful	Chorus (i)
Yellow	Intellectuality	Clear thought	Energetic	Man (iii)
Orange	Pride	Conceit, pride	Confidence	
Red	Anger	Anger	Strength	Man (iii)
Scarlet	Noble anger			
Rose	Love	Unselfish love		
Blood-red	Sensuality	Sensuality		Man (iii)
Black	Malice		Grief	
Grey	Depression		Motionlessness	Chorus (iv)
Brown	Avarice	Animal passion		
Grey-green	Deceit			Woman (iii)
Yellow-green			Lunacy	Man (iii)
White			Purity, joy	

In conjunction with the earlier discussion of Schoenberg's opera, the table shows the composer's indebtedness to theosophical colour theory. Whereas the light-crescendo in the third scene, showing the transformation of the Man's emotions, can be interpreted fairly well in terms of Kandinsky's assignment of meanings, there are other colour associations which demand a reading by means of other sources. At the end of the third scene, in particular, the stage is illuminated by 'a pale, greenish-gray light' when the Gentleman appears with the Woman; here, Leadbeater's attribution of deceit to the colour appears crucial. Similarly, the Chorus is illuminated with grey-blue in the final scene ('somewhat tinted with red') as they preach renunciation to the Man; the use of grey may well suggest depression.[66] The consistency with Leadbeater as well as his future artist-friend, Kandinsky, suggests a close reliance on theosophical sources for Schoenberg as early as 1908.

Other details as well suggest a source of Schoenberg's imagery in theosophical writings. The hideous monster that gnaws at the Man's neck in the first and fourth scenes recalls a description that Steiner gives of the relation between the 'inner' and the 'outer' worlds according to theosophy's esoteric claims: 'Just as someone in the physical world entirely surrounded by mirrors could observe his physical body on all sides, so too, in a higher world, man's soul-being confronts him as a mirror image.' Hence, 'Passions seated in man's lower nature may assume the forms of animals or similar figures which hurl themselves upon the individual concerned.'[67] The resemblance is close enough to be more than coincidental. More broadly, Schoenberg's use of the terms 'inner' and 'spiritual' conforms to theosophical usage, where the 'inner world' offered the point of contact with the 'spiritual': the 'outer world' was material and evil, as it was for Kandinsky.[68] We may conclude, therefore, that Schoenberg was influenced by theosophy throughout the period 1908–12, and that *Die glückliche Hand* in particular was a pre-eminently theosophical work.

To say this, however, is to place the influence of theosophy on Schoenberg much earlier than is generally acknowledged. The influence of Kandinsky on Schoenberg after 1911 is well established, and the relevance of the theosophical ideas of reincarnation and karma for the unfinished oratorio, *Die Jakobsleiter*, has been suggested.[69] In general, however, a number of diverse sources have been suggested for Schoenberg's concept of a new music without identifying the precise contribution of each.[70] But a more direct influence of theosophy on Schoenberg's thinking, beginning in 1908, would account for a number of puzzling aspects of Schoenberg's new style. Not only does it explain the emphasis on visual colour in *Die glückliche Hand*; it also makes the parallel emphasis on tone colour in the Five Orchestral Pieces intelligible. The creation of tone-colour melody, which must surely appear one of the oddest aspects of the New Music, is explicable if seen as something requiring 'the development of the spirit'[71] – in a theosophical sense. The connection between colour and music was, after all, important to Alexander Scriabin, and he is known to have been a theosophist.[72] More fundamentally, however, theosophy explains the doctrine of self-expression out of 'inner need', together with the particular characteristics of the new musical language Schoenberg created. This spiritual movement, to which Schoenberg like Kandinsky likely turned for solace, was the crucible in which the New Music was forged.

The emancipation of dissonance is the most obvious characteristic of the New Music. The connection of theosophy with this is easy to see in the writings of other composers who contributed to Kandinsky's almanac in 1911. Theodore von Hartmann, for example, a known theosophist, stated baldly in his essay, 'On Anarchy in Music': 'External laws do not exist.' He then continued:

> In all the arts, and especially in music, every method that arises from an inner necessity is right. The composer wants to express what at the moment is the intention of his intuition. At this moment he might feel the need for a combination of sounds, which, according to present theory is regarded as cacophonous. It is obvious that such a judgment of theory cannot be considered an obstacle in this case.

Once again, the emphasis on 'inner necessity' is used to justify a repudiation of any merely 'outer' law of tonality or consonance. Accordingly, Hartmann redefined beauty as 'the correspondence of the means of expression with inner necessity'.[73] This resembles Kandinsky's own redefinition of beauty: 'That is beautiful which is produced by the inner need, which springs from the soul.'[74]

Thus, 'spiritual harmony' was quite different from harmony in the traditional sense. For Kandinsky, harmony in the spiritual sense consisted in the juxtaposition of contrasts, not in the properties of proportion, balance or order: 'The strife of colours, the sense of balance we have lost, tottering principles, unexpected assaults, great questions, apparently useless striving, storm and tempest, broken chains, antitheses and contradictions, these make up our harmony.'[75] In short, theosophists tended to employ words to mean exactly the opposite of the traditional meaning. Hence, Hartmann could conclude that 'any combination of sounds, any sequence of tone combinations is possible'.[76] In Schoenberg's language, dissonance was emancipated, but here not on any ground of historical inevitability; rather for the purpose of expressing the 'inner need' of the theosophical composer.

What, then, was this theosophy that was so important for the formation of both modern abstract painting and atonal music? Conceived in the 1870s by Madame Blavatsky, theosophy attained a wide following in Europe and the United States by the beginning of the twentieth century. As Rudolf Steiner explained it, following Madame Blavatsky, theosophy was a 'spiritual' system of understanding, based on a 'hidden wisdom' recovered in the East. In truth, it is a syncretistic system that takes some Western ideas about the soul and combines these with elements of Buddhism and Hinduism, especially the doctrines of reincarnation and karma, the latter being the justice whereby a person is held to live the next life according to what was earned in the present one.[77] There is no belief in God as the Creator, nor in an eternal life spent in a beatific vision of God.[78] For Madame Blavatsky, indeed, theosophy was an alternative to Christianity, to which she was decidedly hostile.[79] For Steiner, however, it was important to attempt a reconciliation of the two, which he accomplished by a docetic understanding of Christ's incarnation: the perfect soul of Christ could not really have been united with the body that suffered.[80] Leaving aside this element, however – although it did cause Steiner to separate from the Theosophical Society – theosophy flourished largely because its insistence on the spiritual appeared as an occult alternative to the positivism of modern science in a world now perceived as meaningless.[81] As a consequence of this occultism, however, its view of reality was deeply non-rational.

The theosophical understanding of the human being begins to reveal the scope of this non-rationality. We shall take Steiner's model of the human being as he presented it in his *Theosophy* (1904) as most relevant to Schoenberg and Kandinsky.[82] Whereas it has been traditional in the West to conceive of human nature as the union of body and soul, theosophy added a third component higher than the soul: the spirit. Each of these was in turn divided into three, but in such a way that there were two cases of overlapping levels.[83] Table 6.2 shows Steiner's schema representing the components of the human being,

Table 6.2   Levels of the soul according to Rudolf Steiner

Spirit	*Soul*	*Body*
1. Spirit-man (the essence of the spiritual)		
2. Life-spirit (spiritual life-force)		
3. Spirit-self = Consciousness-soul (intuitions of the spiritual)		
4.	Intellectual-soul (the 'I': feelings)	
5.	Sentient-soul =	Astral-body (desires)
6.		Life-body (vital life-force)
7.		Physical body (the senses)

together with a translation of their meaning into more familiar langauge. What is important here is that the 'intellectual soul' or the 'I' is defined as feelings, not as intellect having the capacity for rational thought. The self as ordinarily understood thus becomes explicitly emotivist, while the spiritual self remains undefined.

In this table, the spiritual levels function as a mirror image of the three levels of the body; otherwise, they lack definition. Yet it is the spirit, not the soul, that theosophy expected to be reincarnated.[84] The three levels of the spirit were held to constitute 'a perceptible reality as the higher, truly spiritual part of the aura' surrounding an individual.[85] Theosophists claimed that this aura could really be seen, but only spiritually, by someone who was spiritual enough to be clairvoyant. The aura could be depicted very clearly, however: it consisted of an egg-shaped image surrounding the human body, filled with the colours expressive of the person's desires, passions and character. Both Annie Besant and Charles Leadbeater supplied illustrations of such auras in their books, it being for this purpose that they developed their theories of colour expression.[86] Kandinsky's painting, *Dame in Moscow*, makes use of precisely such auras.[87] But the spotlights on a stage could even more effectively create the appearance of auras: hence Schoenberg's use of coloured lights in *Die glückliche Hand*. The use of colour was not simply as an adjunct means of expression in the opera; rather, it supplied the *essential* spiritual content. Music represented the passions of the soul, but the colours took the expression to the yet higher dimension of the spiritual.

In spite of the fact that the spirit was theoretically indefinable, it was nevertheless supposedly perceivable. As a mirror image of the physical part of human nature, it reflected the desires and vitalist life-force of the human body. Desires, passions and feelings were therefore the fundamental constituents of human nature for the theosophists: reason had no place. Self-expression was necessarily the expression of emotions, and perception of 'the spiritual' the sensual awareness of feeling. The anti-rationalism of the theosophical understanding of human nature is what lies behind Expressionism in both art and music.

The question of why it seemed necessary for Schoenberg to reject a rationally intelligible beauty in the name of self-expression has now received an initial answer. It was not simply his personal crisis that precipitated the development of a new style of music that was highly dissonant, atonal and unmelodic. Although the events of 1907–08 and his reactions to them supplied him with material for composition over the next several years, the doctrine of self-expression by which the musical representation of his private pain was justified stemmed rather from a theosophical understanding of the self. Theosophy saw the self as purely emotive and non-rational, surrounded by an aura that revealed the inner nature of the human person. The 'inner need' for expression, therefore, was not so much an inner drive or compulsion as a logical necessity: the outward expression could only reflect the inner self. Thus the outward appearance – in music, the sonic surface – could not matter. Beauty became irrelevant to the representation of 'spiritual truth'.

Theosophy, then, played a crucial role in the birth of musical and artistic modernism. It supplied the ideology which demanded the replacement of beauty with the doctrine of self-expression. This role of theosophy has not been understood, for even when Schoenberg's interest in esoteric spirituality has been noted, the temptation has always been to see theosophy as similar to other religions; the modern distance from religious faith fosters a view of one religious belief as being equivalent to another. But Judaism and Christianity both understand man to be made in God's image and after His likeness (Gen. 1:26), and the main traditions of Christian theology have understood the image of God to be reason itself.[88] It does make a difference, therefore, what kind of spirituality Schoenberg sought in the depths of his crisis in 1908 and after.

Theosophy is a gnostic religion; it denies the goodness of the materiality of the world in order to ensure the purity of the human spirit. Its conception of the spirit is as alien to the sensible world: Madame Blavatsky conceived the divine spirit as showering 'its radiance on the inner man', so that the human soul would seek its immortality by ascending to absorption in the spirit and losing its personality. Nevertheless, for both Blavatsky and Steiner the spirit was never to come to rest in heaven, but would be reincarnated, thus preserving its alienation perpetually.[89] But with the separation of spirit from soul, theosophy sees the soul as comprised of feelings and passions, corrupted by bodily existence. Existence in this life, therefore, becomes fundamentally suspect because of the imprisoning nature of matter. But if matter is thus the enemy of the spirit, the spirit ceases to be sensually perceivable, and the perception of material order ceases to be important. Hence follows a radical transformation of the conception of human nature, for when materiality is stripped away from what matters in perception, the comprehension of patterns found in material form ceases to be the task of perception. The irony of theosophy, then, is that in denigrating the material world in order to seek the spiritual, the human spirit itself ceases to be definable. The search for spirituality becomes a quest for the unknowable, and the perception of knowable order becomes that of a prison. This is the reason for the deep anti-rationalism of theosophical aesthetics in its rejection of the order of beauty.

To say all this, however, is to raise an important philosophical question, one that cannot be avoided in any honest assessment of the historical origins of modernism. The replacement of the aesthetic of beauty with the doctrine of self-expression not only becomes intelligible in light of the influence of theosophical spirituality; it also necessarily becomes suspect from the traditional point of view, because it rests on the rejection of reason as the defining characteristic of human nature. As we have seen, to deny human rationality is not simply to reject the philosophical tradition that has undergirded Western civilization; it is to deny human nature altogether. For musical and artistic modernism, then, the question is not merely one of historical influences, or a matter of setting one aesthetic against another and noting the differences. Instead, the question demands to be asked: which one is an adequate understanding of human nature?

Atonal music turns out to be deeply non-rational, both in the implicit lack of order in the rejection of consonance, a tonal centre and melodic organization, and in its origins and its justifying ideology. But the denial of order in the music is a repudiation of the association of music with the metaphysical categories defining the good: unity, harmony and ordination toward a *telos*. To deny the good is, however, to deny the goodness of existence itself. Moreover, since any claim for the truth of the Expressionist aesthetic necessarily entails a view of human nature as fundamentally non-rational, its claim for truth in understanding of human nature is subject to judgement of its truth and adequacy; therefore, the Expressionist aesthetic itself will also be subject to the same judgement. Such a judgement ceases to be a matter simply of personal taste.

Given the influence on other composers, however, Schoenberg's development of atonality as a consequence of theosophical inspiration must rank as one of the determinative events for the history of music in the twentieth century. It is nevertheless true that Schoenberg's development of the New Music did not stop with simple atonality; he went on to develop the Twelve-Tone Method, which seemed to impose a degree of rationality and order on the compositional process. To what extent it did so in fact becomes the crucial question: did it really alter the nature of atonality? Certainly no consideration of the problem of atonality would be complete without an examination of its subsequent history, for its later forms might suggest that the initial stage of its development was too fragile to endure long as a quest for spiritually significant music. But the importance of this question cannot be overestimated for another reason: Schoenberg's development of the Twelve-Tone Method guaranteed the long hold of the avant-garde on the world of art music. Thus a close scrutiny of the next stage of Schoenberg's development becomes imperative.

Notes

1. Arnold Schoenberg, *Theory of Harmony*, trans. Roy E. Carter (Berkeley: University of California Press, 1978), p. 10.
2. Ibid., p. 9.
3. Ibid., p. 324. Later, Schoenberg provides a fuller citation of the passages in question, where the voice-leading clearly refutes his own argument (p. 327). He concludes: 'It is certain that harsh harmonies, since they appear in Bach and thus surely cannot be aesthetic flaws, are actually requirements of beauty, if beauty is itself a requirement' (p. 328). This misses the point, for the traditional aesthetic of beauty required the resolution of dissonance, not its avoidance. The dissonances in the examples he cites do in fact resolve.
4. Ibid., p. 325.
5. Cf. John C. Crawford and Dorothy L. Crawford, *Expressionism in Twentieth-Century Music* (Bloomington: Indiana University Press, 1993), p. 1.
6. G. W. F. Hegel, *Vorlesungen über die Ästhetik*, ed. E. Moldenhauer and K. Michel, *Werke in zwanzig Bänden* (Frankfurt am Main: Suhrkamp Verlag, 1970), vol. 15, p. 133, vol. 13, pp. 204–10; *Aesthetics: Lectures on Fine Art*, 2 vols, trans. T. M. Knox (Oxford: Clarendon, 1975), vol. 2, p. 889, vol. 1, pp. 154–8.
7. The affair was first related briefly by Joan Peyser in her book, *The New Music: The Sense Behind the Sound* (New York: Delacorte Press, 1971), pp. 23–5. Documentary evidence of Schoenberg's suicidal inclinations at the time is provided in Crawford and Crawford, *Expressionism*, pp. 69–70. Both studies emphasize the role of Schoenberg's psychological troubles in his development of atonality, as does Carl E. Schorske in his *Fin-de-siècle Vienna: Politics and Culture* (New York: Random House, 1981), pp. 354–5.
8. Arnold Schoenberg, 'Composition with Twelve Tones (1)' in *Style and Idea*, ed. Leonard Stein, trans. Leo Black (Berkeley: University of California Press, 1984), pp. 216–18. Anton Webern similarly argued for the historical inevitability of a style based on complete dissonance in *The Path to the New Music*, ed. Willi Reich, trans. Leo Black (1963; London: Universal, 1975), pp. 36–9. Both, however, rest on assumptions of linear progress and historical determinism, which must be rejected theoretically, just as they are belied by the particular example of Schoenberg's own choices.
9. 'Verklärte Nacht,' from Richard Dehmel's 'Weib und Welt', is given as the preface to the score of *Verklärte Nacht: Sextett für zwei Violinen, zwei Violen und zwei Violoncelli* (Berlin: Verlag Dreililien, [n.d.]).
10. Author's translation of George's text in Stefan George, *Werke*, 2nd edn, 2 vols (Munich: Helmut Kupper, 1958), vol. 1, p. 293.
11. The doctrine of the resurrection of the body in both Judaism and Christianity precludes this kind of absorption into the divine. In particular, Christian teaching insists on the preservation of the intellect and the will, the essential constituents of the human person, in the life of the world to come. Cf. St Thomas Aquinas, *Summa Contra Gentiles*, Book IV, Chapter 92, and Book III, Chapters 47–53. For

a brief description of ancient gnostic belief regarding the salvation of the spirit, see Hans Jonas, *The Gnostic Religion: The Message of the Alien God and the Beginnings of Christianity*, 2nd edn (Boston: Beacon Press, 1963), pp. 44–5. As we shall see, this will become central to Schoenberg's view of life.

12.   Schorske's discussion of this work remains one of the best in the literature, as he recognizes its pivotal importance; see his *Fin-de-siècle Vienna*, pp. 345–54.

13.   On the origin of the text, see Alan Philip Lessem, *Music and Text in the Works of Arnold Schoenberg: The Critical Years, 1908–1922* (Ann Arbor: UMI Research Press, 1979), pp. 67–8.

14.   It was Anton Webern who first called attention in 1912 to the 'giving-up of all thematic work'. For a discussion of the literature on this, see John C. Crawford's essay, 'Schoenberg's Artistic Development to 1911', in *Arnold Schoenberg, Wassily Kandinsky: Letters, Pictures and Documents*, ed. Jelena Hahl-Koch, trans. John C. Crawford (London: Faber and Faber, 1984), p. 184. As the Crawfords point out in their *Expressionism*, p. 83, there are symbolic leitmotives employed, but they are very short and do not suffice to make up a motivic construction of themes.

15.   This discussion is based on the translation of the drama given in *Arnold Schoenberg, Wassily Kandinsky*, pp. 91–8.

16.   Ibid., pp. 97–8.

17.   See Crawford and Crawford, *Expressionism*, pp. 70, 95, and 178 respectively.

18.   Arnold Schoenberg, 'Das Verhältnis zum Text', in *Der blaue Reiter*, eds Wassily Kandinsky and Franz Marc, new edition ed. Klaus Lankheit (Munich: R. Piper Verlag, 1965), p. 75; 'The Relationship to the Text', in *The Blaue Reiter Almanac*, ed. Wassily Kandinsky and Franz Marc, trans. and ed. Klaus Lankheit (1974; reprinted New York: Da Capo Press, [n.d.]), p. 102.

19.   Leon Battista Alberti, *On Painting*, trans. Cecil Grayson (London: Penguin, 1991), p. 60.

20.   'Das Verhältnis zum Text', *Der blaue Reiter*, p. 74; 'The Relationship to the Text', *Blaue Reiter Almanac*, p. 102.

21.   'Breslau Lecture on *Die glückliche Hand*', in *Arnold Schoenberg, Wassily Kandinsky*, p. 107. The translation of 'glückliche' as 'fateful' is corroborated here by Schoenberg's pessimism.

22 .   *Die glückliche Hand*, in *Arnold Schoenberg, Wassily Kandinsky*, p. 95.

23.   'Breslau Lecture', in *Arnold Schoenberg, Wassily Kandinsky*, p. 105. Curiously, in spite of the emphasis that Schoenberg placed on the lighting effects in the opera, these have received little attention in the literature. Jelena Hahl-Koch virtually ignores the matter in her essay, 'The Stage Works', in this volume, pp. 152ff, and the Crawfords do not mention it at all in their discussion of the opera in their *Expressionism*, pp. 84–6. Only Karl H. Wörner takes it seriously; see his *Die Musik in der Geistesgeschichte: Studien zur Situation der Jahre um 1910* (Bonn: Bouvier, 1970), pp. 156–60.

24.   Baudelaire's poem, 'Correspondances', asserted that 'Les parfums, les couleurs et les sons se répondent', a claim that became fundamental for the Symbolists; see Andrew G. Lehmann, *The Symbolist Aesthetic in France, 1885–1895* (Oxford: Basil Blackwell, 1950), pp. 166ff. Joris Karl Huysmans made the synaesthetic experience the central element of the aestheticism of his Decadent novel, *A Rebours* (1884). The ultimate source of this strange notion was Emanuel Swedenborg, who thought that 'it is not just everything in the human body that corresponds [to heavenly or spiritual qualities], but everything in the universe as well': *The Universal Human and Soul-Body Interaction*, ed. and trans. George F. Dole (New York: Paulist Press, 1984), p. 193. Hence, colours necessarily

symbolized or corresponded to spiritual, moral, and emotional qualities, as well as to other sense perceptions. Swedenborg's occult mysticism was one of the important – and often underestimated – influences on nineteenth- and twentieth-century avant-garde culture, as we shall explore in the next chapter.

25. 'Breslau Lecture', Arnold Schoenberg, Wassily Kandinsky, p. 105.
26. This is the fundamental criticism which must be directed against atonality in music. But here it is pertinent to note that colours cannot be ordered into relationships that are harmonious in any sense analogous to music, because musical consonance depends on ratios of frequency in waveforms that are perceptible because of interference and reinforcement, whereas colours do not have waveforms that are similarly perceptible in their combinations.
27. 'Breslau Lecture', *Arnold Schoenberg, Wassily Kandinsky*, p. 105.
28. Kandinsky, 'Über Bühnenkomposition', *Der blaue Reiter*, p. 190; 'On Stage Composition', *The Blaue Reiter Almanac*, p. 190.
29. *Der blaue Reiter*, pp. 191–2; *The Blaue Reiter Almanac*, p. 191.
30. *Der blaue Reiter*, p. 202; *The Blaue Reiter Almanac*, p. 199.
31. *Der blaue Reiter*, pp. 202, 206; *The Blaue Reiter Almanac*, p. 199.
32. *Der blaue Reiter*, p. 206; *The Blaue Reiter Almanac*, p. 201.
33. Although Karl Wörner is willing to place the beginning of Schoenberg's and Kandinsky's friendship as early as 1909 or 1910 in *Die Musik in der Geistesgeschichte*, p. 187, their first two letters appear to refute this, being dated the 18th and 24th of January 1911. See their correspondence in *Arnold Schoenberg, Wassily Kandinsky*, pp. 21–5. In a footnote to her discussion of this issue, Jelena Hahl-Koch suggests 'that both were influenced by a common earlier source' (note 86, p. 198), but the role of theosophy remains conjectural for her (p. 144). The crucial point is that there appears to have been no mutual influence before January of 1911.
34. Wassily Kandinsky, *Concerning the Spiritual in Art*, trans. M. T. H. Sadler (New York: Dover Publications, 1977), p. 17.
35. Ibid., p. 2.
36. More precisely, there is the possibility of the emotions being controlled by reason. This is a point that Thomas Aquinas makes in the *Summa Theologica*, trans. Fathers of the Dominican Province, 5 vols (1911; Westminster, MD: Christian Classics, 1981), Pt I–II, q.17, art.7, vol. 2, p. 660. Hence he delineates the kinds of emotions felt by the relation one has to the object of feeling: love, desire and joy are awakened by a specific object, these three emotions forming a sequence moving from the psychic union with the object in love to the full possession of the object in joy. A similar movement is found in the contrary sequence of hate, aversion and sadness. On this, see the excerpt from St Thomas's treatise *On Truth*, q.26, art.4, c, in *An Aquinas Reader: Selections from the Writings of Thomas Aquinas*, ed. Mary T. Clark (1972; New York: Fordham University Press, 1988), pp. 256–7.
37. *Concerning the Spiritual in Art*, p. 14.
38. Ibid., p. 16.
39. Will Grohmann, *Wassily Kandinsky: Life and Work*, trans. Norbert Guterman (New York: Abrams, 1958), p. 53.
40. *Concerning the Spiritual in Art*, p. 15.
41. Schoenberg spoke of 'spiritual impressions' in the passage of his 'Breslau Lecture on *Die glückliche Hand*', in which he defined his music as 'the art of the representation of inner processes' rather than an art of 'material meaning': *Arnold Schoenberg, Wassily Kandinsky*, p. 105.
42. *Concerning the Spiritual in Art*, pp. 9, 29, 50 (for example). Kandinsky's use of

the word 'inner' reflects a metaphysical dualism in which the inner or spiritual is contrasted with the outer or material. Hence he speaks of the 'inner life' (ibid., p. 1), 'inner harmony' (p. 15), and 'inner need' (pp. 26, 32); also 'inner sound,' 'inner unity' and 'inner value' in the essay examined above, 'On Stage Composition'.

43. Schoenberg, *Theory of Harmony*, pp. 9, 325.
44. Kandinsky, *Concerning the Spiritual in Art*, p. 16.
45. Ibid., p. 32.
46. Ibid., p. 50.
47. Quoted in *Arnold Schoenberg, Wassily Kandinsky*, p. 98.
48. Ibid., p. 105.
49. *Concerning the Spiritual in Art*, pp. 24–5, 27.
50. Ibid., pp. 38–9.
51. Ibid., pp. 40–41.
52. *Arnold Schoenberg, Wassily Kandinsky*, p. 96.
53. *Concerning the Spiritual in Art*, pp. 24–7. Wörner notes the similarity of Schoenberg's and Kandinsky's interest in the expressive properties of colour, but interprets the colour symbolism in *Die glückliche Hand* without reference to Kandinsky's notions: *Die Musik in der Geistesgeschichte*, pp. 156–60.
54. The New Version of the Five Pieces for Orchestra, by Arnold Schoenberg, is published by C. F. Peters Corp. (New York, 1952) and is the authority for this discussion. On the third movement's original title see Peyser, *The New Music*, p. 29.
55. For discussions of Op. 16, see Carl Dahlhaus, *Schoenberg and the New Music*, trans. Derrick Puffett and Alfred Clayton (Cambridge: Cambridge University Press, 1987), pp. 141–8, and John C. Crawford's essay, 'Schoenberg's Artistic Development to 1911', in *Arnold Schoneberg, Wassily Kandinsky*, pp. 182–3. Both authors treat the concept of *Klangfarbenmelodie* uncritically: Dahlhaus accepts it as a claim for a potential acoustical phenomenon, and Crawford takes Schoenberg's retrospective term 'Impressionistic' at face value. If one understands the bizarre nature of such a claim for tone-colour melody, however, the origin of such a concept demands explanation.
56. *Theory of Harmony*, p. 421.
57. Ibid., p. 422.
58. After a period of travel, Kandinsky settled in Munich in 1908, after which his painting became increasingly experimental. A common influence on both Schoenberg and Kandinsky is claimed in Jelena Hahl-Koch's essay, 'Parallels in Their Artistic Development', *Arnold Schoenberg, Wassily Kandinsky*, pp. 143–4, but without a careful consideration of the evidence for Schoenberg. Wörner correctly identifies theosophy as a source in his discussion of Schoenberg's oratorio, *Die Jakobsleiter*, but fails to consider possible earlier manifestations for the period 1908–12. What follows, therefore, is crucial for understanding the origin and nature of Schoenberg's Expressionism.
59. The English 'spiritual' translates the German 'geistig'. in what is a standard translation. Yet some clarification is in order, since 'geistig' is also 'mental' or 'intellectual' – but no-one translates the word in the literature under discussion in this way, and for good reason. The English 'intellect' would correspond to the German 'Verstand' better than 'Geist'; the critical question in what follows is: what is the human spirit or mind? Like Kandinsky, the writers examined here reject the intellect as the answer.
60. Sixten Ringbom, *The Sounding Cosmos: A Study in the Spiritualism of Kandinsky and the Genesis of Abstract Painting* (Åbo: Åbo Akademi, 1970), pp. 48, 65. The

centrality of this theosophical influence is only hinted at by Kandinsky's own few references to Madame Blavatsky and Theosophy, as on p. 13 of *Concerning the Spiritual in Art*. But the source of modern theosophy lay in the writings of Helena Petrovna Blavatsky: for a brief introduction to her thought, see *The Key to Theosophy: A Simple Exposition Based on the Wisdom-Religion of All Ages* (1889; reprinted Pasadena, CA.: Theosophical University Press, 1995).

61. Grohmann, *Wassily Kandinsky*, p. 41.

62. Ringbom, *The Sounding Cosmos*, pp. 62–3.

63. Ibid., pp. 78–85. In Charles W. Leadbeater's *Man Visible and Invisible: Examples of Different Types of Men as Seen by Means of Trained Clairvoyance* (New York: John Lane, 1903), not only is there an entire chapter devoted to 'What the Colours Mean' (pp. 80–85), but there is a table of colours and their emotional signification as a frontispiece, and other illustrations of colour auras throughout the text. Such occult auras were supposedly visible to the clairvoyant, which has profound implications for the expressive use of colour in Expressionist art. The expression of the colours was meant to be perceivable to the spiritually initiated, but appears groundless to anyone else.

64. Rudolf Steiner, *Theosophy: An Introduction to the Supersensible Knowledge of the World and the Destination of Man*, trans. E.D.S. (Chicago: Rand McNally, 1910), pp. 182ff. Also Steiner, *Knowledge of the Higher Worlds: How Is It Achieved?*, rev. trans. D. S. Osmond and C. Davy (London: Steiner Press, 1969), p. 118; this book is based on two books published in Germany before 1909–10: *The Way of Initiation* and *Initiation and Its Results*. The argument that follows relies upon Steiner, since Kandinsky met him in Munich in 1908, and Wörner argues that Schoenberg came to know Steiner's ideas in the same period in Vienna through his good friend, Dr Oskar Adler: see *Die Music in der Geistesgeschichte*, pp. 182–3. It certainly seems more likely that Schoenberg would have been influenced by Steiner's presentation of theosophy than by Blavatsky, Besant or Leadbeater, for the latter three borrowed heavily from Indian religious concepts and terminology, whereas Steiner was careful to remain within the intellectual orbit of German philosophy, translating Indian terms into more familiar language as much as possible. Thus, while Madame Blavatsky originated modern theosophy, Steiner was the most important agent popularizing it in Germany and Austria in the early twentieth century.

65. Table 6.1 is based on the passages already identifed in the works of Leadbeater and Steiner, and on Kandinsky, *Concerning the Spiritual in Art*, pp. 37–41. Schoenberg's use of colour in *Die glückliche Hand* is identified by the objects illuminated by stage lights; Schoenberg also specifies the colours of clothes, etc., but the illumination is what is crucial here.

66. *Die glückliche Hand*, in *Arnold Schoenberg. Wassily Kandinsky*, pp. 96–8.

67. Steiner, *Knowledge of the Higher Worlds*, pp. 152–3.

68. Ibid., p. 147.

69. Wörner, *Die Musik in der Geistesgeschichte*, pp. 178ff; Crawford and Crawford, *Expressionism*, pp. 87–9.

70. See John Covach, 'The Sources of Schoenberg's "Aesthetic Theology"', *Nineteenth-Century Music* 14 (1996), pp. 252–62: he sees Schopenhauer, Goethe and Swedenborg as the most crucial influences: p. 260.

71. *Theory of Harmony*, pp. 422.

72. See Simon Morrison, 'Skryabin and the Impossible', *Journal of the American Musicological Society* 51 (1998), pp. 283–330.

73. These passages all from Hartmann, 'Über Anarchie in der Musik', *Der blaue Reiter*, pp. 88–9; 'On Anarchy in Music', *The Blaue Reiter Almanac*, p. 113.

74. *Concerning the Spiritual in Art*, p. 55.
75. Ibid., p. 43.
76. Hartmann's essay, *Der blaue Reiter*, p. 89; *The Blaue Reiter Almanac*, p. 114. N. Kulbin's essay, 'Die freie Musik,' *Der blaue Reiter*, pp. 125–31; 'Free Music', *The Blaue Reiter Almanac*, pp. 141–6, expresses similar views.
77. Steiner emphasizes the hidden nature of this wisdom in his *Theosophy*, pp. 2–3. Although Steiner does not acknowledge a dependence upon Blavatsky's own *Theosophy*, he does discuss the Eastern ideas of reincarnation and karma, pp. 59ff. In *An Outline of Occult Science*, trans. Maud and Henry B. Monges (first German edition, 1909; Spring Valley, NY: Anthroposophic Press, 1972), pp. 229ff., Steiner explicitly traces the hidden wisdom back to the people of ancient India. Thus he claimed that this wisdom was not only the same throughout the ages, but had been propagated directly from the origin of time. Hence, Steiner could add elements of Platonism, Christianity and the thought of Kant, Fichte, and Goethe, and claim that his system was a recovery of the totality of wisdom, long fragmented and obscured. Such syncretism is typical of gnostic systems: see Kurt Rudolph, *Gnosis: The Nature and History of Gnosticism*, trans. Robert M. Wilson (San Francisco: HarperCollins, 1987), pp. 54–5. Steiner openly acknowledged his gnosticism, as in *Knowledge of the Higher Worlds*, p. 19.
78. Steiner placed the emergence of the 'Sun Being' rather late in the process of cosmic evolution. He identified this Being as the Fichtean Higher Ego of the human race, and 'the Being in Whom the relationship that the Christ has to the cosmos manifests itself to the human beings of our time': *An Outline of Occult Science*, p. 215. Thus there is no Creator God for him. Neither is there an immortal life after death; there is only cleansing and preparation for the next reincarnation: ibid., pp. 74–85.
79. See, for example, the editors' brief biography in H. P. Blavatsky, *An Abridgment of the Secret Doctrine*, ed. Elizabeth Preston and Christmas Humphreys (Wheaton, IL: Theosophical Publishing House, 1967), p. xiv. For the best scholarly discusssion of modern theosophy, see Maria Carlson, *'No Religion Higher than Truth': A History of the Theosophical Movement in Russia, 1875–1922* (Princeton: Princeton University Press, 1993).
80. Steiner's Christology is discussed as a central element of his thought in Johannes Hemleben, *Rudolf Steiner: A Documentary Biography*, trans. Leo Twyman (East Grinstead, Sussex: Henry Goulden, 1975), pp. 96–100. From the perspective of orthodox Christianity, it may be said that Steiner combined a docetic understanding of Christ's nature with the Adoptionist heresy.
81. On the phenomenon of widespread enthusiasm for the occult since the end of the nineteenth century, see James Webb, *The Occult Underground* (La Salle, IL: Open Court, 1974) and *The Occult Establishment* (La Salle: Open Court, 1976).
82. Leadbeater's model of the soul is much more complicated in *Man Visible and Invisible*, pp. 46ff.
83. This discussion is based upon Steiner, *Theosophy*, pp. 22–58. Table 6.2 summarizes the discussion and is based on the brief outline provided by Steiner on pp. 54–5.
84. Ibid., pp. 78–9.
85. Ibid., p. 51.
86. In Leadbeater's illustrations, the auras enclose the human figure with several colours and sometimes patterns, depending on the type of personality being represented: see the plates in *Man Visible and Invisible*.
87. Ringbom, *The Sounding Cosmos*, p. 94.
88. St Athanasius emphasized this in *De Incarnatione*, Section 3: 'he did not barely

create man, as he did all the irrational creatures on the earth, but made them after his own image, giving them a portion even of the power of his own Word; so that having as it were a kind of reflection of the Word, and being made rational, they might be able to abide ever in blessedness, living the true life which belongs to the saints in paradise'. *On the Incarnation of the Word*, trans. Archibald Robertson, in *Christology of the Later Fathers*, ed. Edward R. Hardy (Philadelphia: Westminster Press, 1954), p. 58. Augustine, Thomas Aquinas, John Calvin and many others repeat much the same point. Here, Word and 'rational' both derive from the Greek *logos*, meaning rational speech.

89. H. P. Blavatsky, *The Key to Theosophy*, pp. 102–3, 129; cf. Steiner, *Knowledge of the Higher Worlds*, p. 43, on the spirit as the eternal core of being, and pp. 209–10 on the necessity of reincarnation. These elements are essential parts of the gnostic nature of theosophy, which will be considered at greater length in the following chapter; cf. Hans Jonas, *The Gnostic Religion*, pp. 42–7.

CHAPTER SEVEN

Order and the Occult in the Twelve-Tone Method

Schoenberg's invention of 'the method of composing with twelve tones' in the period immediately following World War I marked the arrival of a new phase for the New Music.[1] The Twelve-Tone Method guaranteed atonality in a composition, securing the effects achieved in the Expressionist period, but regulating the compositional choices much more rigidly. By setting all twelve tones of the chromatic scale in a given arrangement, and then requiring that all the notes of a composition be derived from the original tone row, its inversion, its retrograde, its retrograde inversion, or any of the transpositions of these forms, Schoenberg was able to create what he felt was a substitute 'for some of the unifying and formative advantages of scale and tonality'.[2] The tone row was not usually a theme, and by avoiding melodic intervals that might suggest triadic harmonies, a traditional sense of melody was precluded. Together with the retention of highly dissonant harmonic writing, music composed according to the method remained as uncompromising in its rejection of beauty as the music composed between 1908 and 1914.

The new systemization, however, strengthened its appeal and won for the method a wide following among Schoenberg's students, such as Anton Webern, Alban Berg, Nicholas Slonimsky, John Cage and Ernst Krenek. After World War II, serialism (especially as practised by Webern) profoundly influenced the second generation of the musical avant-garde, in composers such as Pierre Boulez, Milton Babbitt, Karlheinz Stockhausen – and even Igor Stravinsky after Schoenberg's death. For academic composers, too, serialism became crucial to respectability after World War II.[3] As we have seen, Schoenberg's Expressionist music had achieved a decisive influence on the general acceptance of a high level of dissonance as an element of modernist style; the direct influence on Stravinsky and Bartók provided the avenue for a diffusion of dissonance as the essence of modernism in music. But it was the Twelve-Tone Method that secured Schoenberg's fame and place in the musical history of the twentieth century. It became the most significant model for musical composition in both Europe and America in the fifty years following its invention in 1920.[4] Although serialism is no longer the epitome of avant-garde achievement, its historical importance makes understanding its origin and nature imperative. Moreover, that its influence has not been matched by a comparably frequent performance of twelve-tone works is cause for re-examining the aesthetic premises of the Method.

The Twelve-Tone Method is almost always understood as a recovery of order, a restoration of unity and comprehensibility to the otherwise admittedly chaotic language of atonal music.[5] Certainly this is the way Schoenberg himself wished the Twelve-Tone Method to be perceived: in his theoretical writings of this period, he emphasized that 'composition with twelve tones has no other aim than comprehensibility'.[6] Comprehensibility was to be the result of the unity provided by the relation of all the notes in a composition to the original tone-row; such unity would be thematic or motivic, rather than harmonic, even though the tone-row was not in principle a theme.[7] In this turn to comprehensibility and order as explicit goals of composition, Schoenberg shares in the general turn to a 'New Objectivity' which characterized the arts in the 1920s.[8] Hence, it is often regarded as comparable to the turn to neo-classicism on the part of Prokofiev, Stravinsky, Hindemith and other composers after the end of World War I.[9] In that sense, the development of the Twelve-Tone Technique would seem to take back many of the gnostic features of the New Music.

Yet it is possible to question the method's success in achieving musically perceptible comprehensibility: for tone rows lack the hierarchical pitch organization that seems necessary for both initial thematic perception and its subsequent recognition in a piece. Moreover, in an earlier essay Schoenberg had written that 'comprehensibility as a musical idea is independent of whether its components are made audible one after the other or more or less simultaneously'.[10] But this is a perspective that seriously diminishes the motivic comprehensibility of the use of a row. Webern was even more specific in rejecting the thematic nature of twelve-tone music: for him, the row was usually not a theme, and he found greater freedom in working 'without thematicism'.[11] Finally, the use of constant dissonance, in continuity with the earlier Expressionist style, produces a sonic monotony that will always threaten to overwhelm any attempts to articulate form or to establish an audible order.[12] The aurally evident similarity of style to Schoenberg's earlier Expressionist period compels asking if the Twelve-Tone Method were not equally a rejection of order. If so, it might equally be an expression of a gnostic metaphysic and psychology.

Any assessment of the metaphysical significance of the Twelve-Tone Method necessarily will depend on the answer to this question of its order or disorder. Certainly the fundamental anti-rationalism of the Expressionist style did not emerge until the meaning of the doctrine of self-expression had been established; for this, the origin of the doctrine in non-musical ideas was vital for understanding its nature. It was clear enough that the musical disorder of Expressionist atonality corresponded to Schoenberg's own psychic disorder in 1908, but it was not clear why that personal trauma should have been elevated, in effect, to a status of universality in his works of that period. Only the theosophical view of the non-rational, emotivist self could explain that claim of universality and account for the nature of the new imperative for self-expression. If the Twelve-Tone Method is to be understood as a restoration of order, the nature of that order will need to be clarified; certainly it is a very different kind of order from that of tonality. On the other hand, if it is best understood as a rejection of order, the rigid form in which disorder is cast must be explained. An examination of the theory underlying the method in the context of the works leading to the development of it will show, however, that the new 'order' shared the occult nature of the 'inner unity' of the Expressionist aesthetic. Hence it did not abandon, but continued, the theosophical approach of the earlier period.

Influences on Schoenberg's musical development, 1912–23

Schoenberg first published music written according to the Twelve-Tone Method in the Five Piano Pieces, Op. 23 of 1923. The method, however, had had a long gestation: he had composed the first and third of the Five Pieces at least as early as 1920, and he had used both a six-tone ostinato and a nine-note tone row at the beginning of the oratorio, *Die Jakobsleiter*, the composition of which he had started in 1917, but never finished. Thus the oratorio marks the genuine birth of what became the Twelve-Tone Method. In addition, he claimed to have sketched a genuinely twelve-tone theme for a scherzo movement of a projected symphony in 1915.[13] In fact, the oratorio was originally intended as the finale of that symphony, suggesting that the plans for it and the oratorio are of the utmost importance in understanding the origin, nature and significance of the Twelve-Tone Method.

Schoenberg had begun working on the programmatic ideas for the symphony in 1912, the same year that he finished his most important Expressionist work, *Pierrot lunaire*, Op. 21. Again, the origin of what eventually became the first use of a row at the height of his Expressionist period suggests the essential continuity of his aims and views. He wrote to Richard Dehmel, the poet whose work had inspired *Verklärte Nacht*, asking him to write a libretto on the subject of modern man's struggle to find God, overcoming atheism and finally 'learning to pray'.[14] Dehmel refused, and Schoenberg then sketched his own text. He entitled the first movement, 'Change of Life (looking backward, looking to the future; gloomy, defiant, withdrawn)' – clearly an autobiographical portrait in the same vein as his earlier Expressionist works. The second movement, 'The Joy of Life', was to be based on Dehmel's poem, 'Schöne wilde Welt'. The third movement, entitled 'Death-Dance of Principles,' was to be a monologue that showed the inadequacy of every philosophical position, after the manner of Nietzsche. Finally, the fourth movement was to be *Die Jakobsleiter – Jacob's Ladder*.[15] The textual outline of the symphony, then, together with a few musical fragments, was completed in 1915. Schoenberg's service in the Austrian army during the war interrupted his work; when he returned to the project in 1917, it was *Die Jakobsleiter* – the original finale of the symphony – that claimed his attention. This was the movement in which the religious element would triumph over the atheism of the modern world shown in the projected third movement, and man would be shown 'learning to pray'. The symphony and the oratorio derived from it, therefore, reveal Schoenberg's own spiritual quest more clearly than any other work of this period.

Schoenberg himself identified two sources of inspiration for *Die Jakobsleiter*. In his original letter to Dehmel, he mentioned Strindberg's work, *Jacob Wrestling*, and the description of an ascent into heaven at the end of Balzac's novel, *Séraphita*.[16] Indeed, the first of the Four Songs for Voice and Orchestra, Op. 22 (1913), was entitled 'Séraphita', indicating the strength of Schoenberg's interest in the subject at that time.[17] Balzac's novel, completed in 1835, is based on the theological system of Emanuel Swedenborg (1688–1772), which was much more neo-Platonic in character than gnostic. Although it is sometimes labelled 'theosophical', it has little more in common with Madame Blavatsky's system than the claim for the possibility of occult knowledge and contact with the dead.[18] Swedenborg's belief in contact with angels and heavenly beatitude had appealed to Balzac, providing him with an ideal of beauty and love by which to judge the corruption of an increasingly materialistic world. Hence, although *Séraphita* is little known today in comparison with the merciless depiction of human folly and moral vice in *Père Goriot*, for example, it was nonetheless a novel in which Balzac took great pride.[19] It articulated his vision of the ideal. The same quality appealed to Schoenberg, who professed to be taken with the angel Séraphita's ascension into heaven and the glimpse this gave of life after death.

Indeed, the connection between Schoenberg's perception of this vision and his formulation of the Twelve-Tone Method is of vital importance for understanding the nature and aim of the method. Schoenberg saw the use of tone rows as securing comprehensibility through the underlying unity of all the forms of the row, whether that unity was perceived or not. Since this unity was independent of the tones of the row being heard in a linear order or simultaneously, the unity appears as an occult, inner quality, rather than an audible element. Not even the temporal order of tones, therefore, affected the underlying unity provided by the row: this recalls the 'inner harmony' that Kandinsky posited in the most disharmonious outward appearances.[20] But Schoenberg's conception of musical unity was not merely that provided by the row; rather, the 'two-or-more-dimensional space in which musical ideas are presented is a unit'.[21] That is, 'the elements of a musical idea are partly incorporated in the horizontal plane as successive sounds, and partly in the vertical plane as simultaneous sounds'.[22] The unity of the two planes in one space was what allowed the row to be distributed among melody and harmony without regard to temporal order.

Schoenberg claimed that this concept of musical unity without temporal order was derived from the vision of heaven in *Séraphita*: 'In this [musical] space, as in Swedenborg's heaven (described in Balzac's *Séraphita*) there is no absolute down, no right or left, forward or backward.'[23] In this account of the intrinsic if often imperceptible unity of twelve-tone music, the lack of tonal hierarchy and temporal order corresponded to the absence of hierarchy and order in the Swedenborgian heaven. It should also recall the description of heaven in Stefan George's poem, 'Entrückung', with which Schoenberg's experimentation with atonality began. Thus, we may trace a continuity of interest on Schoenberg's part in this kind of a vision of heaven without the orientation of spatial or temporal order.

The opening lines of *Die Jakobsleiter* are often taken as evidence in support of the claim that the Swedenborgian vision was the specific inspiration.[24] The archangel Gabriel preaches to the souls gathered in heaven as they await their next incarnation: 'Whether right or left, forward or backward, upward or downward, one has farther to go without asking what lies before or behind him. It shall be hidden: you may, you must forget it, in order to fulfill the task.'[25] These lines are set to music that begins with a nine-tone chromatic passage having only one repetition of a tone within that span: B-flat–C–G-flat–D–B–A–G-sharp–D–C-sharp–G (see Example 7.1, where it should be noted that the tones are sung in *Sprechstimme*). But Gabriel's words are clearly not a description of heaven; they are a description of future possibilities of life for souls that will be reincarnated. They must forget their past lives and must not ask what lies ahead in the next life on earth. If these lines are taken as identifying the metaphysical significance of the Twelve-Tone Method, then, they suggest the hiddenness of life's meaning rather than a vision of heaven. The initial ostinato figure (C-sharp–D–F–E–G-sharp–G) is the original six-tone row; it may indeed be interpreted as the musical representation of the repetitive nature of the endlessly reincarnated life. Its lack of development toward a goal then corresponds exactly to the condition described by the archangel. The path to pursue lies hidden; we are forbidden to ask questions.

But not only are Gabriel's words not a description of heaven; the Swedenborgian vision of heaven as described by Balzac is not as Schoenberg characterized it. It is rather a view of heaven with a great degree of hierarchy and order, centred on God as the source of all that exists. Balzac describes what the two principal human characters, Wilfrid and Minna, are allowed to see as the hermaphroditic Séraphita is assumed into heaven and received as an angel, ascending through seven divine worlds:

> The two seers could discern the seraph as a darker object amid deathless legions … . And then, as though all the arrows of a quiver were shot off at once, the spirits dispelled with a breath every vestige of his former shape; as the seraph mounted higher he was purified, and ere long he was no more than a filmy image of what they had seen when he was first

Example 7.1   Arnold Schoenberg, *Die Jakobsleiter*, Gabriel's solo, mm. 11–19

> transfigured – line of fire with no shadow. Up and up, receiving a fresh
> gift at each circle, while the sign of his election was transmitted to the
> highest heaven, whither he mounted purer and purer.[26]

The hierarchy of heaven could not be more clear: the higher one ascends in
heaven, the more purified one becomes.

In fact, however, all worlds in Swedenborg's view – earthly, spiritual and
divine – were ordered by and toward God. As Balzac describes it: 'Each world
had a centre to which tended every atom of the sphere; these worlds were
themselves each an atom tending to the centre of their species. Each species
had its centre in the vast celestial region that is in communion with the
inexhaustible and flaming *motor power of all that exists.*'[27] Only because of
such a teleological ordering could it be said that 'yet all was one' while all
things remained individual.[28] Swedenborg himself thought an individual's soul
was purified in an intermediate spiritual realm after death and there became
worthy of heaven. Swedenborg taught that a person progressed through four
possible states after death: a brief transition was followed by the release of the
inner mind from the fetters of the natural world; the wicked would remain in

the second state, but the virtuous would enter a state of instruction, after which these spirits would enter heaven and become angels. The human spirit attaining angelic beatitude was thus the hallmark of Swedenborgian theology.[29]

In contrast, Madame Blavatsky and Rudolf Steiner rejected such a vision of heaven as a final destination, and such a spiritual, purgatorial realm as its preparation. For Steiner, reincarnation was essential in order to recruit others into the movement as well as to develop one's spiritual powers. But in attacking a longing for heavenly bliss as egoism inimical to the love of others and of the world, Steiner and Blavatsky missed something that Swedenborg, in common with the Christian tradition, understood: there must be a final end, in which love is perfectly shared, or there is no purpose in life on earth.[30] Schoenberg, therefore, could not have been inspired to the creation of the Twelve-Tone Method by Balzac's description of the Swedenborgian heaven, nor by the broader character of Swedenborg's theological system, which is quite different from the theosophical system that had attracted him after 1908. Either he did not read *Séraphita* closely, or he confused his own ideas with those of Balzac. In any case, it is clear that the essence of the method is a decisive rejection of teleological order.

What Schoenberg did find in Balzac's novel was a doctrine of reincarnation that, little faithful to Swedenborg, closely resembled that of Blavatsky's and Steiner's theosophy. Schoenberg's text, while endorsing reincarnation, decisively rejects the conception of its purpose as Balzac describes it. For Balzac, because no one life could suffice to cleanse a soul of the corruption that existence in this world entails, multiple lives would be necessary for a soul to learn virtue and become completely purified. As Séraphita explains, there are seven levels of life through which a soul must pass in order to ascend into heaven: these are the Sphere of Instinct, the Sphere of Abstractions or false science, the life of suffering, the life of loving 'where devotion to the creature teaches us devotion to the Creator', and then the life 'during which we seek, in silence, the traces of the Word, and become humble and charitable'. Finally, there is the life of 'high desire', and the life of prayer.[31] Thus, each stage is seen as a test or trial by which one learns a specific virtue and thereby earns the right to advance to the next. In the novel, Séraphita represented the life of prayer, and at his death, he was finally accorded a place in heaven among the angelic host. In contrast, Schoenberg's libretto for *Die Jakobsleiter* allows no hope for a final repose in heaven.

The oratorio is set in heaven, with the archangel Gabriel listening to the confessions first of the Chorus, and then of six characters who represent progressively higher levels of life. Gabriel's response to each is to indicate that further trials await in future lives. These characters do not correspond to the seven stages described by Séraphita, however: Schoenberg used the general concept of spiritual development, but moulded it to suit his own purposes. Perhaps the closest similarity is the sixth character, the Dying One, who parallels Séraphita's own role as the dying paragon in the novel. But whereas the novel shows his assumption into heaven as a celebration of his virtues – his longing for heaven, his deeds, his faith, his charity, his pious resignation[32] – Schoenberg's Dying One merely complains about life: "A life is fearful; a pain! A sorrow so great that one only feels it.' Death, then, comes as the sole release, and he acknowledges that 'the most blessed dream is fulfilled'.[33] Just at that moment, his part is replaced by a female voice singing pure tones without words; the Dying One's part is labelled 'The Soul', and it is sung simultaneously with Gabriel's response to the Dying One. Gabriel's words, however, offer little comfort: 'Do you come near again to the light? ... Know however, you go steadily forth from here! I know your sorrows and your future sins.'[34] Unlike Séraphita, therefore, The Dying One will continue to experience the endless round of reincarnation. The final chorus makes the point emphatically: 'He must yet long wander!'[35] Thus, the text leaves no hope for heaven as an eternal dwelling in bliss.

Schoenberg's musical sketches ended at this point in 1922, and although he always hoped to return to the work and complete it, he was never able to do so. Like his other great religious work, the opera *Moses und Aron*, it was destined to remain unfinished.[36] Indeed, the performing edition of the score had to be created from the sketches by Winfried Zillig; it comprised only the first half of the projected oratorio. The second half, however, was to be devoted to the life of prayer that Schoenberg had emphasized as his original intent.[37] Since this was the stage of life that Séraphita represented in Balzac's novel before her death and assumption into heaven, it is possible to see that Schoenberg remained faithful to the novel in that one respect.[38] But it was the manner of earthly life, not the vision of heaven, that was important for *Die Jakobsleiter*. On this point Schoenberg instead preserved the ideas of Madame Blavatsky and Rudolf Steiner in rejecting eternal bliss. Thus the modern theosophists are more crucial than Balzac or Swedenborg for understanding the work in which tone rows first made their appearance.

The genesis of *Die Jakobsleiter* and the Twelve-Tone Method is clarified, however, if the oratorio is viewed in light of the other source Schoenberg mentioned to Dehmel in 1912: August Strindberg's prose fragment, *Jacob Wrestles*, written in 1898. This was Strindberg's account of his own spiritual crisis in the face of his troubles as a controversial playwright and a man unable to adjust to married life. That his second marriage had fallen apart, and that he had not written for the theatre since 1892, were only symptoms of a deeper psychological disorder.[39] His intellectual evolution bespeaks a similar instability, for he had passed from socialism and atheism to an enthusiasm for Nietzsche, and finally to an interest in Swedenborg and the occult.[40] By 1897, when he went to Paris to arrange for the publication of some of his plays, he felt himself socially and artistically isolated, cursed by higher powers, and without hope: he thought both the celibate and the married life were equally unhappy.[41] Taking the title of his story about his year in Paris from the account of Jacob wrestling with the angel of God in Genesis 32:24–9, Strindberg saw his own spiritual struggles as similar, and intended to give them an outcome to that would be comparable to the blessing Jacob received from the angel. The angel had told Jacob, 'Your name shall no more be called Jacob, but Israel, for you have striven with God and with men, and have prevailed' (Gen. 32:28). But Strindberg had no such blessing to reflect in his writing; being a Protestant had been an agony, and now he had grown weary of Swedenborg.[42] Hence he was unable to finish the tale in such a way as to integrate it with his earlier, autobiographical *Inferno*.[43] His spiritual struggle had left him merely wounded like Jacob, but without any religious moorings: this was what appealed to Schoenberg.

The main outline of Schoenberg's religious quest closely resembles that of Strindberg. Raised in a half-Jewish household, he had become an unbeliever by 1890. Although he formally converted to Lutheranism in 1898, he had little to do with the church after 1902; yet he did not reconvert to Judaism until 1933.[44] It is the period between 1902 and 1933, then, that is of the most interest, for what filled the vacuum left by the absence of contact with formal faiths was of decisive importance for the development of his musical ideas. Between 1902 and 1911, he read widely in philosophy, procuring many of the works of Kant, Schopenhauer, Nietzsche and Bergson.[45] This list itself suggests that he was wrestling with the problem of unbelief, for Kant's moral argument for belief in an utterly transcendent and unknowable God issued quickly in the atheism of Schopenhauer and the nihilism of Nietzsche.[46] Like Strindberg, Schoenberg appears to have been engaged in a spiritual struggle.

The importance of modern theosophical ideas, therefore, is possible to explain on this longer account of an ongoing spiritual quest. It would be easy to explain it after 1911, when he and Kandinsky became good friends, or after Schoenberg's move to Berlin later that year, where he might have had the opportunity to attend Steiner's lectures. But as we have seen, this is too late to account for the clearly theosophical foundation of Schoenberg's works between 1908 and 1911. At the same time, if the influence of modern theosophy came as early as 1908, it would not suffice to explain the actual impetus for *Die Jakobsleiter* or the projected symphony from which it sprang. There was a new source of inspiration: the parallel to Strindberg's spiritual quest, and the failure of the solutions presented by Swedenborg and Balzac. Like Strindberg, Schoenberg seems to have rejected much of Swedenborg's more optimistic theology.

The resulting spiritual crisis was what lay behind the projected symphony of 1912 and *Die Jakobsleiter*. As we have seen, the third movement of the symphony was to be entitled 'The Death-Dance of Principles', revealing the inadequacy of philosophy, and the fourth movement that became the oratorio was to show the spiritual solution of man 'learning to pray'. Yet Schoenberg could not complete the oratorio to show the life of prayer; instead, *Die Jakobsleiter* as it stands offers bitter accusations against life, beauty, morality and all the conditions of material existence – without, as we have seen, the hope of heavenly beatitude. A closer examination of the text will show that these attitudes, like those of the earlier Expressionist period, are not simply the expression of Schoenberg's private despair, or even a despair shared with other creative personalities such as Strindberg, but rather the essence of the theosophical view of human existence. It is a recognizably gnostic view in its devaluation of this world and of material existence, which will prove vital for understanding the development and aim of the Twelve-Tone Method.

The gnostic character of *Die Jakobsleiter*

The argument of the oratorio takes its bearing from an underlying despair regarding the possibility of happiness in human existence. The opening chorus delivers an indictment of life: 'The unbearable pressure, the hard burden, what fearful sorrow, burning yearning, hot desire … .'[47] Five groups within the chorus then describe life more fully: The Rejoicing Ones speak of 'joy without end', which The Doubting Ones immediately disparage, describing life instead as without joy, always filled with sorrow and doubt. The Unhappy continue the lament of endless sorrow. They yield to The Indifferent, who do not know what direction they will go next; finally, the Gently Yielding preach acceptance of life as they find it: 'O how beautifully it is lived in the dirt.'[48] These choral groups anticipate some of the positions represented by individual soloists later in the oratorio. Gabriel's response to all of them is 'No matter! Farther!' – repeating his initial proclamation that 'one has farther to go without asking what lies before or behind him'.[49] Nevertheless, he calls to those assembled now to approach.[50] Although the purpose of life be hidden, the judgement of heaven might yet be known. The rest of the oratorio presents the archangel's judgements on six different lives.

The first to step forward is The One Who is Called. He has spent his life seeking beauty – a personification, perhaps, of the young Schoenberg. He confesses that his life has been filled with joy and has not been afflicted with suffering: 'The rays of the sun smiled on me and warmed me … . I saw only my sun, heard only the rhythm of beauty!' Gabriel responds, however, that this self-satisfaction is idolatry, that the entire path of torment still awaits him.[51] This rejection of beauty is familiar to us already from Schoenberg's theoretical writings. Yet the opposition developed in the *Harmonielehre* was between beauty and the truthfulness of self-expression, so that beauty simply became irrelevant to the artistic demands of the theosophical self. Here, however, Gabriel calls beauty, joy and the warmth of the sun – a metaphor for all that is good – 'idols'. Thus more than artistic beauty is rejected here: the experience of goodness and beauty in life itself is cast as an idolatrous substitute for genuine spirituality.

But this is an identifiably gnostic position, for gnosticism sees the physical world as essentially hostile to the spirit, lacking in goodness and beauty, so that the material aspect of human existence shares in this evil nature necessarily.[52] In contrast, Judaism and Christianity insist on the goodness of God's creation: 'And God saw everything that he had made, and behold, it was very good' (Gen. 1:31), repeated in the text central to both the Jewish and Christian liturgies: 'Holy, holy, holy is the Lord of hosts; the whole earth is full of his glory' (Isaiah 6:3).[53] While it is certainly possible to make idols of good things, to reject all that is good and beautiful as idolatrous is to attribute to the material aspect of human existence a deceptive and ultimately evil nature. The theosophy that was so influential for Schoenberg was indeed a modern gnosticism. His and the archangel's rejection of beauty, therefore, have roots in a metaphysic utterly opposed to the Jewish and Christian faiths.

A nihilist rebellion against an omnipotent and unitary God is represented in the second figure to step forward. The Rebellious One voices a complaint against the impotence of moral laws that becomes an accusation against God Himself for both creating man with instincts for committing evil deeds, and giving man the Ten Commandments: 'How powerless, however, does the Lord appear in the commandments, when He hands over His creation to torment and persecution, self-created and done by a stranger!' The archangel responds by calling this 'shortsightedness and arrogance', yet he listens, 'astounded; but not to contradict!'[54] The Rebellious One, in other words, articulates a version of the Problem of Evil that uses the instincts arising from physical being to construct an argument against God as the creator of both material nature and the moral law.

Again, this is a gnostic position: gnosticism generally understands the creator of the material world to be distinct from the ultimate source of spiritual existence.[55] Hence Gabriel condemns the spiritual rebellion against God, but refrains from contradicting its essential theological premise. Here it should be noted that Schoenberg's text departs from the Swedenborgian solution to the Problem of Evil in Balzac's *Séraphita*, where the world's emanation from God (in a neo-Platonic sense) explained evil as a result of the distance of the material world from God.[56] Thus, the goodness and power of God could be defended while regarding evil as both necessary and escapable. Such a self-contradictory position can be avoided only by a doctrine recognizing the possibility of human sin, such as Judaism and Christianity possess. For Schoenberg, however, it was matter, not sin, that defined the essence of the human predicament. Gabriel, therefore, allows the gnostic complaint against God to stand, for the archangel will himself emerge as the chief proponent of gnostic spirituality in the oratorio.

The next figure, The Struggling One, articulates Schopenhauer's philosophy of renunciation of willing. He confesses to having once sought happiness, and when that failed, he strove 'toward "painlessness" through renunciation, which also failed'.[57] This is an obvious reference to Schopenhauer, whom Schoenberg read in 1911, but it is also reminiscent of the doctrine Schoenberg put in the lines of the final chorus of *Die glückliche Hand*: 'Can you never renounce? Never at last resign yourself?'[58] In the end, The Struggling One simply accepts unhappiness as the inevitable condition of life. Although he knows the commandments as they are written and has followed them faithfully, he confesses to being 'incapable of avoiding right or wrong' in 'puzzling, conflicting situations'. He concludes, therefore, with an accusation little different from that of The Rebellious One: 'Why was no consciousness given us to respect unsaid laws, no eyes to see them, no ears to hear them?'[59] Although he appears to occupy a higher level than The Rebellious One because he does not regard instinct as all-powerful, he too finds the moral life remote.

The archangel, however, responds less ambiguously than before: he rejects the despair of seeing unhappiness as inevitable, for the more sensitive one is, the nearer is one to spiritual insight.[60] Then he encourages The Struggling One to step nearer, and in the process articulates the central metaphor of the work: 'There is one to lead you against his and your wills .... Whoever is an image and possesses a brightness upon a middle level is similar to One Much-Higher, like the distant overtone is to the fundamental; while other, deeper, even almost-fundamentals are foreign to him ... as coal is to the diamond.'[61] This mysterious and seemingly confused analogy demands elucidation. It is a metaphor of the theosophical cosmogony.

Rudolf Steiner's account of cosmic evolution is revealing, and would have been accessible to Schoenberg before he began writing *Die Jakobsleiter*.[62] For Steiner, there was no God standing at the beginning of the cosmic process; instead, the world began with a first spiritual stage of heat, from which soon afterwards 'certain exalted beings' came to exist through a kind of 'condensation' – the 'Spirits of Wisdom', or Dominions. After that, other spiritual beings were generated: Thrones, Powers, Authorities, Archai (rulers), Archangels, Seraphim, Angels and Cherubim as he identifies them according to traditional terminology.[63] That is, Steiner took over the ranks of angels according to Christian theology and gave them a generative significance.[64] From them, according to Steiner, the world as we know it eventually came into being, but separated by a long and elaborate chain of generation. Some of these beings became human souls; others became 'Luciferic beings' that 'brought to the human being the possibility of unfolding a free activity in his consciousness, but at the same time also the possibility of error, of evil'.[65] The Sun Being, however, was higher than the Luciferic beings; this became the 'Higher Ego' of the human race, that is, Steiner's equivalent of God.[66] But spiritual being was of the same kind as the first being: this was a monistic metaphysic posed as an alternative to both the dualism and the materialism of the late nineteenth century. The apparent monism of Steiner's theosophy, therefore, conceals the enormous evolutionary distance placed between this world and the spiritual world in modern theosophy. But it is a gnostic cosmogony.

Gnostic cosmogony tends to be complex and hierarchical. Ancient gnosticism, as it originated in the Roman Empire, saw the created world as a prison made by powers or archons, who were themselves created by the highest God, but who are separated from God by an unbridgeable chasm. The explanation of this often took the form of an elaborate chain of divine generations in order to guarantee that the world and the lower powers could not know God. These powers, seen as residing in the planetary realm of the heavens, ruled the world by fate and law, so that the order they imposed – the order of nature and natural law – was part of what made the world a prison for man, hostile to the human spirit that was part of the original divine spirit. Material order, therefore, was unspiritual, which explains why spiritual existence must be found in material disorder, or, for the ancient gnostic, frequently in an antinomian rejection of moral law. For the highest God is alien to this world, according to gnosticism: He did not create it and does not rule it. He is unknowable; the equally indefinable human spirit is a part of God's essence, trapped in the material prison of the body, together with an 'astral' soul created by the ruling powers of the world. Thus the astral soul was equally a feature of imprisoning material existence; only the spirit, as a spark of the divine spirit, would be worthy of salvation.[67] The hierarchical theology, then, both explained the alienation of the human spirit from the world in which it dwells and bound together the dualism of matter and spirit in a unity of spiritual generation of the lower powers.

Much of this is familiar from our examination of the theosophy of Blavatsky and Steiner: the indefinable nature of the human spirit, the astral body consisting of desires, and the inhospitability of matter to the spirit are telltale signs of a gnosticism that they openly acknowledged.[68] In one crucial respect, however, modern theosophy may appear surprising, for both Blavatsky and Steiner emphasized the monistic nature of reality. In contrast to nineteenth-century materialism, which seemed to exclude any spiritual dimension, theosophists sought to vindicate the existence of the spiritual by another kind of monism, which would find its proof in the occult.[69] Yet this could be accomplished only by defining matter as a 'condensation' of the spiritual substance, yielding a hierarchy of the degrees of spirituality. The emergence of the material world, therefore, would have to be described in terms of a cosmic evolution not at all unlike the descent by divine generation described in the fantastic theories of the ancient gnostics, in order to guarantee the distance of matter from the purity of the spirit.

The mysterious proclamation by the archangel Gabriel in *Die Jakobsleiter* now, however, becomes explicable in terms of gnostic theology. Those who yearn for the spiritual life are on the middle level of spirituality, and they already resemble the One Much-Higher. Yet the musical analogy employed demands a deeper reading, for if the fundamental is equivalent to God, then the deeper overtones, the 'almost-fundamentals', must be beings who stand metaphysically near to God, but are nevertheless 'foreign to him' – for example, the Luciferic beings of Steiner. In this way the human being who recognizes his spiritual nature 'possesses a brightness' and resembles God. Moreover, because the gnostic God is as unknowable and indefinable as the human spirit, the concept of divinity becomes completely impersonal: hence, 'there is one to lead you against his and your wills ... .' The divine spark of the human spirit, imprisoned in its body, blindly seeks to return to its source.

The musical analogy itself, however, remains problematic. The distant overtone is said to resemble the fundamental, while the deeper overtones are described as 'foreign' – 'as coal is to the diamond'. This is contrary to any intuitive understanding of the overtone series, in which the lower overtones are more likely to be consonant with the fundamental and resemble it. For Schoenberg, the overtone series supplies the basis for understanding consonance and dissonance, but since all overtones generated by a vibrating body contribute to its timbre, he concluded that there was no essential difference between consonance and dissonance. He had raised this point already in the *Harmonielehre* of 1911:

> the overtones closer to the fundamental seem to contribute more or less
> perceptibly to the total phenomenon of the tone – tone accepted as
> euphonious, suitable for art – while the more distant seem to contribute
> less or less perceptibly. But it is quite certain that they all do contribute
> more or less, that of the acoustical emanations of the tone nothing is lost.[70]

From this indisputable fact he concluded: 'Hence, the distinction between them is only a matter of degree, not of kind.'[71] That is, the continuity of the overtone series would overturn the discontinuity in perception of the difference between consonance and dissonance. The acoustical error of this has already been discussed. It was, however, crucial to Schoenberg's argument that dissonance could be and had been 'emancipated' simply because composers' increased use of dissonance familiarized people's ears with these more complex, but not incomprehensible sounds.[72] Familiarity, then, would compensate for the greater complexity, and the modern composer could express himself as he felt compelled to do.[73] Dissonance thus became more important than consonance.

The musical theory, however, does not explain the necessity for rejecting consonance altogether. But the gnostic theology implied in Gabriel's complex metaphor does explain Schoenberg's view of that necessity through the counter-intuitive nature of the archangel's musical analogy. For if the fundamental tone represented the alien, unknowable Spirit as the source of existence, and the deeper overtones, which form consonances with the fundamental, stood for the intermediate and oppressive spiritual beings of gnosticism, then the true nature of consonance would be evil rather than good. In this way, the entire traditional association of consonance with goodness and dissonance with pain and evil would be overturned. Dissonance, then, could indeed be reckoned as somehow similar to the unknown One Much-Higher, as spiritual man approaches the alien Spirit of gnosticism. Read this way, the puzzling inversion of the fundamental and the higher overtones in this passage contains the justification of Schoenberg's emancipation of dissonance and development of the Twelve-Tone Method as a guarantee of dissonance and of the avoidance of a fundamental or tonic.

The response of the archangel Gabriel to The Struggling One, therefore, marks an important dividing point in the oratorio. With that speech, Gabriel has completed the exposition of the gnostic metaphysic; his next three speeches will be devoted to its implications for life and death. There is a corresponding division among the figures who approach heaven's judgement: the first three represented positions that Schoenberg himself had passed through and ultimately rejected or overcome, whereas the last three will represent progressively higher stages of spiritual development (in a gnostic sense). Their remarks and Gabriel's responses will confirm the theosophical character of *Die Jakobsleiter* and will help to explain Schoenberg's overpowering conviction of his own calling in bringing forth the New Music. This conviction, though born of a forceful and unusual personality, was shaped and solidified by the ideology that served as its justification.

The next figure, that of The Chosen One, articulates a sense of being called by the higher powers in heaven, in spite of his own reluctance that is rooted in knowing his creative work will not be understood. In answer to Gabriel's preceding call to step forward to the middle level of the spiritual hierarchy, The Chosen One responds that he must, but explains his motivation with a quintessentially gnostic sentiment: 'I seek to flee matter: the loathing makes it easy for me, hunger forces me back ... .' He seeks to be 'a New Man certainly, a higher one perhaps to represent. They are themes; I am a variation!'[74] Here the pronoun 'they' can only refer to spiritual beings or powers, confirming the theosophical reading of the earlier passages and making it critical for understanding The Chosen One's conviction of being called. The inspiration of the spiritual powers – they who are called the themes – is therefore vital for his work. If the sense of calling is thinly veiled autobiography, so too must be its theosophical theology.

Gabriel responds with a significant account of creativity according to this heterodox theology. He distinguishes carefully between the Highest (Spirit) and the Word: the Word is spiritual but subordinate to the Spirit, and is what enters into an individual to give birth to creative work. Referring to the Word,

Gabriel advises: 'Choose that part which he was able to safeguard. It is not too little, because he is wonderfully merciful – wherein he resembles the Highest – to sacrifice himself in his smallest.' The Word is here understood to make a sacrifice in coming to dwell in a human being. The Word does so, however, because 'He must create, so long as he is impure: out of himself to create!'[75] Here there can be no temptation to understand the Word in a Christian sense, for it is certainly not equally God in substance or being with the Father, and it enters into individuals, this act constituting its sacrifice because of the pollution of its spiritual nature with matter. But this pollution is precisely what impels the Word to create through the medium of those who are chosen. Thus the orthodox Christian association of the Word with God's act of creation is transmuted here to individual, artistic creation made possible because of the impurity of the Word in its incarnation in individual human beings. What will be created, as in the case of the oratorio, will be a revelation of the 'spiritual wisdom', the theosophical gnosis.

If Gabriel responds to The Chosen One with encouragement, he answers the next figure, The Monk, with a judgement and a command. Here the difficulties are spiritual rather than creative, so that the transition between these two levels parallels the transition in the first half of the oratorio between The One Who is Called to create beauty and The Rebellious One. But just as The Chosen One will create spiritually rather than beautifully (for beauty is an alien, material category), so too The Monk is a genuinely spiritual figure rather than a rebel who cannot understand life spiritually. The Monk confesses that he strove in life to be righteous and to be a good servant, yet he accuses himself of arrogance and vanity, and of not bearing his sacrifice gladly. Gabriel, however, rejects the necessity of that kind of self-sacrifice: 'Now you have given up all splendor for a sad knowledge that you do not suffice!' He sends The Monk away from heaven with the words: 'Go; proclaim and suffer: be prophet and martyr.'[76] The life of monastic withdrawal, then, is not the fulfilment of the spiritual side of man. Instead, the active life of a prophet and martyr will be the accomplishment of true spirituality. This is, of course, how Schoenberg considered himself for proclaiming the New Music.[77] But *Die Jakobsleiter* ties this mentality to a spiritual motivation that was theosophical, rather than Judaic or Christian.

As we have already seen, the sixth figure, The Dying One, complains that life is fearful and painful. He looks forward to death and the enlightenment it will bring, yet he is sent forth by Gabriel to live still more lives.[78] This is the expression of the theosophical doctrine of reincarnation; the result, however, is to deny divine mercy altogether, for there is no forgiveness of sin. As Gabriel told The Monk: 'your sins are punished, purifying them.'[79] For the theosophist, as we have seen, divine judgement is justice without mercy; and there is no hope for an ultimate salvation in a beatific vision of a God Who is Love. For the modern gnostic, man is alienated from material existence, but because of the doctrine of reincarnation, the alienation from the world turns out to be perpetual.

The view of death itself is important, however, as the one experience of pure spirituality allowed before the next reincarnation. Hence Gabriel says in response to The Dying One's laments: 'Now you do not complain anymore; you begin to grasp what you must forget again soon. You return again, so leave the complaints behind you. If you do not complain anymore, you are near. Then is the Self extinguished –'.[80] A choir of angels confirms this understanding of the soul's experience of the spiritual life between death and rebirth: 'extinguish the conscience, extinguish the understanding. Extinguish yourself!'[81] Thus, in contrast to both the Christian and even the Swedenborgian conceptions of salvation, Schoenberg allows nothing of the personality to be preserved in even a transcendent, purified form.[82] The understanding, the rational part of the soul in the traditional philosophical view of the structure of the soul, is to be extinguished like a light. Only the Soul as pure spirit – indefinable spirit – survives to be reclothed with a new personality; this closely resembles Steiner's doctrine.[83]

This element of gnostic theosophy has significant musical reflections. For the Soul, The One Who Is Called and The Chosen One, together with some of Gabriel's responses, are the only solo lines in the oratorio not to be sung in *Sprechstimme*. This dissolution of pitch which Schoenberg had first employed in *Pierrot lunaire*, Op. 21 (1912), was the musical symbol appropriate to the material world. Pure tones were reserved for the figures who had some contact with the spiritual world.

The oratorio's view of the spiritual life as the extinction of the personality, therefore, was what was so important for Schoenberg's development of the Twelve-Tone Method. The unity of space he claimed to have seen in Balzac's description of heaven, from which he derived the idea of the unity of musical space as the foundations of the method, was simply not present in *Séraphita*. But to say of the modern theosophists' heaven that 'there is no absolute down, no right or left, forward or backward' would be a valid description, for the absence of a God in theosophy means that there could be no directed focus of heavenly life, as in Balzac's vision, nor any beatific vision, as in Christianity. This recalls, moreover, the vision of heaven already seen in Stefan George's poem, 'Entrückung', which Schoenberg had set to music in his Second String Quartet in 1908. The latter had no need for such ordering, since the soul was stripped of all that could define its personality.[84] Thus the lack of hierarchical order in heaven corresponds to the lack of purpose in life itself: the endless round of reincarnations has no ultimate goal. This correspondence is what Gabriel's opening lines suggested: 'Whether right or left, forward or backward, upward or downward, one has farther to go without asking what lies before or behind him.'[85] The non-teleological, non-hierarchical 'unity' of the Twelve-Tone Method, then, is the musical approach appropriate to the gnostic vision of heaven and of life. It is not, however, true order, precisely because it lacks the teleological nature that is crucial for establishing a true unity toward which all the parts are ordered.

The continuation of gnosticism in *Moses und Aron*

Although the beginnings of the Twelve-Tone Method are to be found in *Die Jakobsleiter*, Schoenberg perfected the Method in other, non-vocal works while he was still occupied with the sketches for the oratorio. Thus the inspiration of the gnostic spirituality informing that text remained critical for the development of the Method. But the gnostic nature of the Method remains evident in Schoenberg's later works as well. Even the opera, *Moses und Aron*, which he began shortly before he reconverted to Judaism in 1933, exhibits the unknown and alien God of theosophy rather than the God Who revealed Himself through His covenant with Abraham, Isaac and Jacob. This thoroughly dodecaphonic work, therefore, develops the link between gnosticism and the Twelve-Tone Method which was so crucial to the emergence of the Method in the years preceding 1923.

Certainly *Die Jakobsleiter* had avoided the central point of God's promise in the story of Jacob's ladder in Genesis 28:11–17. For Jacob's dream of a ladder upon which angels were ascending and descending has as its culmination God's appearance and promise to give the land where he lay to Jacob's descendants. Moreover, Jacob's perception upon waking, that he had been in the presence of God, was certainly absent from the oratorio. But Schoenberg similarly altered the story of Morses and Aaron in Exodus 32–4 to suit his own purposes. The opera functions on one level as an allegory of the conflict between feeling and law, beauty and truth in artistic creativity, yet it is also explicitly a theological work.[86] In it, God remains ultimately unknowable for both Aaron the rebel and Moses the lawgiver.

In both the account in Exodus 32 and the opera, the Hebrew people lose patience with Moses and turn to Aaron, who fashions an idol of a golden calf, while Moses is delayed on Mount Sinai. But Schoenberg interprets the motive according to his own conception: a priest complains of the Law that Moses is supposed to receive from God as an 'Unperceivable command from one who's yet unperceived.'[87] Aaron justifies his idol by saying, 'No folk can grasp more than just a partial image, the perceivable part of the whole idea.'[88] Thus the issue is the perceptibility of God – the same God Who had just led His people out of Egypt. In the opera, however, God is just an 'idea'. Moses concedes: 'Inconceivable God! Inexpressible, many-sided idea ... .'[89] He lectures Aaron: 'To serve, to serve the divine idea is the purpose of the freedom for which this folk has been chosen'[90] – but the divine idea is still the replacement for the living God. Such a divinity not only lacks all the qualities able to inspire worship, but will necessarily remain unperceivable. A divine idea is indeed an abstraction of an inconceivable God.

Moses' final description of God places Him utterly beyond human hope or fear: 'The almighty one (and he retains that quality forever) is not obliged to do anything, is bound by nothing. He is bound neither by the transgressor's deeds, nor by the prayers of the good, nor by the offerings of the penitent'.[91] This defence of divine omnipotence, however, results in a distant and arbitrary God Whose actions would contradict the essence of the Law given to Moses. For the second commandment in particular, against making graven images, concludes by denying the words of Moses in the opera: 'for I the Lord your God am a jealous God, visiting the iniquity of the fathers upon the children to the third and the fourth generation of hose who hate me, but showing steadfast love to thousands of those who love me and keep my commandments' (Ex. 20:5–6). Here, God's omnipotence indeed proves responsive to human deeds. Thus, Schoenberg's God was still not the God of the Torah, but rather the alien, unknown God of gnosticism. Dodecaphony remained gnostic in inspiration.

The nature of Schoenberg's gnostic spirituality, therefore, is essential for understanding the peculiar nature and aim of the apparently new order of the Twelve-Tone Method from its inception through his mature works. Certainly it is non-teleological; on any traditional understanding, then, it cannot truly be an order. For an order requires a goal toward which every element is organized in a perceptibly coherent structure.[92] For music especially, as an art that unfolds in time and that necessarily cannot be grasped at a glance in a unitary perception, that order must be teleological and must arise from a tonal hierarchy. But the Twelve-Tone Method rejects the organizing goal of a tonic together with the perceptible coherence of a tonal and harmonic hierarchy, while maintaining that the row is the representation of a unity of tones defined by their 'relatedness' to one another. Such an arbitrary relatedness is no order; nor can it produce motivic or thematic units that would be an adequate substitute for the teleological quality of tonal melodies.[93] Thus, Schoenberg's hope that the Method would guarantee comprehensibility fails not only because of the sonic monotony of unremitting dissonance, but more fundamentally because there is no teleological order in either the harmonic or melodic dimension.[94]

The rigid yet occult unity of the Method is born, however, of a gnostic hostility to material perception, and of a conception of life as an endless series of reincarnations. Lacking any ultimate good as the spiritual goal, the music arising from this world-view also lacks a *telos*. The posited unity of a twelve-tone row is as indefinable as the human spirit in gnosticism; what is indefinable is also necessarily imperceptible. Hence, the musical parameters of the method reflect perfectly the underlying inspiration crucial to Schoenberg's path to the development of the method.

The anti-rationalism of the Twelve-Tone Method and the gnostic theology that inspired it must not obscure, however, the more serious metaphysical issue common to both. For both involved a rejection of material order as a condition of human existence. By asserting an indefinable spirit in addition to the human soul and making that spirit antithetical to the world of matter, gnosticism sees everything connected with the material world as intrinsically opposed to the needs of the spirit. Hence matter becomes evil in itself; sensually perceptible order is rejected as a manifestation of evil; beauty as the visual or aural splendor of order ceases to be acceptable. But perceptible order in the material world was always understood in the dominant Western philosophical and theological traditions as a metaphor of metaphysical ordering toward God or the good; such ordering is a crucial component of the goodness of actually existing things, individuals and societies. To reject the one is therefore to reject the other, and indeed gnosticism denies the goodness of ordinary being and normal social modes of existence.[95] The denial of the metaphysical goodness of material existence, then, entails a revolt against order and being in themselves. The extinguishing of the personality in the gnostic vision of heaven betrays gnosticism's hostility to all being. But that is to say it is a self-contradictory understanding of the nature of things.

The gnostic metaphysic, however, is what provided the inspiration and justification for both phases of Schoenberg's development of the New Music: his contact with gnostic theosophy was crucial for both his Expressionist period and the Twelve-Tone Method. The creation of a New Music that was atonal, unremittingly dissonant and unmelodic was therefore not simply due to Schoenberg's private troubles, but was the fruit of a metaphysic that denied the goodness of any actual existent, rejecting true order as a contamination of the spirit by matter. The Twelve-Tone Method guaranteed the lack of true order as the foundation of the rejection of beauty by representing dissonance as the metaphor of the occult and alien Spirit of theosophy. Yet, far from reintroducing a teleological element through this spiritual metaphor, the emphasis on reincarnation in theosophy is reflected in the endless possibilities of variation in the forms of the tone rows. In this way, the lack of an ultimate *telos* in theosophy is reproduced as the lack of a temporally realized *telos* in serial music. The lack of the temporality of the ideal becomes the determined avoidance of tonal teleology.

In this rejection of tonality, teleology and temporality, Schoenberg was not alone. His influence among his pupils was of vital importance for the creation of the musical avant-garde in the twentieth century, and his ideology of the historical inevitability of atonality helped to perpetuate the myth of the New Music long after its lack of public acceptance was clear. But it was not only in music that the influence of gnosticism made itself felt: among painters of the period, in addition to Kandinsky, Piet Mondrian, Franz Marc and Paul Klee were all influenced to some extent by the theosophical movement. Thus the development of Abstract Expressionism in that art also owed a heavy debt to an explicit gnosticism.[96] The gnostic revolt against order and being has therefore become the broad foundation of the culture of modernism in the arts.

The question arises more acutely than ever, therefore, why such a gnostic culture has become the prevailing approach to musical and artistic creativity. The character of Schoenberg's modernism, like that of Kandinsky, reveals the essential nature of the avant-garde in its earliest manifestation: for it was a revolt against order in both the Expressionist and the dodecaphonic phases of Schoenberg's stylistic development, and in its rejection of beauty and order, it was a celebration of metaphysical disorder as the release of the spirit of the emotivist self from the confines of imprisonment in the being of perceptible order. Thus the question becomes why such an extension of the nihilist world-view became the accepted condition of musical and artistic solutions to the problem of meaning. What is it about modern culture that has led to the apparent permanence of the gnostic solution, while appearing to confirm the inevitability of its emergence from purely musical and artistic considerations? It is to this final aspect of the modern condition that we must now turn.

Notes

1. Schoenberg's account of the origin and nature of the Twelve-Tone Method is given in his 1941 essay, 'Composition With Twelve Tones (1)', in *Style and Idea: Selected Writings of Arnold Schoenberg*, ed. Leonard Stein, trans. Leo Black (Berkeley: University of California Press, 1984), pp. 214–44. Aware of the newness of the Method, Schoenberg was convinced both of the historical inevitability of his invention and of its historic import. He called it the 'Method of Composing with Twelve Tones Which are Related Only with One Another' (p. 218) – i.e. instead of being related to a tonic.
2. Ibid., p. 219.
3. The process by which the serial avant-garde became the new academic orthodoxy of twentieth-century music is touched upon briefly by Joan Peyser in her book, *The New Music: The Sense Behind the Sound* (New York: Delacorte Press, 1971), p. 176.
4. Peyser, *The New Music*, p. 42.
5. See ibid., p. 43; also H. H. Stuckenschmidt, *Arnold Schoenberg*, trans. Edith T. Roberts and Humphrey Searle (New York: Grove Press, 1959), p. 73; William W. Austin, *Music in the Twentieth Century from Debussy through Stravinsky* (New York: Norton, 1966), pp. 302–3. In Austin's analysis, the method serves to rationalize chromaticism as the particular means of ordering highly dissonant and chromatic music without a pitch centre.
6. 'Composition With Twelve Tones (1)', *Style and Idea*, p. 215. Anton Webern concurred in *The Path to the New Music*, ed. Willi Reich, trans. Leo Black (1963; London: Universal, 1975), p. 18.
7. Schoenberg, 'Problems of Harmony' (1934), *Style and Idea*, p. 280. Webern was

much more radical in his rejection of thematicism; in his view the row itself provided the required unity without the row itself being an entity identifiable as a theme: see *The Path to the New Music*, p. 55.

8.   Cf. John Willett, *Art and Politics in the Weimar Period: The New Sobriety, 1917–1933* (New York: Random House, 1978).

9.   John C. Crawford and Dorothy L. Crawford, *Expressionism in Twentieth-Century Music* (Bloomington: Indiana University Press, 1993), p. 263.

10.   Schoenberg, 'Twelve-Tone Composition' (1923), *Style and Idea*, p. 208. Webern also thought that musical unity was guaranteed by the 'chosen succession of twelve notes' alone: 'For unity is completely assured by the underlying series': *The Path to the New Music*, p. 40.

11.   Anton Webern, 'The Path to Twelve-Tone Composition', in *The Path to the New Music*, p. 54.

12.   See William Thomson, *Schoenberg's Error* (Philadelphia: University of Pennsylvania Press, 1991), pp. 69, 85.

13.   Schoenberg says this twice, in 'My Evolution' (1949), *Style and Idea*, p. 88, and in the contemporaneous 'Composition with Twelve Tones (2)', p. 247.

14.   Cf. Peyser, *The New Music*, p. 35, for a translation of the letter.

15.   The full account of the projected symphony is given in Alan P. Lessem, *Music and Text in the Works of Arnold Schoenberg: The Critical Years, 1908–1922* (Ann Arbor: UMI Research Press, 1979), pp. 177–80.

16.   Ibid., p. 177.

17.   Ibid., p. 171. The poem, however, was Stefan George's translation of a poem by an Englishman, Ernest Dowson, having little to do with the religious aspect of Balzac's novel; it is rather an invocation of Seraphita to help a drowning man: see Ernest Christopher Dowson (1867–1900), *The Poetry of Ernest Dowson*, ed. Desmond Flower (Rutherford, NJ: Fairleigh Dickinson University Press, 1970), p. 86.

18.   One of the few scholarly studies of the Swedish mystic is Inge Jonsson's *Emanuel Swedenborg*, trans. Catherine Djurklou (New York: Twayne Publishers, 1971). She emphasizes the Neo-Platonic nature of his mysticism (p. 179), and admits the occult aspect of Swedenborg's claim to be able to converse with the spirits of the dead (p. 139). Like Henry James, Sr, in the nineteenth century, however, she is at pains to represent Swedenborg as essentially a philosophical theologian, whose interest in theology developed out of his earlier interest in science; cf. Henry James, *The Secret of Swedenborg: Being an Elucidation of his Doctrine of the Divine Natural Humanity* (Boston: Fields, Osgood, 1869). Balzac, however, understood the essentially mystical nature of Swedenborg's theology; Chapter 3 of *Séraphita* contains a thorough summary of Swedenborg's teaching. Significantly, this was one of the chapters that was heavily underlined in Schoenberg's own copy: see Pamela White, *Schoenberg and the God-Idea: The Opera 'Moses und Aron'* (Ann Arbor: UMI Research Press, 1985), p. 64. Schoenberg owned Swedenborg's *Theologische Schriften*, 'but did not write in the book'. One might add that this is not surprising: Balzac's account is much easier to read than Swedenborg's diffuse prose. Thus, Balzac's novel is the direct source of many of Schoenberg's religious ideas after about 1911, although not, as we shall see, the source of the imagery crucial for the development of the Twelve-Tone Method.

19.   Balzac wrote: 'Séraphita, that will be the master-stroke: it shall bring me the cold sneers of the Parisian, but I shall have touched the hearts of all privileged beings … . Those mystical ideas have taken possession of my mind. I am the artist-believer. One can create a Goriot every day, but one creates a Séraphita only

once in a lifetime.' Quoted by David Blow in his introduction to Honoré de Balzac, *Séraphita*, trans. Clara Bell (New York: Hippocrene Books, 1989), p. xi. In fact, Balzac had already written a shorter novel, *Louis Lambert* (1832), conceived as a preface to *Séraphita*. The importance of Swedenborg to Balzac should therefore not be underestimated. On this subject, see Jacques Borel, *Séraphîta et le mysticisme balzacien* (Paris: José Corti, 1967), and Philippe Bertault, *Balzac et la religion* (Paris: Bovin, 1942); as Bertault notes, Balzac had overcome his earlier scepticism and become more sympathetic to Catholicism by 1830, yet the mysticism of Swedenborg (and others) was to define the highest plane of religious sentiment for Balzac (p. 374).

20. Of the forms constituting the 'harmony of the new art', Kandinsky wrote: 'Their external lack of cohesion is their internal harmony': Wassily Kandinsky, *Concerning the Spiritual in Art*, trans. M. T. H. Sadler (1914; New York: Dover, 1977), p. 52.

21. 'Composition with Twelve Tones (1),' *Style and Idea*, p. 220.

22. Ibid.

23. Ibid., p. 223.

24. Crawford and Crawford, *Expressionism*, p. 87; White, *Schoenberg and the God-Idea*, pp. 65–6; Peyser, *The New Music*, p. 36. On the importance of Balzac as the transmitter of this vision, see Dore Ashton, *A Fable of Modern Art* (Berkeley and London: University of California Press, 1991), pp. 96–120.

25. All translations are the author's, based on the text in Schoenberg's score of *Die Jakobsleiter*, ed. Winfried Zillig and Rudolf Stephan for Universal Edition (Los Angeles: Belmont, 1980); this passage is found on pp. 4–5.

26. Balzac, *Séraphîta*, ed. Henri Gauthier, in *La Comédie humaine*, 11 vols (Paris: Editions Gallimard, 1980), vol. 11, pp. 856–7; *Séraphita*, p. 153.

27. *La Comédie humaine*, vol. 11, p. 854; *Séraphita*, p. 150 (italics in original).

28. Ibid.

29. Reincarnation is not mentioned by Swedenborg's modern interpreters: cf. Inge Jonsson, *Emanuel Swedenborg*, p. 180; on purification after death, and for a synthesis of his writings, Sig Synnestvedt, ed., *The Essential Swedenborg: Basic Teachings of Emanuel Swedenborg, Scientist, Philosopher, and Theologian* (New York: Twayne Publishers, 1970), pp. 106–10.

30. See Rudolf Steiner, *Knowledge of the Higher Worlds: How Is It Achieved?*, trans. D. S. Osmond and C. Davy (London: Rudolf Steiner Press, 1969), pp. 209–12. Madame Blavatsky emphasized reincarnation in order to guarantee a law of justice; she saw no justice in the promise of divine forgiveness and heavenly bliss: see Helena P. Blavatsky, *The Key to Theosophy: A Simple Exposition Based on the Wisdom-Religion of All Ages* (1889; reprinted Pasadena, CA: Theosophical University Press, 1995), pp. 110, 223.

31. Balzac, *La Comédie humaine*, vol. 11, p. 844; *Séraphita*, pp. 138–9.

32. *La Comédie humaine*, vol. 11, p. 857; *Séraphita*, p. 153.

33. *Die Jakobsleiter*, pp. 136–7, 140–41.

34. Ibid., pp. 145–50.

35. Ibid., p. 154.

36. The question naturally arises, why Schoenberg's greatest religious works remained unfinished in spite of the composer's manifest intention to finish them. Crawford and Crawford speculate that in the case of the oratorio, a combination of post-war social and political chaos, performance commitments, and the composer's musical development to the full-fledged twelve-tone technique may have been responsible: *Expressionism*, pp. 89–90. Karl H. Wörner is perhaps closer to the mark, however, in noting the shift in Schoenberg's religious interest,

already discernible in 1925. The Four Pieces for Mixed Chorus, Op. 27 (1925), anticipate the subject of *Moses und Aron*: 'in them we do not find subjectivism, but ethical tenets' – and then in 1926–27, he wrote *Der biblische Weg*, drawing on the Old Testament. He reconverted to Judaism in 1933 after leaving Austria and Germany: Wörner, *Schoenberg's 'Moses und Aron'*, trans. Paul Hamburger (London: Faber and Faber, 1963), pp. 20–21. On this view, Schoenberg's religious evolution may have made *Die Jakobsleiter* largely irrelevant. We shall return to the case of the opera later in the chapter to challenge that view.

37.   See Crawford and Crawford, *Expressionism*, p. 89.

38.   Seraphita describes prayer in Balzac's novel thus: 'Silence and meditation are efficacious means of entering on this road; God always reveals Himself to the solitary and contemplative man': *Séraphita*, pp. 141–2. For Swedenborg, prayer was the link between God and man in this life; for Steiner, in contrast, there was no God in the same sense, to Whom one could pray. Hence Steiner emphasized simply meditation in acquiring 'knowledge and vision of the eternal, indestructible core of [one's] being': *Knowledge of the Higher Worlds*, p. 43.

39.   See Evert Sprinchorn's introduction to the volume of August Strindberg's writings from this period, *Inferno, Alone, and Other Writings*, ed. and trans. Evert Sprinchorn (Garden City, NY: Doubleday, 1968), pp. 26–91. See also Martin Lamm, *August Strindberg*, ed. and trans. Harry G. Carlson (New York: Benjamin Blom, 1971), esp. pp. 291–326; this standard biography, however, mutes many of the details of interest.

40.   Strindberg's interest in the occult was not limited to Swedenborg's variety; Paris in the later nineteenth century fairly teemed with occultists, practitioners of black magic, and societies such as Rosicrucians and the Theosophists. Strindberg was interested in black magic already in 1893, while he was still in Berlin, and actively pursued experiments in alchemy during this period. See the note on this subject in Sprinchorn, ed., *Inferno, Alone, and Other Writings*, pp. 160–63.

41.   Strindberg, *Jacob Wrestles*, in *Inferno, Alone, and Other Writings*, p. 317.

42.   Strindberg, *Jacob Wrestles*, pp. 335–40.

43.   Strindberg concluded *Jacob Wrestles* with the observation that it 'is an attempt at a metaphorical description of the author's religious struggles, and as such it is a failure' (p. 345).

44.   White, *Schoenberg and the God-Idea*, pp. 51–4.

45.   Ibid., pp. 67–9.

46.   White regards Schopenhauer as the decisive philosophical influence on Schoenberg after 1911, especially important for understanding the much later opera *Moses und Aron*. Yet, as we shall see, *Die Jakobsleiter* contains a rejection of the Schopenhauerian doctrine of renunciation (in Gabriel's response to the Struggling One, p. 81 of the score). Moreover, White takes Schopenhauer's 'Idea' to be equivalent to a Platonic Idea (op. cit., p. 70), ignoring the way that Schopenhauer used the word to refer to the objectification of the will to live: on this, see Arthur Schopenhauer, *Die Welt als Wille und Vorstellung*, 2 vols, *Sämtliche Werke in 14 Bänden* (Munich: R Piper Verlag, 1924), section 32, vol. 1, pp. 205–7; *The World as Will and Representation*, 2 vols, trans. E. F. G. Payne (reprinted: 1958; New York: Dover Publications, 1969), vol. 1, pp. 174–6. Finally, *Moses und Aron* makes the Idea of God fundamentally unknowable – a Kantian notion, opposed to the atheism of Schopenhauer. Thus, it is clear that Schoenberg read Schopenhauer carefully, but that other influences were in fact more decisive.

47.   *Die Jakobsleiter*, pp. 6–10 (original punctuation).

48.   Ibid., pp. 32–6, 39–42.

49. Ibid., pp. 4–5.
50. Ibid., pp. 44–5.
51. Ibid., pp. 47–63, 65–6.
52. See Hans Jonas, *The Gnostic Religion: The Message of the Alien God and the Beginnings of Christianity*, 2nd edn (Boston: Beacon Press, 1963), pp. 42–3; and Kurt Rudolph, *Gnosis: The Nature and History of Gnosticism*, trans. Robert M. Wilson (San Francisco: HarperCollins, 1987), pp. 59–67.
53. More philosophically, Augustine was emphatic on this point against the Manichean heresy: 'All things that exist, therefore, seeing that the Creator of them all is supremely good, are themselves good. But because they are not, like their Creator, supremely and unchangeably good, their good may be diminished and increased': *The Enchiridion on Faith, Hope, and Love*, trans. J. F. Shaw (Chicago: Regnery Gateway, 1961), p. 12. Therefore, matter cannot be evil in itself.
54. *Die Jakobsleiter*, pp. 68–76, 78.
55. See Jonas, *The Gnostic Religion*, pp. 42, 46; Rudolph, *Gnosis*, pp. 67ff. Rudolph's discussion of gnostic morality and ethics is well nuanced (pp. 252ff.), and he notes gnostic hostility to the moral law (p. 263); the antinomianism of ancient gnosticism was always one potential. Schoenberg's text, however, is not antinomian so much as it is an attack on the concept of an omnipotent Creator-God as the single source of both Law for the embodied spirit and of the spirit itself.
56. The doctrine of emanation is discussed by Balzac as a solution to the Problem of Evil: *La Comédie humaine*, vol. 11, pp. 826–7; *Séraphita*, p. 118. According to Séraphita's account, there could be only two, equally unacceptable, alternatives to emanation: dualism and pantheism (vol. 11, p. 815; p. 104). But this Swedenborgian argument fails to understand either itself or the Christian doctrine of creation *ex nihilo*: emanation always risks pantheism, and creation does not imply dualism. Cf. Augustine, *Enchiridion*, pp. 11–12.
57. *Die Jakobsleiter*, pp. 79–80.
58. *Die glückliche Hand*, in *Arnold Schoenberg, Wassily Kandinsky: Letters, Pictures and Documents*, ed. Jelena Hahl-Koch, trans. John C. Crawford (London: Faber and Faber, 1984), p. 97. Cf. Schopenhauer, *The World as Will and Representation*, vol. 1, pp. 410–12, on the necessity of abolishing the will to live in order to abolish the pain of life. White, in *Schoenberg and the God-Idea*, claims that Schoenberg read Schopenhauer only in 1911 (p. 67), but obviously he was familiar with the essential ideas much earlier. Anyone familiar with Wagner's works, as Schoenberg was, would have been.
59. *Die Jakobsleiter*, pp. 87–91.
60. Ibid., pp. 81–2.
61. Ibid., pp. 92–7.
62. The Preface to *An Outline of Occult Science* is dated December 1909.
63. *An Outline of Occult Science*, pp. 103, 118ff.
64. The order of the ranks is different in Christian theology, however, and in Christianity the angels were created by God and did not themselves create anything. Cf. St Thomas Aquinas, *Summa Contra Gentiles*, Book 3, Part I, Chapters 77–80.
65. *An Outline of Occult Science*, pp. 125, 206.
66. Ibid., p. 215.
67. This summary is based on Jonas, *The Gnostic Religion*, pp. 42–7; cf. Rudolph, *Gnosis*, pp. 53–121.
68. Between 1904 and 1908, Steiner edited a journal called *Lucifer-Gnosis*; he linked

mysticism, gnosticism and theosophy in *Knowledge of the Higher Worlds*, p. 19. Helena P. Blavatsky aligned her theosophy as well with the ancient gnostics (and all other purveyors of esoteric and occult teachings): see her introduction to *An Abridgement of The Secret Doctrine*, ed. Elizabeth Preston and Christmas Humphreys (London: Theosophical Publishing House, 1966), p. xxxii.

69. Cf. Blavatsky, *An Abridgement*, p. 11; her hostility to science is evident in her statement of the aim of the work 'to show that the occult side of nature has never been approached by the Science of modern civilization' (p. xxiv). Similarly, Steiner called his system 'spiritual science' or 'occult science', and claimed that 'Matter evolves out of the spiritual. Prior to this, only the spiritual exists': *An Outline of Occult Science*, trans. Maud and Henry B. Monges (Spring Valley, NY: Anthroposophic Press, 1972), p. 103. That the appeal of theosophy lay in its spiritual monism as an alternative to materialism is seen in Wassily Kandinsky's attack on 'the nightmare of materialism, which has turned the life of the universe into an evil, useless game', and his consequent enthusiasm for Blavatsky's ideas: *Concerning the Spiritual in Art*, p. 2. As Kurt Rudolph shows, however, the idea of a spiritual monism underlay even the dualism of ancient gnosticism: *Gnosis*, pp. 58, 66.

70. Arnold Schoenberg, *Theory of Harmony*, trans. Roy E. Carter (Berkeley: University of California Press, 1978), p. 20.

71. Ibid., p. 21.

72. He claimed this repeatedly in later years as well; see the essays in *Style and Idea*: 'Problems of Harmony' (1934), p. 284, and 'Composition with Twelve Tones (1)' (1941), pp. 216–17.

73. *Theory of Harmony*, p. 417.

74. *Die Jakobsleiter*, pp. 105–9.

75. Ibid., pp. 115–18.

76. Ibid., pp. 119–23; 127–31.

77. Schoenberg was always proud of his invention of the Twelve-Tone Method; see his claim in 'Twelve-Tone Composition' (1923), *Style and Idea*, p. 207. A year earlier, he had remarked to Josef Rufer, 'I have discovered something which will guarantee the supremacy of German music for the next hundred years': quoted in H. H. Stuckenschmidt, *Arnold Schoenberg*, p. 82.

78. *Die Jakobsleiter*, pp. 132–50.

79. Ibid., p. 130.

80. Ibid., pp. 152–6.

81. Ibid., pp. 145–56.

82. On the Christian doctrine of the preservation of both the intellect and the will, see St Thomas Aquinas, *Summa Contra Gentiles*, Book III, Chapters 47–53, and Book IV, Chapter 92. On Swedenborg, see Sig Synnestvedt, ed., *The Essential Swedenborg*, pp. 107–14: after a human soul has become an angel, according to Swedenborg, one possesses knowledge of goodness and truth, participates in a full married life, and lives a life of service, instruction, and love. Balzac preserves the sense of the preservation of the personality in *Séraphîta*, *La Comédie humaine*, vol. 11, pp. 856–7; *Séraphita*, pp. 153–4. Thus, Schoenberg could not have modelled this part of the oratorio on Balzac's or Swedenborg's view of the heavenly life.

83. Cf. Steiner, *An Outline of Occult Science*, pp. 76ff.; pp. 371ff.: on his view, the soul consists of feelings, not intellect, and after death, the astral body (with all its desires) is shed. The remaining spirit lacks intellect, will and (necessarily) personality.

84. Significantly, Stefan George also had ties to the theosophists and was deeply

influenced by occultism between 1907 and 1913: see Claude David, *Stefan George: Sein dichterisches Werk*, trans. Alexa Remmen and Karl Thiemer (Munich: Carl Hanser Verlag,1967), pp. 294–5.

85. *Die Jakobsleiter*, pp. 4–5.

86. On *Moses und Aron*, see Pamela White, *Schoenberg and the God-Idea*, and Karl Wörner, *Schoenberg's 'Moses und Aron'*; the latter includes a translation of the libretto. The opposition of beauty and truth is already familiar from Schoenberg's Expressionist period.

87. Wörner, op. cit., p. 157.

88. Ibid., p. 189. The usual spelling of Aaron's name is retained here; Schoenberg shortened it to 'Aron' for numerological reasons.

89. Ibid., p. 195.

90. Ibid., p. 201.

91. Ibid., p. 203.

92. Cf. Aristotle, *Metaphysics* 1075a, pp. 10–25.

93. Schoenberg conceded the great perceptual difficulty for a listener, 'even if he is musically educated', in his avoidance of repetition of motivic units and other means of achieving melodic and formal continuity: in 'New Music, My Music' (*c.* 1930), *Style and Idea*, pp. 102–3.

94. Thomson emphasizes both of these deficiencies in *Schoenberg's Error*, but without using the concept of teleological ordering. As a consequence, his conception of tonality is considerably weakened.

95. Eric Voegelin argues this in *Science, Politics and Gnosticism* (Washington, DC: Regnery Gateway, 1968).

96. See the essays in Kathleen J. Regier, *The Spiritual Image in Modern Art* (Wheaton, IL: Theosophical Publishing House, 1987).

CHAPTER EIGHT

The Origins of Modernist Aesthetics

The task of understanding the essential character of musical modernism is now largely complete. Critics such as Adorno and Thomas Mann have pointed to the rejection of musical beauty as arising from the inability to love, the collapse of the moral order and the rejection of a good which would serve to ground the course of human action. These developments arose from within an intellectual culture defined by the dominance of instrumental reason and the elimination of the ability to conceive the Idea of the good noetically. Thus the nihilism of Friedrich Nietzsche appeared as an inevitable consequence of the utilitarian reduction of reason to instrumentality, and the influence of both Schoenberg and Stravinsky appears explicable as answering to the configuration of the larger culture. Nevertheless, we have seen that Schoenberg and other artists of his time were motivated by a deeper quest: not satisfied with the utilitarian and instrumental conceptions of modern materialism, they sought a spirituality rooted in a gnostic vision of reality. But the gnostic concept of the self is just as emotivist as Nietzsche's; the gnostic concept of the soul's endless reincarnation is just as nihilist as Nietzsche's eternal recurrence. What differs is the task of music and the arts: they become not only records of the soul's torments, but also, through their sensual disorder, a revelation of the spirit itself.

If the discovery of atonality and the subsequent imposition of the formal procedures of the Twelve-Tone Method are due to the inspiration of a gnostic theosophy, however, the militancy of modernism becomes far more comprehensible than it otherwise would be. For it would be as imperative for the avant-garde composer to represent the ultimately disordered nature of a 'higher' reality as for traditional composers to represent the nature of order in tonality; it would be imperative, moreover, to displace the tonal order by the 'true' nature of disorder, yet to conceal this break with the past metaphysic by means of the thesis of historical continuity. Nevertheless, the success of the avant-garde in persuading the larger intellectual community of the truth of its understanding of musical reality must rest on more than this thesis of historical continuity. For the means by which music is understood have never been exclusively founded on either naturalism or historicism, but rather have required the assistance of aesthetic perception. Thus the modes by which the avant-garde has been justified and accepted as the legitimate inheritor of the musical traditions of Western civilization become a final and crucial element in understanding the nature of the avant-garde and its acceptance as the musical culture of modernity. The aesthetic theories characteristic of modernism will necessarily turn out to partake of the same essential assumptions of the modernist movement.

We have seen that the predominant ways of understanding music as an art in the twentieth century have been formalism and expressionism. Both have a tendency to locate the value of aesthetic perception in the subjective experience of the listener: the one in the pleasure of form, and the other in the need to experience emotional responses to the music. Both thereby abandon the claims to objective value rooted in the older systems of musical aesthetics. Yet both formalism and expressionism have appeared to overcome the great divide between classicism and modernism, enabling philosophical aesthetics to dispense with the task of justifying one style to the exclusion of the other, or of justifying each by totally divergent methods.[1] In other words, the necessity of accomodating the avant-garde has largely decided the question of aesthetic theory in its subjectivist approach.

The divergence between formalism and expressionism, then, comes down to a preference for one or the other mode of modernism. Formalism sees the abstract form itself as the object of musical perception; this corresponds to the neo-classicist phase of modernist culture, which arose in the 1920s at precisely the same time as the emergence of formalism into supremacy in musical aesthetics. Yet the attention given to the concepts of unity, form and comprehensibility in Schoenberg's and Webern's accounts of the Twelve-Tone Method also made formalism appear as the ideal aesthetic for twentieth-century music in even its most radical phase. Moreover, inasmuch as both Schoenberg and Webern had insisted on the historical continuity of the New Music with the increasing chromaticism and dissonance of late nineteenth-century Romanticism, the aesthetic of formalism appeared able to accommodate earlier styles and forms under the same rubric as the avant-garde. In appearing to be the universal aesthetic, then, formalism also legitimated, preserved and disseminated the avant-garde.

On the other hand, the position of finding the expression of emotion as the determinative element of musical art corresponds to the original inspiration of the Expressionist movement itself. If today musical expression is being rediscovered, it is due less to an enthusiasm for the original phase of Expressionism than to the sense that the alternative, abstract formalism, is no less moribund than the Twelve-Tone Technique and similar approaches to musical composition. Hence, it becomes imperative to seek the common elements of modernist aesthetics in order to understand more fully the phenomenon of musical modernism. For the origins of the modernist mentality lie in the philosophical approaches which have defined the twin aesthetic stances of modern aesthetic theory. The result, therefore, will be to call into question even further the adequacy of modernism in musical culture.

The two positions of formalism and expressionism appear to have their origin in the nineteenth century: Hanslick's treatise, *On the Musically Beautiful* (1854), articulated the formalist doctrine in its definitive form, while the expressionist position recalls common elements of the Romantic doctrine of the composer's self-expression. Both positions, therefore, appear to derive from the aesthetic theories current at the height of the common practice period; the historical continuity of aesthetic doctrines from the Romantic period to the modern period would then mirror the continuity of stylistic development that Schoenberg and Webern postulated as the source of atonality in the potential of tonality. Yet neither historical attribution is as persuasive as might appear at first glance. For Hanslick's formalism was descended from Herbart and ultimately from Immanuel Kant in the late eighteenth century, while the doctrine of emotional expression common to Romantic philosophers and composers was, as we have seen, part of a larger construct in which a metaphysical ideal was recognized as giving an overarching goal to characteristic beauty.[2] In that sense, the twentieth-century version could only be understood as representing a loss of the most important element of nineteenth-century idealism. Thus it is necessary to look elsewhere for the antecedent of twentieth-century Expressionist aesthetics.

The source that corresponds most closely to Schoenberg's own aesthetic, and indeed was historically the source of much of the late nineteenth-century Symbolist aesthetic, was Arthur Schopenhauer. Schopenhauer's aesthetic doctrine was laid out in *The World as Will and Representation* (1819), itself deeply rooted in the problems created by Kantian metaphysics. Thus, in order to understand the aesthetic dilemma of the twentieth century, it is necessary to return to the sources of modern metaphysical understanding, Kant and Schopenhauer. Doing so will reveal the degree to which the modernist impulse springs out of the adoption, not just of the expressionist and formalist doctrines, but of the entire metaphysical system of Kantian philosophy. In that sense, the turn to gnosticism so characteristic of early modernism will be seen to have the character of a solution to a problem inherited from the formative period of idealist philosophy itself. The aesthetic systems by which modernism was justified will turn out to be rooted in a metaphysic that has defined modernity.

The expressionist theory of Schopenhauer

The expressionist doctrine of Schopenhauer points to the nature of the metaphysical problem at the heart of modernism. This position is well known, although its connection with his deep pessimism is sometimes not appreciated: music was the highest form of temporary escape from the pain and suffering inevitable in life. Schopenhauer regarded the will, irrational and arbitrary, as the essence of human nature, always springing 'from lack, from deficiency, and thus from suffering'.[3] All the arts offered some escape from the constant pain of life because they were contemplated disinterestedly – a preservation of the Kantian aesthetic – and therefore without attention to one's own willing.[4] But music alone could create a paradise by reproducing 'all the emotions of our innermost being, but entirely without reality and remote from its pain'.[5] The expression of emotion, therefore, was a reproduction of the motion of the will itself, transformed so that it possessed no objects and therefore none of the pain associated with specific objects of desire. But this removes the very element that could make any emotion identifiable; thus, Schopenhauer's doctrine already replaces the concept of discrete feelings with largely unidentifiable moods which are simply the motion of the will in general. Although he conceived music to be a cathartic release from the will's endless pain, it could be so only by having removed from itself the very emotions it was supposed to express.

At the time of the original publication of *The World as Will and Representation*, Schopenhauer had very little influence. His cause was not helped by his argument, derived from the new contacts scholars had with Buddhist writings, that the only permanent way to overcome the pain and misery of life was the cessation of willing altogether. Thus, it was not until the 1850s that a hint of notoriety emerged; it was in 1854 that Richard Wagner read Schopenhauer's masterpiece and took it to heart.[6] But even so, it was really only in the 1880s, with the advent of the Symbolist movement in poetry, that Schopenhauer began to have a significant impact on the world of the arts.[7] The Symbolists' pessimism found an early prophet in the German philosopher, and the concept of art as an escape from life into the realm of the will itself answered to the new need for a transcendental account of the significance of art without invoking a true transcendence. As a consequence, Schopenhauer's influence still looms large, even without the necessity of endorsing his underlying pessimism: art as a removal from the cares of life is still invoked as an easy explanation for the significance of attention to all styles from all periods.[8]

Yet Schopenhauer's account of the arts, and of music in particular, does not make sense without the burden of his underlying pessimism. It is, therefore, precisely his pessimism that deserves to be taken seriously, for it is a precursor of the nihilism that Nietzsche was to discern as the inevitable product of all metaphysical systems. Hence, it will not do to reduce Schopenhauer's attitude to a matter of his personal predilection, although his pessimism was very early a part of his personality.[9] Rather, what is required here is to understand the perception that the essence of life is pain and suffering on the metaphysical grounds Schopenhauer gives it. This means returning to the foundation of Schopenhauer's mature philosophy in his attempt to construct a critique of Kantian metaphysics.

Schopenhauer's doctoral dissertation of 1813, *On the Fourfold Root of the Principle of Sufficient Reason*, was an attempt to revise Kantian epistemology. Kant had sought to solve the epistemological problem – of how knowledge of anything is possible – through the concept of *a priori* categories such as space, time and causality. The certainty of knowledge was to be guaranteed by the postulate of universal principles of the human mind, principles which must be true because they are necessary for the apprehension and understanding of anything in the world. This, however, left the knowing subject radically separated from the realm of objects.[10] Indeed, the most important result of Kant's *Critique of Pure Reason* (1780) was the bifurcation of the realms of phenomena and noumena, that is, of the observed world of appearances and the spiritual world of essences, or things-in-themselves, including the human soul with its freedom of the will. Knowledge was possible only of the phenomenal realm; it was impossible to know even the freedom of the will, because for Kant knowledge depended on sense perception, and the soul's freedom was not in any way sensuous or accessible to the senses.[11] But sense perception by itself was insufficient to ground knowledge of the phenomenal realm, for there is still a gulf between feeling that there is an object in front of one, for example, and assigning it a location or deciding that it was put there by someone else. This kind of knowledge requires the additional concepts of space and causality, which are never observed by the senses, yet are essential to making sense of sense perception. Thus, Kant had proposed solving the problem of how the radically separated subject could know anything about an object through the postulate of *a priori* principles required by the mind.

Kant's epistemology is not subjectivist in an individualist sense, however: it is the human mind itself, not any particular mind, which requires these *a priori* principles. Schopenhauer, however, accepted Kant's hypothesis of *a priori* knowledge, but altered it by resolving the dualism of subject and object into an individualist subjectivism. That is, he considered all appearances as representations created by the knowing subject himself. Thus, appearances ceased to be objectively knowable and became subjective creations of the subject's will. Hence the title of the 1819 treatise: the world has will for its essence, the realm of phenomena being only the will's own representation of itself. Human consciousness is the only true reality, the will the essence of human nature and all of its constructs.

We have already seen, however, that the will for Schopenhauer was fundamentally rooted in pain and suffering, in need and lack. It was an erotic will: Freud would later take that as his first principle. Nevertheless, this perception of the deficiency of the will emerges from the heart of Kantian metaphysics. For although Kant had made the will the faculty of moral choice, its radical separation from the world of objects rendered it lacking in precisely the ways in which it would seek satisfaction. Indeed, Kant rejected any definition of the object of willing according to the moral law in terms of the satisfaction that might be gained. All motivations of happiness, including that of others, were to be rejected as self-interested to some party, and therefore too impure to ground a moral action.[12] Only duty considered in its own right could motivate morality. The result, however, is surely to make the will perpetually unhappy. This is the will, then, underlying Schopenhauer's conception of willing as originating in pain and need.

This is to say that Schopenhauer's considered metaphysical pessimism sprang precisely from the predicament established by Kantian metaphysics in the first place. To place the will beyond even the willing subject's own knowledge, on the grounds that its freedom could not be sensuously perceived nor its morality sensuously contaminated, created a will that would forever be unhappy. Kant's concept of the will has often been criticized on other grounds: he elevates the will to a position of supreme importance in the conception of the human soul, yet leaves the will empty of objects and devoid of ultimate purpose without a concept of the good.[13] But Kant does not deny an ultimate good, a *summum bonum*; he acknowledges the necessity of belief in a happiness which will be merited by moral activity, and places this ultimate good in heaven.[14] It is, however, the condition of the will in this world which is at issue, for here there is no temporal ordering of life by a definable good. Schopenhauer saw clearly the nihilism that must lurk within the soul of a person who could not ever know, that is, sensuously perceive, genuine goodness. Thus, for Schopenhauer, the beauty of the arts becomes simply an escape from suffering rather than a vision of the ideal, as in Schopenhauer's chief competitor for philosophical attention, Hegel. Schopenhauer endorsed the nihilism implicit in Kant, whereas Hegel sought to overcome it.

This means that all doctrines of expressionism in music derived from Schopenhauer conceal an implicit nihilism. If expression be taken as an end in itself, it is in recognition of there being no higher end for expression to serve, no ideal toward which human life might aspire. But the doctrine of expression cultivated by Schoenberg in the early phase of his atonal period was one which emphasized the expression precisely of pain and suffering, to the exclusion of any other emotion. The will according to Schopenhauer was the will Schoenberg represented in *Die glückliche Hand*, *Erwartung* and *Pierrot lunaire*. In these, the autobiographical content was objectified, yet concealed. Musical representation, then, becomes a therapeutic act, for just the reasons Schopenhauer gave: by depriving the represented will of its objects, music would reproduce the will itself. Whether this reproduction was therefore without its pain may, however, be doubted. Schoenberg's autobiographical works, which through their obscurity even threatened the concept of the coherent self-contained work, accomplished the catharsis of pain that Schopenhauer saw in music.

If, however, this reading of Schopenhauer's nihilism is correct, then it becomes possible to see why both formalism and expressionism have at one time or another dominated the aesthetics of musical modernism. For if formalism, descended from Kant, also holds within it an implication of the nihilism Schopenhauer found supported in Kantian metaphysics, then as an aesthetic it, too, is ideally suited to describing the products of the modernist impulse. Yet to claim that aesthetic formalism conceals an intrinsic nihilism must seem a misrepresentation of the position, for the merit of the doctrine that form constitutes the principal object of aesthetic perception is that it removes the content of art from the domain of dispute. If Schopenhauer is correct, however, such a claim cannot be sustained. A deeper understanding of Kantian formalism, therefore, is necessary in order to assess the metaphysical and aesthetic principles underlying modernism.

The formalist theory of Kantian aesthetics

Kant's aesthetic is given in the *Kritik der Urteilskraft* (*Critique of Judgement*) of 1790. This work completed the exposition of Kant's system of critical philosophy, by which the limits of human reason were set forth. As we have seen, in the bifurcated world of phenomena and noumena, Kant had argued already that knowledge can be said to exist only of the phenomenal realm. Because this is the realm of causality, for Kant the fact of causation, although as a category arising from the requirements of the mind itself, was a pervasive feature of all phenomena. Hence, this realm is the realm of determinism; even in matters of human character and choice, it must be said that there are always prior dispositions which fully determine present character, and factors which can be identified as fully compelling actual choices.[15] Even in the sphere of moral action, what a person does must be counted as causally determined according to Kant.

On the other hand, the will must be free if there is to be moral responsibility, and we must posit such responsibility if life is to make any sense or social life be possible. Hence, the noumenal freedom belonging to the will cannot be determined; this freedom must coexist with the phenomenal determinism of the will's choices as an unperceivable, and therefore unknowable, freedom to act in accordance with the universal moral law. This paradoxical situation is both the strength and the weakness of the Kantian metaphysic: the strength because it will not concede human freedom to the arguments of determinism drawn from the birth of modern science, but the weakness in the sense that it makes such freedom as moral actions require entirely unknown while insisting that it is coextensive with phenomenal determinism. The *Critique of Judgement* attempts to bridge the gap between the realms of freedom and determinism by recognizing a more complex relation of the mind to the world than either pure reason or practical reason allows.

Kant's concept of judgement embraces judgements of beauty and purposiveness in the natural world. It supplies a model for thinking about beauty in the arts only incidentally, yet Kant gives an explicit account of the aesthetic judgement applied to the arts in sufficient detail to warrant the extension of his principles to form a coherent aesthetic theory.[16] Kant, therefore, distinguishes 'free beauty', judged only with respect to its form, from 'dependent beauty', in which the judgement of perfection according to a concept of purpose makes such beauty dependent upon the fulfilment of that purpose. A judgement of dependent beauty is 'contaminated' because it is not a matter of perceiving only pure form; hence, the beauty of a human being, a horse, or a building is of a lower order than the free beauty of flowers, birds and sea shells, because in contrast to the latter, the former may be judged according to their fulfilment of a purpose. Kant then claims the 'superiority of natural to artificial beauty', largely because art is a creation of dependent beauty according to a purpose, whereas nature lacks such a purpose.[17] Thus flowers, birds and seashells are natural objects which appear beautiful because their sole attraction lies in their form: they 'please freely and in themselves'. Kant goes on to claim, however, that certain kinds of man-made objects can also be examples of 'free beauty':

> So also delineations à la grecque, foliage for borders or wall papers, mean nothing in themselves; they represent nothing – no object under a definite concept – and are free beauties. We can refer to the same class what are called in music phantasies (i.e. pieces without any theme), and in fact all music without words.[18]

Thus any art that lacks an intelligible concept is purer than an art that possesses intelligibility. Kant assimilates all instrumental music to the purer model, with unmelodic or themeless music being the best example. Presumably, the toccatas and preludes of Bach would illustrate Kant's point; sacred and operatic arias would not. Aesthetic formalism, therefore, already from the very beginning implied a doctrine specifically about the significance of music, together with a restriction of the highest significance to a certain kind of music. It is worth noting that Kant's aesthetic justified only the least important music of his day.

Kant's larger purpose was to vindicate the possibility of making judgements of taste which could lay claim to some kind of universality, in analogy with the universality of practical reason in deciding upon moral action. In this, Kant clung to the eighteenth-century concept of a universal taste while radically subjectivizing the notion of judgement. For he argued that the judgement of taste is always singular, directed at a particular object and not derivable from any general rules.[19] If an object occupies the cognitive powers suitably, then it pleases, and one is compelled to judge it as being beautiful for everyone universally, without, however, being able to persuade or compel anyone else to judge it the same way.[20] This is parallel with moral reasoning in the *Critique of Practical Reason*: the moral law is universal, but only particular actions can be judged according to their conformity to the categorical imperative. Unlike moral choices, however, judgements of taste are essentially private, so that they lack the actual universality which moral choices necessarily must have. But like moral choices, judgements of taste must be disinterested, for only disinterestedness can guarantee freedom in judging and at the same time justify a claim to universality.

By 'disinterested', however, Kant means that 'we must not be in the least prejudiced in favor of the existence of the things, but be quite indifferent in this respect, in order to play the judge in things of taste'.[21] This goes well beyond the typical eighteenth-century argument that beauty ought to be contemplated disinterestedly in the sense of not desiring to possess the beautiful object.[22] In fact, the usual sense of 'disinterested' contemplation would necessarily allow and require approval of the existence of the beautiful object. But Kant's argument here, as in the case of moral judgements, is against any intrusion of pleasure into the act of judging. For if something is pleasing to the senses, then that the judgement of it as pleasant 'expresses an interest in it, is plain from the fact that by sensation it excites a desire for objects of that kind ...'.[23] In other words, Kant equates sensual pleasure with desire. Hence, he condemns anything that is merely charming, that is, pleasurable to the senses: for example, visual colours and tone colours. Instead, 'the delineation is the essential thing'.[24] In both nature and the fine arts, that means the design constitutes the beauty of a thing; the colour is accidental and is always a corrupting influence. Thus, in music, the abstract relations of the notes in a fantasia afford for Kant the purest example of musical beauty because they are uncorrupted by the charm of a melody.

At this point, it is worth reflecting on the significance of Kant's hostility to sensory charm. He betrays exactly the same hostility to the sensory realm as the gnosticism of the twentieth century; only the motive is different. Whereas for modern gnostics, material existence is itself imprisoning and therefore evil, an infringement on the liberty of the spirit, Kant does not allow the true freedom of the human will to be diminished by its material embodiment; it simply remains unperceivable. But Kant is censorious of pleasure on the highest moral grounds: any desire for pleasure is an intrusion of bodily existence, a command of the body exercised over the will and the faculty of judgement. In moral matters, the result is the pursuit of self-interest rather than of the universality of the moral law for its own sake, and in aesthetic judgement, the enjoyment of the object again out of self-interest rather than for its own sake. But the result is the same, for if the world of the senses cannot in fact be enjoyed, then it is forbidden as evil. Thus the rejection of self-interest that appears plausible in the domain of morality becomes a radical revision in the domain of aesthetics. Concretely for music, the resulting hostility to melodic charm prefigures the twentieth-century rejection of it altogether under the influence of a truly gnostic rejection of the claims of sensuous order.

Kant did find, however, a kind of pleasure associated with the contemplation of beauty, but it was a pleasure which he argued arises solely from the activity of the mental faculties themselves in the process of judging the beautiful independently of any concept. Thus the kind of cognitive powers suitably occupied by the act of judging beauty in objects becomes a crucial consideration. Kant insists on the generality of the cognition employed in aesthetic judgement:

> If the determining ground of our judgment as to this universal communicability of the representation is to be merely subjective, i.e. is conceived independently of any concept of the object, it can be nothing else than the state of mind, which is to be met with in the relation of our representative powers to each other, so far as they refer a given representation to *cognition in general*.[25]

Only the kind of judgement that is without a conceptual basis could both be subjective and have universality ascribed to it.

Kant identifies the cognitive powers brought into relation in the judgement of a beautiful object as the imagination, for the intuitive comprehension of all the details perceived, and the 'understanding for the unity of the concept uniting the representations'.[26] It must be emphasized, however, that what is important here for the concept is not the recognition of the actual object represented, as in the leaves and flowers of a wallpaper border, but only the *unity* of it. Thus, the cognitive powers involved correspond to the qualities of variety and unity in the object being judged as beautiful; these are the objective properties of beauty, but defined so broadly as not to offer a real criterion of judgement regarding, for example, the accuracy of representation. Instead, what gives rise to the judgement of beauty is the involvement of the cognitive powers in a joint activity that Kant calls 'free play', and this is the source of pleasure in the contemplation of beauty; indeed, it is the pleasure itself.

> The consciousness of the mere formal purposiveness in the play of the subject's cognitive powers, in a representation through which an object is given, is the pleasure itself, because it contains a determining ground of the activity of the subject in respect of the excitement of its cognitive powers ... without however being limited to any definite cognition ... .[27]

Kant concludes, therefore, that we seek the state of contemplation of beauty as an end in itself, simply in order to occupy the cognitive powers of the mind. But given his conception of the beautiful as lacking intelligible concepts, it is clear that the contemplation consists in simply absorbing the pattern of a flower, a wallpaper, or an abstract design. Hence the utility of Kantian formalism for the abstract art of the twentieth century: on this aesthetic, only the perception of the whole and the constitutive details is permissible in what has come to be called 'the aesthetic experience'.[28]

Once again, it is worth reflecting on how close Kant is to more modern attitudes, not only toward art, but toward the mind itself. For this aesthetic disparages the role of the mind in the contemplation of beauty by reducing beauty to the purely formal qualities of unity and variety. Although as formal qualities, these are in fact traditional – one may recall the emphasis on integrity and consonance of the parts in the concept of beauty for Thomas Aquinas, for example – nevertheless, the dismissal of a conceptual component of beauty is revolutionary. Hegel, it will be recalled, insisted on defining art as the sensuous representation of the truth, so that artistic beauty was the unity of the concept and its representation.[29] Similarly, Victor Cousin in the nineteenth century defended the essence of beauty as an intelligible concept, a moral or a spiritual beauty.[30] Even for St Thomas, the formal qualities which seem so close to Kant must be understood within their context: he was describing the beauty of the Word as the Son of God, that is, as intelligible truth which possesses both a certain form and a radiance by which it is known.[31] Thus, on the authentically traditional view, the formal properties of beauty are the properties through which an intelligible concept is perceived. By eliminating the conceptual element of beauty, Kant takes the dichotomy of sense and spirit and establishes a hostility to the sensual perceptibility of the spiritual element itself, considered as intellectual concept. Thus arises a diminution of the field of rationality which anticipates the truly gnostic suspicion of reason as a faculty for the apprehension of order in the twentieth century. Kantian formalism is therefore not only adaptable to the modernist styles of art arising out of gnosticism; it established a precedent by weakening the case for the perception of intelligible beauty.

The lack of a conceptual content in beauty is mirrored in Kant's notion of the kind of purpose ascribed to a beautiful object. The awakening of the cognitive faculties in 'free play' constitutes the formal purposiveness of a beautiful object. But it is not an actual purpose; it is only an apparent purposiveness to be ascribed to a beautiful object as existing in order to be judged aesthetically.[32] This is why Kant inverts the traditional hierarchy that placed human, conceptual and artistic beauty above natural beauty; by placing natural beauty highest, it was an example of something that objectively lacked a purpose, but could subjectively be described as if it existed for our contemplation. The humanly created examples of 'free beauty' also conformed to this model of purposeless purposiveness: wallpaper patterns and themeless fantasias exist only to be contemplated as abstract patterns engaging the mind in some measure, but without any specific attention or conceptual thought required. It is to these limited models, then, that all the arts are assimilated in the formalist aesthetic.

Kant's treatment of the arts follows from his account of the pleasure arising in the contemplation of the beautiful. Art is 'production through freedom', that is, it proves itself 'purposive as play'.[33] Its only purposiveness lies in being designed for aesthetic contemplation. It is 'free from all constraint of arbitrary rules', and it must be capable of giving pleasure 'without being based on concepts'.[34] Because there are no rules prescribable for art, he insists, genius is the creative analogue of taste, the 'talent for producing that for which no definite rule can be given ... . Hence *originality* must be its first priority.'[35] Here, then, is the origin of the modern emphasis on originality as the defining characteristic of the creative genius. Although the doctrine of originality has come to be taken for granted since Kant's day, it is clear that its origin reveals its limitations. Such a doctrine is what must emerge as the aim of art once the representation of conceptual content is eliminated.

But Kant's view of the arts, it must be recognized, was seriously at odds with the practice of all the arts in the late eighteenth century. For there were certainly conventions, conceived as rules, governing poetry and the fine arts, and composers learned to write music by following the rules of sixteenth-century species counterpoint as given in Johann Fux's *Gradus ad Parnassum*. Moreover, both poetry and painting were still arts pursued primarily in order to communicate ideas; the eighteenth-century emphasis on moral didacticism in the arts was derived from a long tradition.[36] Music, too, partook of this didactic element, the celebratory ending of Baroque and Classical *opera seria* confirming the triumph of virtue and the defeat of vice. Thus, Kant's conception of the purposiveness of the arts is astonishingly one-sided for his day. Taken literally, his aesthetic demands contemplation only of abstract patterns of rhyme and metre, design and balance, or rhythm and tonal relationships. It could not, indeed, have been persuasive to his contemporaries, who tended to regard the high-mindedness of disinterested contemplation as its main asset. Instead, the real influence of Kantian aesthetics could come only with the advent of abstract art in the twentieth century.

In discussing the arts in more detail, however, Kant did make some provision for the communication of moral ideas. He noted that 'if the beautiful arts are not brought into more or less close combination with moral ideas', they must be fated to arouse discontent in the judgement of reason.[37] Hence, he ranked the arts of speech (rhetoric and poetry) above the formative arts (sculpture, architecture, painting, interior design and landscape gardening). Music and the 'art of color' were least in importance, in his estimation, because they offered only a 'beautiful play of sensations'.[38] Indeed he does not define what an art of colour might be; it does not appear to be related to the formative arts, which he has already discussed. In spite of the potential for some arts to be associated with moral ideas, however, he emphasized that 'yet in all beautiful art the essential thing is the form'; form was still primary.[39] Indeed, he made the moral effect of the arts a result of the elevation of the mind above the level of sense, rather than the actual moral ideas found in any particular work.[40] Beauty was only a weak symbol of moral ideas at best.

Hence, only once did he concede that music might be something more than form in the way it is perceived. In a perhaps confused metaphor, Kant observes: 'the form of the composition ... only serves instead of the form of language ... to express the aesthetical idea of a connected whole of an unspeakable wealth of thought, corresponding to a certain theme which produces the dominating affection in the piece.'[41] That is, whereas in language thought is communicated, in music it is simply the idea of a whole consisting of musical details, like a theme which conveys a dominant feeling or affection. But thematic music, it will be recalled, was less aesthetically worthwhile than themeless music. Thus, although the traditional doctrine of music as the expression of feeling could not be banished completely, for Kant the expression of feeling was in no way relevant to the aesthetic contemplation of music. It was rather the form of a connected whole that really mattered.

Kantian dualism and the emergence of modern gnosticism

The consideration of Kant's aesthetic, therefore, reveals what might be called the genetic weaknesses of formalism. Kantian formalism was not primarily aesthetic in nature; rather, it was the ruling paradigm of his epistemology and his moral philosophy as well. If his aesthetic seems objectionably one-sided with respect to the traditional practices of poetry and painting, the consequences are even more dubious in the other fields of philosophical inquiry. If knowledge has any meaning, surely it must lie in the apprehension of the essential characteristics of the object perceived: and that would include, among other qualities, the freedom that Kant postulated as the central quality of the human soul. But Kant conceived that freedom as spontaneity, the ability to choose arbitrarily, rather than the power to choose rationally; thus he thought he could not detect it. But if human freedom is conceived instead as lying in the very rationality of man, in the ability to weigh choices and to decide among alternatives based on experience, then freedom of the will is discernible and the essence of human nature perceivable.[42] Moreover, with this redefinition of reason, the conformity of reason to the phenomenal world would eliminate the radical separation between the human spirit and the material world of experience and appearance. Knowledge, then, would not be reduced to a matter of sensory perception, but would extend from the senses through the use of the intellect. Therefore, the rigid dichotomy Kant saw in the world of appearances and the realm of essences cannot be sustained. Once that bifurcation is rejected, however, the entire motivation of Kant's aesthetic formalism disappears.

The ethical consequences of a rejection of Kantian metaphysics also have implications for assessing aesthetic formalism. For the human good must indeed be definable according to what human nature objectively is; thus the end of moral decision and action is an identifiable good which must include rationality and freedom of the will properly conceived. The form of the moral law, then, is not sufficient as a guide to either action or virtue. But that means that there are indeed moral ideas, not just a moral law, and thus there is a reason for the traditional content of literature and the fine arts in terms of the educational value of literary and artistic representations of those ideas. The stories that become a part of a civilization's cultural tradition help to define and to perpetuate people's sense of what the virtues are and how they are appropriately realized in given situations. Hence, the intellectual content of literature and the arts should in general be central to their practice, rather than peripheral as Kant tried to make it. The purposiveness of art simply cannot be reduced to the contemplation of form as Kant's aesthetic requires.

The metaphysical foundation of the Kantian aesthetic, however, contains within it grounds for a nihilist despair: it is a proto-gnostic dualism. The radical difference between matter and spirit is not itself gnostic; even in the ancient world, Plato had sharply distinguished the two. But Kant's attempt to solve the epistemological problem that arose within Cartesian scepticism retained the foundations of that problem in the incommunicability of matter and spirit. The ancient world, in contrast, had insisted on the essential conformity of the mind to sense perception and the external world. Thus, while Plato, too, had regarded the body as the prison of the soul, the structure of the Platonic soul had the same structure as the body: the mind, the passions and the desires had their counterparts in the bodily organs of the brain, the heart and the liver.[43] The soul, therefore, was not a stranger to the body; the body was intended for the soul as its temporary home. For Kant, however, the identification of knowledge with sense perception leaves the human spirit with its capacity for willing unknowable, so that only the 'prison' of material existence in the phenomenal world is truly perceived. This, if true, would be cause for despair, but its truth ought to be doubted.

The aesthetic Kant proposes to bridge the chasm separating sense perception of the external world and the rational faculty by which moral choices are made rests, however, on an equally dubious faculty of judgement. This faculty becomes as indefinable as the freedom of the will is unperceivable, so that only a perception of the minimal aesthetic characteristics of unity and complexity constitute its exercise. Such a concept of judgement cannot yield a determinate rule for the judging of particular objects as beautiful, for much more is entailed in the judgement of a work of art as beautiful. Victor Cousin was right to insist that the form is always the form of something: with Hegel, he affirmed the essential content of a work of art as truth itself, a moral and spiritual content. That is, the often-repeated accusation that Kant's moral philosophy rests on an empty concept of the human good in this life may be applied with equal force to this aesthetic. By banishing intelligible content from both art and nature, Kant denies, in effect, any meaningful judgement regarding beauty.

The most serious consequence, however, is further to remove the ability to perceive goodness in the world. For if beauty is, as the idealist aesthetic insists, the sensuous manifestation of truth and goodness, then physical beauty affirms the goodness of existence as well as the possibility of moral goodness itself. But if beauty is not a representation of such truths, and if the good cannot be the end of action, then goodness in the world evaporates. This is nihilism itself; Schopenhauer, therefore, only makes explicit what is implicit in Kant. Thus the triumph of Kantianism in the twentieth century is only another phase in the realization of nihilism. But this means that the oscillation between the aesthetics of Kantian formalism and Schopenhauerian expressionism is not a matter of indecision between two utterly opposed points of view. Rather, it is merely an exchange between two related systems rooted in the same nihilistic metaphysic.

Kant's philosophy was founded on the conviction that post-Newtonian physical science produced an understanding of the world as fully deterministic. It took only the further development of modern science, in both physics and biology to confirm this view to all appearances and to produce the spiritual crisis of the late nineteenth century. The quest to find a way to preserve human freedom, then, could only be accomplished by reasserting the Kantian will as 'supersensible' and therefore untouched by the world of the senses, leaving the moral dimension of human existence intact but unperceivable, or by attempting to subordinate the world of nature to the human will or spirit. The latter was the approach of Schopenhauer and Nietzsche; though prophets of nihilism, they rather attempted to find solutions to the condition of despair through the efforts of the will itself – either to escape the suffering of the world (Schopenhauer) or to assert the will over the suffering of the world (Nietzsche).

The emergence of gnostic theosophy was along exactly the same lines: an attempt to discover a solution to nihilism, rather than to allow the human spirit to be vanquished. Yet its assertion of the indefinability of the spirit, together with its identification of emotion, rather than reason, as the constituent element of the soul, mark it as the inheritor of the metaphysics of both Kant and Schopenhauer. If the indefinability of the spirit echoes the Kantian unperceivability of the will, the emphasis on emotions as solely definitive of the personality recall Schopenhauer's definition of the will. Thus, the modern rebirth of ancient gnosticism was well prepared by the philosophical movements of the late eighteenth and early nineteenth centuries.

The emotivist personality prevalent in the twentieth century, therefore, appears already in the work of Schopenhauer as the inevitable consequence of the predicament established for human existence in the rationalist metaphysic of Immanuel Kant. By reducing the soul to private emotions and desires, Schopenhauer made salvation from the pain of existence dependent on the emancipation from these feelings. But modern gnosticism, instead, celebrates them precisely as the key to salvation, for the degree to which the evil of the world is perceived emotionally is the degree to which spiritual health appears possible to be restored. The irony, then, is that the rationalism of Kant necessarily makes the emotional life appear most attractive. Hence, twentieth-century aesthetics of music have just as often celebrated the emotional content as the formal structure of the art. But the emotional content is now usually regarded as created by the listener, rather than communicated by the composer. When emotions are regarded as essentially private in nature, they become incommunicable. Thus, whatever emotions inspired the composer, others may inspire the listener. This, however, places musical aesthetics well on the road to an exercise in solipsism.

Modern aesthetic theories, therefore, participate in precisely the same metaphysical nihilism as the musical movements they seek to accommodate. At the same time, just as gnostic spirituality underlay the decisive movements creating modernism in music (as in other fine arts), so too there is a suggestion of proto-gnosticism in the Kantian metaphysic itself. For the effort to preserve an arena for the human spirit, even though it will turn out to be unperceivable, is not unlike the theosophical attempt to find salvation from the evil of existence in the realm of the indefinable 'supersensible'. The question this raises, however, is how adequate either modernist musical styles or modernist aesthetic theories are with respect to the requirements of human existence. Claims for absolute determinism are no longer central to the practice of either physical or biological science; even at the end of the eighteenth century, such claims represented an exaggeration of the implications of Newtonian mechanics. While it is possible to understand sympathetically the intellectual and social contexts for the rise of modernism, it is time to question the continued relevance of a view of the world and human existence which rests upon a fundamental scientific misapprehension. This is to suggest, moreover, that it is time for our culture to return the question of validity to the realm of the arts: are modernist styles adequate to the task of representing human nature and the nature of the good? If not, modern aesthetic theories will also require reconsideration. The crucial question is whether an ideal as a vision of the good can once again command belief.

Notes

1. Noël Carroll has noted that in general philosophical definitions of art in the twentieth century have been ahistorical, driven by the need to accommodate the avant-garde: 'Historical Narratives and the Philosophy of Art', *Journal of Aesthetics and Art Criticism* 51 (1993), pp. 313–26.
2. For a survey of nineteenth- and twentieth-century musical aesthetics, see Edward Lippman, *A History of Western Musical Aesthetics* (Lincoln and London: University of Nebraska Press, 1992).
3. Arthur Schopenhauer, *Die Welt als Wille und Vorstellung*, Section 38, ed. Paul Deussen, 2 vols, in *Sämtliche Werke* in *14 Bänden* (Munich: R. Piper, 1924), vol. 1, pp. 231–2; *The World as Will and Representation*, 2 vols, trans. E. F. J. Payne

(1958; reprinted New York: Dover Publications, 1969), vol. 1, pp. 196.

4. *Die Welt*, Section 38, vol. 1, pp. 231–2; *The World as Will and Representation*, vol. 1, pp. 196–7.

5. *Die Welt*, Section 52, p. 312; *The World as Will and Representation*, vol. 1, pp. 264.

6. On Wagner's attempt to rely on Schopenhauer's aesthetic, see Deryck Cooke, *I Saw the World End: A Study of Wagner's Ring* (Oxford: Oxford University Press, 1979), pp. 21–3.

7. On Schopenhauer's importance for the Symbolists, see Andrew G. Lehmann, *The Symbolist Aesthetic in France, 1885–1895* (Oxford: Basil Blackwell, 1950), p. 55.

8. See, for example, Alan H. Goldman, *Aesthetic Value* (Boulder, CO: Westview Press, 1995), p. 155, where art is conceived as the construction of an alternative world removing us from the real world of our everyday lives.

9. See Rudiger Safransky, *Schopenhauer and the Wild Years of Philosophy*, trans. Ewald Osers (Cambridge, MA: Harvard University Press, 1991) for a study of the relation between the philosopher's personality and the development of his thought.

10. Cf. Immanuel Kant, *Critique of Pure Reason*, trans. F. Max Muller (Garden City, NY: Doubleday, 1966), Section 16, B: 132–6, p. 79.

11. This is developed in Kant's *Kritik der praktischen Vernunft*, ed. Paul Natorp, *Kants gesammelte Schriften*, 22 vols (Berlin: Preussische Akademie der Wissenschaften, 1908), vol. 5, p. 29; *Critique of Practical Reason*, trans. Lewis White Beck (Indianapolis: Bobbs-Merrill, 1956), p. 29.

12. Kant, *Gesammelte Schriften*, vol. 5, pp. 34, 58; *Critique of Practical Reason*, pp. 35, 60.

13. See G. W. F. Hegel, *Philosophy of Right*, trans. T. M. Knox (Oxford: Oxford University Press, 1952), Section 135, pp. 89–90; also more recently Iris Murdoch, *The Sovereignty of Good*, 2nd edn (London: Routledge and Kegan Paul, 1985), pp. 35–7, 79–83.

14. Kant, *Gesammelte Schriften*, vol. 5, pp. 129–30; *Critique of Practical Reason*, p. 134.

15. *Gesammelte Schriften*, vol. 5, pp. 94–5; *Critique of Practical Reason*, p. 98.

16. For studies of Kant's aesthetic, see Donald W. Crawford, *Kant's Aesthetic Theory* (Madison: University of Wisconsin Press, 1974), and Francis X. J. Coleman, *The Harmony of Reason: A Study in Kant's Aesthetics* (Pittsburgh: University of Pittsburgh Press, 1974). It is notable as a rare event in twentieth-century aesthetic writing that Crawford is willing to venture some criticism of Kantian formalism (e.g. p. 110).

17. Immanuel Kant, *Kritik der Urteilskraft*, ed. Karl Vorländer (Hamburg: Felix Meiner, 1990), Sections 16 and 42, pp. 69, 151; *Critique of Judgement*, trans. J. H. Bernard (New York: Macmillan, 1951), pp. 65, 142.

18. *Kritik der Urteilskraft*, Section 16, p. 70; *Critique of Judgement*, p. 66.

19. *Kritik der Urteilskraft*, Section 33, p. 135; *Critique of Judgement*, p. 127.

20. *Kritik der Urteilskraft*, Section 6, pp. 48–9; *Critique of Judgement*, p. 46.

21. *Kritik der Urteilskraft*, Section 2, p. 41; *Critique of Judgement*, p. 39.

22. On Kant's relation to earlier doctrines of aesthetic disinterestedness, see Crawford, *Kant's Aesthetic Theory*, pp. 37–41; Jerome Stolnitz, 'On the Origins of Aesthetic Disinterestedness', *Journal of Aesthetics and Art Criticism* 20 (1961–62), pp. 131–43; Preben Mortensen, 'Shaftesbury and the Morality of Art Appreciation', *Journal of the History of Ideas* 55 (1994): 631–50.

23. Kant, *Kritik der Urteilskraft*, Section 3, p. 43; *Critique of Judgement*, p. 41.

24. *Kritik der Urteilskraft*, Section 14, p. 65; *Critique of Judgement*, p. 61.
25. *Kritik der Urteilskraft*, Section 9, p. 55; *Critique of Judgement*, p. 52 (emphasis in original).
26. *Kritik der Urteilskraft*, Section 9, pp. 55–6; *Critique of Judgement*, p. 52.
27. *Kritk der Urteilskraft*, Section 12, p. 61; *Critique of Judgement*, pp. 57–8.
28. As, for example, in Suzanne K. Langer, *Feeling and Form: A Theory of Art developed from 'Philosophy in a New Key'* (New York: Scribner's Sons, 1953), who uses the term 'aesthetic experience' on p. 36, and applies her aesthetic of rhythm in an organic whole equally to tonal and atonal music on p. 126.
29. G. W. F. Hegel, *Vorlesungen über die Ästhetik*, ed. E. Moldenhauer and K. Michel, *Werke in zwanzig Bänden* (Frankfurt am Main: Suhrkamp Verlag, 1970), vol. 13, pp. 83, 151–2; *Aesthetics: Lectures on Fine Art*, 2 vols, trans. T. M. Knox (Oxford: Clarendon Press, 1975), pp. 55, 111.
30. Victor Cousin, *Lectures on the True, the Beautiful and the Good*, trans. O. W. Wight (New York: Appleton, 1875), pp. 149, 157.
31. St Thomas Aquinas, *Summa Theologica*, 5 vols, trans. Fathers of the English Dominican Province (1911; Westminster, MD: Christian Classics, 1981), vol. I, Q.39, art. 8, p. 201.
32. Kant, *Kritik der Urteilskraft*, Section 10, p. 59; *Critique of Judgement*, pp. 55–6.
33. *Kritik der Urteilskraft*, Section 43, p. 155; *Critique of Judgement*, p. 145.
34. *Kritik der Urteilskraft*, Section 45, p. 159; *Critique of Judgement*, p. 149.
35. *Kritik der Urteilskraft*, Section 46, p. 161; *Critique of Judgement*, p. 150 (emphasis in original).
36. Didacticism had its origin in Horace's *Ars Poetica*, lines 333–44: 'Poets intend to give either pleasure or instruction/or to combine the pleasing and instructive in one poem'. But 'The poet winning every vote blends the useful with the sweet,/ giving pleasure to his reader while he offers him advice'. Horace's *Satires and Epistles*, trans. Jacob Fuchs (New York: Norton, 1977), p. 92.
37. Kant, *Kritik der Urteilskraft*, Section 52, pp. 182–3; *Critique of Judgement*, p. 170.
38. *Kritik der Urteilskraft*, Section 51, pp. 180–82; *Critique of Judgement*, pp. 168–9.
39. *Kritik der Urteilskraft*, Section 52, p. 182; *Critique of Judgement*, p. 170.
40. *Kritik der Urteilskraft*, Section 59, p. 213, *Critique of Judgement*, pp. 198–9.
41. *Kritik der Urteilskraft*, Section 53, pp. 185–6; *Critique of Judgement*, p. 173.
42. On Kant's notion of freedom as spontaneity, see *Gesammelte Schriften*, vol. 5, p. 99; *Critique of Practical Reason*, p. 103. The alternative of rational voluntariness is Aristotle's; see *The Nichomachean Ethics*, trans. David Ross (1925; Oxford: Oxford University Press, 1980), Book III, Sections 1–5, pp. 48–63.
43. Plato, *Republic* 436a–441c.

Epilogue

The exploration of the metaphysical foundations of musical culture has now reached a point where it is possible to consider the broader problems posed at the outset of this study. The curious nature of a bifurcated culture has received an explanation: the culture of preservation and the culture of innovation rest on diametrically opposed metaphysical premises. The former, the realm of classical music defined by the stylistic practice of tonality, represents a teleological conception of the temporal order, corresponding to the immanence of the good or the ideal. The latter, the realm of the avant-garde defined by the rejection of tonality, represents a rejection of the concept of order altogether, because order is perceived to be the enemy of the human spirit. Hence, Adorno was right to perceive that the avant-garde dissolves temporality, because any conception of a temporal order uniting the past with the present and the future will constitute an order seen to be imprisoning on the gnostic point of view. But Adorno was not correct in seeing the avant-garde as arising out of despair at the collapse of goodness in the wars and miseries of the twentieth century. Rather, as we have seen, the roots predate those events and have their origin in philosophical responses to modern science.

The impulse of modernism in music arises out of an already bifurcated world as described by Kantian metaphysics. It is a world in which the spiritual element most important for defining human nature appears thoroughly unperceivable and therefore unknowable. As a consequence, the spirit appears trapped in the imprisonment of the phenomenal realm, which is conceived as deterministic in all respects. Order, then, will have to be a part of this determinism; to free the spirit will require denying the goodness which classical philosophy associated with all kinds of order. This is to say, however, that on each of their premises, the culture of classicism and the culture of modernism appear justified. If Plato is right about the goodness of order, then music ought to be harmonious in at least the sense of being consonant and melodic. If Aristotle and Leibniz are correct in emphasizing the necessity of teleological order, then music ought further to be rooted in a tonic, so that it becomes a metaphor of temporality itself. But if Kant is right, then music is permitted not to possess any of those qualities, and if Schopenhauer is right, then it should not. The culture of musical classicism persists precisely because it affords an aural way of conserving the sense of the goodness of temporal existence and the concept of the ideal itself. The culture of the avant-garde arose and persists because it appears to correspond to the way in which the post-Kantian modern world must perceive reality. The problem, therefore, becomes one of deciding the truth of rival metaphysical positions.[1]

Precisely such a judgement appears impossible, however. For the Kantian metaphysic appears to correspond most closely to the scientific understanding of the world; it came into existence in order to recognize the legitimate claims of Newtonian science, and it has enjoyed a revival in the twentieth century because it seemed best adapted to the claims of both the phenomenology of modern relativity theory in physics and the Darwinian evolutionary theory in biology. In the former case, the location of the categories of space and time in human perception corresponds exactly to the Kantian location of them in the human mind, while in the latter case, the sense of determinism in biological development appears to endorse Kant's determinism of the phenomenal realm. But this undercuts the traditional arguments in favour of a great difference between the physical and the biological realms. It also undercuts the Romantics' attempt to vindicate the spirituality of the larger world by employing a biological metaphor: the idea of Nature as an organism rested ultimately on the Platonic concept of a World-Soul. For if Nature is ruled by the deterministic law of the survival of the fittest, then there is no soul in it, no genuine freedom of a rational being. The only way to reconcile science and human freedom, then, would indeed appear to be to insist that both are true simultaneously and paradoxically. But then the freedom of the human spirit will necessarily turn out to be not scientifically verifiable; that is, it will not be justifiable in a scientific world. The result will inevitably be denial of the possibility of such freedom.

Freedom, however, surely matters to most people. Hence, either spiritual freedom will have to be asserted all the more vigorously by denying the category of truth, as in Nietzsche, or some attempt be made to subordinate the scientific understanding to a more spiritual, but equally unverifiable, understanding, as in modern gnosticism. It therefore becomes impossible to say that any metaphysical position is true in the modern world. Either way, the goodness of order must be denied, precisely in order to allow the human spirit some room for a genuine existence.

The classical style of tonality, therefore, appears dead. On this Adorno appears right, even if for the wrong reasons. Or rather, even without the disasters of world war and genocide in the twentieth century, classical musical culture as a creative culture would be dead; the horrors of human wickedness only add to the sense of the evil of the phenomenal and material realm. Equally, however, humanity would seem to require the Idea of the good and the teleological order it produces to find the world bearable; what makes individual as well as social existence sustainable is precisely what appears to be precluded by the scientific understanding. This is the deeper reason why C. P. Snow's two cultures, the literary and the scientific, are at war with one another in the modern world: more than their practitioners not being familiar with each other's worlds, those worlds themselves express irreconcilable metaphysical positions. Thus, the bifurcated musical culture of the twentieth century appears absolutely necessary: the preservation of classicism is required in order to confirm the goodness of life, and the creativity of modernism becomes necessary in order to deny the stultification of the human spirit in a world of determinism.

It will not be forgotten, however, that at the very birth of the concept of tonality, Fétis already saw its death on the horizon. For him, the original *ordre transitonique* of the Baroque was outdated by the discovery of both the technical means of borrowing harmonies from other keys and the expressive ends of representing ever more unstable emotions as characteristic of modern life. Thus, the irony is that for both of these seminal figures for the two cultures, Fétis and Adorno, tonality appeared to be exhausted: still a living cultural force in the mid-nineteenth century, it was dead by the mid-twentieth. But Hegel, too, had spoken of the end of art, seeing even at the beginning of the 1820s a process of cultural decay in the appearance of some of the more nihilistic tendencies of Romanticism.[2] It is for good reason, therefore, that modernism is traceable to antecedents in the Romantic age; the nihilism of Schopenhauer was an implicit possibility in the Kantian metaphysic. For music, however, it took the better part of the century for this implication to work itself out in the appearance of the avant-garde. It is no coincidence that it emerged out of the influence of Richard Wagner, who was inspired by Schopenhauer. The avant-garde of the twentieth century has been the legacy of nineteenth-century nihilism.

Yet the decisive end of tonality came only with the advent of an explicitly gnostic denial of the goodness of order. By turning to gnostic spirituality in the form of modern theosophy, Schoenberg hoped to find a release from nihilist despair in a metaphysical framework for understanding the human spirit. Yet, as we have seen, gnosticism only objectifies the nihilist vision of disorder; it makes disorder normative by explaining tangible order as an evil condition of material existence. This leaves tangible disorder as the defining condition of authentic spiritual existence, thereby legitimating the perception of the world as fundamentally disordered. Although both Madame Blavatsky and Rudolph Steiner strove to maintain the language of moral duty and virtue, neither the metaphysical framework of theosophy nor the emotivist self with its indefinable spirit can overcome the underlying nihilism: the endless round of reincarnations possesses no *telos*, no ultimate vision of the good, to motivate spiritual development. In this, theosophy was remarkably close to Nietzsche, who also believed in the 'eternal recurrence' and tried to develop a substitute for morality in the exercise of the will by the emotivist self.[3] Gnosticism, therefore, is the second stage of the nihilist revolt against being and order; the similarities between Existentialism and gnosticism become intelligible as the attempt to will a meaning for life without a *telos* of the good.[4] This is the stage represented in Schoenberg's break with tonality and the subsequent development of the Twelve-Tone Method.

The legacy of Schoenberg's achievement was the end of classical tonality as the ordering of consonance, harmony and melody around a tonic, and the emergence of a school of composers interested in the strict control of all musical parameters. The trend toward the complete serialization of all musical elements after World War II, inspired by Anton Webern's taut control of pitch sequences, only served to deepen the rejection of musical order and being. The necessary result was music that sounds as if it does not matter what happens next. Hence the irony that many have noted: such music is little distinguishable from that produced by the other approach characteristic of the modern avant-garde, the practice of aleatoric composition. Even more explicitly than Schoenberg's New Music, the latter reflects a gnostic revolt against order.

That there is a close relationship of total serialization and aleatoric composition can be seen in the leading composers of the post-World War II generation. The composer perhaps most closely associated with total serialization in the late 1940s and early 1950s was Pierre Boulez, yet he later moved to a position which incorporated some controlled elements of chance by the late 1950s. His aim was to replace tonality with a new musical grammar and syntax; his rejection of the aims of classical music was inspired by a wide range of modernist composers and artists, including Webern, the poet Mallarmé, and the Expressionist painters Kandinsky, Klee and Mondrian.[5] But whereas many of the earlier modernists had been inspired by a spiritual quest – especially the theosophists Mondrian and Kandinsky, and perhaps Klee – Boulez appears to be devoid of such an inspiration. Composition becomes a substitute for spirituality, and style encodes a metaphysic that subsists in its own right without now being held in explicit belief.

In contrast, the composer most associated with the development of aleatoric music was John Cage: yet he was a student of Schoenberg's between 1934 and 1936. Influenced musically by Henry Cowell, and philosophically by Zen Buddhism after 1946, he began experimenting with the incorporation of non-musical noise in his 'works' in the 1930s.[6] The rejection of discrete pitches as the fundamental constituents of musical sound, however, certainly entails a denial of tonal order. Cage discovered the potential of chance elements for music in reading the *I Ching* in 1950; again, an Eastern philosophico-religious source proved crucial to the avant-garde. The introduction of chance operations as an element in determining musical events further undermines the notion of order: what is heard can have no sense of purposiveness, and indeed Cage admitted that his experimental music had no purpose.[7] His indebtedness to Zen Buddhism, however, provides the essential key to understanding his artistic purpose. For Zen finds this life in need of salvation, yet rejects any transcendent order of being. At the same time, it seeks to escape pure nihilism through a mystical contemplation of the nothingness that it sees at the core of existence. It is therefore a religious understanding that is gnostic in its structure: finding the material world evil, it seeks escape through an indefinable spiritual state.

This affords the key to understanding Cage's most famous 'work' that appears to substantiate Adorno's thesis that the work-concept is now defunct: *4' and 35"*. It may be interpreted in several ways: as the removal of the composer's will from the work, or the removal of conceptual thought from music, or the removal of a dichotomy of composed and uncomposed sounds.[8] All, however, are consequences of Zen Buddhism: for the removal of reality in the form of conceptually composed sounds eliminates the possibility of conceiving the uncomposed sounds as music; the removal of the composer's will from the work is a necessary consequence of there being nothing composed. Thus gnostic metaphysics yields its ultimate result in the elimination of musical composition altogether. For Cage, music was to provide the opportunity for contemplating nothingness and the spiritual insight which that experience could supposedly afford.

Thus the avant-garde has been split between two opposing camps itself, the serial and the aleatoric, but both have owed their essential character to an implicit gnosticism, inherent either in the serial approach or in the underlying philosophy. Nor are their creators isolated cases; among the post-war avant-garde composers, Karlheinz Stockhausen has exhibited the most explicit gnosticism while being one of the most influential of the avant-garde composers. Like Boulez, Stockhausen was an early advocate of total serial control; in the early 1950s, he moved into electronic music, and by the late 1950s had begun to incorporate elements of chance. Thus he unites the two apparently opposed approaches of the avant-garde, demonstrating how closely related they truly are. In language reminiscent of Wassily Kandinsky, he speaks of the 'inner self', a 'cosmic force', and the spiritual element in the soul as 'supra-rational'.[9] Like the ancient gnostics, he sees the cosmos – our galaxy, to be precise – in 'terrible disorder', but looks to a cosmic realm beyond our own (the star of Sirius) as the locus of perfection and harmony.[10] His emphasis on 'vibrations' and spiritual intuition echoes the theosophists; he even distinguishes seven centres of the soul in a manner similar to that of Madame Blavatsky and Rudolf Steiner.[11] Finally, his belief in reincarnation and his view of the body as a prison of the soul are all gnostic traits by now thoroughly familiar.[12] It is little wonder, then, that he has rejected order as the foundation of his music, embracing aleatoric procedures within the context of large-scale deterministic structures. But to repeat a point already crucial to understanding Schoenberg: an obsession with control is not to be confused with genuine order. Both chance and Twelve-Tone control are possible realizations of the gnostic metaphysic.

The influence of gnosticism, therefore, has not been limited to the birth of the avant-garde, but has been vital to sustaining the avant-garde's antagonism to form, order and being. Even where it is not an explicit motive, the rejection of tonality and aural beauty betrays an implicitly gnostic metaphysic. Furthermore, even though the self-revelatory motive of Expressionism and the technique of the Twelve-Tone Method have fallen out of favour by the end of the twentieth century, the stylistic achievements of the avant-garde still dominate the creation of new music: melody is absent; the functional harmony has been replaced by tone combinations used for their sonority; and dissonance is still the predominant sonority employed. Thus the style prevailing for much of the twentieth century embodies yet conceals what was crucial to the origin of the avant-garde, so that to understand the significance of the musical choices at the birth of Expressionism and the Twelve-Tone Method is also to understand the significance of the subsequent avant-garde's entire approach to music. The decisive end of tonality came only with the advent of an explicitly gnostic denial of the goodness of order: this is both the genesis and the essence of the avant-garde.

With the arrival of atonality, however, came the end of the sense of the supreme importance of music in cultural life. After Schoenberg, it is no longer possible to say that the creative efforts of contemporary composers much matter.[13] It might be possible to argue that such a development is insignificant: that the canon is closed, and that such closure is a naturally occurring cycle in cultural history. As long as the canon is preserved, there will be the aural evidence of the goodness of order, represented in the compelling beauty of the works composed according to the principles of tonality. Thus, the preservation of the standard repertoire is vital as long as there is no new repertoire which is equally affirmative of the category of goodness. The post-modernist rejection of the classical canon therefore fails to understand the necessary role played by cultural canons in a civilization.

In response to the assessment of the closure of the canon as a result of the departure from tonality, the new efforts of the so-called 'minimalist' composers are sometimes adduced as a return to tonality.[14] As we have seen, however, the mere repetition of a tone does not constitute a tonal order: it cannot be construed as tonality in any of the traditional senses of the word. The repetitiveness of the minimalist style contains no *telos*; it is as much a denial of rationality as the atonal styles of the earlier part of the century. It seeks to evoke a trance on the part of the listener, rather than the love of melodic and harmonic order. The style, therefore, cannot function as a metaphor of the teleological order established by the good. Minimalism remains a problematic style that still warrants the preservation of the classical canon.

Yet the closure of the canon is perhaps not as innocuous as the argument presented here might make it appear. For the natural expectation is that if a style or a point of view is genuinely worth anything, it will be worth the effort to create something anew in that style, to reconfirm in yet an original way the point of view that is universally believed. To say this is to use the concept of originality in its authentic sense, that is, as meaning the creation of a work within the principles identifying a tradition. When a creative tradition dies and works are no longer composed within it, the message implied is that the tradition is not worth so much after all, that the style no longer possesses universal validity. It is thus the case that a closure of the canon must inevitably put the canon on the defensive; the scepticism seen growing today in the phenomenon of post-modernism represents a probably inevitable attack on the position of prestige long enjoyed by classical music. In such a situation, Castalian sterility is not likely to endure forever.

The post-modernist critique of the canon, however, rests on the rejection of the concept of works and the narrativity they embody. As we have seen, this is a matter of rejecting the *telos* of the good and its temporality; post-modernism is the heir of Adorno's despairing nihilism. But these are serious philosophical issues: if human life is ultimately untenable without a vision of the good and the hope of its temporal realization in some degree, the post-modernist challenge must be met not with arguments concerning the musical canon, but rather with an alternative to its celebration of disorder as the demise of the good.

What would it take to reclaim a vision of the goodness of order and temporality? In considering this question, we would inevitably retrace the steps of post-Kantian idealist philosophy. Yet here is precisely the problem: the solutions available at the beginning of the nineteenth century no longer convince at the beginning of the twenty-first. Schelling's reconstruction of Platonism has been decisively rejected in the twentieth century, if for no other reason than his location of the Platonic Ideas in the conceptions of the divine as given by both Greek mythology and Christian theology. But the ascription of a soul to the world, essential to redeem the sense of organic life in Nature, is much more fraught with absurdity. The Hegelian faith in the temporal achievement of the Ideal likewise is simply unavailable, for the reasons Adorno gives. But if there is no achievement of the Ideal, then in Hegelian terms, there is no union of the Concept and its reality, no way of attesting that the Concept of the good could ever be realized. The result, then, is to fall back into the Kantian bifurcation of the phenomenal and noumenal realms, the division between the perceived reality in which life takes place and the unperceived realm of the Hegelian Concept, or the Kantian thing-in-itself. Once essences become unknowable, however, they may as well cease to exist: the spectre of Nietzschean nihilism once again stands at the door.

The dilemma introduced by Kant is real. Either the category of the good is a noumenal existent, and therefore we must despair of ever knowing it, or it does not exist, in which case we simply must despair. Yet, inasmuch as Kant himself recognized epistemological scepticism as unacceptable, it would be well to suspect that there is something falsely framed by this dilemma as it stands. Kant himself attempted to vindicate the sense of teleology in the second part of the *Critique of Judgement*; once again, teleology could only be apparent, not ascribed to the essence of things, but only posited as an 'as if'.[15] Yet without it, the human understanding of existence in the world would be incomplete and unsatisfactory. In what sense, then, could teleology be vindicated?

To speak of the possibility of teleology means above all to return to the concept of narrative. It is human life which must appear to make sense. Thus, if there is to be any way out of the impasse created by Kantian metaphysics, it must be through a reconception of the human spirit: not spirit as an unperceivable noumenal essence, but spirit as knowable rationality. The freedom of will Kant sought to defend must not be conceived as a mere postulate of spontaneity threatened always with contamination by the world in which the will actually chooses, but rather must be as developed precisely in confrontation with the options the phenomenal world presents for rational judgement. This means that rationality itself will have to be reconsidered: it cannot be simply the choice of means to ends deterministically given, but rather must be, as the classical conception had it, the intuitive apprehension of what constitutes goodness itself. The *telos* of human life, then, becomes precisely the development of this kind of rationality, and the narrative of that development is the kind of narrative we can understand as the primary example of teleological ordering toward the good. It is an individual narrative, not a collective progress or a history of the Hegelian World-Spirit. But it just happens to be the kind of narrative which the great literary and operatic works of all time embody. The rise and survival of the work concept reflects precisely the emergence of narratives of the individual realization of the ideal.

Nevertheless, it will be objected that this is still too optimistic: the human spirit might be conceived more rationally than Kant had allowed, yet the fact remains that people are caught in a world not of their own making, in which events unfold with cruel suffering in store for the innocent. It should be recalled, however, that the Greeks, too, believed the cosmos was oftentimes cruel; the fates decided upon by the gods did not always recognize human merit. Oedipus, for example, was accursed long before he could ever be said to have become a hot-tempered man capable of killing his own father in questionable circumstances. Thus, it is not clear that modern science has changed the human perception of the world all that much; only instead of laying the blame on the gods, we ascribe the determinism of fate to Nature itself. Perhaps, then, the Greek example of the tragic sense points to a way out of the impasse apparently created by modern science and Kantian metaphysics. For if the kind of narrative we are seeking as a model of teleology does not have to be simply the story of progress toward the ideal, but may also be the story of the fall away from the good, then it would be possible to allow that tragic narratives are an essential means by which the good is affirmed. For the good must exist if it can be lost, either through an individual's own fault, or through the terror of fate.

We see here an indication of the importance later nineteenth-century opera still possesses in the culture of classical music, for this repertoire consists largely of examples of tragedy. The turn to the tragic in the Romantic era was of cardinal importance for deepening the sensibility of the musical culture of classicism, and it still plays a vital role in maintaining a sense of the possibility of goodness while recognizing the reality of evil and suffering. Thus conceived, tragedy acknowledges a metaphysically existent standard of goodness: it is the ideal, even if real life cannot attain it or keep it. The story of Camelot does not cease to enchant and even inspire, even as we realize its days are no more.

Indeed, however, the striking fact about twentieth-century culture is the general avoidance of real tragedy. In the popular culture of the musical theatre, for example, it has rarely been present. Instead, musical comedy (especially in its American form) has often propagated a vision of a naïve optimism, a faith that life will always turn out well for the individual. This is not to be dismissed, after the manner of Adorno, as mere commercialism or kitsch; it is clearly a defiant celebration of the possibility of goodness, a decision for the Ideal in spite of the strictures of modern nihilists. Yet the critic would be right: there is something missing here. What is missing, however, is the sense of the tragic potential in life, in a way that might affirm the standard of the good, the vision of the ideal, even the possibility of forgiveness and reconciliation on the threshold of death. But, as has often been observed, the twentieth century has not been a century that acknowledged sin; and without a concept of sin, there can be no real sense of the tragic. As Aristotle argued in his *Poetics*, the tragic character must be both noble and flawed; he must not appear to suffer for no reason, yet must not simply deserve his suffering as punishment.[16] Thus, tragedy as a narrative requires both a concept of sin and a concept of fate. It is the former which implies the standard of goodness crucial to all teleological ordering of human life, and it is this which is missing from modernity.

Adorno would proscribe the tragic from the modern consciousness: 'Music must give up the attempt to design itself as a picture of the good and the virtuous, even if the picture is tragic. Instead it is to embody the idea that there no longer is any life.'[17] Yet such nihilism cannot be justified: to banish the tragic sense is also to banish guilt, so that the very horrors of the twentieth century, which ought to be faced with an acknowledgement of guilt, would not be faced, their guilt not remembered. For there is still life, and it will continue. The only question is whether it will continue in a way that once again seeks the good and that at the same time acknowledges the possibility and reality of failure.

A recovery of the possibility of tragic narrative, therefore, offers the largest hope for a return to a musical culture that is creative as well as preservative of the best in the past. That is, the revival of musical creativity in a way that would respond to people's deepest aesthetic instincts would begin with opera, and would almost necessarily reaffirm the traditional elements of tonality which were born in opera in the first place. But the effect on the forms of instrumental music might be quite otherwise than what has come down from the days of symphonic composition informed by the Romantic idealist aesthetic. Instead of a narrative of progress toward the realization of the good, there might well be a far more sober narrative of tragedy affirming the dignity of life, cast in the tonal language redeveloped in opera. It is perhaps useless to speculate, however, on the precise direction a cultural revival might take, and it is even less appropriate for an academic observer to attempt to prescribe a direction. Yet the endorsement of an Adorno has sufficed to place the avant-garde on a pedestal for much of this century. It is time to question its culture of musical innovation, for its underlying assumptions regarding musical perception, the nature of order, and the essence of the human spirit are all open to challenge. It is time to seek an expression of the good adequate for a new century.

Music is an art that takes place in time; in the secular realm, it is an art that seeks to represent the nature of the secular order. The secular order, however, is temporal, and the nature of temporality according to the longest traditions in Western civilization is both cyclic and linear. That is, time is defined first of all by the return of the days, months and seasons of the year, but it is also a narrative of the growth of the human spirit. The *telos* which stands as the ultimate source of ordering of time, therefore, is the good toward which the individual must seek to develop. Thus, music has as its largest purpose the representation of the narrative of growth in the perception of goodness, or the consequences of the failure to realize the good; in doing so, the musical order reflects the larger metaphysical order of the temporality of human existence. If the good be held not to be knowable, however, there will be no musical representation of it, and thus no creative musical culture in the sense of a creativity which meets with acceptance and wide social resonance.

Such is the situation today, in which the culture of classicism preserves one possible and historically important vision of the narrative of the teleological ordering of time. The culture of modernism, however justified in its logic, fails to satisfy the deepest needs of the human spirit for the presentation to itself of the beauty of goodness and truth. If the classical culture of preservation fails, however, then the modern world risks becoming deaf as well as mute: no longer able to sing the praises of the good, we shall then lose our ability to comprehend those who do. This is a sobering choice at the beginning of the twenty-first century; it is the mark of the tragedy of the modern world. Nevertheless, to choose order above disorder, goodness over evil, and the love of nobility rather than the hatred of beauty, would seem in each case to be the more persuasive choice. As the Platonic tradition understood, love in this world is awakened by the perception of beauty: beauty is the being of goodness that is loved. The dignity of human existence and the renewal of civilization depend on the recognition of the beauty of the good, and the awareness of the tragedy of its loss.

Notes

1. Alasdair MacIntyre confronts a similar problem in the concluding chapters of *Whose Justice? Which Rationality?* (Notre Dame: University of Notre Dame Press, 1988), in which rival traditions of moral enquiry and practice inevitably pose the question of truth. He concludes, however, that the capacity to absorb newly successful insights is one test of the adequacy of a tradition, so that the Aristotelian-Thomist account of morality emerges as the best among several alternatives (pp. 402–3). Yet there is perhaps greater pessimism expressed in his subsequent *Three Rival Versions of Moral Enquiry: Encyclopaedia, Genealogy, and Tradition* (Notre Dame: University of Notre Dame Press, 1990).

2. G. W. F. Hegel, *Vorlesungen über die Ästhetik*, ed. E. Moldenhauer and K. Michel, *Werke in zwanzig Bänden* (Frankfurt am Main: Suhrkamp Verlag, 1970), vol. 14, pp. 231–2; *Aesthetics: Lectures on Fine Art*, 2 vols, trans. T. M. Knox (Oxford: Clarendon Press, 1975), pp. 602–11. While I do not see Hegel as pronouncing definitively the end of the romantic art-form, I do see this passage as expressing a genuine concern about the dissolution of the integrity of the styles which had arisen in the context of Christian civilization.

3. Friedrich Nietzsche, *Also sprach Zarathustra: Ein Buch für Alle und Keinen*, *Sämtliche Werke in zwölf Bänden* (Stuttgart: Alfred Kröner Verlag, 1964), vol. 6, pp. 228, 244; *Thus Spake Zarathustra*, in *The Portable Nietzsche*, trans. and ed. Walter Kaufmann (1954; New York: Penguin, 1976), pp. 318, 332.

4. Hans Jonas, *The Gnostic Religion: The Message of the Alien God and the Beginnings of Christianity*, 2nd edn (Boston: Beacon Press, 1963), pp. 320ff.

5. Joan Peyser, *Boulez* (New York: Schirmer Books, 1976), pp. 4–19. See also Peter F. Stacey, *Boulez and the Modern Concept* (Lincoln: University of Nebraska Press, 1987).

6. On Cage, see James Pritchett, *The Music of John Cage* (Cambridge: Cambridge University Press, 1993), esp. pp. 74–8 on the influence of Zen, and Peyser, *Boulez*, pp. 55ff.

7. For Cage's later explanation of non-purposiveness, see his essay, 'Silence' (1961), in Edward A Lippman, ed., *Musical Aesthetics: A Historical Reader*, 3 vols (Stuyvesant, NY: Pendragon Press, 1990), vol. 3, p. 435.

8. Pritchett, *The Music of John Cage*, pp. 59–60, 77, 104–5.

9. Karlheinz Stockhausen, *Towards a Cosmic Music*, ed. and trans. Tim Nevill (London: Element Books, 1989), pp. 4, 45.

10. Ibid., pp. 16–18. His current project in 1989, a seven-day stage cycle, *Licht*, manifests a distinctly gnostic view of the cosmos: see his description, pp. 83–9.

11. Ibid., pp. 53–5. According to Michael Kurtz, *Stockhausen: A Biography*, trans. Richard Toop (London: Faber and Faber, 1992), the composer was interested in Indian spirituality as early as 1949, and had moved to an interest in esotericism in the early 1970s: pp. 24, 190. He also notes the explicit influence of Madame Blavatsky's ideas on *Licht*, which was conceived in 1977: p. 4. See also Robin Maconie, *The Works of Karlheinz Stockhausen*, 2nd edn (Oxford: Clarendon Press, 1990).

12. Stockhausen, *Towards a Cosmic Music*, p. 113.

13. After all the calls for the acceptance of the avant-garde, it must be insisted that none of the approaches we have discussed has even approached the power of the 'classical' canon to move audiences to their acceptance. Hence the irony in one critic's remark, 'The Schönbergs, Stravinskys and Bartóks are composers we ought by now to have assimilated' followed by a lengthy critique of John Cage:

Laurence Davies, *Paths to Modern Music: Aspects of Music from Wagner to the Present Day* (London: Barrie and Jenkins, 1971), pp. 303ff.

14. As, for example, by William Thomson, in *Schoenberg's Error* (Philadelphia: University of Pennsylvania Press, 1991), p. 181.

15. Kant, *Kritik der Urteilskraft*, ed. Karl Vorländer (Hamburg: Felix Meiner Verlag, 1990), Section 75, pp. 262–6; *Critique of Judgement*, trans. J. H. Bernard (New York: Macmillan, 1951), pp. 245–8.

16. Aristotle emphasizes the concept of flaw in the *Poetics* 1453a, but requires goodness of character in 1454a; this is the key to understanding his requirement of a tragic character 'who is neither outstanding in virtue and righteousness, nor is it through wickedness and vice that he falls into misfortune, but through some flaw', that is, through some weakness or grave error. *Poetics*, 1453a, in *On Poetry and Style*, trans. G. M. A. Grube (Indianapolis: Hackett, 1989), p. 24.

17. Theodor W. Adorno, *Philosophie der neuen Musik* (Frankfurt am Main: Europäische Verlagsanstalt, 1958), p. 168; *Philosophy of Modern Music*, trans. Anne G. Mitchell and Wesley V. Blomster (New York: Seabury Press, 1973), p. 181.

Bibliography

This bibliography contains only those works cited as sources in the notes.

Adorno, Theodor W., *Philosophie der neuen Musik* (Frankfurt am Main: Europäische Verlagsanstalt, 1958).

———, *Philosophy of Modern Music*, trans. Anne G. Mitchell and Wesley V. Blomster (New York: Seabury Press, 1973).

———, *Quasi una Fantasia: Essays on Modern Music*, trans. Rodney Livingstone (London: Verso, 1994).

Alberti, Leon Battista, *On Painting*, trans. Cecil Grayson, ed. Martin Kemp (London: Penguin, 1991).

Annas, Julia, *The Morality of Happiness* (Oxford and New York: Oxford University Press, 1993).

Aquinas, St Thomas, *An Introduction to the Metaphysics of St. Thomas Aquinas*, texts edited and translated by James F. Anderson (Washington, DC: Regnery Gateway, 1953).

———, *Summa Contra Gentiles*, trans. and ed. Anton C. Pegis, F.R.S.C., 5 vols (1955; Notre Dame and London: University of Notre Dame Press, 1975).

———, *Summa Theologica*, trans. Fathers of the Dominican Province, 5 vols (1911; Westminster, MD: Christian Classics, 1981).

Aristotle, *Metaphysics*, trans. Richard Hope (1952; Ann Arbor: University of Michigan Press, 1960).

———, *The Nichomachean Ethics*, trans. and ed. David Ross (1925; Oxford: Oxford University Press, 1980).

———, *Poetics*, in *On Poetry and Style*, trans. G. M. A. Grube (Indianapolis: Hackett, 1989).

———, *The Politics*, trans. Benjamin Jowett, ed. Stephen Everson (Cambridge: Cambridge University Press, 1988).

Arnold, Matthew, *Culture and Anarchy*, ed. J. Dover Wilson (Cambridge: Cambridge University Press, 1932).

Ashton, Dore, *A Fable of Modern Art* (Berkeley and London: University of California Press, 1991).

Athanasius, St, *On the Incarnation of the Word*, trans. Archibald Robertson, in Hardy, Edward R., ed., *Christology of the Later Fathers* (Philadelphia: Westminster Press, 1954), pp. 55–110.

Augustine, St Aurelius, *Confessions*, trans. R. S. Pine-Coffin (Harmondsworth: Penguin, 1961).

———, *The Enchiridion on Faith, Hope and Love*, trans. J. F. Shaw, ed. Henry Paolucci (Chicago: Regnery Gateway, 1961).

———, *On Free Choice of the Will*, trans. Thomas Williams (Indianapolis: Hackett, 1993).

Austin, William, *Music in the Twentieth Century: From Debussy through Stravinsky* (New York: Norton, 1966).

Bakhtin, Mikhail M., *The Dialogic Imagination*, trans. and eds Michael Holquist and Caryl Emerson (Austin: University of Texas Press, 1981).

Balzac, Honoré de, *Séraphîta*, ed. Henri Gauthier, in *La Comédie humaine*, vol. 11 (Paris: Gallimard, 1980).

——, *Séraphita*, trans. Clara Bell, ed. David Blow (New York: Hippocrene Books, 1989).

Bayles, Martha, *Hole in Our Soul: The Loss of Beauty and Meaning in American Popular Music* (New York: The Free Press, 1994).

Beardsley, Monroe, *Aesthetics: Problems in the Philosophy of Criticism*, 2nd edn (Indianapolis: Hackett, 1981).

Bent, Ian, ed., *Music Theory in the Age of Romanticism* (Cambridge: Cambridge University Press, 1996).

Bertault, Philippe, *Balzac et la religion* (Paris: Boivin, 1942).

Blavatsky, Helena Petrovna, *An Abridgement of The Secret Doctrine*, ed. Elizabeth Preston and Christmas Humphreys (Wheaton, IL: Theosophical Publishing House, 1966).

——, *The Key to Theosophy: A Simple Exposition Based on the Wisdom-Religion of All Ages* (1889; reprinted Pasadena, CA: Theosophical University Press, 1995).

Bloom, Harold, *The Western Canon: The Books and School of the Ages* (New York: Riverhead Books, 1994).

Blumenberg, Hans, *The Legitimacy of the Modern Age*, trans. Robert M. Wallace (Cambridge, MA: MIT Press, 1983).

Boethius, Ancius, *The Consolation of Philosophy*, trans. V. E. Watts (London: Penguin, 1969).

——, *De institutione musica*, selections in Strunk, Oliver, ed., *Source Readings in Music History* (New York: Norton, 1950), pp. 79–86.

Borel, Jacques, *Séraphîta et le mysticisme balzacien* (Paris: José Corti, 1967).

Brown, Howard M., *Music in the Renaissance* (Englewood Cliffs, NJ: Prentice-Hall, 1976).

Budd, Malcom, *Values of Art: Pictures, Poetry and Music* (London: Penguin, 1995).

Bury, John B., *The Idea of Progress: An Inquiry into Its Origin and Growth* (London: Macmillan, 1920).

Busoni, Ferruccio, 'Sketch of a New Esthetic of Music', trans. Th. Baker (*c.* 1911), in *Three Classics in the Aesthetic of Music* (New York: Dover Publications, 1962).

Cage, John, 'Silence' (1961), in Lippman, Edward A., ed., *Musical Aesthetics: A Historical Reader*, 3 vols (Stuyvesant, NY: Pendragon Press, 1990), vol. 3, pp. 421–36.

Carlson, Maria, *'No Religion Higher Than Truth': A History of the*

Theosophical Movement in Russia (Princeton: Princeton University Press, 1993).

Carroll, Noël, 'Historical Narratives and the Philosophy of Art', *Journal of Aesthetics and Art Criticism* 51 (1993), pp. 313–26.

Chipp, Herschel B., ed., *Theories of Modern Art: A Source Book by Artists and Critics* (Berkeley: University of California Press, 1968).

Cicero, Marcus Tullius, *De re publica, De legibus*, trans. C. W. Keyes, vol. 213 of the Loeb Classical Library (Cambridge, MA: Harvard University Press, 1928).

Clark, Mary T., ed., *An Aquinas Reader: Selections from the Writings of Thomas Aquinas* (1972; New York: Fordham University Press, 1988).

Coleman, Francis X. J., *The Harmony of Reason: A Study in Kant's Aesthetics* (Pittsburgh: University of Pittsburgh Press, 1974).

Collingwood, R. G., *The Idea of Nature* (Oxford: Clarendon Press, 1945).

Cooke, Deryck, *I Saw the World End: A Study of Wagner's Ring* (Oxford: Oxford University Press, 1979).

———, *The Language of Music* (Oxford: Oxford University Press, 1959).

Cousin, Victor, *Lectures on the True, the Beautiful and the Good*, trans. O. W. Wight (1854; New York: Appleton, 1875).

Covach, John, 'The Sources of Schoenberg's "Aesthetic Theology"', *Nineteenth Century Music* 14 (1996), pp. 252–62.

Crawford, Donald. W., *Kant's Aesthetic Theory* (Madison: University of Wisconsin Press, 1974).

Crawford, John C. and Crawford, Dorothy L., *Expressionism in Twentieth-Century Music* (Bloomington: Indiana University Press, 1993).

Dahlhaus, Carl, *Esthetics of Music*, trans. William Austin (Cambridge: Cambridge University Press, 1982).

———, *The Idea of Absolute Music*, trans. Roger Lustig (Chicago: University of Chicago Press, 1989).

———, *Schoenberg and the New Music*, trans. Derrick Puffett and Andrew Clayton (Cambridge: Cambridge University Press, 1987).

———, *Studies on the Origin of Harmonic Tonality*, trans. Robert O. Gjerdingen (Princeton: Princeton University Press, 1990).

David, Claude, *Stefan George: Sein dichterisches Werk*, trans. Alexa Remmen and Karl Thiemer (Munich: Carl Hauser Verlag, 1967).

Davies, Laurence, *Paths to Modern Music: Aspects of Music from Wagner to the Present Day* (London: Barrie and Jenkins, 1971).

Davies, Stephen, *Musical Meaning and Expression* (Ithaca: Cornell University Press, 1994).

Descartes, René, *Discourse on Method and Meditations*, trans. F. E. Sutcliffe (Harmondsworth: Penguin, 1968).

Detweiler, Bruce, *Nietzsche and the Politics of Aristocratic Radicalism* (Chicago: University of Chicago Press, 1990).

Dewey, John, *Art as Experience* (1934; New York: Berkeley, 1980).

Dowson, Ernest Christopher, *The Poetry of Ernest Dowson*, ed. Desmond Flower (Rutherford, NJ: Fairleigh Dickinson University Press, 1970).

Dryden, John, 'A Song for Saint Cecilia's Day, November 22, 1687', text in *Six Centuries of Great Poetry*, ed. Robert Penn Warren and Albert Erskine (New York: Dell Publishing, 1955), pp. 280–81.

Eksteins, Modris, *Rites of Spring: The Great War and the Birth of the Modern Age* (Boston: Houghton Mifflin, 1989).

Ellman, Donald, 'The Symphony in Nineteenth-Century Germany', in Layton, Robert, ed., *A Guide to the Symphony* (Oxford: Oxford University Press, 1995), pp. 124–54.

Fétis, François Joseph, *Traité complet de la théorie et de la pratique de l'harmonie*, 4th edn (Paris: Brandus, 1849).

George, Stefan, *Werke*, 2nd edn, 2 vols (Munich: Helmut Kupper, 1958).

Gilson, Etienne, *God and Philosophy* (New Haven: Yale University Press, 1941).

Giraud, Albert, *Pierrot lunaire*, trans. Otto Erich Hartleben (Berlin: Verlag deutscher Phantasten, 1893).

Goehr, Lydia, *The Imaginary Museum of Musical Works: An Essay in the Philosophy of Music* (Oxford: Clarendon Press, 1992).

Goethe, *Der Sammler und die Seinigen*, in *Werke*, Part I, vol. 33 (Munich: Deutscher Taschenverbund, 1962).

Goldman, Alan, *Aesthetic Value* (Boulder, CO.: Westview Press, 1995).

Gordon, Donald E., *Expressionism: Art and Idea* (New Haven and London: Yale University Press, 1987).

Gounod, Charles, *Faust: A Lyric Drama in Five Acts with English and French Text* (vocal score) (Miami: Belwin, [n.d.]).

Greenberg, Clement, *Art and Culture: Critical Essays* (Boston: Beacon Press, 1961).

Grohmann, Will, *Wassily Kandinsky: Life and Work*, trans. Norbert Guterman (New York: H. N. Abrams, 1958).

Hahl-Koch, Jelena, ed., *Arnold Schoenberg, Wassily Kandinsky: Letters, Pictures and Documents*, trans. John C. Crawford (London: Faber and Faber, 1984).

Hall, James, *Dictionary of Subjects and Symbols*, rev. edn (New York: Harper and Row, 1979).

Hand, Ferdinand Gotthelf, *Aesthetics of Musical Art; or, The Beautiful in Music*, trans. W. E. Lawson, 2nd edn (London: W. Reeves, 1880).

——, *Aesthetik der Tonkunst*, 2nd edn, 2 vols (Leipzig: E. Eisenach, 1847).

Hanslick, Eduard, *On the Musically Beautiful* trans. Geoffrey Payzant (Indianapolis: Hackett, 1986).

Hegel, Georg Wilhelm Friedrich, *Aesthetics: Lectures on the Fine Arts*, trans. T. M. Knox, 2 vols (Oxford: Clarendon Press, 1975).

————, *The Encyclopaedia Logic*, trans. T. F. Geraets, W. A. Suchting and H. S. Harris (Indianapolis: Hackett, 1991).

————, *Introduction to the Lectures on the History of Philosophy*, trans. T. M. Knox and A. V. Miller (Oxford: Clarendon Press, 1985).

————, *Lectures on the Philosophy of Religion*, trans. R. F. Brown, P. C. Hodgson and J. M. Stewart (Berkeley and London: University of California Press, 1984–87).

————, *The Philosophy of History*, trans. J. Sibree (New York: Dover Publications, 1956).

————, *Philosophy of Nature*, trans. A. V. Miller (Oxford: Clarendon Press, 1970).

————, *Philosophy of Right*, trans. T. M. Knox (Oxford: Oxford University Press, 1952).

————, *Vorlesungen über die Ästhetik*, ed. Eva Moldenhauer and Karl Michel, in *Werke in zwanzig Bänden*, vols 13, 14 and 15 (Frankfurt am Main: Suhrkamp Verlag, 1970).

Heidegger, Martin, *Being and Time: A Translation of 'Sein und Zeit'*, trans. Joan Stambaugh (Albany: State University of New York Press, 1996).

————, *The Concept of Time*, trans. William McNeill (Oxford: Blackwell, 1992).

Helmholtz, Hermann L. F., *On the Sensations of Tone as a Physiological Basis for the Theory of Music*, trans. Alexander J. Ellis (1885; reprinted New York: Dover Publications, 1954).

Hemleben, Johannes, *Rudolf Steiner: A Documentary Biography*, trans. Leo Twyman (East Grinstead, Sussex: Henry Goulden, 1975).

Hesse, Hermann, *Das Glasperlenspiel: Versuch einer Lebensbeschreibung des Magister Ludi Josef Knecht samt Knechts hinterlassenen Schriften*, in *Gesammelte Werke*, vol. 9 (Frankfurt am Main: Suhrkamp Verlag, 1970).

————, *The Glass Bead Game (Magister Ludi)*, trans. Richard and Clara Winston (New York: Holt, Rinehart and Winston, 1969).

Hindemith, Paul, *A Composer's World* (New York: Doubleday, 1961).

Hoffmann, E. T. A., *E. T. A. Hoffmann's Musical Writings: 'Kreisleriana', 'The Poet and the Composer', Music Criticism*, ed. David Charlton, trans. Martyn Clarke (Cambridge: Cambridge University Press, 1989).

Horace, *Satires and Epistles*, trans. Jacob Fuchs (New York: Norton, 1977).

Houlgate, Stephen, *Freedom, Truth and History: An Introduction to Hegel's Philosophy* (London: Routledge, 1991).

Hughes, H. Stuart, *Consciousness and Society: The Reorientation of European Social Thought 1890–1930*, rev. edn (New York: Vintage Books, 1977).

Huray, Peter le, and Day, James, eds, *Music and Aesthetics in the Eighteenth and Early-Nineteenth Centuries* (Cambridge: Cambridge University Press, 1981).

Jacobs, Arthur, *Lend Me Your Ears: A Guide to Orchestral Music – From*

Vivaldi to Bernstein (1987; New York: Avon Books, 1990).

James, Henry, *The Secret of Swedenborg: Being an Elucidation of His Doctrine of the Divine Natural Humanity* (1869; reprinted New York: AMS Press, 1983).

James, Jamie, *The Music of the Spheres: Music, Science, and the Natural Order of the Universe* (New York: Grove Press, 1993).

Jefferson, Mark, 'What's Wrong With Sentimentality', *Mind* 92 (1983), pp. 519–29.

Jonas, Hans, *The Gnostic Religion: The Message of an Alien God and the Beginnings of Christianity*, 2nd edn (Boston: Beacon Press, 1963).

Jonsson, Inge, *Emanuel Swedenborg*, trans. Catherine Djurklou (New York: Twayne Publishers, 1971).

Kandinsky, Wassily and Mark, Franz, eds, *Der blaue Reiter*, rev. edn, ed. Klaus Lankheit (Munich: R. Piper, 1965).

———, *The Blaue Reiter Almanac*, trans. and ed. Klaus Lankheit (1974; reprinted New York: Da Capo Press, [n.d.]).

———, *Concerning the Spiritual in Art*, trans. M. T. H. Sadler (1914; reprinted New York: Dover Publications, 1977).

Kant, Immanuel, *Critique of Judgement*, trans. J. H. Bernard (New York: Macmillan, 1951).

———, *Critique of Practical Reason*, trans. Lewis White Beck (Indianapolis: Bobbs-Merrill, 1956).

———, *Critique of Pure Reason*, trans. F. Max Muller (Garden City, NY; Doubleday, 1966).

———, *Kritik der praktischen Vernunft*, ed. Paul Natorp, in *Kants gesammelte Schriften in 22 Bänden*, vol. 5 (Berlin: Preussische Akademie der Wissenschaften, 1908), pp. 1–163.

———, *Kritik der Urteilskraft*, ed. Karl Vorländer (Hamburg: Felix Meiner, 1990).

Karolyi, Otto, *Introducing Music* (London: Penguin, 1965).

Kinderman, William and Krebs, Harald, eds, *The Second Practice of Nineteenth-Century Tonality* (Lincoln: University of Nebraska Press, 1996).

Kivy, Peter, *The Corded Shell: Reflections on Musical Expression* (Princeton: Princeton University Press, 1980).

———, *Music Alone: Philosophical Reflections on the Purely Musical Experience* (Ithaca and London: Cornell University Press, 1990).

Kramer, Lawrence, *Music as Cultural Practice, 1800–1900* (Berkeley and London: University of California Press, 1990).

Kristeller, Paul Oskar, '"Creativity" and "Tradition"', *Journal of the History of Ideas* 44 (1983), pp. 105–13.

———, *Renaissance Thought and Its Sources*, ed. Michael Mooney (New York: Columbia University Press, 1979).

Kurtz, Michael, *Stockhausen: A Biography*, trans. Richard Toop (London: Faber and Faber, 1992).

Lamm, Martin, *August Strindberg*, trans. and ed. Harry G. Carlson (New York: Benjamin Blom, 1971).

Langer, Suzanne K., *Feeling and Form: A Theory of Art Developed from 'Philosophy in a New Key'* (New York: Scribner's, 1953).

———, *Philosophy in a New Key: A Study in the Symbolism of Reason, Rite, and Art* (Cambridge, MA: Harvard University Press, 1957).

Leadbeater, Charles Webster, *Man Visible and Invisible* (New York: John Lane, 1903).

Lehmann, Andrew G., *The Symbolist Aesthetic in France, 1885–1895* (Oxford: Basil Blackwell, 1950).

Leibniz, Gottfried Wilhelm von, *Monadology and Other Philosophical Essays*, trans. Paul and Anne M. Schrecker (Indianapolis: Bobbs-Merrill, 1965).

———, *Theodicy: Essays on the Goodness of God, the Freedom of Man, and the Origin of Evil*, trans. E. M. Huggard, ed. Austin Farrar (La Salle, IL: Open Court, 1985).

Leppert, Richard, and McClary, Susan, eds, *Music and Society: The Politics of Composition, Performance and Reception* (Cambridge: Cambridge University Press, 1987).

Lessem, Alan Philip, *Music and Text in the Works of Arnold Schoenberg: The Critical Years, 1908–1922* (Ann Arbor: UMI Research Press, 1979).

Lester, Joel, *Compositional Theory in the Eighteenth Century* (Cambridge, MA: Harvard University Press, 1992).

Levinson, Jerrold, *Music, Art, and Metaphysics: Essays in Philosophical Aesthetics* (Ithaca: Cornell University Press, 1990).

Lippman, Edward, *A History of Western Musical Aesthetics* (Lincoln and London: University of Nebraska Press, 1992).

Lovejoy, Arthur O., *The Great Chain of Being: A Study in the History of an Idea* (1936; Cambridge, MA: Harvard University Press, 1964).

Löwith, Karl, *Meaning in History: The Theological Implications of the Philosophy of History* (Chicago: University of Chicago Press, 1949).

MacIntyre, Alasdair, *After Virtue: A Study in Moral Theory*, 2nd edn (Notre Dame: University of Notre Dame Press, 1984).

———, *Three Rival Versions of Moral Enquiry: Encyclopaedia, Genealogy, and Tradition* (Notre Dame: University of Notre Dame Press, 1990).

———, *Whose Justice? Which Rationality?* (Notre Dame: University of Notre Dame Press, 1988).

MacIntyre, C. F., trans., *French Symbolist Poetry* (Berkeley and London: University of California Press, 1958).

Machlis, Joseph and Forney, Christine, *The Enjoyment of Music*, 6th edn (New York: Norton, 1990).

Maconie, Robin, *The Works of Karlheinz Stockhausen*, 2nd edn (Oxford: Clarendon Press, 1990).

Mahler, Gustav, 'Nicht Wiedersehen!' in *Des Knaben Wunderhorn and the Rückert Lieder for Voice and Piano* (Mineola, NY: Dover Publications, 1999), pp. 63–6.

——, *Songs of a Wayfarer and Kindertotenlieder in Full Score* (New York: Dover Publications, 1990).

Mann, Thomas, *Doctor Faustus: The Life of the German Composer Adrian Leverkühn as Told by a Friend*, trans. H. T. Lowe-Porter (1948; New York: Vintage Books, 1971).

——, *Doktor Faustus: Das Leben des deutschen Tonsetzers Adrian Leverkühn erzählt von einem Freunde*, in *Gesammelte Werke in zwölf Bänden*, vol. 6 (Oldenbourg: S. Fischer Verlag, 1960).

Mattheson, Johann, *Der vollkommene Capellmeister*, trans. Ernest C. Harriss (Ann Arbor: UMI Research Press, 1981).

Mersenne, Marin, *Harmonie universelle, contenant la théorie et la pratique de la musique*, facsimile edn by François Lesure, 2 vols (1636–37; Paris: Centre national de la recherche scientifique, 1963).

Mill, John Stuart, *On Liberty*, ed. Gertrude Himmelfarb (Harmondsworth: Penguin, 1974).

Milton, John, 'On Time', text in *Six Centuries of Great Poetry*, ed. Robert Penn Warren and Albert Erskine (New York: Dell Publishing, 1955), pp. 241–2.

Mitchell, Donald, *The Language of Modern Music*, 2nd edn (Philadelphia: University of Pennsylvania Press, 1994).

Morison, Simon, 'Skryabin and the Impossible', *Journal of the American Musicological Society* 51 (1998), pp. 283–330.

Mortensen, Preben, 'Shaftesbury and the Morality of Art Appreciation', *Journal of the History of Ideas* 55 (1994), pp. 631–50.

Murdoch, Iris, *The Sovereignty of Good* (1970; London: Routledge and Kegan Paul, 1985).

Nietzsche, Friedrich, *Also sprach Zarathustra: Ein Buch für Alle und Keinen*, in *Sämtliche Werke in zwölf Bänden*, vol. 6 (Stuttgart: Alfred Kröner Verlag, 1964).

——, *Beyond Good and Evil*, trans. R. J. Hollingdale, rev. edn by Michael Tanner (1973; London: Penguin, 1990).

——, *Jenseits von Gut und Böse, Zur Genealogie der Moral*, in *Sämtliche Werke in zwölf Bänden*, vol. 7 (Stuttgart: Alfred Kröner Verlag, 1964).

——, *Thus Spake Zarathustra*, in Kaufmann, Walter, trans. and ed., *The Portable Nietzsche* (1954; New York: Penguin, 1968).

——, *The Will to Power*, trans. Walter Kaufmann and R. J. Hollingdale, ed. Walter Kaufmann (New York: Random House, 1968).

——, *Der Wille zur Macht: Versuch einer Umwertung aller Werte*, ed. Peter

Gast and Elisabeth Förster-Nietzsche, in *Sämtliche Werke in zwölf Bänden*, vol. 9 (Stuttgart: Alfred Kröner Verlag, 1964).

Norton, Richard, *Tonality in Western Culture: A Critical and Historical Perspective* (University Park, PA: Penn State Press, 1984).

O'Regan, Cyril, *The Heterodox Hegel* (Albany: State University of New York Press, 1994).

Osborne, Harold, *Aesthetics and Art Theory: An Historical Introduction* (New York: Dutton, 1970).

Palisca, Claude V., *Humanism in Italian Renaissance Musical Thought* (New Haven and London: Yale University Press, 1985).

Pauer, Ernst, *Elements of the Beautiful in Music*, 2nd edn (London: Novello, Ewer and Co., 1877).

Pelikan, Jaroslav, *The Vindication of Tradition* (New Haven and London: Yale University Press, 1984).

Peyser, Joan, *Boulez* (New York: Schirmer Books, 1976).

——, *The New Music: The Sense Behind the Sound* (New York: Delacorte Press, 1971).

Plato, *Philebus*, trans. Harold N. Fowler, in *Statesman, Philebus, Ion*, trans. H. N. Fowler and W. R. M. Lamb, vol. 164 of the Loeb Classical Library (Cambridge, MA: Harvard University Press, 1925).

——, *Republic*, trans. Robin Waterfield (Oxford and New York: Oxford University Press, 1993).

——, *Symposium*, in *Lysis, Symposium, Gorgias*, trans. W. R. M. Lamb, vol. 166 of the Loeb Classical Library (Cambridge, MA: Harvard University Press, 1925).

——, *Timaeus*, in *Timaeus and Critias*, trans. Desmond Lee, rev. edn (London: Penguin, 1977).

Poggioli, Renato, *The Theory of the Avant-Garde*, trans. Gerald Fitzgerald (1968; Cambridge, MA: Harvard University Press, 1996).

Pritchett, James, *The Music of John Cage* (Cambridge: Cambridge University Press, 1993).

Rameau, Jean-Philippe, *Générations harmoniques*, in *Rameau's Theory of Harmonic Generation*, trans. Deborah Hayes (Stanford University: Ph.D. dissertation, 1968)

——, *Traité de l'harmonie réduite à ses principes naturels* (facsimile edn: New York: Broude Brothers, 1965).

——, *Treatise on Harmony*, trans. Philip Gossett (New York: Dover Publications, 1971).

Regier, Kathleen J., *The Spiritual Image in Modern Art* (Wheaton, IL: Theosophical Publishing House, 1987).

Ridley, Aaron, *Music, Value and the Passions* (Ithaca: Cornell University Press, 1995).

Riemann, Hugo, *Harmony Simplified; or The Theory of the Tonal Functions of Chords*, trans H. Bewerunge (London: Augener, [n.d.]).

Ringbom, Sixten, *The Sounding Cosmos: A Study in the Spiritualism of Kandinsky and the Genesis of Abstract Painting* (Åbo: Åbo Akademi, 1970).

Roochnik, David, *The Tragedy of Reason: Toward a Platonic Conception of Logos* (New York and London: Routledge, 1990).

Rosen, Charles, *The Classical Style* (New York: Norton, 1972).

Rosen, Stanley, *The Question of Being: A Reversal of Heidegger* (New Haven and London: Yale University Press, 1993).

Rudolph, Kurt, *Gnosis: The Nature and History of Gnosticism*, trans. Robert M. Wilson (San Francisco: HarperCollins, 1987).

Safranski, Rudiger, *Schopenhauer and the Wild Years of Philosophy*, trans. Ewald Osers (Cambridge, MA: Harvard University Press, 1989).

Sandel, Michael J., *Liberalism and the Limits of Justice* (Cambridge: Cambridge University Press, 1982).

Schelling, Friedrich Wilhelm Joseph, *Die Philosophie der Kunst*, ed. M. Schröter, in *Werke*, vol. 3 (Munich: C. H. Beck and R. Oldenbourg, 1959).

———, *The Philosophy of Art*, trans. and ed. Doublas W. Stott (Minneapolis: University of Minnesota Press, 1989).

Schiller, Friedrich, *On the Aesthetic Education of Man in a Series of Letters*, trans. Elizabeth M. Wilkinson and L. A. Willoughby (Oxford: Clarendon Press, 1967).

———, *Werke*, vol. 3, *Gedichte, Erzählungen*, ed. Dieter Schmidt (Frankfurt am Main: Insel Verlag, 1966).

Schoenberg, Arnold, *Dossier de Presse de Pierrot lunaire*, ed. François Lesure (Geneva: Editions Minkoff, 1985).

———, *Dreimal sieben Gedichte aus Albert Girauds Pierrot lunaire*, trans. Otto Erich Hartleben, piano score ed. by Erwin Stein (1923; Vienna: Universal Edition, [1984]).

———, *Die Jakobsleiter*, eds Winfried Zillig and Rudolf Stephan (Los Angeles: Belmont Music, 1980).

———, Five Pieces for Orchestra, Op. 16, New Version (New York: C. F. Peters, 1952).

———, *Style and Idea: Selected Writings*, ed. Leonard Stein, trans. Leo Black, rev. edn (Berkeley: University of California Press, 1984).

———. *Theory of Harmony*, trans. Roy E. Carter (Berkeley: University of California Press, 1978).

———, *Verklärte Nacht: Sextett für zwei Violinen, zwei Violen und zwei Violoncelli* (Berlin: Verlag Dreililien, [n.d.]).

Schopenhauer, Arthur, *Die Welt als Wille und Vorstellung*, vols. 1–2 in *Sämtliche Werke in 14 Bänden*, ed. Paul Deussen (Munich: R. Piper, 1924).

———, *The World as Will and Representation*, 2 vols, trans. E. F. G. Payne (1958; reprinted New York: Dover Publications, 1969).

Schorske, Carl E., *Fin-de-siècle Vienna: Politics and Culture* (New York: Vintage Books, 1981).

Schubart, Christian F. D., *Ideen zu einer Ästhetik der Tonkunst* (1806; Leipzig: Reclam, 1977).

Schubert, Franz, *Die schöne Müllerin*, in *Complete Song Cycles: Die schöne Müllerin, Die Winterreise, Schwanengesang*, ed. Eusebius Mandyczewski (New York: Dover Publications, 1970), pp. 2–53.

Scruton, Roger, *Aesthetics of Music* (Oxford: Oxford University Press, 1997).

——, 'Understanding Music', in *The Aesthetic Understanding* (London: Methuen, 1983).

Scudo, Paul, 'Revue musicale', *Revue des Deux Mondes* (1856), vol. 6, pp. 923–36.

Seneca, Lucius Annaeus, *Dialogues and Letters*, trans. and ed. C. D. N. Costa (London: Penguin, 1997).

Snow, C. P., *The Two Cultures; And a Second Look* (Cambridge: Cambridge University Press, 1963).

Solomon, Robert C., 'On Kitsch and Sentimentality', *Journal of Aesthetics and Art Criticism* 49 (1991), pp. 2–13.

——, *The Passions: Emotions and the Meaning of Life* (Indianapolis: Hackett, 1993).

Sophocles, *The Three Theban Plays: Antigone, Oedipus the King, Oedipus at Colonus*, trans. Robert Fagles, ed. Bernard Knox (New York: Viking Penguin, and London: Allen Lane, 1982).

Stacey, Peter F., *Boulez and the Modern Concept* (Lincoln: University of Nebraska Press, 1987).

Steblin, Rita, *A History of Key Characteristics in the Eighteenth and Early Nineteenth Centuries* (Ann Arbor: UMI Research Press, 1983).

Steiner, Rudolf, *Knowledge of the Higher Worlds: How Is It Achieved?*, rev. trans. by D. S. Osmond and C. Davy (London: Rudolf Steiner Press, 1969).

——, *An Outline of Occult Science*, trans. Maud and Henry B. Monges, rev. ed. by Lisa D. Monges (Spring Valley, NY: Anthroposophic Press, 1972).

——, *Theosophy: An Introduction to the Supersensible Knowledge of the World and the Destination of Man*, trans. E. D. S. (Chicago: Rand McNally, 1910).

Sterne, Colin C., *Arnold Schoenberg, The Composer as Numerologist* (Lewiston, NY: Edwin Mellen Press, 1993).

Stockhausen, Karlheinz, *Towards a Cosmic Music*, trans. and ed. Tim Nevill (London: Element Books, 1989).

Stolnitz, Jerome, 'On the Origins of Aesthetic Disinterestedness', *Journal of Aesthetics and Art Criticism* 20 (1961–62), pp. 131–43.

——, 'The Aesthetic Attitude', in Hospers, John, ed., *Introductory Readings in Aesthetics* (New York: Free Press, 1969).

Stravinsky, Igor, *An Autobiography* (1936; London: Calder and Boyars, 1975).

——, *Poetics of Music in the Form of Six Lessons*, trans. Arthur Knodel and Ingolf Dahl (1942; Cambridge, MA: Harvard University Press, 1970).

——, *The Rite of Spring in Full Score*, Foreword by Boris M. Yarustovsky (1965; reprinted New York: Dover Publications, 1989).

Stravinsky, Vera, and Craft, Robert, *Stravinsky in Pictures and Documents* (New York: Simon and Schuster, 1978).

Strindberg, August, *Inferno, Alone and Other Writings*, trans. and ed. Evert Sprinchorn (Garden City, NY: Doubleday, 1968).

Stuckenschmidt, H. H., *Arnold Schoenberg*, trans. Edith T. Roberts and Humphrey Searle (New York: Grove Press, 1959).

Swedenborg, Emanuel, *The Universal Human and Soul–Body Interaction*, trans. and ed. George F. Dole (New York: Paulist Press, 1984).

Synnestvedt, Sig, ed., *The Essential Swedenborg: Basic Teachings of Emanuel Swedenborg, Scientist, Philosopher, and Theologian* (New York: Twayne Publishers, Swedenborg Foundation, 1970).

Taylor, Charles, *Sources of the Self: The Making of the Modern Identity* (Cambridge, MA: Harvard University Press, 1989).

Thomson, William, *Schoenberg's Error* (Philadelphia: University of Pennsylvania Press, 1991).

Tolhurst, William, 'Toward an Aesthetic Account of the Nature of Art', *Journal of Aesthetics and Art Criticism* 42 (1984), pp. 261–9.

Toorn, Pieter C. van den, *Music, Politics, and the Academy* (Berkeley and London: University of California Press, 1995).

Verdi, Giuseppe, *La Traviata*, libretto by Francesco Maria Piave, trans. Edmund Tracey (London: John Calder; New York: Riverrun Press, 1981).

Voegelin, Eric, *Science, Politics and Gnosticism* (Washington, DC: Regnery Gateway, 1968).

Wagner, Richard, *Tannhäuser in Full Score* (New York: Dover Publications, 1984).

Webb, James, *The Occult Establishment* (La Salle, IL: Open Court, 1976).

——, *The Occult Underground* (La Salle, IL: Open Court, 1974).

Weber, Carl Maria von, *Kunstansichten: Ausgewählten Schriften* (Wilhelmshaven: Heinrichshofen's Verlag, 1978).

Weber, Gottfried, *Theory of Musical Composition*, trans. James F. Warner, 2 vols. (Boston: Wilkins, Carter and Co., 1846).

Webern, Anton, *The Path to the New Music*, trans. Leo Black, ed. Willi Reich (1963; London: Universal Edition, 1975).

White, Pamela, *Schoenberg and the God Idea: The Opera 'Moses und Aron'* (Ann Arbor: UMI Research Press, 1985).

Willet, John, *Art and Politics in the Weimar Period: The New Sobriety, 1917–1923* (New York: Random House, 1978).

Wörner, Karl H., *Die Musik in der Geistesgeschichte: Studien zur Situation der Jahre um 1910* (Bonn: H. Bouvier, 1970).

——, *Schoenberg's 'Moses und Aron'*, trans. Paul Hamburger (London: Faber and Faber, 1963).

Index